Scholarly Reprint Series

The Scholarly Reprint Series has been established to bring back into print valuable titles from the University of Toronto Press backlist for which a small but continuing demand is known to exist. Special techniques (including some developed by the University of Toronto Press Printing Department) have made it possible to reissue these works in uniform case bindings in runs as short as 50 copies. The cost is not low, but prices are far below what would have to be charged for such short-run reprints by normal methods.

The Scholarly Reprint Series has proved a valuable help to scholars and librarians, particularly those building new collections. We invite nominations of titles for reissue in this form, and look forward to the day when, with this series and other technological developments, the label 'out of print' will virtually disappear from our backlist.

EMPIRE OF THE

NORTH ATLANTIC

The Maritime Struggle
for North America

SECOND EDITION

GERALD S. GRAHAM
*Rhodes Professor of Imperial History
in the University of London*

UNIVERSITY OF TORONTO PRESS
LONDON: OXFORD UNIVERSITY PRESS
Issued under the auspices of the Canadian Institute of International Affairs

SCHOLARLY REPRINT SERIES

ISBN 0-8020-7051-5

LC 50-14296

Printed in Canada

To the Officers and Ship's Company
of
H. M. S. *Harvester*
lost in the North Atlantic by enemy
action, March 11, 1943, while on
convoy escort duty

"The marine is a new kind of power which has given, in some sort, the universe to Europe. This part of the globe, which is so limited, has acquired, by means of its fleet, an unlimited empire over the rest, so extended."—*Abbé Raynal*

Preface

THIS book is an exploration and an interpretation of an epoch of empire in the North Atlantic. It is concerned chiefly with three centuries of European rivalry and expansion, from the first conquest of the ocean by the armed sailing-ship to the beginnings of the factory age that foreshadowed the end of the wooden ship of the line. Gradually, in competition first with Spain, then with Holland, and finally with France, England achieved command of the seas. During the eighteenth century, this dominance became so constant that, despite Britain's relative weakness in manpower, she was in a position, by the time of the Napoleonic Wars, to extend her empire from its centre in the North Atlantic to the far distant reaches of the Indian and Pacific oceans.

The new and colossal edifice called the Second Empire was, therefore, founded on a unique naval predominance that had been shaken only during the War of American Independence. By determinedly establishing her naval ascendancy in western Europe, Britain had ensured not only her own national security but also a relatively unrestricted freedom to pursue trade, and to garner the strategic posts protecting that trade in every ocean.

An astute analyst of naval history has put it in these words:

> The greatest strength of British sea power in its classical period had lain in the fact that it was able to compress all its manifold offensive and defensive functions into a single task of relatively limited dimensions, the establishment of the 'command' of the Narrow Seas of Western Europe. By establishing her control over the other naval powers along the western seaboard of Europe, Great Britain had been able to ensure simultaneously the security not only of the motherland but of all her widespread colonial possessions, intercepting at the source any possible enemy attack upon her, which at that time could come only across the sea.[1]

[1]H. Rosinski, "The Role of Sea Power in Global Warfare of the Future," *Brassey's Naval Annual, 1947* (London, 1947), 107.

By asserting consistently this "command of the sea," the Royal Navy revealed itself as an instrument of tremendous strength and influence. After the middle of the seventeenth century, it became clear to wise statesmen that absolute superiority gave its possessor the initiative anywhere on salt water. "The sea is one"; there could be no balance of power as on land; when the stronger fleet secured control of sea communications, it had acquired what amounted to an exclusive monopoly. This monopoly was Britain's uninterrupted possession during the Anglo-French wars of 1793-1814 and, as already remarked, it provided the foundation of the Second Empire after 1783.

The Napoleonic Wars marked the end of an era, and this book might have concluded with such an apparent culmination of imperial commercial designs, symbolized by the world-girdling network of strategic bases. Such a conclusion would, moreover, have made unnecessary any reference to later events of far reaching importance, for the introduction of the *Pax Britannica* after 1815 coincided with the beginnings of a new imperial epoch, the industrial age of steam navigation, screw propellors, iron hulls, shell guns, submarine cables, and free trade. These revolutions in technology and economics expedited and paralleled the expansion of British commerce to the Indian Ocean and the Pacific, and served to emphasize the dwindling prestige of the old North Atlantic empire. Steadily the West Indies declined in wealth and importance; the Newfoundland fisheries lost their centuries-old prominence as "the nursery" of English seamen; while British North America became more and more subject to attack by the multiplying disciples of Adam Smith as an unprofitable and burdensome venture.

To end at 1815 might have been logical, but any study concerned with "command of the sea" would have been incomplete which did not consider, even sketchily, the strategic effects of industrial change preceding the dissolution of the *Pax Britannica* in the twentieth century. In the nineteenth century, the Empire was not only vast; it was scattered, and therefore vulnerable. Yet there was no serious naval competition, and Britain could safely undertake to defend colonial trade and territories anywhere in the world. By the beginning of the twentieth century, however, she was unable to maintain alone this two-hemisphere insurance. With the rise of American and Japanese industrial and naval power, the "narrow seas" were no longer the focal centre of universal "command"; and for the sake of the security of the United Kingdom, the two-power standard had to be surrendered in favour of a policy of alliances.

Moreover, the new products of science and industry, such as the submarine and the airship, while in no way diminishing the importance of controlling sea routes, did symbolize the conclusion of another epoch of empire—the empire of the ship of war, won and maintained through four and a half centuries solely by controlling the *surface* of the sea. I hope later to write about the portentous effects of these changes on the technical methods, machinery, and organization of maritime communications and defence within the Second Empire. Here these effects are outlined in two concluding chapters in an effort to give the shape of an epoch.

The premise that the First and Second Empires resulted from Britain's persistent supremacy at sea, presents, however, a far more complicated problem, that of explaining how this enduring superiority came about. It is certainly necessary to go deeper than the easy generality that geography produced what is sometimes termed a "natural sea power," by giving to the English people easy access to the sea and a special aptitude for it. Even if circumstances lead a nation to a seafaring existence by way of natural processes of trade and commerce, the resulting aptitude or skill remains the product of man-made conditions.

Conditions which breed skilled seamen depended in the past (and still depend) on government policy. Backed by adequate resources, the action of governments has been decisive from the time of Colbert to that of von Tirpitz. Both these men succeeded in building strong navies despite the indifference and even the early hostility of public opinion. The English people of the sixteenth century had no great tradition of the sea to compare, for example, with that of the Scandinavians. Such a tradition—even a family tradition—is valuable; but the forbears of the Hoods, of Nelson, St. Vincent, Howe, Collingwood, George Byng, and Blake, were country gentlemen, solicitors, or parsons, with no sea record behind them.

There was in England no traditional popular compulsion to "rule the waves." Britannia's sceptre was a product of Whitehall and Westminster. It was not the English people who recognized the dependence of the Kingdom on sea power, but their rulers, whether king or parliament, who, from mediaeval times, regulated trade and designed Navigation Acts in the interests of ocean commerce. Such leadership was fundamental to progressive naval development.

Nevertheless, the exigencies of domestic politics frequently intruded on governmental policies. The development of an English navy was seriously affected, for instance, by the failure of Charles I to convince his subjects that "Ship-Money" was more than a political manœuvre. During the War of the Spanish Succession, the struggle between Whigs and Tories became in part a struggle between the maritime and territorial interests of the nation. The Whigs, whose strength lay in the seaport and industrial towns, and who were, therefore, keenly interested in foreign trade, believed in the war, and backed a policy of imperial expansion. Few Tories, on the contrary, had much enthusiasm for overseas "big business," preferring to bring the war to an abrupt end. They did so, and even Marlborough, who understood the value of sea power, was a victim of their final triumph. The Jacobites of George I's day, the Little Englanders of Victoria's, the Canadian isolationists of Laurier's, have had to be considered before governments could take energetic action in matters of naval defence.

In brief, the acquisition of naval strength, and thence, naval superiority, is quite as much a political problem as one of professional naval practice. Admirals with their fleets, remarked Sir John Fortescue, "are mere weapons wielded in the hand of the statesman." Admittedly, other elements have influenced the ultimate use of the weapons: ships' design, tactics, hygiene, finance, the military situation on land, the state of public morale at home. But in the long run, statecraft has remained the most potent determinant, and naval history, so-called, is essentially political and diplomatic history. During the greater part of the period covered by this book the Admiralty and the sea officers gave advice, but on all large issues, and sometimes in matters of detail, the statesmen undertook full responsibility. Above all else, remarked Joannès Tramond, in reference to his own Service, "La Marine est La Politique."

Because the theme of this book bears upon a wide field of immense documentary and printed resources, it has been necessary to exercise considerable restraint in dealing with materials, especially documentary materials. Fortunately, the inevitable process of selection has been made less hazardous by numerous French, American, German and Spanish scholars, who have ransacked foreign archives to the great benefit of British imperial history. Indeed, the task of writing this book would have been almost insuperable without the contributions of men like Roncière and Tramond, Duro and Sombart, Castex and Lacour-Gayet, Baxter and Mahan.

My own manuscript sources lay chiefly in the Public Record Office in London. The most important of these were the In-Letters and Out-Letters of the Secretary's Department of the Admiralty (*Ad. 1* and *2*), the Original Correspondence of the Board of Trade (especially the series designated *B.T. 1*), and various Colonial Office series, such as *C.O. 5* and *C.O. 42*, containing communications between the colonial governments and the home authorities. Of the non-official documents, the Chatham Papers (*G. & D. 8*) most repaid a further sifting, since many letters concerned Pitt's strategy during the Seven Years' War.

The Manuscripts Division of the Library of Congress in Washington graciously provided me with its transcripts of the Admiralty Correspondence beginning with the War of the Austrian Succession. The Public Archives in Ottawa afforded transcripts of much of the Colonial Office correspondence (the most important being the *Q Series*), diligently copied over a long period of years. Also useful were the annual *Reports of the Department of Public Archives of Canada*, especially the earlier editions which contain summaries of unprinted documents (Correspondance Générale) from the National Archives in Paris. Many of these, chiefly relating to the fisheries and the fur trade, have been published in *Select Documents in Canadian Economic History, 1497-1783*, edited by H. A. Innis (Toronto, 1929).

Colonial Office papers summarized in the *Calendar of State Papers, Colonial Series, America and West Indies*, were invaluable for the period between 1574 and 1733. *Acts of the Privy Council of England, Colonial Series, 1613-1783*, edited by W. L. Grant and James Monro (6 vols., London, 1908-12) contained items relating to North American trade and its protection by sea. A certain amount of background material was available in a *Calendar of the Haldimand Collection*, based on the collection in the British Museum, and printed in the *Report of the Canadian Archives for 1887* (Ottawa, 1888). The section called *Correspondence with Officers of the Royal Navy, 1778-1783* (Brit. Mus. 21,800) was not, however, as productive as the title seemed to suggest. Printed collections such as the *Correspondence of William Shirley* (New York, 1912) and Dr. Arthur Doughty's massive series on *The Siege of Quebec and the Battle of the Plains of Abraham* (6 vols., Quebec, 1901) were of particular assistance.

After 1783, and especially for the nineteenth century, the Parliamentary Accounts and Papers, the reports of Royal Commissions and of Select Committees of the Commons (including those printed by authority of the House of Commons in Canada), provided detailed information on problems of imperial defence. Various reports of the Royal Commission on Historical Manuscripts (for example, the *Portland, Dartmouth* and *Stopford-Sackville MSS.*) were of value, especially on the diplomatic side; and the publications of the Navy Records Society, based chiefly on documents from private collections, were indispensable to an understanding of specific phases of naval policy and strategy. Reference to these volumes, as well as to the more significant secondary works, will be found in footnotes.

In the general study of the subject, as well as in the writing of the book, I have been fortunate in having the help of many friends. First, I wish to acknowledge the debt I owe to the late Admiral Sir Herbert Richmond, that unique combination of scholar and seaman, who until the last continued to stimulate me with his vigour and his learning, so often expressed in his own execrable handwriting. Rear Admiral H. G. Thursfield has given me constant advice and support ever since I came to this country, and this book owes much to his sustained interest, enthusiasm, and judgment. I have also had the benefit of expert criticism from Commander J. H. Owen, R.N., whose knowledge of eighteenth-century naval history is unrivalled, and who generously put at my disposal many of his own notes.

The manuscript has been read in whole or in part by George W. Brown, A. L. Burt, G. de T. Glazebrook, H. A. Innis, F. C. Jones, Lillian M. Penson, and Gilbert N. Tucker; and their scholarship has saved me from many a literary and historical error. I am indebted to the officials of the Public Archives at Ottawa who, in addition to normal hospitality, provided me with photographic copies of unpublished maps; to the Public Archives of Nova Scotia at Halifax; and to the Public Record Office in London. I owe much to the courtesy and patience of librarians: in the Douglas Library at Queen's University, Canada; in the Library of Columbia University; in the New York Public Library; in the Manuscripts Division, Library of Congress, Washington, D.C.; in the Libraries of the United Service Institution (London), the Colonial Office, and of the Royal Empire Society. The Admiralty Librarian, Mr. D. Bonner Smith, not only spurred my investigations but took endless pains to get me proper charts.

The work was made possible in the first instance by the generosity of the John Simon Guggenheim Memorial Foundation; and, in its later stages, by a grant from the Canadian Institute of International Affairs. The permanent staff of the Institute and of the University of Toronto Press have given me unstinted help over that exacting stage—preparation for publication.

G. S. G.

King's College
July 3, 1949

PREFACE TO SECOND EDITION

In this new publication of *Empire of the North Atlantic* I have undertaken no major revisions of content or interpretation; the book remains essentially as before a study of command of the sea in relation to North American colonization before 1815. The concluding two chapters, as stated in the original preface, are simply an attempt to outline the effects of industry and science on eighteenth century doctrines of empire and sea power culminating in the end of an era—the era of the warship which for more than three centuries was the sole instrument effecting the control of the surface of the oceans, and the major instrument determining the destinies of the British Empire. In relation to nineteenth century commercial expansion, my conclusions have undergone some modification, and the reader may, if he feels so inclined, supplement chapter XIII with an article which I contributed to the *Economic History Review* —"The Ascendancy of Sail, 1815-1885" (vol. IX, no. 1, Aug. 1956). To learned reviewers and critics of many nations whose scrupulousness has enabled me to repair many errors of fact and print— and especially to Mr. A. W. H. Pearsall, Commander W. B. Rowbotham, R.N., and Colonel C. P. Stacey—I offer my deep thanks.

G.S.G.

February 25. 1958

Contents

074886

Maps

EMPIRE OF THE NORTH ATLANTIC

I

The Supremacy of Spain

SOME four hundred and fifty years ago, the chrysalis of the European world was suddenly broken by explorers. Inquisitive men of the Renaissance reached out over a round world unified by great waters, and found vast islands of land mutually accessible by means of sailing-ships. Between 1487 and 1523 European vessels entered the Indian Ocean and the China seas, crossed the Atlantic and Pacific, and circumnavigated the globe. As a result of this exuberant and spectacular activity, the centre of balance in Europe shifted gradually westward. When Christopher Columbus laid the first foundations of a new Spanish overseas empire, he not only brought to light a New World, he bound it by sails to the Old. The ambit of Western European aspirations was transformed by the conquest of the ocean barrier to America.

Although the Atlantic is more than thirty times larger than the Mediterranean, it is, compared with its bordering continents, relatively narrow. On a globe of the world, it resembles a long inland sea rather than an open ocean, and only a globe can give a correct impression of its limited area in relation to the continents which it unites.

This North American moat, as it has become in the age of aircraft, bulges in two directions like an hour-glass southward from the Caribbean, and again northward into the Arctic. The entrance to the southern bulge is a passage-way some fifteen hundred miles in breadth, the approximate distance between Dakar on the west coast of Africa, and Natal, south of the equator on the coast of Brazil. The northern entrance lies between Newfoundland-Labrador and the Scandinavian peninsula, where Atlantic waters finally mingle with the Arctic Ocean.

This northern gateway is broad, but it is broken by islands which give entrance to the Arctic only by a series of wide channels, islands which served before the dawn of modern history as stepping-stones on a great circle route between the New World and the Old. According to Icelandic sagas, this was the route taken by the Norsemen more than nine hundred years ago—Britain to the Faroe Islands, to Iceland, to Greenland, and thence by Labrador and Newfoundland to the eastern shores of North America. One great natural obstacle, however, has impeded the development of the northerly course. The outflow of the Arctic sea, moving past Greenland and bending southward towards Labrador and Newfoundland, releases on the edge of the curving Gulf Stream its accumulation of ice, which in turn contributes to periodic fogs. Until the present day, cold and fog have obscured the significance of this land chain which ties the North American continent to Europe, but as long as surface ships alone bridged the Atlantic, this mattered little. The island stepping-stones could be ignored; the destiny of Canada lay in the hands of the European nation that could control the intervening ocean with fighting fleets.

Once the Atlantic had been conquered by the sailing-ship, North America naturally developed direct sea connections with the European seaboard. But when fishing vessel or merchantman or galleon went out armed or in convoy, and encountered opposition, the issue of "command of the sea" was inevitably raised. And as the defence of overseas commerce became increasingly important to the economic vitality of European states, the struggle for control of communications was intensified until the Atlantic became a field of battle. Thus the birth of modern sea power was a direct consequence of the discovery of America.

If Columbus had sailed westward from Spain instead of taking a route west by south-west from the Canaries, the course of North American history might have been very different. As it happened, he drew back only a corner of the curtain from the western world; and subsequent Spanish conquests, rather than leading to further occupations northwards, only consolidated Spanish interest in the gold- and silver-bearing regions south of Florida. When the first two colonial powers agreed to split up the findings in 1494 (following an earlier suggestion of Pope Alexander) they did so without any knowledge of what lay to the north of the Bahamas. It is conceivable that the Treaty of Tordesillas (June 7, 1494), by pushing the Papal demarcation line 270 leagues farther west, proved a Portuguese knowledge of Brazil which was, under this arrangement, brought within the Portuguese sphere. Whether or not this be true —and the evidence is doubtful—the fact remains that the treaty-makers unwittingly gave North America its first national boundary line. Ownership rights to Canada and Newfoundland, as well as to the west coast of Greenland, went to Spain before Renaissance Europe knew of the existence of such countries.[1] In this sense, then, the first French settlements on what was to become Canadian soil represent a second discovery of America.

For almost forty years after the first expedition of Columbus no European state seriously opposed the claims of Spain; and Anglo-French searches for a north-west route to the East were merely the beginnings of an unostentatious attempt to side-step them. With full papal support, the Spaniards tried to exclude the adventurers of all other nations from the coasts of North America, and short shrift was given to any Normans or Bretons or Englishmen who happened to be caught in the neighbourhood of the Caribbean. Farther south, the Portuguese were equally ruthless in their efforts to preserve a monopoly in Brazil, and few French traders survived the first merciless expulsion of 1504.[2]

The early years of the sixteenth century were, none the less, a period of tremendous French activity in which Normans and Bretons followed the Portuguese around the Cape of Good Hope, or fished for cod off the shores of Newfoundland. It was the growing importance of the cod fishery which first bound northwestern Europe to the Labrador-Newfoundland projection of the North American continent. Long before the search for the mysterious North-West Passage awakened a national competitive spirit, fishermen from the Iberian peninsula and France had visited the area near the Grand Banks. Indeed, French historians have asserted that French fishermen pushed westward to Acadia and that a chart of the Gulf of St. Lawrence was made in 1506 by Jean Denys of Honfleur.[3]

[1]The Norsemen of the tenth century had visited, and may have colonized, the east coast, possibly as far south as 40° N. lat.; but only hazy recordings of their experiences have come down to us, and, whatever their exploits, they bore no historical relation to the discovery of the New World at the end of the fifteenth century.

[2]See E. Guénin, *Ango et ses pilotes* (Paris, 1901), 13-14.

[3]In the Public Archives at Ottawa there is a map, which is assumed to be a copy of the Denys map.

Whether or not this is adequately proven, Honfleur rapidly became for France what Lisbon and Seville had been for the early *conquistadores*, the gateway to adventure in the west. The picturesque little towns along the coast of Normandy and Brittany nourished a seafaring population, as enterprising and as skilled as any in Europe. From Dieppe and St. Malo went forth the Auberts, the Parmentiers, the Cartiers and the Angos: models, in their way, of Renaissance seamen.[4]

As with the Elizabethans, Spanish or Portuguese prohibitions or atrocities in the Caribbean area merely excited these men to reprisals. In 1517 Dieppe rang with the blows of the ship-wrights' hammers, as Ango prepared "un arsenal de course d'où sortaient des flottes à faire trembler les rois."[5] The contraband trade of the Norman ports grew rather than diminished; brigandage at sea became a normal part of overseas trade, while commercial and colonizing ventures across the Atlantic turned into semi-military enterprises, merchandise sharing the decks with guns and ammunition.

In part, this perseverance against odds may be ascribed to French policy, for French kings had never accepted the arbitrary division of the world between Portuguese and Spaniards. Francis I had haughtily protested against any national monopoly of the heritage of Adam, and he backed Verrazzano's efforts to find a route to Cathay, just as he was to support Cartier's ambitious plans.[6] But there was a notable lack of consistency in Francis's maritime policy. At times belligerent in support of his seamen, he could on other occasions, like Elizabeth of England, submit docilely to Portuguese or Spanish threats and warnings. More than once, the overseas exploits of his impatient subjects were conducted against the most severe royal prohibitions.[7]

It would be wrong to suggest, therefore, that the "Canada" expeditions in the first half of the sixteenth century were in any substantial way linked with the European rivalries of France, England,

[4]See C. de la Roncière, *Histoire de la Marine française* (6 vols., 2nd ed., I-III, Paris, 1909-32), III, 244-8; also L. Gérin, "La Première Tentative de colonisation française en Amérique. François I, Jacques Cartier, Roberval," *Report of the Canadian Historical Association, 1931* (Ottawa, 1932), 52.

[5]See J. P. E. Jurien de la Gravière, *Les Gueux de mer* (2nd ed., Paris, 1893), 158.

[6]Dr. Gustave Lanctot offers documentary proof that Cartier made a voyage to the Canadian coast in 1524, and suggests that he probably accompanied Verrazzano. See "Cartier's First Voyage to Canada in 1524," *The Canadian Historical Review*, XXV, Sept., 1944, 233-45.

[7]See G. Gravier, *Examen critique de l'histoire du Brésil français au seizième siècle* (Paris, 1878), 19.

and Spain. From what is known of the period, it seems clear that until almost the middle of the sixteenth century, Spain made no serious effort to stop expeditions directed towards the north-west of the continent. Apparently Cartier's voyage in 1534 caused no more flutter at the Spanish court than did the earlier searches of Cabot and Verrazzano. Only fragments of the diplomatic conversations between London and Madrid regarding Cabot's discoveries are available; and reports on Franco-Spanish and Franco-Portuguese conversations concerning the first Cartier discoveries are similarly incomplete.[8] But such as they are, they suggest no sense of alarm. There seems to have been the comfortable feeling that France was in no position to tackle Spain in the Indies, and that the attempt to plant a colony on the banks of the St. Lawrence was merely a waste of time.[9]

The first apparent sign that the New World had become a serious object of European state rivalries revealed itself after the second Cartier expedition. Only a few months after Cartier's return from the St. Lawrence in July 1536, Charles V discussed with his ministers ways and means of blocking French undertakings on North American territory, and the king and queen of Portugal were informed of the Emperor's intentions. Four years later, he was urging the lethargic Portuguese to take action, for he had learned that Francis I was "openly granting licences to all his subjects to try their fortunes in the Indies in the discovery and conquest of new lands." Meanwhile his spies investigated the whole French coast from Bordeaux to Dieppe to discover the number of armed ships and whether or not they were designed for ocean voyages and commerce raiding. It was on the Breton coast that a secret agent, Don Pedro de Santiago, found his most exciting evidence. At St. Malo a fleet of thirteen sail, with ammunition and artillery, was being fitted out under the direction of Jacques Cartier. Santiago sought an interview, and learned that the intention was to people a country called

---

[8]Regarding Spanish interest in French designs on the Indies, see A. Rein, *Der Kampf Westeuropas um Nord Amerika im 15. und 16. Jahrhundert* (Stuttgart, 1925), 164 *et seq.*; also, *Calendar of State Papers, Spain, 1538-42*, VI, part 1 (London, Public Record Office).

[9]On June 10, 1541, the Cardinal of Seville, who provided the emperor with the advice of an "expert," wrote as follows: ". . . in my judgment they are making a mistake, for with the exception of the fisheries, this whole coast as far as Florida is utterly unproductive. In consequence they will waste their efforts, or at best return with the loss of most of their people and of the greater portion of all they have taken from France." Contained in H. P. Biggar, *A Collection of Documents Relating to Jacques Cartier and the Sieur de Roberval* (Ottawa, 1930), xxxi and 324-6.

Canada. News of this proposed Cartier-Roberval expedition stirred
Charles to action: immediate instructions were issued for the fitting
out of a fleet to attack the French as soon as they set sail.[10] During
the summer of 1541 two caravels were despatched, but both failed
to catch Cartier.

Although the project of a New France fell to the ground with
Roberval's return, the Spanish government was not unaware of its
significance as the first evidence of national rather than individual
enterprise in North American waters. Almost the last advice Charles
V gave his son, the future Philip II, in 1548, was a warning to "be
ever on the watch if the French wish to send an armada thither [to
the Indies] secretly or otherwise, and to notify the governors of
those parts to be on their guard and where and when necessary in
conformity therewith to resist the said French. . . ."[11]

But the French had no thought of trying to break the Spanish
monopoly in the Caribbean. Up to and during the reign of Francis
I, the object was rather to secure a foothold in the New World as far
away as possible from Spanish territory. French projects during
this period were deliberately designed to avoid military conflict with
Spain, and as long as French settlements were confined to the Gulf
of St. Lawrence, some three thousand miles removed from permanent Spanish settlement, they had a fair chance of success. Indeed,
during the first half of the sixteenth century, the north-eastern elbow
of North America was a remote and isolated zone of fishing activity
and colonial experiment, rather than a potential base of attack
against the monopolies of imperial Spain.

Admittedly, the flag was beginning to follow trade to the Banks
of Newfoundland. By 1550 there were reports of minor sea engagements; between 1554 and 1555 twenty-one French ships were cap-

---

[10]*Ibid.*, xxiii-iv, 104-15, 327-87. Cartier's commission (issued October 17, 1540)
read in part: "With the desire to learn and have knowledge of several countries
said to be inhabited and possessed by savage peoples living without knowledge of
God, we have at great expense already sent several good pilots, our subjects, to
discover in the said countries, and among others we sent out our dear and well-
beloved Jacques Cartier, who has discovered great tracts of the countries of
Canada and Hochelaga which form the confines of Asia on the west, which
countries he found productive of good commodities . . . in consideration whereof
we have decided to send back the said Cartier to the said countries of Canada and
Hochelaga, and as far as the land of the Saguenay, should he be able to penetrate
thither" (pp. 128-31).

[11]Quoted in W. Lowery, *The Spanish Settlements within the Present Limits of
the United States, Florida, 1562-1574* (New York, 1905), 18-19. Cf. Biggar, *op cit.*,
xxxvii, who quotes from Ch. Weiss, *Papiers d' état du Cardinal de Granvelle* (Paris,
1872), iii, 296.

tured by Spanish privateers, and St. John's was raided with heavy losses to the French fleet in harbour.[12] But the little battles and raids had no part in a larger strategy of territorial aggrandizement or of national attrition by destruction of commerce; Spanish colonial hegemony in the New World was not in question, for neither Britain nor France could do more than draw projects of empire until they had attained organized strength at sea.

At the same time, it must be understood that no nation as yet was building what might be called "royal navies." No nation knew the meaning or guessed the far-reaching consequences of "command of the sea." Until the campaign of 1588 there were no naval engagements between fleets of large sailing-ships. The sailing-ship as a unit in military strategy was regarded as little more than a vehicle for moving troops, or a means of clearing the sea for an army of invasion. The phrase "Spanish colonial hegemony" merely meant that Spain had more armed sea-going ships than any of the other powers.

Yet, until the English defeat of the Armada, Spanish sea power resting on Caribbean bases was the determining force in the preliminary European conflict for North America. The French often talked of going to the Indies, as Charles V remarked somewhat sardonically to his son, but "we have taken care that their fleets have not lasted."

At the beginning of the second half of the sixteenth century the eastern coast of the continent from Mexico to Labrador was still unoccupied by Europeans. On the St. Lawrence, the Cartier and Roberval settlements had been abandoned before they had taken root, while in France ominous signs of domestic instability foreshadowed the end of any government-supported schemes of colonization. In 1559 the Treaty of Cateau-Cambresis with Spain seemed to indicate that France was prepared to leave the field of North American settlement to her stronger rivals.

Curiously enough, the very troubles which were to put France out of the running for half a century were responsible for provoking a last and spectacular burst of colonial activity. The efforts were

[12]See H. A. Innis, "The Rise and Fall of the Spanish Fishery in Newfoundland," *Transactions of the Royal Society of Canada* (Ottawa, 1931), XXV, sec. 2, 51; also C. B. Judah, *The North American Fisheries and British Policy to 1713* (Urbana, Ill., 1933), 25-7, and Roncière, *Histoire de la Marine française*, III, 140, 280, 589-94.

individual, not national, but they serve to emphasize a salient fact, namely, that the demarcation line of 1494 derived its vitality, not from any papal sanction, but from the supremacy of Spanish ships on the Atlantic.

Before the shock of civil war had shattered the hard-won unity of France, Gaspard de Coligny, Admiral of France, seemed to have sensed impending tragedy. Already in 1555 he had furnished Vice-Admiral Villegagnon with the necessary capital and supplies to begin a little Huguenot refuge on the bay of Rio de Janeiro. But the colony was weakened by religious bickering; it was ill supported from home, and after Villegagnon departed, the Portuguese had no difficulty in destroying it. Meanwhile, Coligny had become openly Huguenot in his faith, and passionate conversion may partially explain his audacious effort to establish a foothold in Florida, next door to the colonial possessions of Spain. On February 16, 1562, his second expedition in charge of Jean Ribaut set out from France; and, after a journey of some two months, reached land, according to the latitude given, somewhere below Matanzas Inlet. Thence it turned northward past Jacksonville as far as the present Parris Island of South Carolina where Charlesfort was established as the first Protestant settlement in North America.[13] Ribaut left the settlement in July of the same year and took part in the renewed civil wars. During his absence mutiny and starvation brought the colony to an end.

Fortunately, the Treaty of Amboise halted the first struggle between Huguenot and Catholic, and since the armistice lasted for four years, Coligny was able to make one more attempt at colonization. René de Laudonnière commanded the expedition which sailed in April of 1564, arriving off the Florida coast in June, not far from the present site of St. Augustine. On the St. Johns River they established Fort Caroline. Once again, disorders, chiefly the product of famine and bad discipline, weakened the colony, and although an expedition under Ribaut arrived in time to strengthen it, Spain had already determined on the extinction of the nest of Huguenots. Profiting by Ribaut's tactical errors, Pedro Menendez assaulted Fort Caroline in 1565, and destroyed it. Survivors from ships which

[13]See J. Ribaut, *The Whole & True Discouerye of Terra Florida*. A Facsimile Reprint of the London Edition of 1563 together with a Transcript of an English Version in the British Museum with notes by H. M. Biggar, and a Biography by Jeannette Thurber Connor (De Land, Fla., Florida State Historical Society, 1927); also, *Deuxième Voyage du Dieppois Jean Ribaut à la Floride en 1565: Relation de N(icolas) Le Challeux, 1566*, ed. G. Gravier (Rouen, 1872), and P. Gaffarel, *Histoire de la Floride française* (Paris, 1875).

had been blown ashore farther along the coast were hunted down and massacred, "not as Frenchmen but as heretics." Not until three years later (1568) did a Catholic Gascon nobleman, Chevalier Dominic de Gourgues, with two ships which he had armed at his own expense, recapture Fort Caroline, hanging the whole garrison "not as Spaniards, but as murderers." But de Gourgues's only aim was revenge; for the time being French schemes of colonization had come to an end.[14]

So long as France was inferior to Spain at sea, no other result was possible. The destruction of Fort Caroline was the first demonstration in modern European history of the use of naval power as an indispensable buttress of colonial settlement. Colonization could no longer be simply a matter of adventuring to win glory and territories in a New World. It was now imperative that a nation keep in close communication with its overseas plantations. Frenchmen or Englishmen might still harry the Spaniard by sea in bold privateering expeditions, but to maintain a foothold in North America without constant military and naval support from home was tempting disaster.[15]

The destruction of the French colony by arms came as the culmination of a series of sporadic individual encounters from the Azores to Newfoundland. As the most dramatic challenge to Spanish hegemony in North America, Coligny's exploits confirmed the struggle for power on the North American continent as a major European issue. For the first time in history, a European state, Spain, was forced to maintain afloat an economic life-line. The whole of Spanish military and administrative efficiency depended upon the safe and prompt arrival of the treasure *flotas* from the Indies. Enemy guerillas that damaged a key port like Vera Cruz, captured a galleon, or threatened Spanish communication from overseas bases, endangered the whole intricate foundation of Spanish continental power.

The evacuation of Florida meant the temporary renunciation of French colonial experiments. Only fishermen maintained the connection with North America, and almost a hundred years were to

[14]A full account of these two expeditions and their destruction is contained in Roncière, *Histoire de la Marine française*, IV, 46-59.

[15]In almost every history of French colonization written by a Frenchman, one comes sooner or later to phrases like the following: "We have failed in Brazil and in Canada by the action of our Government, not by the action of our men who had all the qualities to make excellent colonists." Gravier, *Examen critique de l'histoire du Brésil français*, 22; and, quoting M. de Varnhagen in the same volume: "If the royal government had done its duty in regard to our merchant marine of the 16th century, Brazil would be today an independent nation, which owed its origin to French colonizers" (p. 15).

elapse between the first discovery of the St. Lawrence by Jacques Cartier and the establishment in Canada of permanent colonization. The Normans and Bretons continued to visit Newfoundland and even the Gulf of St. Lawrence. Such small ports as Jumièges, Vatteville, and La Bouille armed as many as thirty-eight ships for the Newfoundland trade.[16] Moreover, the fishermen from Honfleur and Dieppe began to trade with the natives in furs, and the fur trade soon became an object in itself, tempting the fisherman to become a merchant, and drawing him slowly from Newfoundland to the coasts of Labrador, the Gulf, and even the River St. Lawrence.[17]

But it was not the slow transition from "fish to furs" that accounted for the long gap between Cartier's two inland winterings and Champlain's first permanent settlement in 1604. The main obstacles to settlement lay in Europe. Under Francis I the French attempt to win supremacy over Spain on the continent had failed. Admiral Coligny had then carried the struggle briefly into the colonial world, but he was playing almost a lone hand, and his presumptuous challenge to Spanish power had also come to grief. Thenceforward domestic difficulties prevented any government from giving serious attention to affairs overseas. There were, it is true, intervals of peace, but they were transitory, for France had become the battle-ground for rival religions and rival political groups. The war of religion, says M. de la Roncière with some emotion, was the "cursed thing" which forced France to abandon all desire for expansion. "A tenth of the men killed in the least of our civil wars," cried Dominique de Gourgues amid the bloodshed, "would have sufficed to conquer several kingdoms."[18]

That colonial attempts in the sixteenth century failed was not because the French lacked experience or aptitude.[19] On the contrary, they had far more knowledge of Newfoundland and North America than the English, and long tradition bound them to the fisheries. Nor was scientific skill absent. Dieppe had become a city of as-

[16]E. H. Gosselin, *Documents authentiques et inédits pour servir à l'histoire de la Marine normande et du commerce rouennais pendant les XVIᵉ et XVIIᵉ siècles* (Rouen, 1876), 13.
[17]See P. F. X. de Charlevoix, *Histoire et Description générale de la Nouvelle France* (3 vols., Paris, 1744), I, 107-8; C. et P. Bréard, *Documents relatifs à la Marine normande* (Rouen, 1889), 50; J. B. Brebner, *The Explorers of North America, 1492-1806* (London, 1933), 146.
[18]Quoted in Roncière, *Histoire de la Marine française*, IV, 2.
[19]Cf. Georges d'Avenel, *Richelieu et la monarchie absolue* (Paris, 1887), III, 215.

tronomers, geographers, and map-makers, renowned for the intellectual curiosity that compassed oceans. Its school of seamanship was infused with theoretical science, and theory was not separated from the practical teachings of experienced navigators.

But successful colonization depended on three things—careful exploration of bases for settlement, steady emigration to provide local manpower, and finally, protection of communications to the colony by ships of war. Of these elements the last two, and more especially the final element, sea power, depended on the internal stability of the mother country. In France, the period beginning with the reign of Charles IX (1560-74) and lasting until the Edict of Nantes (1598) was one of almost constant administrative confusion; and as long as the bloodshed and tumult lasted, neither a colonial policy nor any form of large-scale enterprise was possible.[20] Even without government impulse and protection, the French might have clung to settlements far up the St. Lawrence, but the fact of remoteness offered of itself only a very precarious form of security. As long as Spanish maritime power was superior to that of France, any French colony separated from its homeland by the Atlantic lay ultimately at the mercy of Spain.

After the St. Bartholomew Massacre, the successors of Admiral Coligny had no chance to carry on his constructive work even had they wished. Shaken by religious schisms, the slender foundations of a royal navy crumbled away.[21] Always self-reliant by tradition, the western coastal towns either announced their independence or

[20]Moreover, the stream of gold and silver which flowed from America through Spain and Portugal had produced a general rise in European prices, which reached its peak in France between 1576 and 1600, thus adding to the financial confusion already produced by administrative corruption. High taxes, even on the lower classes, brought the royal exchequer next to nothing; the debt soon reached a total of 300 million livres (some two billion in terms of pre-1914 values) and there was not sufficient credit to maintain an army for fifteen days. E. J. Hamilton, *American Treasure and the Price Revolution in Spain, 1501-1650* (Cambridge, Mass. 1934), 207; and J. Tramond, *Manuel d'Histoire maritime de la France* (2nd ed., Paris, 1927), 144-5; also H. Pahl, *Die Kolonialpolitik Richelieus und ihre Beziehungen zu seiner Gesamtpolitik* (Heidelberg, 1932), 11.

[21]Henry II (1547-59) was a precursor of Colbert in his understanding of sea power. Alone of the Valois he grasped, like Henry VIII of England, the new significance of the fighting ship. When he came to the throne he found bad ships and low morale, and he worked hard to restore both. Despite the vicissitudes of war, he planned a great scheme of reconstruction and went far to execute it. All told, including galleys and "roberges," he added fifty new vessels, a fleet which formed the beginning of a royal marine. See Roncière, *Histoire de la Marine française*, III, 453-60. Without the work of Henry II, Admiral Coligny could never have risked his Huguenot brethren in the hazardous Florida venture.

joined with the English and the Huguenots, thus surrendering thousands of the best seamen to the foreigner.[22] While the English continued to man their ships with Bretons, Normans, and Biscayans, the seafaring potential of France was reduced to some sixty captains and five thousand sailors. With the exception of St. Malo, the ports fell into ruinous condition; Dieppe was sacked, and both Havre and Rouen were devastated by Dutch and English raiders. At sea, the kingdom was reduced to two obsolete men-of-war. Of merchant tonnage, by 1589 the Atlantic ports held probably less than eighty vessels of one hundred tons, and most of these were independently owned. The rest were small barques, pinnaces and shallops under twenty-five tons.[23] In the Mediterranean, African corsairs destroyed the trade, ravaged the ports of Provence, including Marseilles, and even followed French fishermen to Newfoundland.[24]

In 1577 Troilus du Mesguoez, Marquis de la Roche, was commissioned to establish a colony with merchant support, but an English squadron blocked the enterprise.[25] His second attempt in 1584 was abandoned after his largest ship was wrecked near Brouage, and the final expedition of 1598 ended in disaster on Sable Island. Cartier's nephews, Étienne Charton and Jacques Nöel, had obtained a monopoly of the fur trade in 1588 in return for bringing out colonists, but as a consequence of opposition from Breton merchants their charter was rescinded.[26] Again France failed to find in the New World a base for operations against her rivals of the Old. When Henry IV ascended a shaky throne in 1589, his country had ceased to exist as a maritime power.

Meanwhile, during the first half of the sixteenth century, English adventurers had been cautiously respectful of Spanish claims in the New World. Although the Cabot landfall was recognized by the map-makers of Europe, subsequent failures served to dampen the

[22]The number has been estimated as high as 200,000. See Tramond, *Manuel d'histoire maritime*, 144-5.

[23]See *Correspondance de Henri d'Escoubleau de Sourdis . . . accompagnée d'un texte historique, de notes et d'une introduction sur l'état de la Marine en France sous le ministère du Cardinal de Richelieu* par M. Eugène Sue (3 vols., Paris, 1839), III, 207; also d'Avenel, *Richelieu et la monarchie absolue*, 161.

[24]Roncière, *Histoire de la Marine française*, IV, 426.

[25]*Calendar of State Papers, Foreign, Elizabeth, 1577-8*, XII, nos. 24, 83, 100, 252, 587, 592, 607.

[26]Cartier's sons, Michel and Jean, attempted to follow in their father's footsteps past Gaspé, but were unsuccessful. See Roncière, *Histoire de la Marine française*, IV, 312.

enthusiasm of a still distracted and poverty-stricken England.[27] In 1527, Robert Thorne urged Henry VIII to support an expedition to the Indies via the North Pole, for "there is no doubt but that sayling Northwards and passing the Pole, descending to the Equinoctiall lyne, we shall hitte these Islandes, and it should be much shorter way than eyther the Spaniardes or the Portingals have." Henry responded to the appeal, but his master mariner, John Rut, was beaten back by ice. Other men after Cabot's time sought out the coast of North America; still others, like William Hawkins in 1530, visited Brazil. But the skippers of those days were not literate folk; and even if they could have written about their strange discoveries, many may have preferred to keep secret the position of their fishing grounds or fur trading preserves.

By and large, England was not yet fitted for large-scale navigational exploits. Despite her insular situation, she was still an agricultural country, continental in outlook rather than seafaring and expansionist. Unlike the Norsemen, and contrary to general belief, Englishmen had no deep-rooted tradition of the sea. Apart from the Crusades and an occasional private expedition to Africa, English pretensions to sea supremacy had been confined to the Channel, which was regarded as a part of the feudal domain connecting the kingdom with possessions in France. If, as one writer has piquantly suggested, Admiral Mahan had gathered around him a group of sixteenth-century Crown officials, he might have found difficulty in persuading them that their country's future lay on the oceans.[28] Until Elizabeth's reign, interest was chiefly landward. While English soldiers fought to conquer Scotland or France, Dutch and German and Venetian sailors carried the bulk of English wool to Flanders, almost all the wine from France, the spices from the Levant, and even the fish from Iceland and the Banks.[29] Henry VII had given some slight encouragement to the Cabots, but instead of finding new gold, successive voyages had only led to old fishing grounds. By the end of the sixteenth century, the average Englishman, if he thought of North America at all, most likely thought of it as a fishing station near Greenland.[30]

[27]J. A. Williamson, *Maritime Enterprise, 1485-1558* (Oxford, 1913), chaps. IV, V, and X.
[28]J. U. Nef, *The Rise of the British Coal Industry* (2 vols., London, 1932), I, 238.
[29]See G. B. Parks, *Richard Hakluyt and the English Voyages*, ed. with introd. J. A. Williamson (New York, American Geographical Society, 1928), 3-4.
[30]*Ibid.*, 7.

Not until the fifteen-seventies did Englishmen seriously begin the task of discovering "a passage by the Northe to go to Cataia, & other east partes of the worlde,"[31] a search which Humphrey Gilbert's *Discourse of a New Passage to Cataia* (1576) did much to encourage. Between 1576 and 1587, Frobisher and Davis each made three voyages into the Arctic, voyages which in turn stimulated Hakluyt to publish the records of the first explorers. In making these heroic attempts, English adventurers were not merely trying to find a short-cut to the Far East; their preference for snow and ice was based on a cautious respect for Portuguese and Spanish claims in the temperate and tropical zones.

For the moment, however, little came of these painful undertakings other than the discovery of the Hudson Straits, and the unwelcome conclusion that a road to the East by the north-west was too costly in terms of life and money to justify further experiment. Nevertheless, there was a real connection between this fruitless search for "the Passage" and English colonial expansion. Both Sir Walter Raleigh and Sir Humphrey Gilbert were convinced that the quest for the back door to the Indies could be linked with colonization, and Gilbert's expedition of 1583 was primarily aimed at founding a colony in Newfoundland. Such settlements, as Hakluyt pointed out, could form strategic bases not only for attacks against the possessions of Spain, but for further searches, "that by these colonies the north west Passage may easily, quickly and perfectly be searched oute as well by river and overlande as by sea."

The establishment of an English military outpost in North America was obviously very much subsidiary to the search for the Passage; at the same time, it was no coincidence that the search for the North-West Passage immediately preceded the initial establishment of the British overseas empire. Repeated failures to find a northern route were bound to deflect the energies of English explorers and their merchant backers towards the North American continent. Moreover, as Hakluyt made plain to his countrymen,

... if we did not fortifie ourselves aboute Cape Briton, the Frenche, the Normans, the Brytons or the Duche or some other nation, will not onely prevent us, of the mighty Baye of St. Lawrence, where they have gotten the starte

[31]See G. B. Manhart, "The English Search for a Northwest Passage in the Time of Queen Elizabeth," in A. L. Rowland and G. B. Manhart, *Studies in English Commerce and Exploration in the Reign of Elizabeth* (Philadelphia, 1924), 14.

of us already, but will deprive us of Newfoundland which now wee [sic] have discovered.[32]

The argument was impressive; yet without constant support by sea colonies such as Raleigh attempted at Roanoke in 1585 had little more chance of success than Admiral Coligny's enterprises in Brazil and Florida. Nevertheless, national interest was beginning to invade the Atlantic jousting ground of private combat. As overseas trade, whether in fish or precious metals, developed, jealousy on the part of the "have-nots" inevitably raised the question of exclusive rights to specified regions. Already the English had begun to prey on Spanish and French shipping to the Banks, and these sporadic undertakings had a pronounced national flavour. English freebooting, like English trade and exploration, was becoming more and more a racial activity.

Yet statesmen in England were slow to grasp the strategic importance of destroying the commerce of a rival; few men, apart from John Hawkins, could have believed that the mere stopping of treasure ships would reduce the military capacity of a great land power. The expeditions of the Elizabethan sea-dogs were essentially semi-piratical attacks on the rich cargo ships and bullion depots. Hopes of profit and hatred of Popery counted for much more than any comprehensive design of impoverishing Spain by eliminating her fleets. There was no suggestion that naval warfare might be in any way decisive, or that the armed ship as an instrument of war could affect the result of the struggle on land.[33]

Not until the eighties did a series of daring and seemingly haphazard English raids on Spanish commerce begin to strike a pattern that had the ear-marks of conscious strategy. This pattern first showed itself soon after 1585 when plans were drawn up for attacks on such significant points as San Domingo, Cartagena, and Panama. There were discussions too on the possibilities of occupying Havana and blockading Mexico.[34] These were no mere schemes of pillage, but projects involving an organized offensive designed to cut at the roots of the Spanish colonial empire and the sources of Spanish economic strength.

[32]*The Voyages of the English Nation to America before the year 1600*, ed. Edmund Goldsmid (4 vols., Edinburgh, 1889-90). Vol. IV contains *Discourse of Western Planting* by R. Hakluyt.   [33]See Appendix A.

[34]See document entitled "Plan of Campaign" in J. S. Corbett, *Papers Relating to the Navy during the Spanish War, 1585-1587* (London, Navy Records Society, 1898), 69.

Drake's West Indian onslaught of 1585-86 helped to bring Philip II close to bankruptcy; it paralysed his campaign in Flanders by depriving Parma of the money to keep up the army. In 1590, when Frobisher and Hawkins waylaid the annual *flota*, Spain had to forego her anticipated invasion of France. Even the plundering of Spanish coastal harbours, when viewed in retrospect, seems to be something more than a beard-singeing diversion. "The truth is," wrote the Venetian ambassador in 1587, "that he [Drake] has done so much damage on these coasts of Spain alone, that though the King were to obtain a signal victory against him he would not recover one half the loss he has suffered."[35]

The first evidence of a groping towards some tactical scheme for sailing-ships revealed itself in the duel with the Spanish Armada. Many Spaniards still regarded the new sailing-ship or galleon as a means of conducting land warfare at sea. The Armada was a collection of armed transports rather than a fleet of battle-ships, and if fighting was inevitable, boarding would be the method chosen. The English, on the other hand, refused such hand-to-hand tactics; and while it is possible to exaggerate the effects of ragged gun-fire on masts and rigging, it can be said that English seamen in 1588 learned the value of the ship, not merely as a vehicle for carrying men, but as an instrument of seamanship designed to fight other ships at a distance.

Had it been a galley battle, Philip would have won; on the decks of the seagoing sailing-ships, his first-rate soldiers were pathetic figures in a pageant from the Age of Chivalry. The defeat of the Armada was, in short, the defeat of land levies at sea. The technique of the land battle-field was not transferable to deep water. On the heaving decks of a galleon, the knightly hero of mediaeval Spain became merely an absurd fore-runner of Don Quixote.[36]

Although naval warfare remained for many years a highly individualistic procedure, the battle of the Armada had, nevertheless, demonstrated the value of the armed sailing-ship as an instrument of state policy, and pointed the way to future state-owned fleets manned

---

[35]See Corbett, *Papers Relating to the Navy*, xliii.
[36]See M. J. Bonn, *Spaniens Niedergang während der Preisrevolution des 16. Jahrhunderts* (Stuttgart, 1896), 3-4, 197; also Tramond, *Manuel d'Histoire maritime*, 97-8; J. S. Corbett, *Drake and the Tudor Navy* (2 vols., London, 1917), I, 388-9; *The Naval Tracts of Sir William Monson*, ed. M. Oppenheim (5 vols., London, Navy Records Society, 1902-14), I, (vol. XXII) 13-14; J. A. Williamson, *Sir John Hawkins* (Oxford, 1927), 426.

by professional fighting seamen. Already a warship had ceased to be regarded as a mere transport for troops engaged in land operations. In the new era of battle at sea, the ship of the line became accepted as exclusively a fighting vessel by all seafaring nations. By the end of James I's reign, the day of the armed merchantman—the cog or the carrack—was over. Squadrons of warships, divided into rates according to the number of guns they carried, took the place of the improvised fleets of Elizabeth's time, and professional seamen were soon wrestling with the problem of deploying large numbers of ships to achieve concentration and thus utilize the full force of their fire power.[37] In other words, schemes of naval tactics—for example, the formal development of "line-ahead"—began to supplant the undisciplined *mêlée* of "hammer and tongs."

A new element had thus entered into the international equilibrium —sea power. In the past, territorial extension founded on military force had been the principal issue of European rivalry. With the seventeenth century, competition on the seas gradually superimposed itself on the traditional pattern of continental relationships.[38] As a consequence of the opening of the Atlantic, there developed a duality in national interests. Expansionist policies concerned with sea routes and colonies were bound eventually to conflict with policies of continental conquest. Thus every state with a frontage on the Atlantic had at least to revise its estimates on the sources of national power. In the new era of trans-Atlantic colonization, overseas trade was to become an essential constituent of a country's prosperity and strength, and the wealth from the huge colonial empire over the horizon would be garnered only by those nations that possessed numerous and well-armed ships. Hence, from overseas trade competition arose the struggle for command of communications, a chronic contest that was to exert a constant and compelling influence upon the external policies of Spain, the Netherlands, France, and England.

In short, by the beginning of the seventeenth century, the statesman was beginning to take the place of the adventurer as the principal advocate of commercial expansion and colonial wealth. In the new

[37]The merchantman continued to carry armament of a sort, and at the time of the first Dutch War it was still in use, but very rarely as a unit in the line of battle. In squadron battles it had little chance against the new three-decker with a hundred guns. Moreover, its value as a cargo carrier by far exceeded its worth as an auxiliary combat vessel.

[38]See C. von Maltzahn, *Naval Warfare: Its Historical Development from the Age of the Great Geographical Discoveries to the Present Time*, trans. J. C. Miller (London, 1908), 31.

epoch of European rivalries a nation's accumulated and organized power at sea was to count far more than all the individual skill and initiative and daring of men like Villegagnon, Ribaut, de Gourgues, Gilbert, and Hawkins, who so unceremoniously initiated the struggle for North America.   Slowly but surely, expanding colonial rivalries were to force the pace of maritime commerce, hasten the acquisition of overseas bases and plantations, and stimulate the growth of state navies as a means to one end—national power.[39]

[39]See in this connection, W. Sombart, *Der Moderne Kapitalismus* (3 vols., Munich and Leipzig, 1916-28), I, 761; also, by the same author, *Studien zur Entwicklungsgeschichte des Kapitalismus.* Vol. II: *Krieg und Kapitalismus* (Munich, 1913), 190.

II

Foundations of French Sea Power

ALTHOUGH the defeat of the Armada was a heavy blow to Spain, Spanish influence continued to count heavily in continental affairs, and almost every European state had its "Spanish party." At the end of the sixteenth century Spain was still to all outward appearances the first power in Europe.[1] Her overseas connections were still intact, and the lesson of 1588 expressed itself in new modern ships and trained crews of fighting seamen. During the last years of Elizabeth's reign, Ireland was invaded and English squadrons in the Channel were repeatedly driven off by superior forces. Indeed, until the end of the war (1604) England, far from continuing her command of the sea, had failed even to break the Spanish trade monopoly.[2]

By the time of Philip II's death in 1598, however, Spain had ceased to be aggressively strong, and the end of her hegemony was near. Among the manifold reasons why the nation which bestrode Europe and North America like a colossus should sink ingloriously to the rank of a third-rate power, two are particularly relevant to this study.

In the first place Spain did not adapt herself easily to the medium of the sea. The average well-bred Spaniard preferred to be a soldier, an official, or a cleric rather than face the routine tasks of ocean commerce and colonization. He remained, on the whole, disciplined and was still prepared to die, if need be, for the state; but this was the discipline of the battlefield carried over into civil life where it took the form of bureaucratic supervision and restriction, with rigid

[1]See Bonn, *Spaniens Niedergang*, 3-4.
[2]See J. S. Corbett, *The Successors of Drake* (London, 1900), vi.

21

monopolies. In matters of ship-building or naval administration, the maritime system of Spain remained inelastic and unimaginative. Supremacy at sea could not be maintained merely by improvisation in an age when constant change in organization was required to meet the exigencies of new naval warfare.

Moreover, during the first half of the seventeenth century, there was a growing disinclination on the part of seamen and traders to participate in the yearly *flotas* to the New World, and this decline in seafaring morale undoubtedly played a part in the steady decay of the merchant marine. By the middle of the century its ruin was nearly complete. At one time the fleets had reached 9,000 tons; after 1651 it was a triumph if one of 3,000 tons could be sent every second year.[3] During the Thirty Years' War, Spain lost some 280 ships; by 1680 she possessed only seven or eight ships of the line,[4] and her great colonial territories in the New World lay at the mercy of the first aggressor.

In the second place, there never was a strong economic basis for Spanish sea power. There was no solid foundation of agriculture, expanding industry, and healthy finance—a condition which goes far to explain the rapidity of disintegration, and to account for the decline in population of the peninsula during the seventeenth century from a probable total of over nine millions to a little over five millions.[5] Spanish hegemony had rested fundamentally on control of the Netherlands, Portugal, and other states within the Hapsburg orbit. In other words, an acute distinction existed between the national or regional and the imperial Spain, between the Iberian peninsula and the far-flung Hapsburg empire. No amount of industrial growth could have made the peninsula a focal area of European commerce; the great regions of commercial and industrial development lay to the north, and even good Atlantic ports could not have made Spain the terminus of the great continental trade routes that ran from the south, the south-east, and the east. Since medi-

[3]C. H. Haring, *Trade and Navigation between Spain and the Indies in the Time of the Hapsburgs* (Cambridge, Mass., 1918), 211-15; see also Hamilton, *American Treasure and the Price Revolution in Spain*, 304.

[4]See Tramond, *Manuel d'histoire maritime*, 96-9.

[5]See R. Altamira, *Historia de España* (4 vols., Barcelona, 1928-9), III, 486-90; IV, 254. R. B. Merriman in *The Rise of the Spanish Empire in the Old World and in the New*, IV (New York, 1934), estimated the total population as a little over nine millions in 1594 (p. 448). Most of the figures for the early seventeenth century are in dispute, although there is no denying the rapid decline; cf. R. T. Davies, *The Golden Century of Spain, 1501-1621* (London, 1937), 272.

eval times these routes had converged on the north, and in the seventeenth century, Amsterdam, not Seville, was to be the centre of the giant trading web. Amsterdam became not only the money and staple market of Europe but the *entrepôt* of the world, whence merchants of all nations brought their cargoes for warehousing and redistribution.[6] Such treasure as the Mexican *flotas* continued to bring to Spanish ports ultimately crossed the peninsula to the profit of Holland, France and England, who were, in a sense, the part-creation of Spanish riches.

Yet, apart from Jamaica, Hispaniola, and a few smaller islands, the Spanish-American empire was to remain curiously intact. Remoteness, however, rather than naval power was the key to immunity, for the area of competitive colonization had shifted to the north of the Caribbean. In these circumstances, the Spaniards were able to maintain their claims to a complete monopoly of discovery and trade in the West Indies. When Henry IV of France came to terms with Philip in 1598 at the Peace of Vervins, all mention of overseas claims was left out of the treaty; likewise, when James I made peace in 1604, the agreement gave no more than the right to trade with all "Kingdoms, Dominions and Islands of the King of Spain to which before the war there was commerce according to the ancient treaties."

Meanwhile England had failed to exploit the lessons which had been taught in 1588. The significance of sea power which the Elizabethans had begun to grasp was no longer appreciated; the first Stuart king was intent on peace with Spain, and for him the "Overlordship of the Ocean" held small attraction.

The actual beginnings of the greatest colonizing movement in English history had, therefore, none of the glamour associated with the sixteenth century. The foundations of Virginia were laid precariously in 1607 amid circumstances that were almost squalid, and only the decline of Spanish sea power enabled them to endure. Sixteen years later, William Alexander made his first unfruitful visit to Nova Scotia. The first large-scale migrations of the British peoples, which led to the founding of New England, were essentially the product of religious differences. In Newfoundland, the main effort had been protective rather than colonizing. During the years be-

[6]C. Wilson, *Anglo-Dutch Commerce and Finance in the Eighteenth Century* (Cambridge University Press, 1941), 3-4; also R. Ehrenberg, *Capital and Finance in the Age of the Renaissance*, tr. H. M. Lucas (London, 1928), 357-63.

tween Gilbert's voyage of 1583 and John Guy's colony of 1610, the English were content with a foothold from Cape Bonavista to Cape Race, leaving to the French the whole of the south shore. At the same time, a large part of the Newcastle coal trade, the Greenland fisheries, the herring fisheries—almost all except the Newfoundland trade—gradually passed to the hands of the Dutch. Algerian pirates and "Dunkirkers" swept the Channel in search of galley slaves and booty; the only attempt at retaliation in James's reign was the naval expedition of 1620—a vain effort against the Moslem nests in North Africa.

And with the power, the glory had departed. The defeat of the Spanish Armada was accepted as an incident of stormy weather.[7] After the execution of Raleigh, the age of heroics was succeeded by an era of apathy. By stopping the war with Spain and insisting on peace at any price—which meant the end of privateering—James effectively blocked the development of the English navy. It remained for the moment a kind of sea militia, still dependent on the merchant service at a time when few merchants were anxious to rent or lend to a poverty-stricken Stuart. By 1614, "there were not ten ships of two hundred tons left belonging to the river of Thames fit for the defence of the kingdom."[8] By 1625, when Charles I came to the throne, the country possessed only seventeen comparatively modern ships, and most of these were far too slow to deal with Moorish pirates or Dunkirk privateers.[9]

Hence it happened that a small, fiercely aggressive and loosely federalized republic, but recently freed from Spanish control, grasped a "command of the sea" that after 1588 had seemed destined to be England's. It was the Dutch and not the English who broke the traditional trade barriers of Spain. In 1609 under the terms of a twelve-year truce, Spain agreed not to interfere with Dutch trade in any regions that were not in the effective occupation of the subjects of the king of Spain. This agreement—for there were no written stipulations—was guaranteed by England and France. While exist-

[7]The lesson was learned but slowly. Even before the death of Elizabeth the story had gained currency that the Armada had been defeated by the winds of God, rather than by the fireships and guns of Howard and Drake. The commemorative medal bore the inscription: "Flavit Deus et dissipati sunt."

[8]Oppenheim, *The Naval Tracts of Sir William Monson*, III (1913), 431.

[9]M. Oppenheim, *A History of the Administration of the Royal Navy and of Merchant Shipping in Relation to the Navy from 1509 to 1660* (London, 1896), 251-2.

ing Spanish possessions in North America and the Indies were safe-guarded by compact, the unoccupied seas and lands were now open to competition. This tremendously significant admission meant that Spain no longer felt herself powerful enough to shut out her rivals from overseas trade. The monopoly sanctioned by the Pope in 1493 had been extinguished at last.

Usurping the position of the declining Hanseatic League in the Baltic Sea, the Dutch came close to eliminating English competition, as well as gaining a near-monopoly on Baltic timber and other essentials of naval construction. With ships built at a third the cost of the English, and with a low rate of interest upon which to capitalize their undertakings, their fleets quickly gained control of the Baltic and the North Sea.[10] Ranging into the oceans, they soon acquired an empire in both hemispheres, and laid the basis for a powerful navy.

By 1570 the total tonnage of Dutch merchant shipping probably equalled that of Spain and Portugal combined.[11] For a great part of the seventeenth century, the physical volume of Dutch shipping was probably as great as that of the English in the eighteenth. By 1600 Holland controlled over one thousand merchant ships; within a decade the number was around three thousand, along with some three thousand fishing craft.[12] States such as Spain, Russia, Sweden, and Prussia, which were in an embryonic stage of commercial development, found the Dutch carriers indispensable; and while England cramped or dissipated her strength to meet the exigencies of Stuart personal rule, Holland slowly but surely appropriated the carrying trade of Europe.

One fact which was to have a profound effect on subsequent naval as well as commercial competition was the technical advance made by the Dutch in the art of ship-building. After 1590 Spain instituted few changes in ship design, and little progress was made towards improving the sailing qualities of English vessels till the time of the Petts in the reign of Charles I. The Dutch, however, constantly experimented in a realistic effort to meet the problems of

[10]R. G. Albion, *Forests and Sea Power* (Cambridge, Mass., 1926), 156.

[11]A. P. Usher, "Spanish Ships and Shipping in the Sixteenth and Seventeenth Centuries," in *Facts and Factors in Economic History* (Cambridge, Mass., 1932), 211-13.

[12]Figures quoted by Pahl in *Die Kolonialpolitik Richelieus*, 9; based on calculations by E. Baasch, *Holländische Wirtschaftsgeschichte* (Jena, 1927).

the new sea-borne commerce, and Dutch ships of the early seventeenth century—especially the famous "bus," a cargo carrier—represented a significant break with older traditions.[13]

In the Indian and Pacific oceans, and also across the Atlantic, the Dutch were interested not in colonization, but in trade; and until 1664 their West India Company controlled at New Amsterdam a base of immense strategical importance, not only because of its harbour, but because the connecting Hudson River gave convenient inland communication with the St. Lawrence. They also possessed a fleet which was strong enough to have taken Quebec at almost any time during the century. As it happened, however, the security of the Republic depended (until Louis XIV invaded the country in 1672) on good relations with France. Any attempt to assault Canada laid Holland open to retaliation in Europe. Hence the Dutch preferred to confine their main attentions to distant and more profitable waters. In the long run, rivalry for North America was to take the form of a duel between France and England.

By the beginning of the seventeenth century, the disheartening impression left in France by the disasters in Brazil and Florida and the failure to follow up Cartier's plans with regard to Canada had begun to fade. Henry IV had brought an end to religious war, but the country came out of the struggle with little money in the exchequer, next to no ships in the harbours, no colonies, little commerce, and a minimum of prestige. When Sully was embarking for Dover to negotiate a treaty, French ships lowered their colours as an English man-of-war conducted the chief minister out of his native port.[14]

Lack of money made the task of reorganization, and especially the building of a fleet, enormously difficult. Henry IV made a start by getting an advance on Marie de Medici's dowry. This gave him six galleys, while a tax on brothels and the sale of military orders covered the cost of repairing several obsolete ships.[15] But despite such ingenious efforts, Henry IV cannot be said to have created a navy. Apart from twelve or fifteen galleys at Marseilles, the Atlantic fleet consisted of some dozen badly armed and badly equipped

[13]Usher, "Spanish Ships and Shipping," 195; also B. Hagedorn, *Die Entwicklung der wichtigsten Schiffstypen bis ins 19. Jahrhundert* (Berlin, 1914), 93.

[14]E. Levasseur, *Histoire du commerce de la France* (2 vols., Paris, 1911-12), I, 252.

[15]Tramond, *Manuel d'histoire maritime*, 145; Roncière, *Histoire de la Marine française*, IV, 5-6.

ships, of which only one, *La Vierge*, was regarded as capable of fighting the best English, Dutch, or even Spanish ships.[16] Moreover, the decline of the merchant marine meant a shortage of manpower, since many good seamen like Champlain had entered foreign service.[17]

It is probable that Henry IV, like Champlain, saw a future in North America for the French race. What would have happened had he not fallen victim to an assassin in 1610 must be a matter for speculation; but like all French sovereigns he felt the tug of continental interests, and even with a fuller purse and more secure frontiers, it is almost certain that European obligations would eventually have triumphed over North American. A continental policy meant enlarging the army and economizing on the navy, and without a navy the main pillar of overseas commerce and colonization was lacking.

Nevertheless, Henry established the precedent of state-supported commercial companies. Company efforts at colonization were by no means a novelty. Private associations of merchants had founded the first establishments on the coast of Africa, and this method had been adopted in the fruitless effort to colonize Brazil. But under Henry IV's system, the state was required to play a more substantial part. It was required to help in the task of organization, to sanction the regulations, to supervise their execution, to invest as much money as it deemed wise, and to take nominal responsibility for protecting the territories occupied against attack by rival powers. In a sense, the colony was regarded as a fief, the merchant companies being the "grand feudatories." There was the important difference, however, that the merchant feudality was the creation of the sovereign, who might at any time cancel the grant. In further distinction, since the holders were overseas, they were hardly in a position to nourish the traditional dynastic ambitions of their class in opposition to the king.[18]

Since the risks of the merchants and shipowners in meeting the main costs and in doing the work were large, it was natural that their privileges should be extensive. Because the government was reluctant to spend money, and usually too deeply involved with its European responsibilities to take more than spasmodic interest, the "company" remained as before, the chief instrument of colonization. On the other hand, the colony was ultimately dependent on the state,

[16]H. Pigeonneau, *Histoire du commerce de la France* (2 vols., Paris, 1889), II, 403.
[17]In 1599 Champlain undertook his first reconnoitring trip to the West Indies under the Spanish flag. *The Works of Samuel de Champlain*, ed. H. P. Biggar (6 vols., Toronto, The Champlain Society, 1936), I, 3-80.
[18]Pigeonneau, *Histoire du commerce de la France*, II, 331-2.

not only for armed support but for immigrants, and without the urge of religious persecution colonists of the right kind were hard to secure. As long as the search for precious metals took precedence over agricultural settlement, governments and company directors were often satisfied to ship out criminals rather than farmers or artisans. In 1605 De Monts established Port Royal in the Annapolis basin, but even had there been sufficient financial support, the colonists were not of the type to found a lasting community with roots in the soil.

The history of Canada proper began only with the settlement at Quebec in 1608 under Samuel de Champlain. In Champlain the French possessed not only a great explorer and seaman, but a first-rate leader with unusual skill in native diplomacy and with the idealism of a true imperialist. Born into the Norman tradition of seamanship, and trained in the Spanish service, he remains still the model explorer and colonizer. Champlain had shifted his original plan from Acadia to Quebec, partly because the St. Lawrence post meant easier control of the fur trade, and partly because Quebec would serve as a base from which to find a route to the Western Sea and the Spice islands. In 1609 he worked down the approaches of the Hudson River; by 1615 he had opened up the Ottawa River and pushed on to Georgian Bay and Lake Huron and Lake Ontario.

But colonists were unwanted luxuries; the private company with the royal charter was interested in trade, and there lay the tremendous temptation and the danger. While good fortune gave the English a strip of land on the sea coast, forcing them to crowd their settlement east of the Appalachians, Champlain's successors, with less practical forethought but with brilliant vision, drove up the long rivers in search of the beaver. With a kind of continental strategy they saw the vital points that are vital to this day; and they perceived the strategic possibilities of a great circle of river and lake stretching from the Great Lakes to New Orleans which would shut out the British and eventually give them the continent. Unfortunately, nothing but the most constant support from Europe could have made the achievement of this French idea possible. Without the support of a strong navy, any French possessions in North America were bound to be hostages to the English fleet. The leadership of men like Champlain was of no avail if the communications with the mother country were endangered. Freedom from the menace of Spain meant nothing if France remained inferior to England at sea.

Five years after Champlain founded Quebec, Captain Samuel Argall at the request of the government of Virginia raided and destroyed all the French settlements in Acadia, including Port Royal. Although little more than a buccaneering raid, it marked the beginning of the long contest in arms which was to endure until 1760. Reparations were demanded by the French government, and the Council of Virginia was asked to declare the limits of that colony in respect of previous French claims.[19] But James made no concession to French clamours. Indeed, eight years later he granted the whole area, under the name of Nova Scotia, to a favourite, Sir William Alexander of Menstrie; and in 1624, somewhat forgetfully extended the charter of the New England Company to the forty-eighth parallel, thus overlapping the Alexander grant as well as the claims of France.

In 1623 Sir William sent off his first expedition to take possession of the country. The emigrants wintered in Newfoundland, and in the following spring made their way to the Bay of Fundy. There they discovered that the French had returned in somewhat formidable numbers. This discouraging intrusion compelled them to return to England, where they published an exciting account of the country they had seen only dimly from the decks of their ships.[20]

James's successor, Charles I, renewed the Alexander charter, establishing at the same time the Order of the Knights Baronet of Nova Scotia, to encourage settlement by discriminating offers of titles as well as free land. Several prominent London merchants backed this private venture, chief among them being Gervase Kirke. In the spring of 1628, three ships under the command of Kirke's son, David, accompanied by his two brothers, Lewis and Thomas, set sail from England, furnished with letters of marque from the king giving them authority to capture or sink any French vessels they might encounter, and to destroy French settlements in Nova Scotia or Canada. After calling at Newfoundland, in the hope of getting news of Richelieu's grand expedition, Kirke set sail for the St. Lawrence, ravaging settlements and forts in the neighbourhood of Cape Tourmente on his way thither.

Meanwhile, in April of the same year, twenty vessels laden with stores, food, guns, and ammunition had set out from France under

[19]H. de Montmorency, Admiral of France, to James I, October 18, 1613, in *Calendar of State Papers, Colonial, America and West Indies, 1574-1660*, ed. W. N. Saintsbury (London, 1860), I, 15.
[20]See H. Kirke, *The First English Conquest of Canada* (2nd ed., London, 1908), 53-5.

the command of Admiral de Roquemont. Thanks to Richelieu's zeal there was no problem of colonists on this occasion; emigrants of both sexes, free from criminal records, crowded the decks, along with priests and trained artisans. Unaware of the blockade, the French fleet ran into Kirke's forces above Tadoussac. Although most of his guns were stowed in the holds, and his unwieldy transports deep in the water, De Roquemont refused to surrender. After delivering a broadside through the stern of the admiral's ship, Kirke grappled and boarded her. Two more ships were captured with equal rapidity and the battle was over. Embarrassed by the richness and number of his prizes, which included 138 cannon for the defence of Quebec, Kirke rifled and burned ten of the smaller vessels, sending the salvaged stores with the remainder of the captured ships to Newfoundland. He himself sailed for Acadia, where he sacked Port Royal before returning to England. Lacking means of retaliation in the form of warships, Paris could do little about it except burn the Kirke brothers in effigy and shout for revenge.[21]

In the following year, a new and larger expedition was fitted out by Sir William Alexander, son of the original grantee.[22] Once again, under the command of David Kirke, six well-armed ships and three pinnaces made their way from Gravesend in March of 1629, arriving off Gaspé on June 15. From here Kirke sent his two brothers to visit the Acadian settlements, while he himself, in company with one ship, went up the St. Lawrence to Tadoussac, which he intended to use as a preliminary base for an attack on Quebec.

Champlain was already in desperate straits. As if to provide a second object lesson in the use of sea power, Kirke had captured the solitary supply ship on which the French leader had depended for provisions and powder. Moreover, to defend the crumbling towers of the small *château* which he had erected, there remained only a handful of able-bodied men, a few missionaries, and the women and children. The squadron despatched by the Company was too feeble to dare a rescue; Kirke barred the way up the St. Lawrence. Hence for Champlain there was no alternative to surrender. On July 20, 1629, the Cross of St. George was hoisted above the citadel.[23]

[21] *Ibid.*, 66.

[22] See in this connection a paper headed, "The State of the Business of Canada or New France, 1628," *Historical Manuscripts Commission, Cowper MSS.* (3 vols., London, 1888-9), I, 374-7.

[23] See "Depositions of Captains David and Thomas Kirke," in *Calendar of State Papers, Colonial, America and West Indies, 1574-1660*, 103, see also 98-9, 129, 131.

Peace had already been signed before Quebec fell, but this fact hardly explains the restitution of Canada, Cape Breton, and undefined Nova Scotia in the final settlement. One key to the riddle lies in Charles's own domestic circumstances. Already challenged by a grim and parsimonious Parliament, the king was in desperate need of money; and Richelieu was in a position to bargain with a few captured English ships and the unpaid half of Henrietta Maria's dowry.[24]

For the first time, North American territories had become counters on the European diplomatic board. With the signing of the Treaty of St. Germain-en-Laye on March 29, 1632, France and England recognized, by implication at least, each other's colonies in North America.[25] No boundaries were mentioned, but it is a significant commentary on the decline of Spanish sea power that, for the first time, a treaty acknowledged the existence of French and English settlements in the New World. Despite the written and verbal objections of merchant and fishing interests, emphasizing the danger to British overseas connections, a deal had been arranged, and French sovereignty, which might have been extinguished for all time, was re-asserted.[26] France recovered Quebec, all her fishing stations on the St. Lawrence, Port Royal, and the whole province of Acadia.[27] A disaster not unlike that of Florida and Brazil had been repaired as though by a miracle, and this time the foothold of the French was to be deep and enduring.

[24] See *Lettres, instructions diplomatiques et papiers d'état du Cardinal de Richelieu*, ed. M. d'Avenel (8 vols., Paris, 1853-77), III (1858), 477-8.

[25] S. F. Bemis, *A Diplomatic History of the United States* (2nd ed., London, 1942), 7n.

[26] See *Calendar of State Papers, Colonial, America and West Indies, 1574-1660*, 106, 128; also *ibid.*, 152, where correspondence reveals the anxiety of English merchants to remove the French from Nova Scotia and Canada. Although dated July, 1633, the following proposition in the handwriting of Secretary Coke is worth noting as expressing the general attitude of the mercantile community: "The new discoveries of Virginia, New England, New Scotland, and the rest employing above 300 English ships, have been often interrupted by the French and of late by the Dutch. The English should possess fit places in Canada and elsewhere, to protect the fishermen and inhabitants." (*Ibid.*, 170.) Imagination and acquisitiveness combine in another petition from London merchants, dated April 21, 1636, requesting the right to obtain sea-horse teeth, "a merchant's commodity not yet looked after." (*Ibid.*, 232.)

[27] In compensation for his losses, Alexander, son of the original grantee (who became Viscount Stirling in 1633 and an earl in 1637), received an order for £10,000 from the Treasury, with the grant of "all that part of the mainland in New England from St. Croix, adjoining New Scotland, along the sea to Pemaquid and so up the river to the Kinnebequi (Kennebec) to be henceforth called the Country of Canada." J. B. Brebner, *New England's Outpost: Acadia before the Conquest of Canada* (New York, 1927), 26.

Perhaps because the French possessions were restored with such alacrity, or because Kirke's expedition was little more than a private foray, there has been some tendency to ignore the significance of the first capture of Quebec. This demonstration of the use of sea power as the foundation of colonial dominion received scant attention in the England of the time; on the other hand, the implications of the event did not pass unnoticed in France. Linked with the lesson of La Rochelle, the capture of Port Royal and Quebec strengthened Richelieu in his design to build a French navy.

With the fall of Quebec, France was left almost destitute of colonies and overseas commerce. The Newfoundland fishery was disorganized; in the Arctic, the Spitzbergen whale fishery had been abandoned; and in the North Sea only a venturesome few pursued the herring. In the Mediterranean, Algerian pirates ravaged the shores of Provence, while in the Atlantic, Huguenot rebels attacked the western coasts, occupied the islands of Ré and Oléron, threatened Bordeaux, and blockaded the Gironde from their base at La Rochelle.[28] Moreover, the English were now firmly entrenched on the Atlantic coast; Virginia was an established colony; the Pilgrim Fathers had landed at Plymouth, and the greatest of English colonies, Massachusetts, was about to come into existence.

In one sense, the future of French naval policy may be said to have hung on the siege of La Rochelle. The frantic efforts of Richelieu to collect ships and sailors and guns made obvious to the whole country his conviction that only a strong French fleet could break the Huguenots by cutting them off from outside help. By hiring, buying, and borrowing, a makeshift royal squadron was finally assembled, but not until the harbour was closed by means of a stonework mole in 1628 did La Rochelle, after a fifteen months' siege, finally capitulate.

Sea power alone could not guarantee France against disunity and weakness, but in securing the fall of La Rochelle it did push home the lesson that only by means of a competent navy could France maintain independence of action. "He who is master of the sea, is master of the land" is an exaggerated maxim that occurs more than once in Richelieu's *Memoirs*. Nevertheless, naval strength meant

[28] See Pigeonneau, *Histoire du commerce de la France*, II, 403-4; also G. Lacour-Gayet, *La Marine militaire de la France sous le règne de Louis XV* (2nd ed., Paris 1910), 5.

at least increased European leverage, and after 1628 a deep-sea fleet policy was pushed ahead, stimulated by political division and civil war in England, and accelerated by great statesmanship at home.[29]

According to Richelieu, Providence had offered France the "empire of the seas" by generously providing her with excellent harbours on two coasts—the Atlantic and the Mediterranean; and no one could deny the commercial advantages of this double-frontage. A southern exposure gave France the luxury trade of the Middle East and the opportunity to build an empire in North Africa; the other offered her a share in the discoveries and commerce of the New World. Moreover, she was economically self-sufficient. Far richer in natural resources than Spain, she was able, as time was to show, to recover from devastating defeat with amazing speed and resilience. Admittedly, her best harbours were not the junction points of great continental thoroughfares; rivers such as the Rhône and the Loire were of little value to Marseilles and Nantes because they were not easily navigable. But such obstacles were of minor importance in comparison with the commercial advantages that a double sea-front assured.

Strategically, however, geography gave France few of the advantages which belonged to her as a commercial nation in time of peace. In terms of naval power, two sea coasts meant dispersion— a French navy divided between the Mediterranean and the Atlantic. During the long wars with Britain, the problem of concentrating two fleets for offensive operations was constant, and presented itself acutely after the English established themselves at Gibraltar and Minorca. Until England was able to afford a permanent fleet in the Mediterranean, the decisive fleet engagements took place either in the Channel or on the Atlantic; and from 1688 until 1805, one campaign after another revealed the difficulties of joining two widely separated forces. Every projected descent upon England depended on the junction of the fleets of Toulon and Brest; and, as it happened, each one failed. In 1692, La Hogue might have won for France the command of the sea had the two French forces been able to unite. In short, for offensive operations, apart from the needs of home security, France required a two-ocean navy.

As far back as 1616, when a member of the Council, Richelieu had demanded an inquiry on the state of the navy. The inquiry did

[29]See Pahl, *Die Kolonialpolitik Richelieus*, 78 *et seq.*; also A. T. Mahan, *Naval Strategy* (Boston, 1911), 85-6.

take place, and it was on this occasion that the *prévôts* and aldermen of Paris addressed a memorandum to the king expressing their humiliation at the condition of the kingdom.

We see how much the neighbouring states have gained by distant voyages; places hitherto unknown and half lost in the waves of the ocean have been settled by the Dutch and the Spaniards, and these have become so prosperous that they now exceed some of the most esteemed provinces of Europe . . . and while Holland and Spain steadily increase their power and authority, that of France seems to be proportionately shaken and diminished.[30]

"My heart grieves," wrote Isaac de Razilly, "when I consider how the foreigners talk about France. They say to me: 'What power has your king? Even with all his armies, he has not been able to conquer one of his own noblemen without the assistance of England, Holland or Malta.' " France, he went on, had ports, forests, agriculture and great seamen.

But who in France encourages these brave men? The nobility so prompt to relieve the wounds of their own amour-propre, do not believe that there is any prestige to be had in founding colonies: we have our ships built in Holland; more than 200,000 mariners serve abroad, to be labelled fools and hypochondriacs by the foreigner. What has hindered the upper classes from casting their bread upon the waters is that those who have governed the state have heretofore mocked at the very idea of sea power. I make bold to say that the government has acted towards the inhabitants of this country as the savages of Canada act towards God. They do not fear him, and they do not serve him, because they have no respect for him; they prefer, on the contrary, to serve the devil abroad. . . .[31]

Interest in naval affairs had always been spasmodic; naval administration had never been a natural or accepted function of government. In this sense the navy could be regarded as a sort of barometer of national vitality. It was, according to Richelieu, the indicator which revealed whether a government was strong enough to raise itself above party profit and subordinate the particular to the general interests of France. When he came to power in 1624, the barometer was far down. Most of the ministers, nobles, and civil servants openly asserted that France could get along without a navy. "Those

---

[30]Levasseur, *Histoire du Commerce de la France*, I, 252.

[31]Quoted in Roncière, *Histoire de la Marine française*, IV, 491. Isaac de Razilly, chevalier of Malta and a captain in the French navy, had had a distinguished naval career, and his experiences undoubtedly taught him to appreciate the intimate connection between sea power and colonization. He became one of the original members of the Company of One Hundred Associates, and after 1628 was their naval commander. Between 1632 and 1635, the time of his death, he was governor of Acadia. (See Le R.P.L. Le Jeune, *Dictionnaire Générale de Biographie . . . du Canada* (2 vols., University of Ottawa, [1931] 506-8.)

who have controlled the state in the past," said Richelieu, "have mocked at sea power. Instead of encouraging the good citizens who risk their goods or their lives for France, . . . they reserve their favours for all the vicious and importunate who follow the court." To him, French salvation depended on the impulse given by the chief of state, and this he was prepared to supply.[32]

In 1626, under the title of grand master, chief, and superintendent-general of navigation and commerce, he took over complete control of French maritime affairs. In doing so, he suppressed the old office of "Admiral of France," and took away from the provincial governors the special admiralty rights which they had arrogated to themselves. Up to this time, owing chiefly to the absence of a fleet, the office of Admiral of France had been a peace-time sinecure which profited its possessor through the sale of subordinate posts, such as that of vice-admiral and coast-guard captain. Moreover, the Admiral had held enormous administrative powers within the limits of royal jurisdiction. He directed commercial as well as military affairs at sea; his right of judgment on all questions relating to maritime law gave him an almost sovereign administrative authority. For the Admiral, the sea was a realm from which he and his agents drew lucrative revenues in the form of prize money, rights to shipwrecked vessels, confiscations, sale of passports, and letters of marque.

After redeeming this post,[33] Richelieu went on to eliminate, one by one, the provincial admiralties. In 1631 the *parlement* of Brittany surrendered its special privileges; Provence succumbed under threat of arms, while the Viceroy-Admiral of New France lost his emoluments as well as the symbols of authority. Finally, by taking under his personal jurisdiction the ports of Havre and Brest and Brouage, Richelieu may be said to have wiped the slate clean of maritime feudalism.[34]

The new broom extended its sweep to colonial administration. Like Henry IV, Richelieu was undoubtedly influenced by English and Dutch precedents. The brief history of European commercial companies had shown both men what might be achieved by private corporations working under the auspices of national governments.

[32]*Ibid.*, 7.
[33]The Admiral of France, Henri de Montmorency-Danville, renounced his office in return for a payment of 1,200,000 livres.
[34]See d'Avenel, *Richelieu et la monarchie absolue*, 172; Levasseur, *Histoire du commerce de la France*, I, 253; and Roncière, *Histoire de la Marine française*, IV, 558.

But Richelieu made a more significant shift in emphasis than did Henry IV. His projected company would not be cast adrift with merely perfunctory supervision; it would receive the constant and energetic backing of the state. In 1626, at his house in Rueil, he signed a contract with the delegates of an organization called the Company of New France, and launched Champlain on his great experiment. With this action there began a second epoch in French colonization—one which may be termed the period of "Company" control and monopoly. It was to last almost continuously until 1665 when New France became a royal colony.

But men and money for speculative overseas experiments were not easy to find; and the urgent invitation of the "grand master" to subordinate personal profit and convenience to the general interest of the nation would have accomplished little without strong administrative pressure combined with plums in the form of titles of honour.

The merchants of Paris, Rouen, and Bordeaux were tempted. The Bretons alone remained aloof. Even the populace of the Breton ports, a grand seaman class, were too attached to their native soil and too independent to leave it willingly at the call of Paris. The Basques were fishermen rather than adventurers; the Bordelais preferred trade to colonization; the Rochelois were excluded by their religion from overseas settlement. So it was to Normandy that the Cardinal turned for his crews, his colonists, and his leaders, to provide the foundation of New France over the Atlantic.[35]

But with all this new enthusiasm and vigour, French colonial policy continued to be bound up with European foreign policy to a far greater extent than that of England or Holland. Unlike her rivals, France was to be constantly pulled to and fro between imperial dreams and continental attachments. The latter more often predominated, and French colonization became in the long run a by-product of European activities.[36] Cartier's final expedition had been possible only because France had for the moment renounced her policy of appeasement with Spain. The Angos of Dieppe, the Cartiers of St. Malo, the Denys of Honfleur were called the "noblemen of the sea" but they and their *confrères* rarely won the influence which ordinarily accompanied such rank in Paris.[37]

[35]See G. Hanotaux, *L'Energie française* (Paris, [1902],) 249-50; Roncière, *Histoire de la Marine française*, IV, 505.
[36]Pahl, *Die Kolonialpolitik Richelieus*, 95.
[37]See Guénin, *Ango et ses pilotes, passim*.

In Richelieu's writings there is comparatively little mention of colonies or colonial policy, and it may be doubted if he was ever deeply interested in North American trade and colonization. Nothing in his *Memoirs* would indicate that he shared the imperial enthusiasm of a Colbert. Nevertheless, his anxiety to build a fleet makes it clear that he intended France to be more than a great continental power. Like Bismarck in the eighteen-eighties, he wanted to make his country at least play a part with other colonial powers in the occupation of the unclaimed portions of the world.[38] He recognized full well that neither money, nor quality of colonial leadership, could weight the balance in favour of France, if communications were in doubt. Without fighting strength at sea, French possessions in North America were little more than hostages to English or Dutch fleets. Despite the constant protests of ambassadors, French traders and fishermen even in times of peace had had to suffer physical depredations as well as vexatious restrictions at the hands of the stronger powers.[39] It was essential to Richelieu's ambitions, as well as to his pride, that France should become a naval power.

The design of a French navy did not, of course, originate with Richelieu. Others, besides Henry IV, had seen the need for a fleet, and had had the wisdom to begin the task. Philip the Fair, Charles V, Louis XII, Henry II, all at least pondered the idea; but Richelieu alone had the energy and resources to turn this idea into wood and iron, flesh and blood.[40] His best informed collaborator was Isaac de Razilly, formerly in command of the Brittany squadron.[41] Razilly was the man chiefly responsible for translating Richelieu's ambitions into action. Indeed, Razilly's *Memoir* of November 26, 1626, had the same inspirational effect, and emphasized the same sort of fundamental doctrines of sea power, as did Captain Mahan's first expositions of almost three hundred years later. At an Assembly of the Notables in January, 1627, he summarized his case for a navy which should enable the king to win the mastery of the sea. The assembly was convinced, and on February 8, 1627, voted monies for the establishment of a fleet of forty-five war vessels along with an appropriate number of galleys.[42]

[38]See *Mémoires du Cardinal de Richelieu* (10 vols., Paris, Société de l'Histoire de France, 1907-31), I, 398, 438, and VII (new ed.), 26.
[39]See *Lettres du Cardinal de Richelieu*, III, 478.
[40]Tramond, *Manuel d'histoire maritime*, 149.
[41]See p. 34.
[42]Tramond, *Manuel d'histoire maritime*, 150-1.

Meanwhile, Richelieu's inspectors visited the ports, counted the number of vessels and the amount of equipment, the condition and size of the harbours, and the number of sailors and carpenters. On this basis, the Cardinal determined the quota of sailors to be furnished by each province, and the amount of money that might be levied for ships and equipment.[43] Heretofore, custom had allowed certain individuals or special interests to build vessels and rent them to merchants for their protection. From now on, the navy became a state affair. No vessel could bear arms without the royal permission; every port was made accountable to the king for ammunition, armament, and all manner of war materials.[44]

Moreover, at a time when the sciences of gunnery and fleet tactics were barely beginning to take shape, Richelieu established a school of navigation and pilotage where Father Fournier wrote the classic treatise on hydrography in 1643.[45] He arranged for a professor of mathematics to teach the "secret of longitudes," created new ports, enlarged others, and finally established four great naval arsenals at Le Havre, Brest, Toulon, and Brouage, the latter a tumbledown walled-in village of some 250 inhabitants.

Richelieu got his forty-five ships of war, varying from 600 to 1200 tons. Ten years after he came to power, the Royal fleet on the ocean included sixty-four ships; that of the Mediterranean thirteen round ships and twelve galleys.[46] Meanwhile the budget climbed from 800,000 livres (the total when he took office) to 4,300,000 at the time of his death. Altogether it was a sum sufficient to make France powerful at sea without unduly stretching her financial resources. Indeed, the cost of the navy per unit went down greatly when the government began to build or buy instead of borrowing or

---

[43]See "Summary of Voyage made by Sieur d'Infreville in all the ports and harbours of France" by command of M. Cardinal Richelieu, following a commission given in May, 1629, in *Correspondance de Henri D'Escoubleau de Sourdis*, III, 176-221. *Normandy:* At Dieppe, there were available 6 vessels of 100 and 150 tons which could serve in war, as well as 300 sailors and 20 carpenters; at Havre de Grace 50 captains, 46 pilots, 50 carpenters. At Honfleur, there were 2 well-equipped ships of 8 cannons each; at Granville there were 20 Newfoundlanders. *Brittany:* At Saint-Malo there were 40 ships from 200 to 300 tons and some of 400, armed as the average merchant vessel with iron cannon (from 10 to 26 pieces); also 60 barks and lesser vessels. At Port Benie, there were a dozen Newfoundlanders; at Saint-Malo, 400 sailors, 500 carpenters, 200 gunners, 50 good masters. *Picardy:* At Cayeux there were 200 sailors and fishermen; in all, 850 sailors and 8 carpenters.

[44]See F. C. Palm, *The Economic Policies of Richelieu* (Urbana, Ill., 1922), 103-4.

[45]Another text-book used by young officers was Samuel Champlain's "Traité de la Marine et du devoir d'un bon marinier," in *The Works of Samuel de Champlain*, VI, 253-347.

[46]See Pigeonneau, *Histoire du commerce de la France*, II, 408.

renting. Outright ownership was the first step in breaking the dependence on foreign sources; the second was the construction of French ships in French ports.[47]

Unfortunately, France failed to compete with other nations in the art of ship-building. Yards were finally established at Honfleur, Le Havre, and Dieppe; and a number of ships of around 400 tons were successfully launched from the ports of Brittany. But most of these were built according to Dutch design, and although she no longer obtained whole squadrons from the Netherlands as had been done up to 1626, France continued to buy the larger vessels until Colbert's time. Even the Royal flagship *Saint Louis* of 1000 tons came from Holland.[48] Using wood and other materials from the Baltic, the Dutch built their ships at least a quarter more cheaply than the French. With the exception of the great *Couronne*,[49] the largest and fastest ship of the line of that day, which took twelve years to build, most of the large commercial vessels, as well as warships, continued to be bought outside France.[50]

Meanwhile, Richelieu combed the ports for seamen, and tempted back from Holland, Spain, England, and Sweden those who had previously found it more profitable to work away from home. He began to build up an officer class, without care for social caste or religion. Rough Huguenot masters from La Rochelle were given commands, along with their former adversaries from St. Malo or Dieppe. He drew in lawless adventurers, tamed them, and made them loyal French officers.[51] "I prefer," said Richelieu, "strong brave seamen nourished on salt water and the bottle rather than powdered dandies, for such people will better serve the king."

With all the authority of a dictator, Richelieu had foisted a naval policy on the nation. By the force of his own personality backed by the authority of his office, he had pressed the country into maritime enterprises which it was not wholeheartedly prepared to accept.

[47]Under the latter conditions, it was estimated that 45 ships would cost the government in a year what 50 ships would cost in rent for six months. D'Avenel, *Richelieu et la monarchie absolue*, 186-7.

[48]Roncière, *Histoire de la Marine française*, IV, 592-9.

[49]Credit is given to the builders of the *Couronne* for the discovery of the fact that a comparatively small number of guns with roomy quarters is more advantageous than a much greater number so crowded together that there is no space to work them properly. J. K. Laughton, *Studies in Naval History* (London, 1887), 65.

[50]D'Avenel, *Richelieu et la monarchie absolue*, 167-8.

[51]Roncière gives, as an example, the story of the Dunkirk pirate who turned from his evil ways and ended by marrying a lady of quality. *Histoire de la Marine française*, IV, 599-600.

Through him the king had become ship-builder, shipowner, merchant-trader, and colonial adventurer. It is easy to suggest that his system lacked the vigour and spontaneity which more individual initiative might have contributed, but even had semi-private "Company" enterprises been a success, the state had to lay the foundation, for basically naval power is an artificial creation. Assuming a sufficiency of national resources, the making of a navy depended, as it still depends, primarily on the action of government. If Richelieu's achievement was ephemeral, it was because his successors in power did not continue his policies, and not because Frenchmen lacked a love of salt water or a sense of adventure.

In so many ways France was, like England, an amphibious state. Both countries possessed long coast lines bordering rich agricultural and mineral interiors; both cou d build on fine maritime stocks, for the seamen of St. Malo and Honfleur were in every respect as good as those of Bristol and Plymouth and in many ways showed greater versatility. In the opinion of contemporary English officers, French crews could man a gun or make and furl a sail as smartly as those of any other country.

It would be a mistake, therefore, to designate England as a "natural" sea power, and to exaggerate French propensities for war on land. Maritime pursuits were just as natural to France as to England. The essential difference lay in the attitudes of kings and governments; but these, in turn, were largely prescribed by the facts of geography. In the building and maintenance of fleets, British governments were to show greater constancy than did the French, simply because, thanks to the English Channel, there were no continuous and exhausting conflicts of interest. Because of long interior frontiers, France was repeatedly drawn deep into Europe. The age-old rivalry of Bourbon and Hapsburg drew like a magnet on the arms of France, and made French sea power a thing of intermittant enthusiasms. For three centuries France was to be torn between continental and maritime ambitions, and the periods of maritime ardour were never long enough to compensate for the prolonged intervals of indifference and neglect.

III

The Rise of English Sea Power

FOR England the epoch of imperial expansion which had opened inauspiciously with the beginning of the seventeenth century, appeared likely, by the end of the reign of Charles I, to end disastrously. The Dutch were looming up as a threat not only in the North Sea, but on the estuary of the Hudson River, at New Amsterdam. It seemed possible that Holland, in the first flush of prosperity and power, might engulf not only Spanish possessions in the Caribbean but also the struggling English colonies to the north and south of the Hudson. Although the Dutch threat in North America never fully materialized, it is not surprising that Englishmen of the time viewed with apprehension the efforts of a powerful maritime state to establish colonial ascendancy on the North American coast, as well as in the region of the Grand Banks.[1]

At a time when the fate of Quebec lay in the diplomatic balance, English naval power had reached possibly its lowest ebb. Indeed, if Canada had not been surrendered, it is difficult to believe that Charles I would have been in a position to have held that country against the rising strength of Richelieu's squadrons. England itself lay open to invasion from the sea. Hardly a harbour or a colonial convoy was safe from the ravages of the "Turks," as the Algerian Moslems were called. While Dunkirk pirates practically blockaded the eastern ports, sometimes raiding the lower reaches of the Thames, the "Turks" raided the south and west coasts in search of galley slaves.[2]

[1]See Judah, *The North American Fisheries*, 86, 88, 90.
[2]See *Calendar of State Papers, Domestic, Charles I, 1625-26*, 415; and *ibid., Apr.-Aug. 1640*, 438. Occasionally they were caught, but even then fear of reprisals

When Charles came to the throne in 1625, the English fleet on paper consisted of some forty vessels of which twenty-six were ships of the line. Seventeen of the forty were comparatively new;[3] but most of the remainder were either unseaworthy or far too slow to catch such enemies as fast-sailing pirates. These numbers could, of course, be greatly increased by "commissioned" merchant ships which, as in Tudor times, were still called out to strengthen the fighting fleet. The expeditions between 1625 and 1628 were made up largely of these armed cruisers, but such a mixture could scarcely be called a national navy. It was an *ad hoc* service in the transitional stage, a sort of hybrid combining the characteristics of a regular force with those of a sea militia.[4]

Charles was interested in his heterogeneous fleet, and he was intelligent enough to see the necessity of maintaining it in a high state of efficiency both in peace and war. This was the justification for his levy of the famous "ship money" in 1634, a general tax for the support of the fleet. In view of Charles's convictions on the need for a permanent, state-owned navy, it was unfortunate that the Service should have become thus tangled in a battle of political ideas. To the public of that day, ship money appeared to be merely one more example of the King's determination to get money by evading control of Parliament. Only after the Restoration was the policy of a standing navy, in peace as well as war, accepted by king and Parliament, ". . . so long as the English Navy was the King's own navy, it was seldom if ever called the 'Royal Navy' "; paradoxically, it became the Royal Navy during the reign of Charles II, who had ceased to own it.[5]

Yet, the nucleus of a standing navy, as opposed to the old sea militia composed of King's ships and merchantmen, was to be the grand product of the Interregnum years. Sheer necessity—the urge to survival—led the Commonwealth in the first three years of its existence to create a fleet that could challenge the Dutch for the command of the seas, and eventually deprive them of their maritime commercial monopoly.

compelled the government to treat them gently. An expedition of 1637 rescued some 300 or 400 English captives—the only active success of Charles's naval administration.

[3]Oppenheim, *A History of the Administration of the Royal Navy*, 251; also d'Avenel, *Richelieu et la monarchie absolue*, 159.

[4]See D. Hannay, *A Short History of the Royal Navy* (2 vols., London, 1898-1909), I (1898), 171.   [5]Lewis, *England's Sea-Officers*, 51.

Under Charles I the resources of the Crown alone had been unequal to the construction of ships during wartime, while in peacetime the launching of one or two at most was the cause of some pride and satisfaction. Under the Commonwealth they were ordered ten at a time; and in one year, 1654, twenty-two new men-of-war left the slips, apart from merchantmen and various prizes subsequently added to the English naval service. In Charles's reign the preparation of a single fleet for a peaceful summer cruise in the narrow seas required a year of preparation. During the Commonwealth, in addition to a powerful reserve kept on the Downs ready for immediate action, and numerous cruisers patrolling the coasts, there was a Mediterranean squadron, a modest West Indies squadron, and the small beginnings of a North American Station.[6] The days of individual enterprises and private pillaging excursions were over; the era of national undertakings had begun.

The problem of finance, which had worried Charles I and wrecked his plans, was of small moment to the Puritans and their leader. A navy was urgently needed to keep the republic alive. After the execution of the King in 1649, his family and friends had retired to the continent with the intention of raising forces and returning as soon as possible to England. Indeed, Rupert had already raised eleven ships, and begun a privateering war. The best means to prevent royalist plans from materializing was to bar the North Sea and the Channel.[7] The immediate obstacle was expense; but the new government got the money roughly and quickly by means of monthly assessments, deliquents' fines, and the sale of private or corporate property. The system was reckless and improvident, but it raised an income of five and a quarter millions a year as against the million a year raised by Charles, and it did provide ships. For the campaign of 1652 in the First Dutch War, Parliament voted forty thousand pounds sterling a month; in the following year this grant was increased. Under Cromwell's direction, ship-building became a national industry. Between 1649 and 1654, Parliamentary committees dispensed enough money to buy or build 71 ships. All told, during the Dutch war, England was able to put 131 ships to sea[8]; from 1649 to

[6]See Oppenheim, *A History of the Administration of the Royal Navy*, 302.
[7]See G. Lacour-Gayet, *La Marine militaire de la France sous les règnes de Louis XIII et Louis XIV* (Paris, 1911), 206.
[8]See Oppenheim, *A History of the Administration of the Royal Navy*, 338; and Tramond, *Manuel d'histoire maritime*, 113.

1660, 103 new vessels (excluding prizes) were built or purchased, and 69 of these were from 26 to 100 guns.[9]

At the same time, the Service was made more tempting by all-round raises in pay, special prize-money benefits, and improved victualling. By 1653 the number of enlisted sailors had reached 30,000. But the great problem was to get officers. After the King's death a majority of this class had embraced the royal cause, and had joined Prince Rupert in carrying on the fight in the Mediterranean, across the Atlantic, or off the west coast of Africa. Faced with this embarrassing problem, Parliament had to improvise hastily. In well-nigh desperate straits it turned to the land forces, and there found the answer. Austere Puritans, for the most part with very limited experience at sea, but with a well-developed sense of discipline and an urge for the offensive, became the officers of the "New Model" Navy. Parliamentary colonels like Blake and Monk and Deane and Popham were transformed overnight into admirals; they learned their trade and proved themselves in three years of uninterrupted fighting against the Royalists under Prince Rupert.[10] The story of Monk's first signal to his squadron, whether or not apocryphal, is at least symbolic of the new amphibian: "By the left, march."

Of the "Generals at Sea," as they were officially known,[11] who were in charge of fleets, Blake soon rose supreme. He had had some experience on merchantmen but, as with Beatty, it was a peculiar blend of instinct, energy, and audacity that made him a great leader. Few of England's eminent captains have received so little attention as Robert Blake, although there are distinguished naval officers who would rank him next to Nelson as a commander, and Nelson himself wrote, "I do not reckon myself the equal of Blake." Certain it is, in any event, that as a sailor Blake, like Cromwell the soldier, found

[9]"Great ships" existing in 1649 were: 1 of 100 guns, 1 of 88 guns, 3 of 70 guns, about 30 of 20-60 guns. See *Lists of Men-of-War, 1650-1700*, Part I, *English Ships, 1649-1702*, Compiled by R. C. Anderson (Cambridge, Society for Nautical Research, 1935), 1-5.

[10]On February 20, 1649, Parliament recalled the Commission under which the Earl of Warwick had been named Lord High Admiral. One week later Colonels Edward Popham, Robert Blake, and Richard Deane were appointed Commissioners with powers to order, manage, and command the fleet and execute martial law. Popham, who had been a naval officer, was succeeded at his death by George Monk; and Deane, who seems to have had some sea experience as a youth, was followed after his death by William Penn. See R. Beadon, *Robert Blake, Sometime Commanding all the Fleets and Naval Forces of England* (London, 1935), 59-61; also Beadon, "Robert Blake, General and Admiral," *Journal of the Royal United Service Institution*, Feb. 1932, 124 *et seq.*

[11]The term "General at Sea" was not a rank but an appointment.

his true vocation. In April of 1649, at the age of fifty-one, he hoisted his flag and, except for one period of sick leave ashore, spent the remainder of his life at sea.

That the navy existed to protect trade as well as territory had become a firmly established principle of English policy; already there was a manifest tendency to identify the fruits of overseas commerce with military strength. The competition for colonies and colonial trade had not yet become a major element in the European balance of power, but there were signs to indicate that the wealth of the New World would soon be recognized as an important, if not vital, means of influencing that balance. Although the Navigation Act of 1651 was not ostensibly a measure of military security, it was designed to curb the commercial competition of the Dutch. By forbidding the carriage of English goods in ships other than English, by confining the imports of Asia, Africa, and America to English ships, and by stipulating that European goods must come in either English ships or ships of the country producing them, the Act aimed at protecting English shipping interests and indirectly crippling the Dutch. "National animosity," says Adam Smith, "at that particular time aimed at the very same object which the most deliberate wisdom could have recommended, the diminution of the naval power of Holland, the only naval power which could endanger the security of England."[12]

The old view that the Navigation Act of 1651 was merely an excuse to make an attack upon the Dutch hardly holds water today, although the resentment aroused by the wide-spread competition of Dutch trade all over the globe made a clash almost inevitable. Certainly national feeling in both countries, aggravated as it already was by political sympathies and colonial rivalries, made any contentious subject a possible *casus belli;* and when Tromp appeared unexpectedly with a large squadron off the coast of Kent (under pretext of sheltering from the storm), and ran into Blake who was at anchor near the South Foreland, the flashpoint in international relations had been reached. History has not determined which commander fired the first shot; suffice it to say, the two squadrons fought until nightfall without any definite result, and shortly afterwards official hostilities were declared.

---

[12]The effectiveness of this Act in damaging Dutch trade, and hence contributing to war, has been questioned by recent historians. See G. N. Clark, "Historical Revisions: The Navigation Act of 1651," *History*, Jan. 1923, 282-6.

The war of 1652-54 which ensued, ushered in the era of great naval battles. There was little long-range strategy; the proximity of their coasts threw the belligerents into contact almost as soon as they left port.[13] Both nations were intent on controlling the sea lanes in the interest of national wealth and colonial expansion; and both peoples possessed a vein of bull-dog tenacity, which was largely responsible for the sanguinary slogging matches fought so determinedly and pitilessly.

In terms of ready rather than potential power, the war seemed likely to be an unequal duel. While Cromwell's country was still facing bankruptcy, Holland was at the height of her power. The foundations of her colonial empire had been securely laid in the Spice islands of the East; she had taken over the old Hanse trade of the Baltic; thanks to efficient carriers and low freight rates, she had gained almost a monopoly of the European coastal trades. Until 1651 England received the bulk of her imports in Dutch ships. Moreover, although Dutch military organization may have been faulty, the fleet had not been put on a peace footing at the end of the Thirty Years War (1648). On the contrary, it had been substantially increased; and by reason of their carrying trade the Dutch had probably four times as many seamen to draw upon as had the English.[14] Admittedly, the English navy had also been reorganized and reinvigorated, but poverty of both manpower and gold was still a millstone that hampered the persevering efforts of Blake and Monk.

On the other hand, the parochial rivalry between the Dutch States was responsible for a shocking lack of unity in high command. Admiralty authority was divided between five provincial admiralty boards, and centralized direction was continually deflected by political animosities, which sometimes led to the sacrifice of good captains. Furthermore, although the Dutch had more ships than the English, their insistence in the first year of hostilities upon using line-of-battle ships to convoy merchant fleets through the Channel prevented them from concentrating a heavily preponderant fleet capable of winning a decisive victory. Dutch revenues depended on sea-borne trade that was now subject to the strangulating operations of English squadrons lying athwart Dutch routes to the Atlantic.

[13]See R. Castex, *Les Idées militaires de la Marine du XVIIIe Siècle: De Ruyter à Suffren* (Paris, 1911), 9.
[14]Oppenheim, *A History of the Administration of the Royal Navy*, 306.

It was fear of risking this vital income that tempted the Dutch to put so much effort into convoy protection.

This refusal to divorce battle strategy from trade protection almost certainly influenced the outcome of the war. The narrow margin by which Blake was saved in 1652 might be represented by the strength that the Dutch consumed in trade protection. It is easy to be wise after the event; at the same time it is not unreasonable to suggest that, after Blake's defeat off Dungeness in November 1652, if the Dutch had ignored convoy escort and employed their temporary command of the Channel to complete a concentration, they might not have lost the Battle of Portland in the following February. Indeed, with sufficient forces, which were actually available, they could have prevented the English ships from joining and might have destroyed them squadron by squadron. And if the English fleet had been so crushed, it is doubtful if sufficient money and material equipment could have been provided to renew the struggle.

Five major actions were fought, and in four of these the English were completely victorious. The battle off the Gabbard Shoal to the east of Harwich, in June 1653, was the heaviest naval engagement in the history of either power,[15] and it was followed by a blockade of the Dutch coast that caused for a time the complete cessation of the Dutch trade. "The English are masters of us and the seas," said de Witt dolefully as the end approached; but it was only the end of the first round. When formal peace came in 1654, the Dutch navy was still a powerful instrument, strong enough to leave the question of trade rivalry still unsettled, and pointing the way to a further contest for command of the Channel. Two more wars were to be fought, and the Thames was to suffer a second humiliating blockade.

With the Restoration there came a further expansion in English naval ship-building. The first great Naval Defence Act of 1677 provided for the building of 30 new ships. By 1688 the navy had grown within twenty-five years from 156 vessels to 173. Moreover, the Stuarts built larger vessels, and by the end of the century the 1000-ton ship of the line had become, despite certain nautical weaknesses, almost a standard type. In 1660 there were no more than 30 ships of

[15]The Commonwealth fleet consisted of 105 vessels of which 59 were above 30 guns, 5 were fireships, and 34 were hired merchant ships of 46-28 guns. See *Papers Relating to the First Dutch War, 1652-54*, V, ed. C. T. Atkinson (London, Navy Records Society, vol. XLI, 1911), 16. For a full list of the Navy, excluding hired merchant ships, see *ibid.* VI (vol. LXVI, 1930), 49.

the first three rates; by 1688 the number had doubled. In 1660 the total tonnage was 62,594; by 1688 it had risen to 101,032. Although calibres remained approximately the same throughout the century, the number of guns had risen proportionately in ratio to the size of the ship that received them. Vessels of the first rate carried as many as 100 guns, but beyond that lay the danger line. Already, by Blake's time, it was something of a problem to control a three-decker of more than 100 guns in a bad sea.[16] Although ranges were still meagre—650 to 750 yards at maximum—the gun was becoming more dangerous as it gained in accuracy and precision. Boarding was still possible through surprise attack, or as a means of taking a disabled adversary, but it no longer played an important role in sea engagements.

At the same time, it is curious to notice that the art of ship-building, which had risen to considerable heights in the days of Charles I and Phineas Pett, seemed to have sadly declined. Pepys remarks that

... in 1663 and 1664 the Dutch and French built ships with two decks, which carried from sixty to seventy guns, and so contrived that they carried their lower guns four feet from the water, and to stow four months' provisions, whereas our frigates from the Dunkirk-build, which were narrower and sharper, carried their guns but little more than three feet from the water, and for ten weeks' provisions.[17]

English shipwrights tried to catch up, but in the Third Dutch War it was evident that the enemy retained their advantage. Corruption combined with lethargy prevented even Pepys and the Duke of York from making radical progress in design. It may be doubted, wrote David Hannay, whether any form of organization could have prevented dishonesty. "The prevailing sentiment of the time looked upon robbing the State very much as otherwise quite honourable people still look upon a little smuggling."[18]

Yet it would be a mistake, as Dr. Tanner has pointed out, to accept the period of the Interregnum as one of piety and efficiency and that of the Restoration as immoral and utterly slack. Except for the years 1679-84, "there was no abject incompetence and some steady progress."[19] A sense of the importance of sea power had now

[16]For a comparison with the eighteenth century, see Appendix B.
[17]Hannay, *A Short History of the Royal Navy*, I, 332.
[18]*Ibid.*, 316.
[19]J. R. Tanner, *Samuel Pepys and the Royal Navy*, Lees Knowles Lectures, delivered at Cambridge, 1919 (Cambridge, 1920), 77.

become part of the consciousness of all politically-minded English-men; the renewed Dutch Wars were to reinforce this feeling. More-over, the Stuart kings were interested in maritime as well as colonial affairs. Charles II took delight in sailing down the Thames to inspect the fleet, while his brother James II has been called an "expert" on ship-building matters.[20] Both took an interest in the details of ad-ministration, and both took a hand in the transaction of naval business. Had James not played the fool in the political sphere, he might have remained on the throne and revived within the fleet that discipline in which he so firmly believed, and which the navy of his time so frequently lacked.

The Second Dutch War (1664-67) saw the end of Dutch dominion on the North American continent. In 1664 Admiral Holmes had little difficulty in seizing the settlement of New Amsterdam with its 1,500 inhabitants, and this conquest gave England control of the whole Atlantic coast from Nova Scotia to Virginia. In retaliation, de Ruyter, after attacking the African coast colonies, raided New-foundland in June of the same year. Shipping and shore equipment were destroyed in the out-ports, and de Ruyter capped his exploit by sailing boldly into St. John's harbour, which was protected only by a cable.[21] Efficient escort work prevented further damage to fishing convoys in transit, although Dutch privateers continued to be a nuisance to the trade, and as late as 1673 plundered Ferryland, destroying cattle and burning seventy fishing vessels.[22] Owing to the recall of English ships on the Atlantic station during the Third Dutch War (1672-74), a Dutch squadron was able to evade the English home fleet and recapture New York, as it was now called; but the triumph was short-lived. The final decision was won at the council table, and under the terms of peace the old Dutch colony was once again returned to England.

In Canadian history, the elimination of another competitor for North American territories is especially significant. England had de-feated a sea power more commercially and imperially minded and far more business-like than Spain, a power which had already es-tablished itself at the mouth of the Hudson River, astride the coastal

[20]*Ibid.*, 19.
[21]See James, Duke of York, to Sir William Penn, July 2, 1665, *Historical Manuscripts Commission, Portland MSS.* (2 vols., London, 1891-3), II, 102-3; also P. Blok, *The Life of Admiral de Ruyter*, tr. G. J. Renier (London, 1933), 195.
[22]*Calendar of State Papers, Colonial, America and West Indies, 1675-6*, IX, 197.

communications of the English Atlantic colonies whence it looked up the long inland waterway that led to the heart of Canada at Montreal. It may be that the Dutch would never have developed the incentive nor the power to establish a far-flung North American domain in the face of French opposition in Europe. The settlement on the Hudson had never been a really flourishing entity, chiefly because it never received the same vigorous attentions from the state as did the East Indian colonies. But whether or not the Dutch could have succeeded in building an enduring American empire, the fact remains that a Dutch triumph would have greatly favoured Louis XIV's design of exorcising English dominion from the New World. At a time when the population of the coastal colonies was small, and when existence depended utterly on constant communication with the mother country, an English defeat would have given a tremendous impetus to the expansionist plans of Colbert, and Talon in New France might have gained his cherished winter port in New York.

Meanwhile, the lessons of the Dutch wars were to have a fundamental effect on English colonial policy. Blake had demonstrated that only supremacy at sea could secure England's undisturbed control of trade routes; and now, for the first time in English history, the destruction of the naval forces of the enemy in time of war had become the accepted means to this end. The primary purpose of naval warfare was no longer the mere pillaging of ocean commerce, but the destruction of the instrument that defended and guaranteed the existence of that commerce. Once the opponent was reduced in battle or starved by blockade, his colonies, as well as his trade routes, were at the mercy of the victor. The fight for command of the sea was, therefore, gradually coming to be recognized as the basic principle of the new naval strategy.

Moreover, in time of peace, commercial rivalry on the oceans was tacitly admitted to be an unofficial process of war, a chronic feature of the struggle for wealth and power. "The intention of its framers," wrote S. R. Gardiner, in reference to the Navigation Act of 1651, "by the nature of the case was not to make England better or nobler, but to make her richer."[23] The navigation laws of Charles II carried this intention still farther. The Act of 1660 was even harsher in some of its clauses than that of Charles's Puritan predecessors. Indeed, Restoration ministers had begun to grasp the close con-

[23]*History of the Commonwealth and Protectorate* (London, 1894), I, 83.

nection between sea power, colonies, and commerce, which subsequent Hanoverian governments were to accept as a matter of course. Further proof is the fact that although hard pressed by France and Spain to restore Nova Scotia and Jamaica (which the Protector's Major Sedgwick had captured in 1655), Charles refused. Even his marriage with Catherine of Braganza had a possessive imperial flavour about it: ". . . the principal advantages we propose to ourself by this entire conjunction with Portugal are the advancement of the trade of this nation and the enlargement of our territories and dominions."[24]

During the period of the Restoration, trade dictated colonial policy, and the ground was laid for commercial uniformity as expressed in the Navigation System. Since colonies were more dependable sources of production than foreign countries or their dependencies, the acquisition and security of colonies became a prime objective of naval policy. "Trade and sea power, trade as nourishing sea power, and sea power as safeguarding and extending trade, that was the main outlook of Charles II's reign."[25]

In the circumstances, if the demands of colonial trade expansion were to be met, the development of a permanent professional sea force was inevitable. Between 1642 and the accession of Charles II in 1660, the old sea militia of King's ships had gradually taken shape as a national navy paid for by the nation. Parliament and Protector had found it wise to keep a considerable number of ships in commission even in peacetime, send them forth on cruises and make them operate together. There was no distinction as yet between the merchant seaman and the regular fighting seaman; but at least it could be said that, during the years of the Commonwealth, a great many crews rarely, if ever, served afloat except in a warship. Although landmen continued, even after the Civil War, to be given naval appointments, and though a permanent corps with gradations of rank had not been formally established, a class of men who could handle ships and guns and exercise military command had been formed at last. Henceforth, the navy was to develop into a service quite distinct from the merchant marine, and although the average merchantman continued to carry some arms, its value as an actual fighting vessel became less and less as its cargo-carrying capacity increased.

[24]Quoted in J. A. Williamson, *A Sho tHistory of British Expansion* (2nd ed., 2 vols., New York, 1931), I, 256.
[25]C. Lucas, *Religion, Colonising and Trade: The Driving Forces of the Old Empire* (London, 1930), 52.

Against ships like the *Sovereign of the Seas* (built in 1637) which carried 104 guns on her three decks, the armed merchantman was of little or no avail. In the new age of sea warfare, improvised armaments were no longer sufficient; and by the end of the seventeenth century, fleets were disinclined to join battle unless they could oppose the enemy's line with an equal number of ships of the same class. Experience in the Dutch wars proved that the mixture of the true and the improvised might be more dangerous than useful, and henceforward homogeneity became an indispensable requirement for the battle line. Like the Dutch, the English abandoned the makeshift squadron or fleet for a standard organization designed exclusively for war.[26]

With the birth of the permanent navy came the development of tactical schemes, for which the Elizabethans had vaguely groped. Gradually and almost instinctively there was evolved the theory of ships attacking, not independently of each other, but in "line ahead," paralleling the enemy line, and thus avoiding the risk of masking each other's broadside fire.[27] Under the first two Stuarts, the new theory had made little progress, because under James little attention was paid to the navy, and under Charles more care was given to ships than to training in tactics. Not until the First Dutch War did the single "line ahead" become a formal battle formation, and only after a year of uncertain fighting did the admirals of the Commonwealth, in March of 1653, establish it as part of the *Fighting Instructions*. Both Blake and de Ruyter preferred when possible to engage "in line," close-hauled to the wind, and their approval lent authority to a battle formation which Elizabethan experts like Monson had hitherto scorned.

Unfortunately, exact geometric dispositions had a habit of becoming stereotyped simply because they were neat, precise, and logical. Cautious and uninquisitive commanders preferred to work according to set-piece formulae. On the sea, says Castex in *Les Idées militaires de la Marine*, "where geometry seems to have a natural ascendancy, one had to possess a highly developed sense of military strategy to resist the delight to the eye and the spirit, of a line in perfect order of battle."

[26] See M. Lewis, *The Navy of Britain: A Historical Portrait* (London, 1948), 110-111.
[27] See Corbett, *Fighting Instructions*, 76.

During the First Dutch War both Blake and de Ruyter regularly began battle in close line according to the book, but neither lost his ability to depart from the formal and methodical. Almost from the beginning de Ruyter put his finger on the weakness of tactical uniformity. He appreciated the wisdom of arranging ships so that they could fire freely from the broadside, and keep in contact with one another; but he regarded *line of battle* as a formation primarily useful as a means of approaching the enemy. Once the moment for actual engagement arrived, he never hesitated to abandon it.

Castex suggests that the English, having at their disposal more efficient ships and personnel, could control a rigid line more easily than the Dutch; but he admits that there was a difference of opinion on the use of it from the very start. Monk and Rupert, for example, saw its merits under certain circumstances. After the Battle of the "Four Days," (1666) de Guiche could say: "Nothing equalled the fine English order at sea. Never has a straighter line been drawn than that made by their vessels. . . . They fought like a line of cavalry manœuvred according to rules."[28] But both Monk and Rupert were too intelligent not to recognize that rigidity could be fatal, and that initiative and originality should be encouraged. They were among the first to declare that "line or no line, signals or no signals, the destruction of the enemy is always to be made the chiefest care!"[29] Like Nelson and, to a lesser degree, Rodney, both Monk and Rupert recognized the advantage of concentration, the value of the sudden and overwhelming push at one point, "the crown," as Castex has called it, of all naval manœuvre.[30] In such circumstances a premium was placed on leadership, and the flash of inspiration, later called the "Nelson touch," frequently brought decisions impossible to obtain within the narrow confines of "line of battle" tactics.

Unfortunately, in the words of his brother Charles, the Duke of York was "as stubborn as a mule." Both he and his colleague William Penn were unbending in their belief that there was no other way of fighting a battle; and the Duke of York's Instructions of 1665 gave precise and almost imperative meaning to this rigid theory of naval tactics. Before long the tradition of audacity and opportunism established by Monk and Rupert and Blake fell into dis-

[28]Quoted in Castex, *Les Idées militaires de la Marine*, 14.
[29]See Corbett, *Fighting Instructions*, 92, 120.
[30]Castex, *Les Idées militaires de la Marine*, 67.

repute. At the beginning of the Third Dutch War (1672) amending articles, which allowed a certain amount of flexibility, disappeared. In 1688, Admiral Russell, the opponent of Tourville at La Hogue discarded them entirely, and returned to the old *Instructions of 1665*. A "false pattern of action" had won acceptance and approval at a time when, owing to the decline of the French navy, the cessation of fleet actions on a grand scale favoured its perpetuation.[31] Formalism and pedantic adherence to system came to dominate the tactics of sea battle. Admittedly superior English seamanship frequently lent flexibility to the "line"; mastery in the handling of individual ships often compensated for weakness in general tactics; but until well into the eighteenth century few English commanders possessed the courage or the genius to depart from orthodoxy. By 1672 "line of battle" had taken on an almost sacrosanct character.

Meanwhile, there had been a rapid expansion of English merchant shipping. Statistical comparisons show quite clearly that the general growth of English commerce dates from the period of the Protectorate, and that growth was particularly active after the Restoration.[32] During Elizabeth's reign the American voyages had added enormously to the number of sea-going commercial ships; but these belonged to Spain, whose sea power was, in a sense, a product of the American discoveries. The gold and silver of Mexico and Peru had enabled Spain to maintain a tonnage far larger in the sixteenth century than that of France and England combined. Even had the French and English planted their colonies soon after 1500, they still would have lacked the readily transferable wealth of gold and silver that Spain obtained with such ease. As compared with the Spanish colonies, the mainland of North America provided small encouragement to the English carrying trade.

From the middle of the seventeenth century, however, the development of coastal commerce, the long-distance fishing trade, the Baltic timber trade, the French wine trade, and the growing intercourse with India led to a steady expansion of English merchant shipping. The absolute and proportional figures of tonnage increases show:

[31]See A. T. Mahan, *Types of Naval Officers* (Boston, 1901), 72.
[32]See A. P. Usher, "The Growth of English Shipping 1572-1922," *The Quarterly Journal of Economics*, XLII, May, 1928, 465-78.

	absolute tonnage	proportional
At the end of the 16th century.........about	50,000	100
At the end of the 17th century.......at most	300,000	600
At the end of the 18th century..............	1,725,000	3,450
At the end of the 19th century..............	9,280,160	18,560[33]

In 1582 England possessed more than 1500 sea-going merchant ships; by 1701 the number had risen to approximately 3,281. Since the number of ships had little more than doubled and the tonnage total had expanded about six times, there must have been a general increase in the average tonnage of the merchant ships.

Yet the increase in individual ship's tonnage is by no means striking. Until the beginning of the nineteenth century, no merchant vessel exceeded 1200 tons; and there were relatively few in the group between 400 and 1,200.[34] Indeed, England rather more than other European countries persisted in her use of small ships; in the seventeenth century probably one quarter of her entire shipping was under 200 tons.[35] The average North Sea and cross-Channel carrier varied usually between 100 and 250 tons, as compared with the Indiaman of 300 to 600 tons. Under 100 tons there came the steadily multiplying host of coastal craft.

During this time the mutual dependence of merchant marine and fighting navy was strengthened rather than diminished. As armament and fighting technique became more specialized, the merchant vessel could no longer be conscripted indiscriminately for war service; nevertheless its value as an auxiliary for transport, victualling, and convoy escort was still considerable. Of even greater importance, the trading vessel furnished the best breeding ground for English seamen. The ability to man the ships of the Royal Navy in time of war depended to a great extent on the prosperity of the merchant marine. A large and thriving "nursery" in the shape of a flourishing carrying trade meant a well-stocked recruiting ground at the constant disposal of the Admiralty.

The colonial trades, and especially the Newfoundland fisheries, have been traditionally exalted as the most productive nurseries for

[33]Sombart, *Der Moderne Kapitalismus*, I, 300. In 1572 the total number of merchant ships in England was 1383, with a total tonnage of 50,816; of these 86 were 100 tons or over and 869 were under 40 tons. See *Calendar of State Papers, Domestic, Elizabeth, 1566-79*, VII, 441.

[34]According to Sir William Monson, at the time of the death of Elizabeth there were not four merchant ships of 400 tons or over.

[35]Usher, "The Growth of English Shipping," 476-7.

seamen[36]; but their importance in this respect has been exaggerated. The new Royal Navy gained the bulk of its recruits from the coastal vessels, and more particularly the colliers. The coal trade was a "nursery" that no other of the expanding continental powers possessed. In the eighteenth century, Adam Smith claimed that it employed "more shipping than all the carrying trades of England."[37] This is clearly an over-statement; Smith may have been thinking in terms of manpower rather than tonnage, in which case he was probably influenced in his judgment by Charles Povey, a London coal merchant, who wrote in 1700:

> The Colliery-Trade brings up a greater number of Seamen than all our Navigation elsewhere, and it must be acknowledged that when Owners and Masters of Vessels gain by Trading to Newcastle, then, and then only, our Trade to foreign Parts is in a flourishing Condition.[38]

It is impossible to estimate with any accuracy the total number of seamen employed in the coal trade during the reigns of the later Stuarts,[39] but some idea of accumulating manpower may be gained from the fact that in 1550 the traffic to London employed only two native ships; by the end of the seventeenth century, more than 1,500 sea-going colliers were being used, and all those engaged in coastwise trade were English owned. Nor is it entirely without significance that the first great period of naval expansion should have paralleled the rapid expansion in the coal trade. Unlike the long-distance trades to Jamaica or Newfoundland, the seamen of the colliers could be summoned with only a few days' notice; they represented a

---

[36]In James I's reign the Newfoundland fisheries employed only about 150 sail; the Iceland fisheries, approximately 120.

[37]See Adam Smith, *Wealth of Nations*, II, chap. v.

[38]Quoted in J. U. Nef, *The Rise of the British Coal Industry*, I, 238; see also 239-40, and II, 141.

[39]In 1774 Captain Robert Tomlinson in his "Essay on Manning the Royal Navy without Recourse to Impressment" wrote as follows: "I apprehend it will be admitted, that the Northern coal trade in England, exclusive of Scotland, will raise twelve thousand seamen the first three years of a war. Wales and Whitehaven, at least four thousand more, in their coal trade. The Newfoundland-fishery, at least fourteen thousand. All the other trades in Great Britain and Ireland, suppose only twenty thousand, which added together, make fifty thousand seamen." *The Tomlinson Papers*, ed. by J. G. Bullocke (London, Navy Records Society, LXXVI, 1935), 162 *n.* On p. 156 *n.*, however, the author makes it clear that his Newfoundland total is entirely theoretical, based on information "by some gentlemen, who must be allowed to have some knowledge of the Newfoundland fishery," and on the assumption that his own "or a similar plan" was enforced so as to raise the seamen. In actual fact the Newfoundland fishery never fulfilled its function as the great "nursery for seamen." See in this connection, G. S. Graham, "Fisheries and Sea Power," *Report of the Canadian Historical Association for 1941* (Toronto, 1941), 27 and 30.

standing reserve of able recruits; and as the manpower problem became more acute, beginning with the wars of Louis XIV, the seagoing coal trade gained correspondingly in strategic importance.[40]

Meanwhile between 1500 and 1660 the total tonnage of the English navy increased almost six times.[41] That the merchant carriers should provide a foundation for this great expansion of the military marine is obvious; but that the development of the Royal Navy should accelerate the growth of merchant ship-building is more questionable. According to Werner Sombart, concentration on the building of warships stimulated the growth of merchant shipping, since the government recognized the advantages of being able to charter useful transport and auxiliary craft in time of war, while the merchants appreciated that they would profit by it.[42] In other words, military interest counted more heavily than purely trading interest in the expansion of commercial ship-building. But even in an age of chronic war, so sweeping an explanation must be taken with caution, because, for the period lasting almost to the end of the century, there is no ready or accurate means of estimating the extent of collaboration between Royal Navy and merchant marine. By the time of William III there are at least lists of expenditure; until then, authoritative evidence can hardly be said to exist.

But no statistics are necessary to prove the intimate relationship that government assumed to exist between navy and merchant service. In an era of tremendous commercial expansion, empire was conceived as a blend of trade and sea power—a combination of two interacting and mutually expanding elements. "As trade and commerce enrich," wrote Bolingbroke in 1738, "so they fortify our country. The sea is our barrier, ships are our fortresses, and the mariners that trade and commerce alone can furnish are the garrisons to defend them."[43] William III's Board of Trade and Plantations continued from 1696 to 1782 to symbolize the pre-eminence of trade over colonization; and it was the growth of world trade that now stimulated the expansion of the Royal Navy. "The Navy is of so great importance" wrote Lord Halifax in 1694—and the Trimmer was not given to dogmatic generalizations—"that it would be disparaged by calling it less than the life and soul of Government."[44]

[40]See Nef, *The Rise of the British Coal Industry*, I, 237-8.
[41]Sombart, *Der Moderne Kapitalismus*, I, 762 and 766.
[42]Sombart, *Krieg und Kapitalismus*, 180-2, 190.
[43]*Letters on the Spirit of Patriotism and on the Idea of a Patriot King* (Clarendon Press, 1917), 116.
[44]*The Complete Works of George Saville, First Marquess of Halifax*, ed. Walter Raleigh (London, 1912), 175.

IV

The War of the League of Augsburg

BY the time of the Stuart Restoration, the first foundations of maritime power so magnificently raised by Richelieu had begun to crumble. At the end of Mazarin's administration, France had once more ceased to count at sea. New construction had fallen behind, maintenance had been ignored, and vessels rotted on the slips. "I would rather tend cows than command a force so badly organized and disciplined as this one," wrote a provincial vice-admiral.[1] When Colbert took office in 1661 the French navy was reduced to less than twenty seaworthy ships.

Sixteen years later, the total French establishment included more than 250 vessels of war. Of these, 68 belonged to the first three rates (of not less than fifty guns, and of at least eight hundred tons burden), and there was money for new construction.[2] Here was a navy capable of matching the combined fleets of England and Holland; and this incredible achievement was, as nearly as it could be, the performance of a single man.

Colbert was the second architect of French maritime eminence. It was Colbert who was chiefly responsible for the establishment or renovation of arsenals at Dunkirk, Brest, Rochefort, and Toulon; Colbert who made ship-building a national industry, and who, in an effort to abolish pressing, not only made recruitment a systematic feature of state administration but urged enlistment as a patriotic

[1]Quoted in Tramond, *Manuel d'histoire maritime*, 171.
[2]See *Select Naval Documents*, ed. H. W. Hodges and E. A. Hughes (Cambridge University Press, 1922), 80; also J. K. Laughton, *Studies in Naval History* (London, 1887), 46. Cf. Tramond, whose total figures are slightly higher (*Manuel d'histoire maritime*, 207).

obligation. Following in the footsteps of Richelieu, he introduced order and continuity in place of indifference and incoherence.[3] Whether or not he fully understood all the implications of the "command of the sea" which absolute superiority alone can provide, the fact remains that he was the first Frenchman, and possibly the first statesman of any country, to solder together what Mahan has so aptly called the "three rings" in the chain of maritime supremacy —ships, colonies, and commerce.

As early as 1647, at a time when the wars of the Fronde were shortly to undo the great work of Richelieu, Colbert had begun to interest himself in political affairs. His progress had been rapid, and after the death of Mazarin he became successively counsellor, intendant, controller-general of finances, and finally in 1669 minister of marine, an office which he had actually administered since 1665. He never held either the title or the attributes of "First Minister," for this was against Louis XIV's principles, but his responsibilities must have embraced at least ten departments. He possessed, says Tramond, an authority almost without limit.

Indefatigable worker, methodical in details, as hard on others as on himself, without hates and without affections, he exercised a decisive influence on the life of France; for nearly two centuries, his theories and his opinions were to remain as incontestable dogmas for administrators and statesmen.[4]

Like Richelieu, Colbert had to work slowly in the beginning. Like Richelieu, he had to create order out of the internal confusion brought about by the corrupt administration of his predecessor Fouquet. The population was groaning under heavy taxation; yet the state was on the verge of bankruptcy, and commercial activity on the oceans was almost at a standstill. The carrying trade of France, both coastwise and foreign, had fallen almost entirely into the hands of the Dutch. Some 150 Dutch ships disputed the French West Indies trade, and out of a probable total of 20,000 vessels in the merchant marine of Europe, Colbert estimated that some 16,000 belonged to Holland.[5] The measure of his success in reforming the administration is apparent in his earliest navy budgets. In 1663 the grant was three million livres; within a few years, this sum was doubled and then trebled. In 1671, the total budget was thirteen

[3]See Lacour-Gayet, *La Marine militaire de la France sous le règne de Louis XV*, 7.
[4]*Manuel d'histoire maritime*, 174-5.
[5]S. L. Mims, *Colbert's West India Policy* (New Haven, Conn., 1912), 3.

millions, and Colbert made sure that the money went to its allotted destination.[6]

Like Richelieu again, he imported essential materials and borrowed brains. Reserves of naval stores and masts were purchased in Sweden and the Baltic; model ships were purchased from Holland, and skilled Dutch workmen were hired to teach the art of shipbuilding to the native French. Colbert was aiming at self-sufficiency, as is further evidenced by his successful plans for construction in New France. Quebec and other colonial ports continued to supply ships for the French navy until the loss of Canada in 1763.[7] Although Colbert failed to make French ship-building independent of the Baltic, his pertinacity stimulated far-reaching improvements in design; thenceforward, through the eighteenth century, French naval architecture was superior in almost every respect to that of the English.[8]

France was thus prepared in ships, men, and administration, as never before in her history. Moreover, the absolute monarchy, which was to reach its zenith under Louis XIV, seemed to give her all the advantages of quick initiative, without the delays and hesitations which over-indulgence in parliamentary debate seemed to demand. Only by continual encouragement and supervision was the French nation likely to develop that tradition of sea warfare which was slowly becoming a part of the politically conscious Englishman. As it happened, however, it was lack of constant direction that in the long run ruined Colbert's great work. Under Louis XIV the navy was bound to be a royal instrument, subject to personal whims and political exigencies. A change of ministers was sufficient to suspend a whole programme. Before his death Colbert had failed to create within the nation a crusading maritime spirit sufficient to resist the more seductive concepts of land conquest and European hegemony.

For a time, however, his policy bore good fruit. In campaigns which lasted off and on for ten years, DuQuesne won control of the Mediterranean, while in the Channel both Dutch and Spanish suffered reverses. This period saw the full tide of French naval prosperity, and at the outbreak of the War of the League of Augsburg (which substituted a Dutch-English combination for a Spanish-

[6]Laughton, *Studies in Naval History*, 44.
[7]See Albion, *Forests and Sea Power*, 75.
[8]See Hodges and Hughes, *Select Naval Documents*, 80.

Dutch) the French fleet was probably unequalled. It was an auspicious introduction to the new "Hundred Years' War" that was to
become in the eighteenth century a struggle for empire in Asia as
well as North America. Until the battle of the Boyne (1690) consolidated William's position, Tourville's victories on the sea seemed
likely to shatter the Dutch alliance before it had a chance to ac-
cumulate strength.

The first stake in the struggle should obviously have been command
of the sea, for only by controlling the Channel could the French open
and safeguard an invasion route to England. As it happened, the
significance of the early naval operations seems to have been over-
looked both in France and in England. Since the war was not,
except incidentally, a fight for colonies and commerce, it was inevitable that naval operations should be regarded as subsidiary to
land operations; but whatever the role of the navy, it was a mistake
to neglect its true function and to ignore the decisiveness of battle
as a means of eliminating the enemy at sea. Both sides, however,
seemed content with partial or local control of such areas along the
coasts as were required for the transport and landing of troops, a
perfunctory naval strategy that almost suggests a retrogression
towards pre-Armada doctrine.

In France, this false conception of the aims of naval warfare was
firmly cemented by La Hogue in 1692. La Hogue spelt the end of
the great invasion attempt, and although France, like Spain after
1588, repaired her losses, something of the sea-spirit, which men like
Richelieu and Colbert had momentarily been able to fan into life,
had gone forever. "La Hogue," says Michelet, "insignificant at first
glance, changed the course of history." Regarded superficially, it
was but a temporary check. Scarcely more than thirteen French
ships had been lost; in 1693, Tourville still held the sea with seventy
ships of the line.[9] Yet the apparently haphazard manner in which
the English followed up their victory, their withdrawal to the defensive (apart from a few spasmodic raids), and the ultimate
dispersal of their great fleet served to confirm official French
opinion of the secondary importance of naval battle, and the folly
of sacrificing men, time, and money in the pursuit of command of
the sea.

The building and arming of the great French fleets at Brest and
Toulon had borne hard on the exchequer, and the returns had been

[9] R. Daveluy, *L'Esprit de la Guerre Navale* (2 vols., 2nd ed., Paris, 1909), I, 246.

negligible. Between 1662 and 1690, some 216 million livres had been spent on the navy; "to what effect?" urged the military party which included Louvois and Vauban. Expenditure on a fleet was a foolish form of patriotism. Recent experience had demonstrated, in their opinion, that neither successes nor defeats at sea had any great effect on final military results.

According to Saint-Simon, "la jalousie de Louvois écrasa la marine." Louvois had a passion for war on land, and the man who spoke of replacing ships of war with regiments for coastguard duty had obviously little interest in maritime and colonial ambitions.[10] Whether or not it was Louvois's policy that triumphed, the significant fact is that Louis XIV's decision to extend the area of his European dominions enabled England to regain at leisure the supremacy of the sea which for a time she seemed to be in some danger of losing. No longer subject to the counsels of Colbert and his son Seignelay, the king turned for solace to the victors of Namur.

With La Hogue, the navy ceased to play a part in "la grande politique." Morale and maintenance declined, and the real power of the fleet after 1692 hardly corresponded with the impressive totals of guns and ships. Since the squadrons rarely left harbour, officers and crews grew rusty on navigation, gunnery, and general sea knowledge. Moreover, the recruiting system of Colbert was unnecessarily perverted for the sake of quick and easy conscriptions. Not only experienced seamen, but also peasants, dock-workers, barge-men, and fishermen, were impressed. Seafaring peoples on the coasts were forbidden to change their occupation, and children of ten years were listed as recruits for subsequent service—a so-called efficiency plan which meant the practical enslavement of the coastal districts. Theoretically, it provided a greater number of men than ever before; official figures give the number as 90,000[11]; but the bulk of the recruits were poor stuff completely lacking in nautical experience, and with little chance of obtaining it in the future. By the end of the century, the French navy was a strong force on paper, but only on paper.

Guerre de course as a species of naval strategy was indirectly a product of La Hogue. With the decline of the French navy, there

[10]See Lacour-Gayet, *La Marine militaire de la France sous le règne de Louis XV*, 8.
[11]See Tramond, *Manuel d'histoire maritime*, 279.

developed the new and vicious tendency to spare ships for commerce raiding rather than risk them in decisive battle.

The object of *guerre de course* was to whittle away the strength and resources of the stronger power, so that the weaker might eventually be in a position to concentrate at the opportune moment with some hope of success. As systematized by the French, this scheme was in essence an expansion of ordinary privateering, for which there were many precedents. When the Low Countries revolted against Philip, the Dutch, who had been crushed on land, took to the water as *Sea-Beggars*, where they were joined in their forays by many English privateers from the West Country. Many of Drake's men were trained in this school of guerilla warfare, for he and Hawkins organized what was in many respects a strategy of *guerre de course*. Charles I tried it for a time. Always short of money and cramped by Parliament in his efforts to enlarge the navy, he sent some of his lighter vessels to sea with the object of enriching his own purse; but the experiment was not a great success, and after Charles's reign England abandoned the strategy of raids upon commerce as a principal objective of war.

Not so the French. Under Louis XIV *guerre de course* broadened from the destruction of commerce by individual corsairs to become a principal objective of war.[12] Renouncing orthodox efforts to win command of the sea, the French government unleashed its corsairs in the Channel and the North Sea. From 1693 until 1714, this system of commerce raiding was continued to an extent, and with a success, unparalleled in the age of sail. The ships, most of them taken from the royal marine, were fast cruisers, heavily armed, and capable of staying at sea for several months. Until the end of the War of the Spanish Succession, they cruised in every ocean; and while it is impossible to give accurate estimates of the destruction they wrought, one reckoning has it that England alone lost 4,200 vessels before the end of the war.[13] For several months in 1693, English commerce with the Levant was almost completely stopped, and in London and Amsterdam insurance rates increased by thirty per cent. *Guerre de*

[12]The famous captain, Robert Surcouf, advised Napoleon: "Sire, in your place, I should burn all my ships of the line and never give battle to the British fleet, or show fight to British cruising squadrons; but I should launch on every sea a multitude of frigates and light craft which would very soon annihilate the commerce of our rival and deliver her into our hands." Quoted in W. B. Johnson, *Wolves of the Channel* (London, 1931), 1.

[13]See Tramond, *Manuel d'histoire maritime*, 289; also, in this connection Ehrenberg, *Capital and Finance in the Age of the Renaissance*, 365.

course was one contributing factor in the creation of the Bank of England.

On the other hand, France was bound to sacrifice her own ocean commerce and, in the long run, as successive alliances wore down her strength in Europe, *guerre de course* became a strategy of delaying defeat rather than pursuing victory; it became a device for making the best of bad circumstances. In the Mediterranean, France was able to hold her position, but outside the gates of Gibraltar she surrendered all that Colbert had dreamed of realizing. The remnants of the royal marine mouldered in harbour, and France became once more a nation of provincial ports, each with its own privateering flotilla, its own parochial discipline, and its own local prosperity founded on pillage.[14]

In 1663 Louis XIV had dissolved Richelieu's old Company of New France which had continued an erratic existence for more than thirty years; and Canada became a royal colony. National prestige was involved in the transfer, for the French stake in the New World had old roots. Canada had been a French possession for more than half a century; yet the population was less than 2,500.

Within the next ten years, Colbert made valiant efforts to stimulate immigration, establish industries, and promote commerce. During that period the population trebled, and under the direction of a great intendant, Jean Talon, the foundations of scientific agriculture and domestic manufacturing were laid. Unhappily, the predicted three-cornered trade between Canada, the West Indies, and France involved too many risks to be successful; despite all Talon's efforts Canada could not produce enough food-stuffs or lumber to make the export total balance even the small imports of West Indies rum, sugar, and molasses.[15] Ship-building made some progress, but on the whole New France failed to make substantial contributions to Colbert's self-sufficient empire. Essentially the colony remained a fur-trading base, with extending lines of communication west and south in the direction of the retreating beaver, on whose skins the solvency of the community depended.[16]

[14]Tramond, *Manuel d'histoire maritime*, 290-1.
[15]See Mims, *Colbert's West India Policy*, 318.
[16]The beaver trade suffered severely from periodic slumps, as French markets failed to absorb the over-supply of furs. After the price collapse of 1674 Colbert encouraged the manufacture of cloth as well as hats from beaver fur. See C. W. Cole, *Colbert and a Century of French Mercantilism* (2 vols., New York, 1939), II, 81, 203-4; also H. A. Innis, *The Fur Trade in Canada* (New Haven, Conn., 1930), 63-4.

None the less, the arrival of regular troops, the Carignan Salières, was evidence of continuing royal interest. The aggressions of the Iroquois both southward and westward were stemmed, and soon the imperialistic dreams of La Salle led to an expansion of French claims down the Mississippi Valley as far as the Gulf of Mexico. The staking out of so much territory in the rear of the English coastal colonies was clear-cut evidence that France intended to assert herself, in appearance at least, as the dominant North American power. Under the leadership of a great governor, Count Frontenac, a network of small fortifications and blockhouses gradually extended itself below the Great Lakes in defence of French claims and French trade, and plans began to take shape for carrying the offensive from those outer posts into the heart of enemy country—to New York and the sea.

As for Acadia, it had been handed back to France in 1667, to resume its precarious existence as eastern bastion of the empire of the St. Lawrence.[17] Three years later, Port Royal, the chief fortified settlement of the colony, boasted one hundred and sixty settlers, and barely another hundred were to be found in the half dozen fishing stations between Canso and the Penobscot River. While Frontenac bent his feverish energies towards the military consolidation of New France, the seaboard province was either ignored or treated as an administrative annex of Canada, from which it was almost as isolated as from France. The only available overland communications were routes passable by expert trappers and Indians.

Moreover, the whole peninsula was exposed by sea and land to its next-door neighbour, New England; yet without ready assistance from Canada it was expected to form a base of attack against the left flank of the New England colonies, whose fishermen trespassed constantly on local waters or raided and pillaged Acadian ports. Each year some three hundred or more New England fishing vessels visited Acadian waters. "It grieves me to the heart," wrote a governor of Acadia, M. Subercase, "to see Messieurs les Bastonnais enrich themselves in our domain; for the base of their commerce is the fish which they catch off our coasts, and send to all parts of the world."[18] For the next twenty-five years, "the chronicle of the time is a confused record of raids on frontier villages, and on formal fortresses, of fights

[17]Following the conquest of forts and settlements by Major-General Sedgwick of Massachusetts in 1654, Britain had nominal control of the coast of Acadia from Cape Canso to New England, the French retaining their foothold on the shores of the Gulf and on the Island of Cape Breton.
[18]F. Parkman, *Half Century of Conflict* (2 vols., Boston, ed. 1894), I, 107.

between fishing vessels; of seizure of trading ships or of looting of them; and finally, of semi-official piracy and privateering."[19] At a time when Colbert was practising a new colonial policy, Acadia remained curiously aloof from help and almost destitute of protection; by 1690 the garrison at Port Royal comprised about sixty men.

The first French colony in Newfoundland was in a similarly precarious position. Ousted by Britain from the territory between Cape Race and Bonavista, the French government had decided as early as 1655 to fortify Placentia (Plaisance) as a base of operations on the south coast. West of the Avalon Peninsula and protected by a deep bay, Placentia was a makeshift port of wooden houses, set among the rocks and hillocks, when the first governor, Sieur de Kereon, made his unsuccessful attempt to organize a permanent establishment among the migrant fishermen. Seven years later, Fouquet sent out du Perron with a party of emigrants, thirty soldiers and eighteen pieces of ordnance, and this little garrison took possession of the falling earthen entrenchments, somewhat ludicrously named a fort.[20] But at least du Perron was strong enough in 1665 to frighten away de Ruyter and his three men of war, a signal example of the advantages of even primitive local defences against chance raiders.[21]

As the French Newfoundland fishing fleet grew lustily to 400 ships with 18,000 men (as compared with the English total of 300 ships with 15,000 men),[22] additional efforts were made to buttress the French position on the south shore. In 1687 more troops were sent out under the command of Philippe de Pastour de Costebelle, in company with an engineer, who was given the task of putting garrison and inhabitants to work on new fortifications. But the soldiers, already turned fishermen, refused to work without special indemnity, and the governor, faced by revolt from within and alien aggression from without, was able to preserve his position only by treating with the English, who agreed to victual the settlement in return for fish. This arrangement kept the peace until formal war was declared on May 17, 1689.

The first blow came from an unexpected quarter. On the night of February 25, 1690, Placentia was surprised by an English raiding

[19]Brebner, *New England's Outpost*, 47.
[20]R. Le Blant, *Un Colonel sous Louis XIV, Philippe de Pastour de Costebelle, Gouverneur de Terre-Neuve, puis de l'Ile Royale (1661-1717)* (Paris, 1935), 52.
[21]*Calendar of State Papers, Colonial, America and West Indies, 1661-68*, V, 558.
[22]*Ibid.*, 559.

party from Ferryland who took complete possession of the town and port, killing two soldiers and wounding another. After gustily proclaiming their threat to kill all the males and carry off the women, they contented themselves with burning sulphur matches between the fingers of the governor, destroying the gun emplacements, and throwing the cannon into the sea.[23] This triumph was short-lived. The timely arrival of a detachment of marines enabled the poverty-stricken garrison to renew their labours on the fortifications, and plan their own offensive. In the early autumn of 1692 a small "commando" ravaged Trinity Bay, while Costebelle succeeded on September 6 in driving the English from Trepassey. One week later, however, five men-of-war under Commodore Williams anchored in Placentia Bay and called upon the garrison to surrender. With only fifty soldiers in the fort, and practically no ammunition, Placentia seemed doomed, but after a sharp cannonade, the English squadron suddenly withdrew.[24] In August of the following year, a squadron of nineteen vessels, under the command of Admiral Wheler, appeared and prepared for an assault. They anchored within musket-shot of the fort, but bad weather finally forced them to take to the open sea, and in the end Wheler satisfied himself with pillaging St. Pierre.[25]

Had the conflict in North America been a matter to settle between the colonists themselves, there can be little doubt that the professional soldiers of New France would have been more than a match for the numerically preponderant but ill-disciplined farmers, traders, fishermen, and soldiers of fortune in the English colonies. Both sides depended ultimately, however, on overseas assistance; the Atlantic remained the vital channel of communication for men and supplies. While the French under Frontenac were able to make immediate gains by reason of initiative, training, and leadership, in the long run the fate of the western continent was settled on the sea. None the less, the war in North America is significant as being the first in which English and French colonists played a concerted part in company with their mother countries. For years, English, French, and Indians had conducted what might almost be called

[23]See Le Blant, *Un Colonel sous Louis XIV*, 67.
[24]See B. Murdoch, *History of Nova Scotia or Acadia* (3 vols., Halifax, 1865-7), I, 213; also L. A. Anspach, *A History of the Island of Newfoundland* (London, 1819), 96.
[25]Le Blant, *Un Colonel sous Louis XIV*, 82.

private raiding parties on coastal or boundary settlements, frequently without the knowledge or approval of the European rivals across
the sea.   In 1689, began the first colonial effort at waging world war.
On their own responsibility the New Englanders set about the task
of destroying the privateering haunts of Acadia, and finally of assaulting the very centre of French power in North America—Quebec.

Owing to the exhaustion of the treasury as a consequence of
previous military expenditures under Governor Andros, the provisional government of Massachusetts was not keen to make the
venture at the public expense; and it was hoped that private traders,
tempted by plunder and potential trading privileges, might not only
undertake the work of organizing the expedition but also pay for it.
Hence, the order of January 4, 1690, which was passed by the
General Court

> For the encouragement of such gentlemen and merchants of this colony as
> shall undertake to reduce Penobscot, St. John's, and Port Royal, it is ordered,
> that they shall have two sloops of war for three or four months at free cost,
> and all the profits which they can make from our French enemies, and the
> trade of the places which they may take, till there be other orders given from
> their Majesties.[26]

Such a speculation was too novel and too hazardous to tempt the
merchant community; hence it was finally resolved to make the attempt "at the public charge and with all speed."   An immediate
appeal was made for recruits, and when volunteering failed to provide the requisite number, the General Court, on March 22, gave
power to impress young males to the number of five hundred.   As
the principal rendezvous of the privateers who preyed on the coastal
and fishing vessels, Port Royal was made the first objective.[27]   The
command was given to the Honourable Sir William Phips, who had
offered himself when such an expedition had first been considered.

Phips had an incredible career, and his story is the saga of a self-
made man, whose unique talents were in the long run more than
counter-balanced by a monstrous egotism.   With little or no edu-
cation, this man who had been a ship's carpenter won the ear and the
financial support of three kings—two Stuarts and Dutch William.
With little or no sea experience, he had himself appointed captain
of a King's ship to search for Spanish treasure in the Spanish Main.

[26]Quoted in F. Bowen, "Life of Sir William Phips," *The Library of American
Biography*, ed. J. Sparks (New York, 1839), VII, 38.
[27]Governor Simon Bradstreet to the Earl of Shrewsbury, March 29, 1690,
Calendar of State Papers, Colonial, America and West Indies, 1689-92, XIII, 240.

With only the vaguest notion of where the galleons had gone down, he fished almost directly over the wreck of a treasure ship, from which he garnered £10,000 as his personal share, and a knighthood on his return home.[28] Seeking more adventure in the colonies, he went to Massachusetts where he became High Sheriff, and finally in 1692, through the influence of Increase Mather and the Puritan divines, Governor-in-Chief and Captain-General of the province, which then included the colony of Plymouth, the provinces of Maine and Nova Scotia and all the country between these two. But so rapid an advance to power could not have been accomplished without allies. Shortly after his arrival in the colony, he seems to have developed grave anxieties as to the state of his soul, a predicament from which Increase Mather was pleased to save him. Thenceforth the devout Phips held a secure place in the theocracy, and trod the rosy path of a Boston "Ward" politician under the watchful eyes of the ministers.

Phips had intelligence, toughness, and tremendous perseverance; in addition, his "tours de force" were blessed with uncanny luck. "He succeeded in enterprises so hopeless at first sight that men of sober judgment would never have engaged in them, and after failures and discouragements, which would have caused persons of ordinary prudence to give up the attempt."[29] None the less it is clear from the evidence that he was totally unfit either to lead an army or to govern a province.[30]

Phips's instructions, signed by Governor Bradstreet of Massachusetts, were handed to him on April 18, 1690. Apart from routine directions on such matters as daily religious services, they were principally concerned with the punishment to be meted out to Port Royal. Sir William was empowered to offer the garrison fair terms:

. . . which if they obey, the said terms are to be duly observed; if not, you are to gain the best advantage you may, to assault, kill, and utterly extirpate the common enemy, and to burn and demolish their fortifications and shipping;

[28]*Calendar of State Papers, Colonial, America and West Indies, 1693-6*, XIV xxi-xxii.
[29]Bowen, "Life of Sir William Phips," 100.
[30]Phips was always a bit of a brute, and success made him savagely pompous. In the end, when growing irascibility led him to break his cane on the head of one of his captains, he lost popular support and finally left Boston in November, 1694. Once again, he prepared to return to his old business of fishing for sunken treasure. Somewhere in the West Indies a treasure ship carrying the Spanish governor, Bobadilla, had been cast away; but before he could make a start, he caught cold and died in February, 1695, at the age of 45.

having reduced that place, to proceed along the coast, for the reducing of other places and plantations in the possession of the French into the obedience of the crown of England. . . .

Phips set sail from Nantasket on April 28 with a frigate of forty-four guns, two sloops, four ketches, and a total force of about seven hundred men. He arrived at Port Royal on May 11. Taken by surprise, there was little the governor, M. de Meneval, could do. His outer defences, consisting chiefly of a single palisade, lay close to the water, completely exposed to the fire of invading enemy ships. The garrison, which had been reduced to eighty-five men, possessed eighteen cannon, but none of them had been mounted,[31] and, lacking a single officer, they had no one with sufficient knowledge to fire them effectively. Nevertheless, de Meneval stood his ground until the New Englanders had landed, and then, according to his own story, surrendered on condition that private property should be respected and French prisoners guaranteed transport to a French port.

If such were the stipulations, they were certainly not observed. The spirit of the enterprise is best expressed in a diary of one of the militiamen. "We cut down the cross, rifled the church, pulled down the altar and broke their images. (May 13) Kept gathering plunder all day."[32] The invoice of pillage is still preserved in the State Archives of Massachusetts, and the account includes: "twenty-four girdles; two caps; one hood; twenty-four canonical gowns; four more gowns with silver clasps and laced; beds and bedding; one white coat; two pair of shoes; one red waistcoat; fourteen old kettles, pots and stew-pans." Allowing for the value of such miscellaneous plunder, it was estimated that the expedition cost £3000.

After demolishing the flimsy fort and leaving a small garrison in the town, Phips set out for home, stopping en route to proclaim the *pax Britannica* in various fishing settlements that dotted the coast as far as the Penobscot. It was a grand parade, but this Massachusetts triumph was little more than a flash in the pan, and the annexation of Acadia in 1692 no more than a gesture. In 1691 the French once more took possession of Port Royal and the surrounding country and, despite further marauding raids, managed to hold

[31]See "Extract of a Letter to Mr. Jon Usher from Boston, [May 27, 1690]," along with "Journal of the Expedition under Sir William Phips against Port Royal, 1690," *Report of the Work of the Archives Branch for the Year 1912* (Ottawa, 1913), App. E, 64; see also Murdoch, *History of Nova Scotia*, I, 185.
[32]*Calendar of State Papers, Colonial, America and West Indies, 1689-92*, XIII, xii and xiii; see also "An Abstract of a Lre from Mr. James Lloyd, Mercht, Boston, 8th Jany. 1690-91," *Report on Canadian Archives, 1912*, App. E, 64.

it. In August 1696 an old Indian fighter, Benjamin Church, got as far as the Bay of Fundy but, beyond burning Chignecto, accomplished little before returning home.

Nevertheless, the success of the Phips expedition emboldened the government of Massachusetts to "cut off the fountain of trouble at the head." If a Quebec expedition were organized immediately, the enemy would have less time to absorb the lesson of Port Royal and prepare adequately for a siege. The number of Frenchmen of military age was known to be small, and there was comfort in the thought that Frontenac's Indian allies were of little value on the defensive within a fortified town. Moreover, it was hoped that a land expedition consisting of some 1000 militia and 1500 Indians might support the fleet by marching overland to attack Montreal by way of Lake George.

Two days before the return of Phips, the Massachusetts House of Deputies, on May 28, 1690, had passed a bill for "the encouragement of volunteers for the expedition against Canada." To promote enlistments it was ordered that, in addition to pay, "one just half part of all plunder, taken from the enemy, should be shared among the officers, soldiers, and seamen, stores of war excepted." Phips was once more appointed commander-in-chief, with Major John Walley his second-in-command.[33] Lack of money in the treasury still remained a major difficulty, although the motley pickings from Acadia showed that a campaign of plunder might support itself. In any event, a combination of political pressure and publicity won subscriptions from the Boston merchants varying from one to three hundred pounds; the same traders had also been induced by threat of impressment to fit out 32 vessels, "4 of them Ships about 100 Tunns; the rest sorry things," and to supply three months' victuals.[34] Even so, the government was forced to introduce paper currency to make up the deficiency in cash, a method of finance which was subsequently to embarrass the industrious and frugal people of Massachusetts.[35]

Meanwhile, it was discovered that the expedition lacked competent pilots with a knowledge of the St. Lawrence River, and efforts to conscribe experienced navigators in Port Royal were unsuccessful.

[33]See Sir Williams Phips to the King, June 30, 1691, *Calendar of State Papers, Colonial, America and West Indies, 1689-92*, xiii, 478.
[34]"Abstract from a Lre from Mr. James Lloyd Merch^t in Boston, dat. 8th Jany, [1690-91]," *Report on Canadian Archives, 1912*, App. E, 65.
[35]W. Douglass, *A Summary, Historical and Political, of the First Planting, Progressive Improvements and Present State of the British Settlements in North America* (2 vols., Boston, 1755), I, 314n.

To add to misfortune, the expected supplies of arms and ammunition from England had not arrived. However, in view of the lateness of the season it was finally decided to make the venture, come what might, and on August 9 Phips set sail from Nantasket.

The fleet was divided into three squadrons. The largest of thirteen sail was under command of Captain Sugars in the frigate *Six Friends*; the other divisions of nine sail each were commanded by Captains Gilbert and Eldridge. At the request of the government the churches observed a general fast throughout the colony "for the welfare of the army sent into Quebec"; according to Cotton Mather, they kept "the wheel of prayer in continual motion."[36]

A few prizes were picked up in the early stages of the voyage, and arrangements made for their delivery to Boston; but the worst delays were the result of Phips's passion for dramatic landings on uninhabited bits of coast to set up the English flag. Consequently three weeks were consumed before the fleet reached the mouth of the St. Lawrence, and thenceforward progress was even slower. Apart from the need for caution (for they were still without pilots), further delays were caused by adverse winds and by Phips's chronic urge to make periodic stops in order that "councils of war" might discuss plans for the attack, matters which should have been decided in Boston or else left to the discretion of the commander-in-chief. An added inconvenience was the presence of smallpox, which apparently had been picked up in Boston; and this, in company with the usual fevers which attached themselves to ships' crews in those days, added to the distress of the confused and frustrated officers. However, the fleet reached Tadoussac on September 23, and on October 5 (Old Style), nine weeks after embarkation, they finally appeared before Quebec.

These recurring delays were a godsend to the French, for at the end of September Frontenac was still at Montreal awaiting the anticipated attack by land from New York.[37] Had this projected invasion of Canada been carried forward, the inevitable division of the French forces would have left Quebec in a highly precarious situation. As it happened, disputes between the commissioners of the governments of New York and Connecticut made close cooperation impossible and, as a climax to domestic trouble, when the

---

[36]"Relation de Cotton Mather," in Ernest Myrand, *1690: Sir William Phips devant Québec, Histoire d'un Siège* (Quebec, 1893), 112.
[37]See p. 71.

New York force of some 1,000 men and 1,500 Indians finally reached the borders of Lake George, they found no boats. This, together with a continuing desertion of Indian allies, effectively damped the offensive spirit, and the commander gave the order to retreat.

On hearing of this decision, at the time when Phips was slowly feeling his way up the St. Lawrence, Frontenac immediately embarked with such troops as were at hand, and hastened towards Quebec. He found a disheartened garrison of less than two hundred men with twelve pieces of artillery and almost no ammunition. Lahontan, who was on the spot, has suggested that if Phips had landed on the day he anchored off Quebec, he could have taken the town without a shot,[38] but this may be an exaggeration. In any event, instead of making an immediate assault, the whole of Sunday and the next day were passed in quiet contemplation of the Rock, during which time French reinforcements, including Indians, filtered into the besieged town to aid in the work of repairing the walls and mounting the guns. On October 6 a young officer, Major Thomas Savage, was sent on shore with a summons to surrender. What transpired is best described in the caustic words of a Boston merchant:

. . . noe sooner Landed him but carrys him blind fold into a stately Hall full of brave Martiall men, who finding a pumpkin ffleet with ye Union flag Commanded by a person never did Exploit above water; bid them take their demands from their great Gunns, & would not Surrender to Canoes, wch startled our men being preached to other things."[39]

Meanwhile, Phips decided to make his landing about three miles below Quebec on the Beauport shore. Command of the assault force was given to Major Walley. Sir William himself, with four of the larger ships, planned to create a diversion by sailing up the river, and bombarding the lower town. Provided Walley succeeded in crossing the St. Charles River, two hundred men were to be landed, under cover of ships' guns, to breach the defences, whilst Walley moved in simultaneously on the right flank.

On October 7, despite a heavy wind which prejudiced landing operations, Walley made his first attempt. In view of the ravages of fever and disease, only some 1,300 troops could be spared for the

[38]"Outline of a Project to Capture Quebec and Placentia," *The Oakes Collection, New Documents by Lahontan concerning Canada and Newfoundland*, ed. with an introd. by Gustave Lanctot (Ottawa, Public Archives of Canada, 1940), 33; see also Murdoch, *History of Nova Scotia*, I, 192.

[39]"Abstract of a Lre from Mr. James Lloyd, [8th Jany. 1690-91]," contained in "Journal of the Expedition to Quebec," *Report on Canadian Archives, 1912*, App. E, 65.

task, and of these, many were in lamentably bad condition. As might have been anticipated, while the boats were able to leave the ships, they were almost unmanageable close to the shore where the surf endangered lives as well as scanty stores of ammunition. On the following day the attempt was renewed and this time with success. Unfortunately, a shelving beach forced the troops to wade ashore, an exhausting experience which chilled them to the bone. And hardly had they landed when they were forced to fight their way through woods and swamp, sporadically sniped by a French ranger detachment. But the New Englanders were used to bush fighting, and despite fatigue and cold they were able to drive the enemy back with a loss of only five killed to the enemy's thirty.

The French retired to a small village on the English flank, and Walley, finding himself short of ammunition, preferred to stay his advance rather than try to drive them out and seize their warm and comfortable quarters. This meant that the New Englanders had to bivouac in the open air in weather which was unusually severe for that time of year; rivulets had already frozen up and there were no provisions. On landing, each man had carried with him three quarters of a pound of powder, about eighteen shot, and two biscuits. The biscuits had long since disappeared, as well as most of the powder and shot, but help was expected at midnight. Unhappily when the ferries arrived, they brought, instead of needed supplies, six brass field guns which in the then weakened physical condition of the troops were more of a burden than an aid. Without horses, it was absurd to expect chilled and famished men to drag the pieces across the marshy ground which separated them from St. Charles River. Moreover, the addition of half a barrel of powder and a hundred-weight of bullets would hardly suffice to clear the advance.

The explanation of this scarcity of ammunition is simple, but fantastic. Phips with his four ships had sailed up the river, and begun his assault on the lower town. The attack was premature, for Walley's forces had not crossed the St. Charles; yet the useless cannonade against rocks and stone buildings was kept up till night-time, when all but two rounds of powder had been exhausted. Thence, having suffered considerable damage to their hulls as a result of vigorous enemy counter-fire, the ships dropped down the river again.

Short of supplies and powder, Walley's position was a desperate one. Several of his men were suffering from frozen hands and feet, and others had succumbed to the relentless smallpox. The banks of the St. Charles were steep and commanded by at least one battery, and beyond them were the walls of Quebec defended by troops probably double the strength of the attackers. Under the circumstances, a vigorous assault by the French might well have routed Walley's forces then and there. Fortunately for this helpless commander, the enemy preferred to skirmish, thus allowing the New Englanders to withdraw in some semblance of order.

The main problem now was that of avoiding annihilation by removing the troops from shore to ships. Retreat to the beach where the troops had previously landed was skilfully accomplished after midnight on the 11th; but the presence of substantial French forces made it far too dangerous to embark in daylight, and the boats were ordered back. The succeeding day was spent in driving off enemy detachments, and then when nightfall came, despite a withering fire from the surrounding woods, most of the survivors were able to regain their ships, leaving behind five guns.[40]

On October 12 a council of war decided, in view of the exhaustion of the troops, to postpone a new attack; but by the time morale and energy had been recovered, Phips was spared further humiliation through a timely intervention of the elements. A sudden storm scattered the fleet, and drove the ships helter-skelter down the river with loss of anchors and cables. All the way home, winds beat upon them, so that the retreat became a rout. One vessel went down, a second was wrecked, and a third was burned at sea. Others were blown so far from the Atlantic coast that they did not reach Boston until five or six weeks after the more fortunate Phips had landed.

"Thus, by an evident hand of heaven," declared Cotton Mather, "sending one unavoidable disaster after another, as well-formed an enterprize, as perhaps was ever made by the New-Englanders, most unhappily miscarried. . . ."[41] More severe judges explained everything by the fact that a Church of England chapel in Boston had been allowed to stand undisturbed. Considering the failure of the land campaign against Montreal, the absence of pilots, the lack of ammunition, bad leadership, and bitter weather, the wonder is that the expedition returned at all.[42]

[40]See Major Walley's "Journal," in T. Hutchinson, *The History of Massachusetts Bay, 1628-1750* (2 vols., 3rd ed., 1795), I, App.; also, *Documents relative to the Colonial History of the State of New York*, ed. by E. B. O'Callaghan (11 vols., Albany, 1855-61), IX, 455-62.
[41]"Relation de Cotton Mather," 111.
[42]See Major Walley's "Journal."

The elation of the French was naturally proportionate to English gloom. Quebec was safe, and Port Royal had been recovered. At the moment when the new charter of Massachusetts announced the incorporation of Acadia to the Commonwealth, French privateers were harassing the shores of New England, and threatening "with Assistance from Europe" to assault Boston itself.[43]

Thenceforth, along the coasts of the mainland and Newfoundland, the war became a matter of hit-and-run attacks on the part of the French. It was a period of enthusiastic *guerre de course*; the English seemed utterly impotent to turn their superior strength on sea to good account. Despite shortages of food and munitions, the French base at Placentia became the centre for a series of raids that by 1697 had destroyed every English settlement on the eastern coast of Newfoundland except Bonavista and Carbonear. In August 1694 five French ships of forty and fifty guns attacked Ferryland.[44] Two years later, when the French returned in stronger force, all the ports came close to being within their grasp.

In 1696, the Marquis de Nesmond was ordered to join his ten ships to the Rochefort squadron and proceed to Newfoundland. Eluding the Channel fleet, he reached Placentia towards the end of July, whence he set sail for St. John's. The English squadron refused to come out of harbour, and Nesmond, preferring not to risk an assault on the town, returned to France without firing a shot. Meanwhile, however, a second French squadron arrived at Placentia on September 24, where it was learned that Ferryland had fallen to an expedition from Saint-Malo. Proceeding separately to St. John's, the two forces had no difficulty in conquering the ill-fortified port, whose garrison suffered from want of equipment as well as food. At the same time Pierre le Moyne d'Iberville, with a detachment of Canadians, ravaged or burned most of the isolated outposts along the eastern coast.[45] The English foothold in Newfoundland was now reduced to Trinity and Conception Bays, and the Royal Navy faced the prospect of losing "the most considerable trade and training for seamen."

In the face of incessant and vehement demands from London and

[43]*Acts of the Privy Council of England, Colonial Series, 1613-1783*, ed. by W. L. Grant and J. Monro (6 vols., London, 1908-12), II, 203.
[44]*Calendar of State Papers, Colonial, America and West Indies, 1696-7*, XV, 222; see also, *Acts of the Privy Council, Colonial Series*, II, 289.
[45]*Ibid.*, 211, 224, 314; also, Murdoch, *History of Nova Scotia*, I, 222-5.

West Country fishing interests, the English government felt compelled to act vigorously.[46] Preparations were begun early in January 1697, but as a consequence of delays in arranging convoys and the difficulties of pressing men for the King's ships, it was not till mid-April that a squadron under Commodore John Norris consisting of ten men-of-war, a fireship, and two bomb-ketches, with some 760 men, set sail for Newfoundland, arriving at the southern extremity of Conception Bay on June 7.[47] Here they learned that, apart from Bonavista and Carbonear, nothing had escaped the "barbarous fury" of the enemy: St. John's had been gutted; Ferryland, the "best harbour and pleasantest place in the whole island," was deserted; and only two or three inhabitants remained in Bay Bulls.[48]

From the beginning the expedition appears to have suffered from lack of supplies, although the authorities in Whitehall had urged Massachusetts to provide as much aid as possible in ships, men, and stores.[49] Although St. John's was secured, no attempt was made to destroy French settlements on the south shore. When Nesmond reappeared in August with an augmented squadron of sixteen ships of war, ten of which mounted sixty guns or more, Norris, after reluctantly taking the advice of a council of war, skilfully moored his ships in the shape of a half moon, broadsides to the harbour mouth. However uninspired, his tactics in the face of superior enemy forces were to be justified by events. After plying up and down for a whole day, Nesmond sent in a fifty-gun ship and a bomb-ketch to test the defences. At the end of a short exchange of broadsides, the two

[46]Hitherto resentful of government interference, the West Country now united with the London interests in demanding speedy and effectual aid before the French, "destroy all their garrisons and ruin the country." For petitions, warnings, and complaints from the West Country and elsewhere, see Calendar of State Papers, Colonial, America and West Indies, 1696-7, XV, 211, 224, 347, and 440; also L. F. Stock, Proceedings and Debates of the British Parliaments respecting North America [1542-1739] (4 vols., Washington, 1924-37), II, 178 and 181; and D. W. Prowse, A History of Newfoundland from the English, Colonial and Foreign Records (London, 1896), 211 et seq.

[47]Calendar of State Papers, Colonial, America and West Indies, 1696-7, XV, 320, 377, 433-5, 440, and 452.

[48]Colonel Gibsone in command of the land forces to Council of Trade and Plantations, June 28, 1697, in Calendar of State Papers, Colonial, America and West Indies, 1696-7, XV, 522.

[49]"The possession of Newfoundland by the French being of most near concern to our colony of New England, we expect you to give this expedition all the assistance that lies in your power, and that such ships and land forces to be sent to our said colony, as may be spared with respect to the safety thereof, to join with our other ships and forces between Cape Race and Bonavista on the eastern coast of Newfoundland." Letter from the King to the Governor of Massachusetts, March 18, 1697, in Calendar of State Papers, Domestic Series, William and Mary, 1697, VIII, 62; also ibid., Colonial, America and West Indies, 1696-7, XV, 403.

vessels hauled off, and on the following day the entire French squadron withdrew.[50] St. John's had been saved; but the French position in Newfoundland was stronger than ever by the time the Treaty of Ryswick restored peace and the *status quo* to the suffering inhabitants.[51]

A strategy of *guerre de course* was almost certain to be profitable in distant local sea areas where local protection was thin; amphibious operations against isolated towns and fishing harbours could hardly fail. Yet the struggle for Newfoundland, like the struggle for Canada, was bound eventually to turn on the command of the sea. No amount of fortifications could save Newfoundland if naval supremacy were lost. As the Committee of the Privy Council for Trade and Plantations reported in 1675:

> That besides the Charge of Forts, and of a Governor which the Fish Trade cannot support, 'tis needless to have any such defence against Forreigners, the Coast being defended in the Winter by the Ice, and must in Summer be the resort of your Majesties Subjects, for that place will allwayes belong to him that is superior at Sea.[52]

Similarly in Hudson Bay, where the English posts were badly fortified and poorly garrisoned,[53] the final decisions were not influenced by *guerre de course*. There too, naval warfare was a matter of surprise raids and landing parties, with most of the laurels going to the French, who put forth most of the effort. In retrospect, there is something fantastic about these amphibious contests in or about the dark waters of the Bay; they were so remote from the struggle in Europe as to appear almost beyond the periphery of human experience. Yet the flag was bound to follow trade even to the far north. Like Newfoundland, the area around Hudson Bay was not an object of territorial conquest; nor was it considered as a field for settlement. Acquisition was not intended to mean the occupation of a colony, but merely the establishment of fortified posts for the benefit of the beaver trade. As a source of economic strength, the

[50]See Colonel John Gibsone's somewhat prejudiced narrative of the expedition to Newfoundland in *Calendar of State Papers, Colonial, America and West Indies, Oct. 1697-Dec. 1698*, XVI, 39-42; also *Historical Manuscripts Commission, House of Lords MSS.*, (new series) 1697-99, III, 312-53; and J. Burchett (Secretary of the Admiralty), *A Complete History of the Most Remarkable Transactions at Sea from the Earliest Accounts of Time to the Conclusion of the Last War with France* (London, 1720), 562-4.

[51]See G. S. Graham, "Britain's Defence of Newfoundland," *The Canadian Historical Review*, XXIII, Sept., 1942, 268.

[52]Report of Committee of the Privy Council on Newfoundland, 1675, in *Acts of the Privy Council of England, Colonial Series*, I, 622.

[53]See *Minutes of the Hudson's Bay Company 1679-1684: Part I, 1679-82*, ed.

beaver, like the cod, could be identified with military power in Europe.

On May 2, 1670, Charles II had granted about a quarter of the North American continent to a company of English courtiers headed by Prince Rupert. The grant covered all the land drained by the waters flowing into the Bay and the Strait, and this included, generally speaking, a great horse-shoe belt extending southwards to the present states of Minnesota and North Dakota. The object of the Company, according to the terms of the charter, was the discovery of a new passage into the South Sea, and the furtherance of trade in furs, minerals, or other native commodities. The first posts were built at the mouths of the Rupert and Moose Rivers on James Bay, and on the estuary of the Albany.[54] Thence they attracted a downstream traffic in beaver skins, which by 1681 severely cut into the French trade based on overland routes to Tadoussac, and Three Rivers on the St. Lawrence. In the opinion of Intendant Duchesneau, the French could effectively oppose the English only by competing in Hudson Bay itself.

> The sole means to prevent them from succeeding . . . would be to drive them by main force from that bay, which belongs to us; or if there would be an objection to coming to that extremity, to construct forts on the rivers falling into the lakes, in order to stop the Indians at these points.[55]

But European considerations delayed the beginnings of the struggle for the Bay. The Company had been founded in the year of the Treaty of Dover, and the French alliance provided immunity until France made peace with Holland in 1678. After that date, as political relations cooled, commercial antagonisms were sharpened, and in May of 1682 Louis XIV informally gave notice of the coming conflict by granting a charter to the Compagnie du Nord.[56] The ensuing competition led inevitably to a traders' war, and culminated in the de Troyes expedition of 1686. The force led by the Chevalier de Troyes was more than a mere raiding party of adventurers; it was a well-organized military expedition, stiffened with regular troops, and supported by the government of New France.

---

by E. E. Rich (Toronto, Champlain Society for the Hudson's Bay Record Society, 1945), App. A, 245, 292.
[54]See *Documents relating to the Early History of Hudson Bay*, ed. by J. B. Tyrrell (Toronto, Champlain Society, 1931).
[55]*Documents Relative to the Colonial History of the State of New York*, IX, 166; see also *Minutes of the Hudson's Bay Company*, xliii.
[56]*Minutes of the Hudson's Bay Company*, xlv-xlvi.

In the circumstances, it is not surprising that it easily conquered the "Bottom Bay," leaving the Company with only Port Nelson and its new post on the Severn.[57] In 1693 Fort Albany fell before a visiting English squadron, but such triumphs were bound to be short-lived unless the English were prepared (as they were not) to fortify their trading posts and garrison them adequately. When Pierre le Moyne d'Iberville, with three ships, captured Fort York on the Nelson River in October 1694, it was a case of trained men and artillery against dispirited civilians behind wooden palisades.

The resulting contest for command of the Bay centred about Fort York and the outlets to the Hayes and Nelson Rivers, which drained the best beaver region in the country. So long as the French could hang on to York, they held a strategic position from which they could keep pressure on their rivals in the "Bottom Bay" and ultimately, perhaps, drive them out again.[58] As a consequence, when the English recaptured the Fort in 1696, the French crossed the Atlantic in force the following year under the Marquis de Nesmond,[59] and not only harassed the long tormented outposts of Newfoundland but under d'Iberville's direction fought the only full-dress naval battle of the whole northern war. Details of this curious engagement were kept by a French officer, Bacqueville de la Potherie, who was serving under d'Iberville in the *Pelican*, and were subsequently printed in Paris in 1716 under the general title *Histoire de l'Amérique septentrionale*.[60]

The first encounter between French and English forces took place at the entrance to the Bay on August 25 (New Style), 1697, but ice

[57]See A. S. Morton, "The Early History of Hudson Bay," *The Canadian Historical Review*, XII, Dec., 1931, 416; see also *Report on Canadian Archives, 1883*, Note C, 173; and I. Caron, *Journal de l'expédition du Chevalier de Troyes à la Baie d'Hudson en 1686* (Beauceville, Que., 1919).

[58]Morton, "The Early History of Hudson Bay," 418.   [59]See p. 77.

[60]A later edition was published in 4 volumes in Paris in 1753; see also J. R. Douglas and J. N. Wallace, *Twenty Years of York Factory, 1694-1714: Jérémie's Account of Hudson Strait and Bay* (Ottawa, 1926), containing a sketch of the battle by one of d'Iberville's associates. The editors point out that there is no account of this sea fight written from the English side, and "it is impossible to avoid the conclusion that, for some reason, the whole story has not been told (p. 29, *n.* 41). According to Jérémie's statement, the *Pelican* "ran alongside the flag-ship of 50-guns, and fired a broadside so accurately and with such effect that, before they had time to tack, they saw half the sails of the Englishman in the water, and the ship sinking before the eyes of his countrymen. . . ." (p. 29). D'Iberville reported: "I fired my broadside and sank her immediately, and ran alongside the *Hudson's Bay* to board her, but she struck her flag." The Canadian historian, William Kingsford, whom the authors also quote, is sceptical of the French accounts, on the grounds that no broadside could, so instantaneously sink a ship like the *Hampshire*. In his view the flagship was struck by a squall and capsized.

brought both squadrons to a standstill before they were within range. On the following day, however, the English flag-ship, *Hampshire* (52 guns), and two armed merchantmen, *Dering* (30 guns) and *Hudson's Bay* (32 guns), were able to break loose, and attack the French frigate *Profond* with heavy broadsides. Leaving her for lost, the English squadron made off in the direction of Port Nelson. Meanwhile, the *Profond* had broken clear with hull intact, and, accompanied by the *Wasp* and the *Violent*, made her way towards the entrance of the Churchill River in an effort to avoid the English and make necessary repairs. D'Iberville in the *Pelican* was the last to get clear of the ice; assuming that the rest of the squadron had sailed for Port Nelson rather than the Churchill, he followed with all haste, arriving on September 3. On the 5th three ships appeared on the horizon and believing that these were his missing colleagues, he weighed anchor and went out to meet them, only to find that they were English. With one 50-gun ship he faced an English squadron combining 114 guns.

A stiff on-shore gale was blowing, which probably favoured d'Iberville in his lone encounter, for he was a skilful navigator and tactician. Failing to manœuvre him into shoal water, the captain of the *Hampshire* allowed his own ship to be trapped to leeward. Lacking sea-room which might have enabled him to tack to safety, and suffering from a *Pelican* broadside, the *Hampshire*, for reasons which are still far from clear, suddenly foundered with all hands. Shortly afterwards, the *Hudson's Bay* surrendered and the *Dering* took to flight. Fort York capitulated and kept its new name, Fort Bourbon, until 1714.

Not on the sea, but around the council table of the peace-makers, was Hudson Bay eventually regained for England; and it was a happy coincidence that a former governor of the Company of Adventurers, John Churchill, Duke of Marlborough, should have made so handsome though indirect a contribution towards its recovery.[61] Nevertheless, the English government's neglect of small local defences in the Bay as well as in Newfoundland was unwise and costly. Modest fortifications and small garrisons would have more than halved, if not eliminated, the destruction wrought by visiting raiders.

Various factors—climatic, political, financial, and military—were responsible for this condition of neglect; but they are of minor consideration in comparison with the French failure to appreciate the

[61]See Morton, "The Early History of Hudson Bay," 420.

importance of superiority at sea. Louis XIV's renunciation of "command" left not only Fort Bourbon, but Quebec, Port Royal, and Placentia, at the mercy of the Royal Navy. *Guerre de course* might mean the ravaging of St. John's or the sudden capture of Fort York, but it could not prevent an ill-informed and badly led Massachusetts expedition under Phips from reaching the ramparts of Quebec, or, for that matter, any other expedition that sailed in reasonable strength. Although the French colonies in North America were almost a century old, already the consolidation of English sea power threatened their extinction. Like the Spanish colonies to the south, they now existed on sufferance; like Turgot's metaphorical "ripe fruit" they were, sixty years before their time, ready to drop off, because the roots which nourished them crossed the Atlantic.

V

The War of the Spanish Succession

APART from leaving most of the factories on Hudson Bay in the hands of the French, the Treaty of Ryswick (1697), which concluded the War of the League of Augsburg, effected no changes of European sovereignty in North America. In contrast, the War of the Spanish Succession, which followed four years later, was to produce a major rearrangement of colonial boundaries. Essentially the war was an attempt to defeat the dynastic ambitions of Louis XIV and restore the European balance of power. In an effort to prevent France from gaining the full inheritance of the Spanish Empire, England, Holland, and Austria came together in 1701 in a Grand Alliance. This alliance had positive objectives, however, beyond the limits of national security. It was designed to prevent France from monopolizing the Spanish Indies and consequently Spanish sea power, and to regain, for England especially, the commercial privileges which had been enjoyed within the old Spanish empire. For Louis had not only put his grandson on the throne of Spain and thereby upset the delicate European equilibrium; he had immediately taken over the rich *asiento*, and his navy (which the English Admiralty was inclined to over-estimate) had been ordered to protect all trade between the Spanish colonies and the French kingdom.

It was this excess of colonial power and wealth which weighed so heavily in the minds of commercially minded Whig statesmen. Both Dutch and English would probably have consented, with reluctance, to see a Bourbon at Madrid; but even had the barrier fortresses never been seized or Holland's sovereignty never threatened, it is doubtful if England would in the long run have allowed France to take over the monopoly of Spanish trade in the New World. Indeed, Article VIII of the agreement which produced the Grand Alliance stipulated that France should never be allowed to enjoy the exclusive commerce of the West Indian colonies.

On the continent of North America, however, England had been willing to compromise. The Treaty of Ryswick (1697), which restored the *status quo ante*, and incidentally recognized Acadia as a possession of France, was accompanied by a gentleman's agreement that both powers should seek to preserve an amicable neutrality in America. But neither Massachusetts nor New York was prepared to submit quietly to such instruction; in North America, as in Europe, the issues were being drawn, and colonials were again making plans to rid themselves of a restless neighbour who worried their frontiers by sea and land.

The Phips expedition had been the first large-scale naval operation in North American waters, and its failure had given the French a momentary feeling of hope and confidence. But no wise Frenchman could ignore the fact that Port Royal had changed hands four times, and that its existence still hung by a thread. Any English attack was almost certain to come from the seaward; and to hold his province the governor of Acadia rarely had under his command more than two *stationed* frigates. Moreover, he could expect little in the way of reinforcements. Concentration on military objectives in Europe left less and less money available for the French navy.[1] No new vessels were being built, and those already afloat frequently lacked essential materials for repairs. In the circumstances, he was bound to depend on privateers from home ports, or on the energy and constancy of the corsairs, who came up from the French West Indies to make a living off Boston shipping. At the same time, it was realized in France that any permanent English occupation of the peninsula lying athwart the St. Lawrence basin must inevitably prejudice the safety of communications to Canada.[2] It was thus the vulnerability of Port Royal, rather than its strength, that led the French to launch their offensive south of the borders of Acadia. Attack was the best defence.

In July 1704 an expedition of Quebec French and eastern Indians advanced southward in the region between the Piscataqua and

[1]A budget of eighteen million livres, which was insufficient in 1700, dropped to seven or eight million as the war progressed. See Tramond, *Manuel d'histoire maritime*, 306.

[2]M. Pontchartrain, Minister of Marine, to M. de Beauharnois, Intendant of Rochefort, probably December 24, 1711, quoted in Murdoch, *History of Nova Scotia*, I, 328.

Connecticut Rivers. But Governor Dudley of Massachusetts had been warned, and his frontier forces not only broke up the attackers but carried the war into enemy country. In co-operation with several local sloops and brigs and two frigates, Colonel Church headed a plundering raid against Acadia. Beyond the burning of the village of Minas, little was accomplished, although the governor declared that the addition of one fifty-gun ship (for which he had asked) would have meant the reduction of Port Royal.[3] His assumption was probably correct. Both Port Royal and Quebec were short of provisions because of the capture of victualling ships, and it is of significance that in the following year the Canadian governor, Vaudreuil, proposed a new scheme of North American neutrality.[4]

But proposals for a colonial peace merely stimulated New England to further effort, and projects for attacking both Port Royal and Quebec continued to make semi-official appearances.[5] In the spring of 1707, an expedition was finally got under way. It consisted of approximately 1,000 militia (including a contingent from Rhode Island), in twenty-three transports, mainly sloops and brigantines, and convoyed by the fifty-gun man-of-war, *Deptford*. On June 6, a landing was made on the headland at the entrance to Port Royal, and on the following day the commander-in-chief, Colonel John March, disembarked with 750 men on the south or harbour side, a league below the fort.[6]

Although Subercase had initiative, courage, and imagination far beyond that of any other governor in the history of Acadia,[7] his position was a cheerless one. The invading force was strong, well-equipped, and optimistic. Indeed, Boston was already preparing for a public celebration of victory, when the city received the astounding news that, after advancing to the gates of Port Royal,the attackers had retired without firing a shot, apart from the slaughter of a few hundred cattle.[8] A curious haze surrounds the last days of this expedition, making a conclusive verdict on the cause of failure almost impossible. A clamorous Boston blamed the leadership, and

[3]*Calendar of State Papers, Colonial, America and West Indies, 1704-5*, XXII, 213 and 273; see also T. Hutchinson, *History of Massachusetts Bay, 1628-1750*, II, 132-5.
[4]October 1705, *ibid.*, 662.
[5]*Calendar of State Papers, Colonial, America and West Indies, 1706-8*, XXIII, 29-32.
[6]Murdoch, *History of Nova Scotia*, I, 286.
[7]See Brebner, *New England's Outpost*, 50.
[8]*Calendar of State Papers, Colonial, America and West Indies, 1706-8*, XXIII, xxiii, 560-87.

openly insulted the troops as they marched through the streets after
disembarkation. Colonel March and Captain Stukely of the *Dept-*
ford denied charges of cowardice and offered as excuse the strength
of the French garrison and the lack of heavy artillery.[9] Incompe-
tency in the high command and lack of trained troops is probably
the answer, although there is food for thought in a letter (dated
Philadelphia, January 10, 1708) written by an observer, Colonel
Quary, to the Council of Trade and Plantations:

> I am sure yr. Lordships will be strongly surprised . . . that not withstand
> ing all the misery that hath happened, and still threatens New England from
> the settlement of the French at Port Royall, yett there hath been and still is a
> trade carried on with that place by some of the topping men of that Govern-
> ment, under the colour of sending and receiving Flaggs of Truce.[10]

Meanwhile, Colonel March, after re-embarking his troops, sailed
to Casco Bay, where he was met by an additional regiment of militia
and given fresh orders to take Port Royal. In August, an already
dispirited outfit appeared off Port Royal, under the command of
Captain Wainwright, who had previously been second-in-command
under March. Although fortifications had been strengthened, and
the number of defenders augmented by conscribing the crew of a
frigate, there had been apparently some talk of surrender. But
Subercase would have none of it, and his resolution and spirit seem
to have been intuitively recognized by the invaders. For, after a
quiet fifteen-day siege which cost the French three men killed and
wounded, Wainwright gave orders to withdraw.

Meanwhile, news of the failure was followed in New England by
rumours of reprisals. Subercase's genius for organization was already making itself felt in Acadia, and it was rightly assumed that
he believed attack to be the best form of defence.[11] From Massachusetts came petitions for additional ships,[12] money, arms, munitions, soldiers. Strong pressure was brought to bear on the Council
for Trade and Plantations, and prominent individuals like Samuel
Vetch of New York went to England to beg assistance for the reduction of Acadia and Canada. It was Vetch who pictured the New
Englanders looking out over their abandoned north-eastern lands,
their fur trade lying in ruins, while privateers from Subercase's nest

[9]*Ibid.,* 560.   [10]*Ibid.*
[11]See Subercase to Pontchartrain, December 20, 1707, in "Correspondence
générale, Acadia," 1707-8, VI, c. 11, in *Report on Canadian Archives, 1887,* ccliv
and cclv.
[12]*Calendar of State Papers, Colonial, America and West Indies, 1706-8,* XXIII,
739.

at Port Royal poached on their fisheries and paralysed their sea-borne trade with the Sugar Islands.[13] According to Vetch, the time was ripe to take the offensive, before the French should grasp the initiative and attack Maine; and his suggestions for ending the menace were introduced by a lengthy review of the case for expelling the French bag and baggage from North America. The situation of Port Royal, wrote the Council of Massachusetts to the Queen,

> . . . makes it a Dunkirk to us with respect to navigation, it lying so apt and commodious for the intercepting of all shipping coming to, or going from hence to the eastward, and is a fit receptacle for privateers, who can soon issue out thence and are near hand to send in their prizes, as also to annoy our Fishery, whereof we have had frequent experience, to the very great hurt of the trade of our Nation.[14]

These urgent appeals were not without effect, and in 1709 the British government finally agreed to support an expedition against both Port Royal and Quebec. Unhappily political and European difficulties postponed the arrangements until the following year, to the chagrin of Massachusetts, Connecticut, New Hampshire, and Rhode Island, whose leaders had been organizing and drilling their impatient forces. For a time, indeed, it seemed as though the whole scheme would be abandoned. The Sacheverell impeachment eventually led to the overthrow of the Whig ministry and a new Tory ministry under Harley was soon to begin negotiations for peace with Louis XIV. As it happened, an accumulating series of disasters in Newfoundland produced an emotional explosion of parliamentary and public opinion that impelled action.

On June 24, 1702, shortly after the outbreak of war, Captain John Leake, already commissioned governor of Newfoundland, had been given a small squadron and ordered to secure possession of the whole island. Leake sailed from Plymouth in July, and his almost casual adventure was entirely successful. He not only captured twenty-nine enemy fishing and merchant vessels, but harried the southern coast settlements, destroying French establishments at Trepassey and Saint Mary's, and razing the small fort on St. Pierre.[15]

---

[13]"Canada Survey'd or the French Dominions upon the Continent of America briefly considered in their situation, strength, trade and number . . ." (Received July 27, 1708), *Calendar of State Papers, Colonial, America and West Indies, 1708-9*, XXIV, 41-51.

[14](Received May 25, 1709), *ibid.*, 316.

[15]Anon., *The Naval History of Great Britain* (4 vols., London, 1758), III, 21, 298; also Anspach, *A History of the Island of Newfoundland*, 120.

But the English triumph was short lived. In 1703, after a half-hearted attempt against Guadaloupe, an expedition under Vice-Admiral Graydon was directed to Newfoundland in response to agonized calls for help from the inhabitants. By the time the fleet arrived in early August, the French had been reinforced, and in view of the lateness of the season, a council of war declared an attack on Placentia to be impracticable. On Graydon's return to England, his failure was investigated by a committee of the House of Lords, and his conduct of the campaign severely criticized. While there can be no doubting the lack of leadership and initiative, the opinions of Graydon's captains cannot be ignored. The ships were in bad shape, rigging was crumbling, the crews were sickly and short of provisions. Faulty administration at home was as much responsible for the humiliation as leadership on the spot.[16]

None the less, the misfortunes of the expedition provided a welcome stimulus to the French. Early in 1705, an expedition of five hundred men led by Acadia's Subercase set out swiftly from Placentia to attack St. John's. The town was in a poor position to withstand a serious assault. Heavy storms had left their mark on new fortifications, and discipline had gone steadily downward. While officers added to their incomes by trade, the soldiers hunted, fished, and drank. According to the chaplain, whose life seems to have been in danger even in the pulpit, they embezzled the king's stores and threatened the lives of the inhabitants. "These debauched libertines and blasphemous wretches are the plague of the whole harbour and a disgrace to mankind."[17]

Short of arms, ammunition, and clothing, with but one shoe to ten men, without any medical care whatsoever, cheated out of their pay by government agents and goaded to desperation by the ill-treatment and neglect of their commanding officers, many troops deserted; others mutinied.[18] In an early effort to bring some order out of the chaos, the commodore of the annual convoy had been made commander-in-chief of the land forces. But even if this naval officer had been blessed with the highest order of political tact and humanity, both the army and the merchants were bound to resent his control and obstruct his administration. Chiefly as a consequence of

[16]See Minutes of Council of War, September 3, 1703, in *Calendar of State Papers, Colonial, America and West Indies, 1702-3*, XXI, 667.
[17]*Calendar of State Papers, Colonial, America and West Indies, 1701*, XIX, 549; see also *ibid., 1702-3*, XXI, 479.
[18]*Ibid., 1701*, XIX, 556; *ibid., 1704-5*, XXII, 269; *ibid., 1710-11*, XXV, 71-2.

intensified bickering, the home government's attempt to achieve some efficiency through unity was abandoned at the very time when Subercase was preparing his lightning stroke.[19]

In St. John's no watch had been kept, most of the guns were covered with snow, and only the presence of mind of a drunken soldier prevented a complete surprise. Happily, discipline did improve under fire, and after a half-hearted siege of five weeks the mixed company of Canadians and Indians marched on to destroy Ferryland, pursuing their devastating course as far north as Bonavista.[20] In the summer and autumn fresh raids were made on the remaining English settlements, and it was echoes from these little forays which slowly awakened the House of Commons to the "great declension of the British interest in and lucrative trade to Newfoundland."

By 1708, the British Cabinet was at last ready to act. In July, arrangements were begun to detach "a competent number of ships with 2 regiments . . . to seize Newfoundland, and take the post of Placentia, which we are assured may very easily be done with that force. . . ."[21] The expedition was to proceed direct from Ireland to Placentia, where it was hoped to secure the French fishing fleet prior to its departure. Meanwhile, the Dutch were to guard the Flanders coast to prevent any alliance between the Dunkirk and Brest squadrons, which might upset the plan. Once again, however, bad weather combined with bad organization delayed the expedition until the lateness of the season made the project impossible.[22]

Left to his own resources, Major Thomas Lloyd, the commander of the garrison at St. John's, strengthened his meagre forces by conscribing civilian inhabitants. He was optimistic because he was stupid.[23] Placentia, he reported to the home authorities, was weakly

---

[19] *Ibid., 1704-5.*, XXII, 525.   [20] *Ibid.*, 501.

[21] Lord Godolphin to Captain Byng, Windsor, July 9, 1708, in *The Byng Papers, Selected from the Letters and Papers of Admiral Sir George Byng, First Viscount Torrington and of his Son, Admiral The Hon. John Byng*, ed. B. Tunstall (3 vols., London, Navy Records Society, 1930-3), II, 159 and 206.

[22] *Ibid.*, 212.

[23] Under Lloyd's command, discipline reached a new low level. "Since his return," read a memorial of 1708, "the people are worse us'd than before. They are compelled like slaves to go into the woods on Sundays to cut timber for his service; are spit upon, kickt, beaten, wounded, overladen with unequal quartering of soldiers. . . ." (See *Calendar of State Papers, Colonial, America and West Indies, 1706-8*, XXIII, 686. In June, 1708, Queen Anne took a hand, informing him personally that he would be examined for his misdemeanours, and if found guilty, would be punished. (*Ibid.*, 740.) Two years later Lloyd was dead, but an order of the Queen-in-Council addressed to the Board of Ordnance and the Committee for Trade forbade any payments "due to the late Major Lloyd." (*Ibid., 1710-11*, XXV, 71-2.)

garrisoned, and no danger from the French need be apprehended. "If the enemy hurt us this year, I'le allow ye fault to be laid to my charge."[24] Five weeks later, St. John's was surprised and taken by a force of a hundred and sixty from Placentia under the command of Joseph de Brouillan. Lloyd was wounded and, along with other hostages, taken to Placentia. The forts were demolished and the guns removed; subsequent raids on Carbonear and Ferryland were less successful, largely owing to stiff resistance on the part of the inhabitants.[25]

News of the disaster reached London in February 1709; further information suggested treachery on the part of Major Lloyd, whose actions for some time past had been under suspicion. His guilt was never proven, but the records establish a negligence so flagrant as to approach treason.[26] Fact and rumour together precipitated a storm of public memorials and official resolutions, a storm so violent that a reluctant Cabinet was forced to take drastic action. Under the command of Captain George Martin, a small squadron left Plymouth in May "for the reduction of Canada and other places in America."[27] Two months later, the new secretary of state, Lord Dartmouth, appointed Viscount Shannon to command an additional force, which it was planned should join the original expedition for the final attack on Quebec.

In July, the first British squadron appeared in Boston harbour—six ships carrying a regiment of marines and supplies of ammunition. Colonial enthusiasm mounted, to be abruptly checked on the last day of August by the news that contrary winds had delayed the departure of the additional force under Viscount Shannon. On October 14, five regiments were actually embarked at Portsmouth, but after lying for some weeks waiting for a fair wind, it was wisely decided to abandon the journey in view of the lateness of the season. In the meantime, however, the decision had been taken to make the assault on Port Royal. On September 18 (O.S.) the expedition set

[24]Lloyd to Council of Trade and Plantations, October 22, 1708, in *Calendar of State Papers, Colonial, America and West Indies, 1708-9*, XXIV, xlii, 115-16.

[25]*Ibid.*, 216, 524-5, 544; also Anspach, *A History of the Island of Newfoundland*, 130-2.

[26]See testimony forwarded to Admiralty, received December, 1709, in *Calendar of State Papers, Colonial, America and West Indies, 1708-9*, XXIV, 543-50; also Le Blant, *Un Colonel sous Louis XIV*, 128.

[27]*Calendar of State Papers, Colonial, America and West Indies, 1710-June 1711*, XXV, ix. Since, according to the Old Style calendar, the New Year began on March 25, the expedition left in May of 1710.

sail from Nantasket under the command of Martin, as commodore of the squadron and captain of the *Dragon* (50 guns). Apart from thirty-one transports the squadron consisted of the *Falmouth* (50 guns), the *Lowestoft* (32 guns), the *Feversham* (36 guns), and one bomb-ketch; subsequently there was added the *Chester* of 50 guns.[29] Colonel Francis Nicholson was in charge of the land forces, with Samuel Vetch as his adjutant-general. In addition to a regiment of four hundred English marines, there were two regiments from Massachusetts, and one each from Connecticut, New Hampshire, and Rhode Island, all four colonial contingents being commissioned and armed by the gift of Queen Anne.

The *Chester* had been sent in advance to intercept any supplies which the enemy might attempt to send to Port Royal; but any forebodings as to the flourishing condition of the garrison were without foundation. Port Royal had received no supplies from France for three years.[30] Although the expedition had been late in leaving, and did not reach the harbour until September 24, Subercase had no adequate means of preparation and no chance of holding out against some 3,500 men with his ill-trained garrison of three hundred, many of whom were certain to desert when the first shot was fired. Against English artillery, he had only tumbledown ramparts mounting six guns and two mortars.[31] The fort was in no shape to stand any kind of siege. Consequently, on October 1, when three batteries opened fire within a hundred yards, Subercase surrendered with all the "honours of war." After changing the name of the town to Annapolis Royal in compliment to Queen Anne, Nicholson returned to England, leaving Vetch in charge with a garrison of five hundred troops.

For the third time, Port Royal had succumbed to New England militiamen. Sedgwick in 1654 and Phips in 1690 had sailed unmolested to the narrow harbour on the Bay of Fundy. Surprise has always been an influential factor in amphibious warfare, and while it had little direct connection with the success of the Acadian expeditions, where the objective was so clearly marked in advance, nevertheless, as compared with the slow mass movement through bush and swamp and lake country towards Montreal, the advantages

[29]See Anon., *The Naval History of Great Britain*, III, 138-40; also Murdoch, *History of Nova Scotia*, I, 311; and Parkman, *Half Century of Conflict*, I, 145. See also Appendix B.
[30]*Calendar of State Papers, Colonial, American and West Indies, 1710-June 1711*, XXV, 220-1. [31]See Brebner, *New England's Outpost*, 55.

of mobility and relative tactical freedom on the sea were highly significant. Port Royal, without proper fortifications and garrison, was at the mercy of any English Atlantic squadron. Like Newfoundland it would "allwayes belong to him that is superior at sea."

The capture of Port Royal brought welcome relief to the New England coast, although privateers were still as "thick as bees," and Indians and French still raided the unprotected land frontiers. No "settled repose" could be expected until Canada, that "American Carthage," was finally subdued.[32] Accordingly, a second series of petitions for a renewal of the attempt upon Quebec began to filter in to England, where Colonel Francis Nicholson had betaken himself to press the need for an immediate conquest. Such appeals betokened no sudden colonial affection for the British regular soldier; from 1707 onwards the New England governments simply recognized the absolute need for professional troops as well as heavy ships, if the capital of New France was to be taken. From all reports Quebec had been greatly strengthened, information which confirmed the necessity of a disciplined and seasoned force. It is true that the colonies had asked for help before; but apart from a few bungling efforts as, for example, the projected Shannon expedition of 1710, the government was not enthusiastic about weakening the home fleet for the sake of local operations in North America. Had it willed to take Quebec, and made adequate preparations for conquest, the town was theirs for the asking.

Two facts help to account for the sudden English zeal to support a full-dress attack against Quebec in 1711, and both are related to Marlborough's victories on the continent. On the one hand, France no longer maintained even a pretence of an active fleet; hence British ships could be spared from home waters.[33] On the other hand, the Tory leaders, Harley and St. John, saw the prestige of Marlborough as their greatest obstacle to political victory, and looked to a Tory conquest of New France as one means of deflecting public interest.

But in the course of planning a military triumph, they made one fundamental error. While the cream of Marlborough's armies—seven veteran regiments—was earmarked for service, they allowed the Queen's new favourite, Mrs. Masham, to insinuate her brother

[32] *Calendar of State Papers, Colonial, America and West Indies, 1710-June 1711,* XXV, 335.
[33] See J. H. Owen, *War at Sea under Queen Anne, 1702-1708* (Cambridge University Press, 1938), 50.

as commander of the troops; and Brigadier Jack Hill had won his rank by social and not military competence. To make matters worse, the naval command was given to an almost unknown admiral, whose subsequent failures alone redeemed him from obscurity. Sir Hovenden Walker was "a gentleman of letters, good understanding, ready wit, and agreeable conversation," but he was "no more a Saunders than Hill was a Wolfe."[34]

Meanwhile, Colonel Nicholson had sailed for America, to make arrangements with the participating colonial governments in New England, New York, Jersey, and Pennsylvania, and to organize under his own leadership an expedition against Montreal by land. Unfortunately, adverse weather delayed his arrival until June 8, 1711. The council of war which met in New London on June 21 had little time to concert arrangements before the arrival of Admiral Walker's squadron at Boston, some four days later, with thirty-one transports carrying 5,300 troops.[35] Walker found little but con-

[34]*Ibid.*
[35]The Line of Battel [sic]

Frigates and small Vessels	Ships	Men	Guns
Basilisk*	Swiftsure*	440	70
Loestoff, N.J.	Sunderland*	365	60
Tryton's *Prize* J.S.R.	Enterprize J.S.R.	190	40
	Sapphire CB.	190	40
Granada *Bomb*	Kingston J.S.R.	365	60
	Mountague*	365	60
	Devonshire* Pr. B.S.L.	520	80
	Edgar*	470	70
	Humber* Pr. B.S.L.	520	80
	Windsor*	365	60
	Dunkirk*	365	60
	Feversham NJ.	190	36
	Leopard CB.	280	54
	Chester CB. Pr. B.S.L.	280	54
	Monmouth*	440	70

Memorandum, That when the *Humber* and *Devonshire* leave the Fleet, the *Windsor* and *Mountague* close the Line. Dated abord her Majesty's Ship the *Humber* in *Nantasket* Road, near *Boston* in *New England*, the 24th of *July* 1711.   H.W.

N.B. The Ships mark'd thus [*] sailed with me from *Boston*: Those mark'd [CB] join'd me off *Cape Breton*: Those mark'd [Pr. B.S.L.] parted from me in the Bay of *St. Lawrence*: Those mark'd [J.S.R.] join'd me at *Spanish* River: Those mark'd [N.J.] never join'd me.

Contained in H. Walker, *A Journal: Or Full Account of the Late Expedition to Canada; with an Appendix containing Commissions, Orders, Instructions, Letters, Memorials, Courts-Martial, Councils of War, etc. relating thereto* (London, 1720) App., 246. On pp. 190 and 191 are listed "The several Transports, Storeships, etc that came to Plymouth and sailed from thence, with the Number and Disposition of the Soldiers." On p. 245 there is "A list of the Vessels taken up for her Majesty's Use as Transports for the forces of the Massachusetts, in the present Expedition."

fusion and an absence of that "hearty zeal for the service which he had expected." The colonists were loyal and firm in their decision to take Quebec, but the growth of a national spirit more American than English was already apparent.

One of Hill's officers wrote to Mr. Secretary St. John:

'Tis certain if the Government here had made that dispatch which they ought to have done, and which our General constantly press'd them to do: I believe we might have sail'd from hence a fortnight ago. But all has been done with indolence and indifference with a thousand scruples and delays.[36]

It proved to be a difficult business to round up the colonial contingents, unearth pilots and transport, and tempt from reluctant farmers the stores of fresh provisions. Already there were signs of the friction between inhabitants and regulars which was to reach its head in Braddock's day. There is nothing unique in the lust of civilian inhabitants to make money out of the army. It became as standard a privilege in modern Aldershot as in early eighteenth-century Boston. It was inevitable that the army which lay encamped on Noddle's Island in Boston bay should find the cost of victuals gradually ascending. Much pressure and constant bickering finally prevailed upon the colonial government to force prices down to a somewhat less extravagant level. Only a man of General Hill's good will, remarked one of his loyal aides, could have overcome "the interestness, ill-nature and sourness of those people, whose Government, doctrine and manners, whose hypocrisy and canting are insupportable."[37] Hill did show tact, for his *Journal* records an appearance at Harvard Commencement, "for no other reason than to put the people of the colony in humour to comply with the necessary demands of the troops. . . ."[38]

Meanwhile, charts of the St. Lawrence and maps of Quebec were studied by the higher command;[39] siege trains were prepared, along

[36]*Calendar of State Papers, Colonial, America and West Indies, July, 1711-June 1712*, XXVI, 40.

[37]*Ibid.*, xi.

[38]*Ibid.*, 61.

[39]A chart of the St. Lawrence contained in *The English Pilot: The Fourth Book* (London, 1706) between pp. 4 and 5, represents probably the only English chart available to Walker on this journey. The group of rocky islets known as *Ile aux Oeufs* on which he subsequently met disaster are not indicated, nor does the guide itself contain navigation directions for the St. Lawrence River. The edition of 1716 contains a revised chart (between pp. 6 and 7) showing the Seven Islands some forty-five miles distant from L'Ile aux Oeufs, as well as various anchorages in the neighbourhood, but there are still no sailing directions. The 1760 edition provides an exact reproduction of the chart of 1716, indicating that Saunders must have depended on captured French charts when plotting his expedition to Quebec

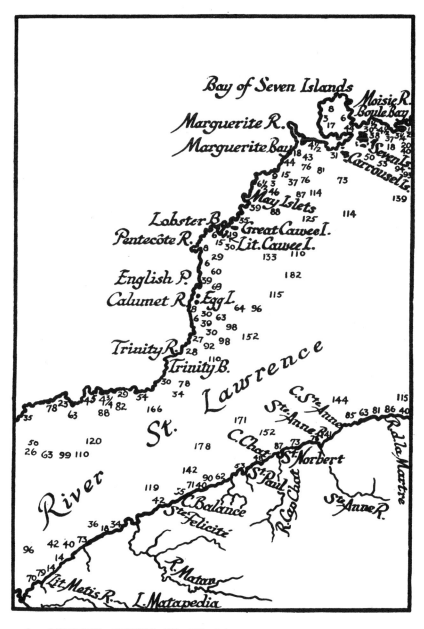

Bay of Seven Islands

Moisie R.
Boule Bay

Marguerite R.

Marguerite Bay

Carrousel I.

Sevent.

May Islets

Lobster B.

Great Cawee I.

Pentecôte R.

Lit. Cawee I.

English P.

Calumet R. Egg I.

Trinity R.

Trinity B.

St. Lawrence

C. Ste Anne

Ste Anne R.

R. de la Martre

C. Chat

St. Norbert

River

St. Paul

Ste Anne R.

St. Felicité

C. Balance

R. Cap Chat

R. Matan

Lit. Metis R.

L. Matapedia

I. MODERN CHART OF ST. LAWRENCE RIVER SHOWING
EGG ISLAND

with cranes and other engines to be used in hoisting cannon, mortars, and ammunition up the cliffs; the countryside was combed for provisions and stores. The main problem, however, was to find pilots to navigate the St. Lawrence. Phips had succeeded through good fortune rather than scientific skill; and Phips's old seamen told Walker hair-raising stories about the difficulties which would be encountered.

> That from Tadous[s]ac to some leagues above Quebec the water ebbs and flows with that prodigious rapidity it will carry a ship above a league and a half an hour: that we must have a sufficient gale of wind to stemm this tide, or it will drive the ships on shoals and rocks, which are in vast numbers all along the river: and that there's every day, especially in the latter season, such squalls of wind that the stoutest ships are hardly able to resist them.[40]

Somewhat alarmed by all he heard about treacherous winds and tides and shoals, Walker decided not to risk his eighty-gun ships; hence, after transferring his flag to the seventy-gun *Edgar*, he sent the *Humber* and the *Devonshire* to cruise for a month at the mouth of the St. Lawrence to guard his rear during the attack.[41]

The fleet sailed from Boston on July 30 (O.S.), and carried close to 6,500 troops. Up to this time, strict measures had been taken in the colonial ports to ensure secrecy; but there is good reason to believe the French had knowledge of the project before Walker left England. In any event, French suspicions must have been finally confirmed by the action of the General Court, which issued a public proclamation for "a general fast" to promote the success of the expedition.[42]

From the beginning Walker acted as though Providence alone were a sufficient guide. Despite his nightmares about navigating

---

in 1759. It is conceivable that French charts may have been acquired by Walker, but judging by his *Journal* whatever charts he possessed gave no reference to L'Ile aux Oeufs. Moreover, since neither for 1716 nor for 1760 does the authoritative *English Pilot* contain sailing directions, it seems most unlikely that any first-rate information was acquired from the French before 1759. In the Admiralty Library, there is a captured French chart dated 1758, which may have been available to Saunders, but which was certainly not acquired in time to serve the editors of *The English Pilot* in 1760.

[40]Colonel King to Secretary St. John, July 25, 1711, in *Calendar of State Papers, Colonial, America and West Indies, July, 1711-June, 1712*, XXVI, 39.

[41]See Walker, *A Journal*, 117. The eighty-gun *Torbay* had been sent back to Plymouth shortly after the expedition left England "for she being the worst man'd Ship, I did believe it better for the Service to send her back, because I could not Man her from the rest, without disabling them." Hovenden Walker to Josiah Burchett, Secretary of the Admiralty, May 8, 1711, in Walker, *A Journal*, App., 195.

[42]See *Calendar of State Papers, Colonial, America and West Indies, 1710-June, 1711*, XXV, xiv.

the river, he had no pilots with first-hand experience of the St. Lawrence. Captain Cyprian Southack, commander of the Massachusetts province galley, was probably the most competent navigator in the fleet; yet, shortly before the fleet put out, he was sent to Annapolis Royal to pick up artillery stores and marines from the resident garrison. Colonel Samuel Vetch, the original designer of the enterprise, professed a good general knowledge of St. Lawrence tides and channels, and shortly before passing Gaspé (August 18) he was invited to lead the way. But Vetch was unwilling, unless he could stay in his own ship, rather than change to the small frigate, *Sapphire*, which was in the van. For some obscure reason, Walker did not insist; apparently Vetch received no further orders, and followed behind the flagship, watching her course, as he admits in his *Journal* with growing uneasiness and foreboding.[43] Vetch later asserted that had he led the fleet, disaster could have been avoided. Whether or not this bold speculation is justified, his argument that the weather was too rough to change ships is as curious, under the circumstances, as Admiral Walker's incredible failure to compel him to move.[44]

The fleet reached the neighbourhood of Gaspé on August 16, and sighted Anticosti, but was prevented by contrary winds from entering the river. As a consequence, the admiral made for Gaspé Bay, and dropped anchor to await more favourable weather. On August 20, the wind veered westerly, and he prepared to move, but on the following day a fog blew up which continued to thicken. From noon of the 21st until noon of the 22nd, the fleet made only thirty-four miles.

On the following day a strong gale blew up from the east, and this, combined with more fog, made it impossible to steer any course with safety. In Walker's own words:

. . . having neither Soundings or sight of Land to help us, or any Anchorage within sixty Leagues, and that not safe, it was therefore by the Advice of the Pilots then abord, both *English* and *French*, the best in the Fleet, (who agreed in their opinions) that I made the Signal to bring to with our Heads to the Southward, at eight a-clock at Night, by which posture it was reasonable to believe we should not have come near the North Shoar, but have been

[43]*Ibid., July, 1711-June, 1712*, XXVI, xii. For the "Journal" see *ibid.*, 152-7.
[44]Midway on the voyage, Vetch wrote a letter to Mr. Secretary St. John (August 10, 1711) "off Cape Brittoun" in which he said: "The getting to which place [Quebec] by reason of the difficulty of the navigation I look upon to be the difficultest part of the enterprise, being myself if not the only att least the best pilot upon the Expedition, although none of my province." *Ibid.*, 70.

driven by the stream in the Mid-Chanel; but quite contrary, as we were with the Winds easterly and our Heads to the Southward, in two Hours time we found our selves upon the North Shoar amongst Rocks and Islands, at least fifteen Leagues farther than the Logg gave; where the whole Fleet had like to have been lost.[45]

Walker is correct in saying that he ordered the fleet to be brought-to, heading to the south. Had they kept this position until morning, eventual disaster might have been avoided. But shortly after ten, fearing he was getting too close to the south shore, Walker ordered the fleet to wear and bring-to heading north. During this procedure, the admiral was preparing to go to bed, when one of the army officers reported seeing breakers to leeward. According to log readings this was fantastic, but the officer insisted on calling the admiral, who finally came on deck in dressing-gown and slippers. By that time the whole fleet was standing north, and ships in the van were already on the edge of the breakers.

Once recovered from the shock, Walker immediately attempted to get clear by hoisting all available sail, but such ships as saw the signal failed to get about, and were forced to anchor in seven fathoms. Within a cable's length on either quarter the surf was dashing high over the reefs of the Île aux Œufs[46]; and for the rest of the night the darkness was broken with flashing distress signals and the faint cries of despairing men whose ships splintered on the rocks.

Up to the moment of anchoring (shortly after 10.30 p.m.) a gale was blowing almost directly on shore. Had it continued, it is doubtful if any of the ships could have been saved. Mercifully, the fleet

[45]Walker, A Journal, 44-5. See also W. M. Morgan, "Queen Anne's Canadian Expedition of 1711," Queen's Quarterly, XXXV, May, 1928, 460 et seq.

[46]Admiralty hydrographic surveys of the present day describe Egg Island as "a group of four low, rocky islets, bare of trees, together with some above-water rocks. . . . North reef, which is always above water, is situated about half a mile northward of Egg Island. Rocks, that dry 6 feet in places, extend about a quarter of a mile southward from North reef. Northeast reef, with depths of less than 3 fathoms over it, extends about 6 cables north-north-eastward from the northern end, of Egg Island; there are depths of less than 6 feet near its outer end, and rocks that dry 3 feet in places; the sea generally breaks over these rocks. Great care is necessary when in its vicinity, as it is steep-to on its seaward side.

"There are considerable depths along the western side of Egg Island and North reef, which decrease gradually, towards the mainland. The bottom, in the deep water, on the eastern side, is of clay, and in depths of 9 fathoms or less, it is of sand. The best anchorage is in depths of 9 fathoms, the best position being with the southern end of Egg Island bearing about 120 degrees, and the inner edge of North reef bearing about 020 degrees. A good scope of cable is advisable, on account of the violent squalls off the land that occur, at times." St. Lawrence Pilot: Comprising the Gulf and the River St. Lawrence, the Banks of Newfoundland, the Approaches to the Gulf by Cabot Strait, the Strait of Belle Isle, and the Gut of Canso (London, 10th ed., 1943), 206-7.

was spared from complete destruction by a providental lull, followed by a shift of wind. At 2 a.m. the wind, which began to rise again, shifted to the north, and at 5 o'clock it backed directly off-shore, enabling most of the ships to weigh or slip their anchors and sail out. It spoke well for the seamanship of Walker's crews that only eight transports and one sloop were lost. These transports carried in all 1,383 soldiers and seamen, of whom only 499 were saved.[47]

Despite freshening gales, Walker stayed in the neighbourhood for two days, in order to save what men and stores he could. On August 25, the customary council of war was held, and it was agreed, by reason of the lateness of the season, the scarcity of supplies, and the ignorance of the pilots, that it was wholly impracticable to reach Quebec.[48] It was resolved instead to attempt the reduction of Placentia in Newfoundland, and a message was dispatched to Colonel Nicholson (who had managed to reach Lake George), requesting him to abandon his advance on Montreal. With a force of 2300 colonial militia and Indians Nicholson had made excellent progress, and the recall was a bitter blow. Contemporaries relate that he burst into a rage, threw his wig upon the ground and stamped on it, denouncing the fleet and its leaders with cries of "Roguery—Treachery."[49] In any event, there was nothing for him to do but burn the forts he had built on the way, and retire to Albany, where he disbanded his army.

On September 4, the fleet cast anchor off Spanish River in Cape Breton, where a second council of war discussed the validity of an intercepted letter from the governor of Placentia to M. de Pontchartrain, the minister of marine in Paris. According to Costebelle's letter, the garrison, consisting of some 2,000 men, was prepared to give a far different reception to the enemy than that accorded them at Port Royal.[50] Impressed by this advance information (which may very well have been intended for English consumption), fearful of renewed bad weather and short of provisions, the council agreed to give up the enterprise. After sending a detachment to relieve the colonial garrison at Annapolis Royal, and setting up a cross at Spanish River, with a modest inscription dedicating the surrounding country to the Queen, Admiral Walker returned to England to face the music.

[47]See T. Lediard, *The Naval History of England . . . from the Norman Conquest in the year 1066 to the conclusion of 1734* (2 vols. in one, London, 1735) 854.
[48]Anon., *The Naval History of Great Britain*, III, 150.
[49]See P. Kalm, *Travels into North America* (3 vols., London, 1770) III, 135.
[50]*Calendar of State Papers, Colonial, America and West Indies, July, 1711-June, 1712*, XXVI, 94-5.

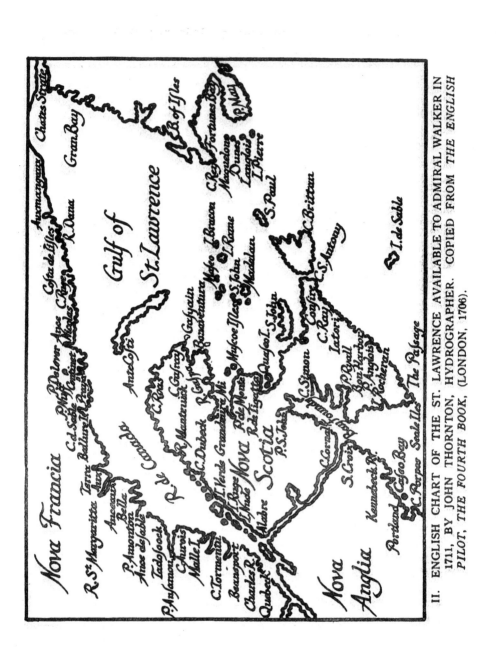

II. ENGLISH CHART OF THE ST. LAWRENCE AVAILABLE TO ADMIRAL WALKER IN 1711, BY JOHN THORNTON, HYDROGRAPHER. COPIED FROM THE ENGLISH PILOT, THE FOURTH BOOK, (LONDON, 1706).

On October 9, the fleet reached England, where shortly afterward, as a climax worthy of the most purple detective fiction, the flagship *Edgar* blew up with most of the crew and all the admiral's journals, charts and papers, including Sir William Phips's Journal of his Canada expedition.[51] Possibly for want of evidence and possibly too for political reasons, Walker was not struck off the Flag List, but was sent to Jamaica. From there, however, he was recalled in 1712 to stand trial, and afterwards was dismissed from the service and denied his pension.

It is not unlikely that the fall of his patron was Walker's final undoing, for his only crime, says the Tory John Charnock, was that he was a friend of Bolingbroke's.[52] That he owed some of his unpopularity to the fact that he was a teetotaller and a vegetarian,[53] and his final dismissal to political vendetta, hardly alters, however, the fundamental fact that he undertook the navigation of the St. Lawrence with pilots whom he knew to be ignorant of their task. Among the various petitions for redress after the event, from widows and owners of transport, there is one addressed to the Admiralty by Thomas Coulthurst, dated June 21, 1714, for reimbursement on the ship *Neptune*, lost "by being forced up the River Canada without a Pilot [,] to carry Provisions to Her Majesty's Forces there."[54]

The Walker expedition fitted into no carefully wrought scheme of imperial expansion; it was rather an act of retaliation, begun chiefly at the instigation of the New England colonists. Faulty leadership contributed largely to its failure, but bad leadership neither explains, nor should it obscure, the imperfections of colonial organization. Years of bitter border warfare had not taught the colonies the wisdom of co-operation either among themselves or with the forces of the mother country. The advantages of overwhelming numbers had not been utilized to offset the strength which the French still derived from professionally trained troops under centralized feudal control.[55]

However, failure does not diminish the significance of a great joint enterprise. It was the first substantial operation directed

[51]See Walker, *A Journal*, 155-6; also Douglass, *A Summary, . . . of the British Settlements in North America*, I, part 2, 313.
[52]*Biographia Navalis; or Impartial Memoirs of the Lives and Characters of Officers of the Navy of Great Britain* [1660-1795] (4 vols., London, 1795), III, 455ff., 466.
[53]See Lediard, *The Naval History of England*, II, n (*K*) 855.
[54]*Acts of the Privy Council of England, Colonial Series*, II, 659-60.
[55]See Brebner, *New England's Outpost*, 49.

against Canada from across the Atlantic. Weighed down by European and subsequently by domestic difficulties, English governments had hitherto been reluctant to exercise their power in the New World. Ordinarily, when the colonies made their periodic calls for help, they were told that all available manpower was required for campaigns on the continent. In other words, colonial interests did not come first; they were very much subsidiary to English and allied interests in Europe,[56] and during Queen Anne's war, the colonial theatre hardly counted; the focus of naval activity was the Mediterranean. But sea power has often been most influential when it has been least conspicuous, and during the War of the Spanish Succession this was true in the North Atlantic where the carrying trades drew heavily on the Royal Navy for convoy escort.

Between 1702 and 1712, the French had pursued relentlessly a strategy of *guerre de course*, and the injuries to English and colonial shipping were serious. Moreover, because local defences had been neglected, the Newfoundland fishery and the fur trade to Hudson Bay had at times been brought close to extinction. Yet, the French plan of campaign had totally failed. The object of *guerre de course* whether in Hudson Bay, the Gulf of St. Lawrence or in the Channel had been the infliction of such losses as would strain the resources of the enemy, and thereby hasten a favourable peace. This objective had not been achieved. On the contrary, England (unlike Holland), had prospered in war; English overseas trade had gradually expanded, while that of France had been slowly extinguished. By the end of the reign of Louis XIV, it had, for all practical purposes, ceased to exist.[57]

[56]See Admiral Sir H. Richmond, *Statesmen and Sea Power* (Oxford, 1946), 96.
[57]Tramond, *Manuel d'histoire maritime*, 306.

VI

Beginnings of the Duel for Empire

A T T H E beginning of the seventeenth century, England had become a vigorous and unified small nation; but as yet she held no territories overseas. A little more than a hundred years later, the first British Empire had been almost completed, and the new sea-girt Britain, which the Union with Scotland had brought into being, was able to assert a maritime and commercial ascendancy over the rest of the world. By establishing and gradually consolidating naval superiority over the other powers of western Europe, she not only was able to ensure her own immunity, but had unrestricted freedom to pursue trade and acquire possessions on a world-wide scale.

The War of the Spanish Succession had been, in a sense, a "business man's war." Indeed, it had been waged quite as much to determine who should possess the Spanish trade, as who should possess the Spanish Crown.[1] The sequel was naturally enough a "business man's peace," a peace that made ample provision for Britain's commercial expansion. Although nothing can excuse the guileful manner in which the war was concluded, historians now regard the Treaty of Utrecht (1713) as a fair and moderate product of arbitration. Under its terms Britain gained Acadia (excluding Cape Breton Island), the huge but undefined Hudson Bay territories, Newfoundland (with a reservation to the French of fishing rights on the northeast shore),[2] St. Kitts in the West Indies, and two Mediterranean stepping-stones, Gibraltar and Minorca. By a sordid agreement,

[1]See A. M. Wilson, *French Foreign Policy during the Administration of Cardinal Fleury 1726-1743* (Cambridge, Mass., 1936), 42.
[2]Under Article XIII, the French were allowed "to catch fish, and to dry them on land, in that part only, and in no other besides that, of the said island of Newfoundland, which stretches from the place called Cape Bonavista to the northern point of the said island, and from thence running down the western side, reaches as far as the place called Point Riche."

known as the *asiento*, she won the sole right to trade in slaves with Spanish America.[3]

This extension of the empire greatly enlarged the network of naval bases which now served British communications in every part of the globe. Free from continental entanglements, Britain was able to concentrate her attention on the oceans, and, under the protection of her fleets, to direct into her own treasury the growing stream of overseas riches. As a consequence, the trading and financial interests on whose support the Hanoverian dynasty relied so heavily began to consider naval defence as necessary business insurance. The records of the Admiralty alone reveal their ubiquitous activity and mounting influence. "Of the greater part of the regulations concerning the colony trade," wrote Adam Smith, "the merchants who carry it on, it must be observed, have been the principal advisers."

While Holland's strength declined during the War of the Spanish Succession and French and Spanish commerce was swept from the seas, the British mercantile community could look upon war as an exceedingly profitable undertaking. Twenty-five years after the Treaty of Utrecht merchants formed the vanguard of citizen patriots who so vociferously demanded the complete breaking of the Spanish colonial monopoly. Not many years later, the safety of a West India convoy was sufficient to influence Cabinet policy in determining the movements of a fleet. Indeed, there were merchants who regarded the security of the West Indies as almost vital to the successful pursuit of a war. In the opinion of the elder Pitt, the capture of each French island represented a double gain, since the resulting increase of English trade was accompanied by a proportionate weakening of French trade. If France and Spain were to be completely cut off from their West Indian or North American markets and sources of supply, the losses sustained, it was believed, could be so severe that one or other would be unable to keep on with the war.[4]

This far-flung colonial trade was regarded not only as essential to national prosperity, but as an actual foundation of naval strength.

[3]The *asiento* provided for the annual delivery of 4,800 African slaves to Spanish America for a period of thirty years. A minor concession in itself, it came to be a landmark in the history of British commercial expansions, for it laid the basis for Britain's leadership in the slave trade until the end of the eighteenth century.

[4]See H. W. Richmond, "The Land Forces of France,, June 1738," in *Naval Miscellany*, III (London, Navy Records Society, 1928), LXIII, 51; also H. J. S. Brownrigg, "Naval Bases in Relation to Empire Defence," *Journal of the Royal United Service Institution*, LXXVII, 1932, 47.

Since the merchant ships were the nurseries of the fighting fleets, it was proper to assume that commercial expansion advanced national security, just as a powerful fleet safeguarded commercial expansion. In other words, colonial trade and sea power were indissoluble, and both were held equally to be the objects of national policy. Although this view came to be generally accepted by European powers, complete identity of interests was possible only in a thalassic state. Unlike continental countries, Britain could afford, because of the English Channel, to neglect her army, add to her responsibilities all over the globe, and still remain a first-class power. Her pre-eminence was, for this reason, unique, and, judged in retrospect, unassailable.

In contrast, Holland had been almost destroyed by the very wars which, in alliance with Britain, she had so successfully helped to conclude. The little country which had at one time possessed a fleet equal to the combined navies of England and France was now reduced to a fraction of her former naval strength. During the War of the Spanish Succession, Holland had seldom more than fifty warships at sea;[5] by 1740 there were only twenty-nine. The Dutch, wrote Lord Chesterfield, had no other than a courtesy title to the name of a sea power.

Geography demanded of the Dutch both a first-class army and a strong navy. Overseas trade still supported an army, but the earnings were no longer shared with the navy. In an era of increased trade competition and larger professional armies, the financial strain required to maintain both was too great. Moreover, during the forty years after 1672, the Dutch had always to face the awesome prospect of another French appearance on the left bank of the Rhine. At times their army had risen to 150,000 men, double that of France in proportion to population. Even after Utrecht, the expensive "barrier fortresses" had to be maintained, and at times fear of French invasion kept the English alliance almost as warm as in the days of Louis XIV.

Lack of a strong navy may have affected Dutch morale by curbing the old spirit of individual adventure, but naval decline meant no decay of trade. Thanks to the past efforts of her explorers and traders, Holland remained a wealthy empire. Provided she was allowed to keep her colonies there was a steady revenue, and Amster-

[5]Tramond, *Manuel d'histoire maritime*, 323.

dam remained a financial centre with deep roots in the European trading economy. Despite the Navigation Acts which excluded her from British colonial trade, she became again the great neutral carrier. With a mercantile marine far larger than required for domestic needs, she competed vigorously in the international field, and before the middle of the eighteenth century had achieved a near-monopoly of the Baltic carrying trade. In his *Wealth of Nations* Adam Smith could say that the Dutch carrying trade exceeded that of any other nation.

In time of war, of course, the "great carrier" existed only on sufferance, dependent on the goodwill of her rivals and their interpretations of non-belligerent rights. The position was an uneasy one for a nation bereft of sea power, but as long as the British were under pressure, as they were during most of the War of the Austrian Succession, the Dutch could hope to maintain their profitable neutrality.[6]

Spain too had her resurgence of maritime life. Although the navy had hardly justified its existence during the War of the Spanish Succession, as soon as the domestic situation had been cleared up by the Treaty of Utrecht, Philip V began to give it his attention. With the backing of his chief minister, the Cardinal Alberoni, a veritable renaissance took place.[7] In 1713 Cadiz was commercially a city of the dead, with hulks rotting in the harbour, and its arsenal destitute of supplies. Alberoni sent his young lieutenant, Joseph Patiño, to inspect the situation; three months later, ships were at sea headed for Buenos Aires, Havana, and Vera Cruz.[8] A naval college was established, regulations for recruiting were drawn up, and building yards were started in Galicia and Catalonia. By 1737, the Spanish Navy counted thirty-four ships of 60 to 114 guns, nine frigates, and sixteen small craft, divided between the ports of Cadiz, Ferrol, and Carthagena.

[6]They were free, for example, under the Contraband Treaty of 1674, to ship food and naval stores into the unblockaded ports of the French West Indies, thus enabling the French to refit their naval squadrons and arm their merchantmen. See H. W. Richmond, *The Navy in the War of 1739-48* (3 vols., Cambridge University Press, 1920), 51*n.*, 75-7, 149-50, 168.

[7]The financial revival is examined by E. J. Hamilton in "Money and Economic Recovery in Spain under the First Bourbon, 1701-1746," *The Journal of Modern History*, XV, Sept., 1943, 192-206.

[8]G. Desdevises du Dezert, "Les Institutions de l'Espagne au XVIIIe Siècle," Chap. VII, "Histoire de la Marine au XVIIIe Siècle," *Revue Hispanique* (Paris, 1927), LXX, 443.

Moreover, efforts were made to encourage Spanish manufactures, and to find foreign as well as colonial markets for their produce. In 1728 the Caracas Company was founded, and this new organization concentrated its energies in a diligent attempt to revitalize the merchant marine. The whole tempo of Spanish life quickened under the galvanizing impulse of Alberoni, and for a moment there was a return of the old martial spirit which had characterized Spanish arms in the sixteenth century. As evidence, within two years following the outbreak of war with England in 1739, the new navy took 372 prizes. While Spanish privateers cruised blithely in the North Sea and the Channel, men-of-war convoyed treasure ships and merchantmen or escorted troops.[9] In Britain, long before the exhibition of Captain Jenkins's ear, merchant petitions had poured into Westminster demanding redress of grievances.

But Spain was no more capable than Holland of wresting from Britain the mastery of the seas. Britain's duel for empire was to be fought with France, whose ability to recuperate rapidly has always been a source of astonishment and sometimes embarrassment to her enemies and rivals. France was a rich country whose real strength lay not in precarious alliances or brittle dynastic ties with Spain, but in the indigenous resources of land, and more especially of population, which enabled her to equip a powerful army and maintain it for prolonged periods. By the beginning of the century her population was more than 20,000,000 as compared with Britain's 5,000,000 and Holland's 2,500,000. The wars of Louis XIV had left her exhausted, but territorially she had suffered little damage. With the exception of a few fortresses, her possessions were intact, and there was in consequence less disposition to expedite *revanche*. Economic convalescence was what France needed above all else, and for this an *entente* with Britain (1717-31) offered a unique opportunity.

Although the French navy, for all practical purposes, had ceased to exist, its resurrection was certain, assuming considerations of empire were not violently subordinated to political ambitions on the continent. The connection between overseas commerce and sea power was now admitted by most French statesmen, and especially

[9] R. Beatson, *Naval and Military Memoirs of Great Britain from 1727 to 1783* (6 vols., London, 1790-1804), I, 122; W. Coxe, *Memoirs of the Kings of Spain of the House of Bourbon, 1700 to 1788* (5 vols., London, 1813), III, 25.

by Cardinal Fleury, who saw in trade and colonies the necessary and dependable instruments of a European military policy.[10]

But until Fleury became chief minister, the re-creation of a fleet was a slow and uphill struggle. Six years after Utrecht, there were only forty-nine vessels of all rates,[11] and most of these were in a sad state of disrepair. During the same period, the arsenal at Toulon had not sent a single vessel down the ways. Between 1717 and 1723 only two ships were built at Brest, a number quite insufficient for replacements. By 1730 there were fifty-one ships from first to sixth rates, divided among Toulon, Rochefort, and Brest; but not all of these were kept in commission. By the end of 1739 the number of ships of the line had grown to about fifty at a time when Britain's total was eighty.[12]

There were, however, other factors which made French naval experts hopeful that they could overcome the handicap of Britain's numerical superiority. For example, France continued to lay weight on technical superiority, and from the early days of Louis XIV until the end of the Third Empire under Louis Napoleon, she kept her lead in the application of science to the art of war.[13] The average French ship of the line was the product of skilled architects, and it was capable of heavy fire power without loss of weatherliness. The same could not be said of English-built ships of similar rating.

Permit me to assure you, My Lord, [wrote an expert artillerist to Lord Anson at the Admiralty, in 1744] the knowledge every officer has of the great disproportion that is at present between our 60 to 70 gun ships and the enemy's fills him with concern . . . an English ship of war of 70 guns cannot take a French or Spanish ship of the same force, whereas it is pretty apparent our 70 gun ships are little superior to their ships of 52 guns.[14]

Thus, it is not surprising that many British warships were modelled on vessels captured from the enemy.[15] Indeed, all through the wars of the eighteenth century, British captains sought with unique eagerness to command French prizes.

[10]Wilson, *French Foreign Policy*, 45, 55-6, 298.
[11]See Appendix B.
[12]Richmond, *The Navy in the War of 1739-48*, I, 14-51. Including fifty-gun ships, Britain's total was 124; but of these, 44 were unfit for service, and of the remaining 80, only 35 were actually ready for sea.
[13]This opinion is supported by a shrewd military historian; see *The Logs of the Conquest of Canada*, ed. by W. C. H. Wood (Toronto, Champlain Society Publications, 1909), IV, 37.
[14]Quoted in Hodges and Hughes, *Select Naval Documents*, 121.
[15]Regarding French and Spanish claims to superiority, see J. Charnock, *An History of Marine Architecture . . . especially of Great Britain . . . from the earliest period* (3 vols., London, 1800-2), III, 17? ?

As for the merchant marine, although ship-building statistics indicate a sustained effort, Colbert's dream of a large maritime "nursery" for the King's navy did not materialize. In 1718, according to Voltaire, the French merchant marine consisted of 300 vessels, excluding small fishing and coastal craft; in 1738, his estimated total of large merchant ships was 1,800.[16] In October 1730, an official report gave a total of 3,060 ships of all sizes, and 37,976 seamen.[17] The Levant trade eventually employed some 800 ships annually, but outside the Mediterranean a large part of the overseas and even the coastal trade was still carried by British, Dutch, and Hamburg merchantmen. On the coast of Africa and in the West Indies, the traffic to France was chiefly in French hands, but at the peak it rarely occupied more than 500 ships.[18] Hence, even more than in Britain, the problem of naval recruiting defied satisfactory solution. True enough, Colbert's system of registering all men with sea experience was renewed and improved, but shortages forced the government to widen classifications; peasants and artisans were included, and, in time of stress, mercenaries were hired in the markets of Genoa, Nice, and other Mediterranean ports.[19]

During this time, French naval strategy remained, as after La Hogue, essentially concerned with husbanding resources—the retention of a "fleet in being." The importance of sea power was everywhere acknowledged, but a chronic inferiority of numbers encouraged scepticism of the effectiveness of sea battle. Much in the manner of the Germans after Jutland, the French were inclined to count an indecisive engagement as a victory, provided they saved their ships. By the middle of the eighteenth century, the art of sparing ships in battle had become firmly welded into strategic doctrine.

France had repudiated "command of the sea," on the shaky assumption that certain ends, such as the invasion of England or the acquisition of a West Indian island, could be achieved without the preliminary elimination of her opponents' fleets. In short, the conquest of territory had become a more important object of naval strategy than the destruction of the enemy at sea.[20] An eighteenth-century naval authority, Audibert Ramatuelle, expressed this concept as follows:

[16]*Oeuvres complètes de Voltaire* (52 vols., Paris, 1883-85), XXXVII, 529.
[17]Wilson, *French Foreign Policy*, 315.
[18]W. L. Dorn, *Competition for Empire 1740-1763* (New York, 1940), 115.
[19]See M. Loir, *La Marine royale en 1789* (Paris, 1892), 40.
[20]See Castex, *Les Idées militaires de la Marine*, 36.

La marine française a toujours préféré la gloire d'assurer ou de conserver une conquête à celle, plus brillante peut-être, mais certainement moins réelle, de capturer quelques vaisseaux; et, en cela, elle s'est rapprochée davantage du véritable but de la guerre.[21]

Certainly, the strategy of taking territory had some validity for continental operations, where it was sound practice to garner spoils as hostages for lost possessions overseas. What the seaman lost at war, the diplomat might retrieve at the peace. But the whole history of French colonial policy should have revealed the sophistry of the doctrine as applied outside Europe. It should have been clear to any intelligent minister of the eighteenth century that if the conquest of a colony were made by means of overseas transport of men and supplies, its possession could be assured only by the maintenance of communications with the sources of supply.

As it happened, the French continued to build their empire without securing it by sea. The colonies themselves, Canada especially, were militarized as far as money allowed; indeed, it became part of French policy to extend the land war to the North American colonies. But because French policy opposed decision by battle whenever battle could be avoided, the colonial life-line in time of war could be kept intact only by emergency expeditions of succour, and these depended for success upon eluding an enemy that held command of the sea. On many occasions in the eighteenth century these expeditions were successful; but consistent success cannot be built on the chance game of hide-and-seek. That Canada remained French as long as it did was due not so much to the wisdom of French strategy, which could only delay a decision, as to lack of ambition on the part of British governments.

Although doctrine might dampen initiative, the Frenchman was never a bad seaman; certainly the British Admiralty correspondence does not convey the impression that the Royal Navy felt any overweening sense of superiority in personnel. The great Suffren had many imitators to show that, despite the hampering effects of national policy, quality could reveal itself not only in ships but also in men. Statistics of losses sustained by the British merchant marine pay tribute to the exploits of Jean Bart, Forbin, and Duguay-Trouin. It became almost a habit for raiding squadrons to "steal out" of port and elude superior English forces; but the impressive thing is not the

[21]Quoted in Castex, *Les Idées militaires de la Marine*, 30. This dogmatic philosophy finds expression constantly in Ramatuelle's *Cours élémentaire de tactique navale* (Paris, 1802), which was dedicated to Bonaparte.

fact that they got away but the near-punctuality with which, for example, the squadrons of Toulon and Brest or Rochefort made their rendezvous before crossing the Atlantic. Apart from the cramping bonds of doctrine, the chief French handicap was not lack of skill but lack of ships. Had France been able to build ships as well as armies, she might have won the Seven Years' War.

The Comte de Maurepas, who administered the navy from 1723 to 1749, appreciated the importance of numerical strength; but he hesitated to oppose with any vigour the traditional continental commitments which demanded the strongest army in Europe.

I submit that it is principally on the sea that one must make war on a maritime power [he wrote to the King]. I agree that in France land forces are necessary and demand great expense in time of war, but are not naval forces equally so when the war is against a maritime power and should they not be given preference from the moment when they serve to procure by means of commerce public revenues without which land forces cannot be maintained? I have often heard foreign ministers say that our navy is too much neglected, that it would better if the King had 50,000 less troops and 50 more vessels.[22]

But Maurepas realized that he would be fighting a losing battle and he preferred not to press his argument. He was perhaps reluctant to play the crusader at the risk of losing his job and the perquisites which accompanied it. When he did fall from power in 1749, it was because he offended the Pompadour, and not through any zealous opposition to the continental policy of his master.

In the long run, it was the unavoidable logic of geography that finally shaped policy. Like the Dutch, the French could not escape the political dilemmas which confronted any continental state. The long coastline with its front on two seas did stimulate the commercial instinct of the people of the ports and direct their enthusiasm towards horizons overseas, but no French statesman could take his eyes for long from *le sol de France*. An enemy might threaten English communications, or even attack a colony, but the soil of England was rarely in danger. France, on the contrary, was always at the mercy of an enemy coalition, which a shuffle of the diplomatic cards might provoke at any time. For this reason she was never in a position to concentrate wholeheartedly on winning command of the sea, which alone could guarantee a policy of imperial overseas expansion.

Not that French statesmen in an era of mercantilism were unaware of the military importance of maritime trade in producing a

[22]Quoted in R. Jouan, *Histoire de la Marine française* (Paris, 1932), I, 223.

favourable balance of power in Europe. ". . . it is the colonies, trade, and in consequence sea power," wrote Choiseul, "which must determine the balance of power upon the continent."[23] But France was not an island, and the whole problem of overseas expansion was far more complicated for France than for Britain. France wanted continental power and security, and she wanted an overseas empire; but she had not the resources to obtain both.

The British declaration of war against Spain in October 1739, made war with France almost inevitable. In both countries there was growing unrest, and a feeling that the armistice was coming to an end. For sixteen years after the Treaty of Utrecht Europe had been preserved from any vital disturbance by an *entente* between France and Britain. At any time between 1715 and 1731 there could have been a great war, and as a matter of fact there were little wars, but the *entente* held. Thanks to French co-operation, Britain was able to keep Spain and Austria from aggression, while maintaining at the same time her own naval, colonial, and commercial supremacy.

But a change came with the War of the Polish Succession in 1733. Spain and France defeated Austria, and both powers attained what they wished without Britain's help. Despite the Emperor Charles VI's demands for assistance, Walpole, who was responsible for British foreign policy, refused to enter the struggle. The Family Compact of 1733—the alliance of the Bourbons—gave the death-blow to his design of "peace with honour"; and Britain was left in isolation, without a single trustworthy ally. Yet Walpole refused to be disillusioned, and as late as 1738 he still hoped to keep the peace by means of new treaties and conventions. His diplomatic ideas were original and, for the period in which he lived, unique. He really believed what Ambassador Lichnowski told his German masters in 1914, that nothing could be so mad, nothing so foolish, as war by a trading nation.

But the mood of the country was against him. Men more emotional, yet wise, men who were uninfluenced by the clamours of the herd, saw war as inevitable. They rightly judged that the Family Compact was very much concerned with colonial questions and commerce. Spain, quickened into new life, was trying desperately to hold her South American monopolies, which enterprising British and New England captains and traders were doing their best

[23]Quoted in Rosinski, "The Role of Sea Power," 103.

to sabotage. Under the Compact Spain bound herself to deprive Britain of all lawful commercial privileges in America and to transfer them to France in return for help in taking Gibraltar.

A more fundamental cause of British restlessness was a growing fear of the intentions of imperial France. However unjustified it may have been, there was an apprehension, amounting almost to conviction, that French trade was gaining rapidly at the expense of British, and that peace under such circumstances was dangerous to security. There was open concern about the flourishing condition of the French fishery at Newfoundland and at Cape Breton, the development of the French East India Company, the competition of the French in the sugar trade and in the slave trade, and the seeming prosperity of the French fur trade. Fear of French commercial expansion in all these spheres alarmed the English merchants and roused talk about a preventive war.[24]

The French government was aware of this attitude. Many high officials were certain that the Spanish War was but a preliminary move against their own colonial trading interests, and had as its ultimate object the destruction of French maritime power. "France," in the words of one of her historians, "could not look on with an indifferent eye at a quarrel in which her interests were so much involved: to allow the English to destroy the Spanish settlements in America, establish herself there and take possession of their trade, was to permit the ruin of a flourishing French commerce."[25] In other words, it was beginning to dawn on both French and English governing classes, that two empires could no longer endure side by side.

Burke has remarked that the War of Jenkins's Ear was a war for plunder, but there was a deeper issue. In the seventeenth century, colonial problems had been purposely left outside the orbit of European diplomacy. There was an instinctive desire on the part of all the colonial powers to keep colonial rivalries from complicating their European policies.[26] European powers, as Professor Penson has remarked, "put to blind eyes" the telescopes that pointed towards the areas of conflict in distant possessions. In 1686 the North American Treaty of Neutrality between France and Britain stated that "if ever any rupture should occur in Europe . . . (which God forbid),"

[24]Wilson, *French Foreign Policy*, 290-3.
[25]M. Sautai, *Les Préliminaires de la Guerre de la Succession d'Autriche*, quoted in Richmond, *The Navy in the War of 1739-48*, I, 76.
[26]L. M. Penson, *The Colonial Background of British Foreign Policy* (London, 1930), 15.

no acts of hostility should take place in any part of America, but "true and firm peace and neutrality shall continue . . . as if no such rupture had occurred in Europe".[27]

By the beginning of the eighteenth century, however, the scope of British foreign policy had extended itself beyond the continent, and now embraced the whole world. The desire to expand commercially, and at the same time stifle the trade of foreign rivals, counted far more heavily than any dynastic tie such as attached Britain to Hanover. The balance of trade had become part and parcel of the balance of power.

Britain's interests were bound to conflict with those of any other nation possessing overseas colonies which by reason of their strategic position might threaten or cramp her own expansion and commerce. The paths of expanding empire were already clearly marked. Gibraltar and Minorca were stepping-stones to the East; on the west coast of Africa trading settlements pointed the way to the Cape or across the Atlantic to the Caribbean. In North America twelve colonies straggled unevenly from the Penobscot to the Savannah River, and Georgia was in the making; athwart the approaches to Canada lay Acadia, Newfoundland, and the Hudson Bay territories. From the north, the south and the east, a semicircle of British posts and settlements enfolded the wide but thinly stretched dominions of France.

The War of the Spanish Succession had been in many respects a localized conflict. There had been fighting in North America, and in the end certain territories had changed hands; but neither Britain nor France had engaged full strength. Naval engagements in North American waters had been isolated enterprises having little connection with the decisive theatre of operations in home waters. But by 1739 statesmen, as well as merchants, had begun to react to the fatalistic doctrines of eighteenth-century mercantilism. The implications of world-wide trade competition pressed themselves relentlessly on the pattern of strategy. The colonies were now regarded as almost integral parts of the national economy. The focal sea areas in their neighbourhood began to acquire a strategic importance, which more than ever justified the presence of small permanent squadrons and stationed ships as guardians of local trade routes. It is at this point, then—the beginning of the War of Jenkins's Ear—that the

[27]F. G. Davenport, *European Treaties Bearing on the History of the United States and its Dependencies* (3 vols., Washington, D.C., Carnegie Institution, 1917-34), II (1929), 322-3.

history of naval policy is absorbed almost completely into the history of commerce, a conjunction of interests which led Admiral Sir Herbert Richmond to the conclusion that, in the shaping or deflection of strategy, the effect of commercial considerations was even greater in the eighteenth century than in our own.[28]

The second phase of the struggle was marked by the entrance of France, and the merging of the War of Jenkins's Ear with the War of the Austrian Succession.[29] Far up the Rhine near the little village of Dettingen, in June of 1743, the two principals fought their first battle in the long-drawn-out duel for maritime and colonial supremacy. That British forces were so engaged, deep in the continent, clearly pointed to the absence of any comprehensive imperial design. In the beginning British statesmen were too deeply immersed in continental affairs to attend properly to the empires that lay, waiting for the winner, outside the European cockpit. Moreover, the protection of sea communications to the continent, and the blockade of French and Spanish ports, left few ships available for colonial expeditions on a grand scale. As a result, British strategy on the seas was confined almost entirely to the defensive; the War of the Austrian Succession covered a period of indecisive naval warfare, relieved only by one dramatic event, and that a retaliatory stroke by the colonists themselves—the capture of Louisbourg.

The inhabitants of Massachusetts had long looked fearfully and covetously at the Cape Breton fortress. Years of savage border warfare had left a legacy of hatred which recent coastal raids from that privateering base had revived and sharpened. The capture of Canso and one or two other minor posts seemed to demonstrate that the possession of Nova Scotia was in doubt as long as the French were allowed to exert their naval force from so formidable a *point d'appui*. In the opinion of the shrewd and aggressive governor of Massachusetts, William Shirley, the expense of defending the British colony, as well as the New England fisheries, would in the long run equal the cost of reducing Louisbourg. If the mother country would undertake to contribute ships, Shirley was prepared to organize a colonial expedition to make the conquest.[30]

---

[28]Richmond, *The Navy in the War of 1739-48;* see especially III, 243-52.
[29]In 1740, France, after signing the Pragmatic Sanction (1735), which guaranteed Maria Theresa's dominions, broke the treaty and, along with Spain, Bavaria, Prussia, and Saxony, began the task of dividing the Austrian Empire.
[30]William Shirley to the Duke of Newcastle, Boston, January 14, 1745, in *Correspondence of William Shirley, Governor of Massachusetts and Military Commander of America 1731-1760,* ed. by C. H. Lincoln (2 vols., New York, 1912), I, 161-5; also Shirley to the Lords of Trade, July 10, 1745, *ibid.,* 242-4.

VII

The First Conquest of Louisbourg

Separated from the peninsula by the narrow Strait of Canso, the island of Cape Breton points north-east towards Newfoundland from which it is separated by a narrow arm of the sea. Strategically placed at the entrance of the Gulf of St. Lawrence, indented with deep harbours and supporting in large areas good soil and rich forest growth, Cape Breton seemed destined to become not only a military bulwark of New France, but a trading *entrepôt* which would ultimately compensate for the cession of Acadia and the loss of Placentia. It was a natural base for the protection of the profitable French fisheries, a distributing centre to rival New England's Boston, and a spring-board for the oft-dreamed recovery of Nova Scotia.

From this base even an assault by sea against New England was not impossible, provided the French could gain a temporary command of the sea. Ships from Louisbourg could cut Atlantic communications with Nova Scotia or Newfoundland, and threaten the coast from Maine to Rhode Island. Already the attacks on colonial fishing ports had shown the potential peril of a base in a focal sea area, from which the French could harry the trade and disrupt the fisheries.

The English, [declared the former Minister of Marine, Count Pontchartrain] are worried about the importance of this post. They see that it prejudices their commerce and that in time of war it will menace their navigation. After the outbreak of hostilities, they will lose no time in trying to seize it. . . . If France should lose the Island, such a loss would be irreparable, for it would take with it all our possessions in America.[1]

By controlling Cape Breton, the French believed they could secure their own Canadian domain, and eventually drive the British

[1]G. Hanotaux, *Histoire des colonies françaises* (6 vols., Paris, 1929), I, 231.

and New Englanders from the Banks, thereby increasing the value of their own fishery as a nursery of sea power.

Île Royale or Cape Breton had been frequented from time immemorial by Basque and Breton fishermen. Two Scots, Lochinever and Ochiltree, in 1621 and 1629 respectively, had tried to establish a colony there, but both had failed, and the island eventually fell to Nicholas Denys, who established several fishing ports, including Ste Anne and St. Pierre, which were used by "La Compagnie de Pêche Sedentaire."[2] In 1672 Colbert conceived the plan of exploiting the whole resources of the island, using the oak for ship construction and the abundant coal for distilling West India molasses. But industrial development was negligible, and by 1710 it was proposed that a fortified port should be established to serve as a clearing house for trade to France, the West Indies, and Quebec. By making Cape Breton rather than Quebec their port of call, ships from the West Indies could make two round trips a year and avoid the dangers of early freeze-ups in the St. Lawrence.[3]

Following the Treaty of Utrecht and the loss of the Acadian peninsula, the new plan was immediately set in motion. A former governor of Placentia, the Sieur de Saint-Ovide, was dispatched in 1713 with an engineer and surveyors; he found the island in possession of twenty-five or thirty Indian families and one Frenchman. After many surveys and prolonged hesitation, it was finally decided to found the new wilderness capital on the eastern tip, at the entrance to a bay long known as English Harbour. The new establishment was renamed Port Saint Louis.

In 1720 the French began the work of fortification, a project which eventually was to cost more than two million pounds sterling, despite the fact that the original plans, drawn up according to Vauban's ideas, were never fully executed. Corrupt administration, poor supervision, and dishonest labour were largely responsible. Cut stone and solid bricks were carried from France in the fishing fleet, but large quantities of these and other good materials went into the building of the governor's and intendant's quarters or were sold to

[2]Denys came out to Acadia in 1632 with Isaac de Razilly who was official representative of the king and of the Company of New France. On his return to France several years later he published an extremely useful book, *The Description and Natural History of the Coasts of North America*, ed. and trans. W. F. Ganong (Toronto, 1908).
[3]Regarding Louisbourg's function as a distributing centre, see *Select Documents in Canadian Economic History, 1497-1783*, ed. H. A. Innis (Toronto, 1929), 128-44.

New England traders and replaced by feeble substitutes. Even mortar became a source of profiteering, as crumbling walls were subsequently to testify.[4]

The fortress proper occupied over a hundred acres. On the harbour side it extended about three quarters of a mile, and over half a mile on the land side facing the sea. Near the centre stood the *Bastion Royal*, or citadel, which contained the governor's house, barracks for the garrison, an arsenal, powder magazine, and well-built casemates. Beyond a moat in the rear lay the greater part of the town, consisting chiefly of wooden houses built on foundations of stone sometimes to a height of six feet.[5] Here were installed the families of the garrison from Placentia (which had been surrendered to the British under the Treaty of Utrecht) as well as many fishermen from the south shores of Newfoundland and St. Pierre.[6]

The harbour ran nearly two miles north-east and south-west, and was almost landlocked. The two small peninsulas on either side of the entrance were a mile apart, but the actual fairway was reduced to little more than a quarter of a mile, on the one side by Goat Island, and on the other by numerous reefs off Lighthouse Point. This approach was protected by a strong fortification on Goat Island known as the Island Battery which mounted some thirty-nine guns, and by the Royal Battery on the mainland which could bring thirty guns to bear.[7] Temporary entrenchments, with a few gun emplacements, were established to the south-west of the town facing Gabarus Bay, but the garrison was never strong enough to permit effective defence outside the walls. As long as enemy fleets remained outside the harbour to face the fogs and storms of an open roadstead, the fortress was in little danger; but landings to the south-west along Gabarus Bay or on the north-east peninsula, where the lighthouse stood, could immediately threaten both town and fort.[8]

An additional weakness lay in the failure of Louisbourg and its environs to achieve anything like self-sufficiency. The newly settled

[4]See W. Wood, *The Great Fortress* (Toronto, 1915), 6.
[5]Beatson, *Naval and Military Memoirs*, III, 57.
[6]Hanotaux, *Histoire des colonies françaises*, I, 231-3.
[7]"Ships or floating batteries inside the harbour could enfilade the whole left flank and centre of a besieger's approaches; while a frontal attack had to be made against a double tier of well-protected guns. The weak points were, however, particularly vulnerable to attack by superior sea power; for no ordinary garrison had either sufficient numbers or mobility to defend both the lighthouse peninsula and the landing places along Gabarus Bay. Wood, *The Logs of the Conquest of Canada*, 64.
[8]See map on p. 121.

inhabitants preferred fishing to farming, partly from laziness, and partly because no reliance could be placed on crops; prevalent fog and rain seemed to prevent the grain from ripening properly.[9] A host of complaining letters from intendants and governors suggest that the colony received little help from France and was kept alive by importations of foodstuffs from Canada, Acadia, Île St. Jean (Prince Edward Island), and New England. In normal times most of the beef and pork came from France, but during war this connection was often broken for many months at a time.[10] In 1743, 172 vessels came to Cape Breton from the West Indies or Europe; in 1744 the number had dropped by 50.[11] By that date the cloistered garrison at Louisbourg had reached a peak of discontent that bordered on mutiny.

Even with the best of food, isolated existence on an island beset with cold and fog was bound to play havoc with morale. Added to this were the vicissitudes of cramped quarters behind rotten defences, a dreary landscape, and corrupt leadership. The mental and physical condition of garrison and townsfolk in the year 1745 is not hard to comprehend. Not until the end of 1744 did the French government, realizing that a British assault was probable, make plans to reinforce the fort and send out fresh stores.

On learning of these plans in December, Shirley immediately wrote the Admiralty urging the interception of the relief ships as a "killing blow" to enemy designs; at the same time he proposed to the General Court of Massachusetts the immediate preparation of an expedition to capture Louisbourg. To await help from England would be to throw away advantages which the present weakened condition of the place seemed to offer.

From the best information that can be had of the circumstances of the Town, [he told the Court] and of the number of the soldiers and Militia within it, and of the situation of the Harbour, I have good reason to think that if

[9]See "Correspondance générale, Île Royale," 1741, XXIII, *Report on Canadian Archives, 1887*, cccxxxii *et seq.*, which contains a synopsis of manuscript documents relating to Canada examined at the Ministère de la Marine, Paris, by M. Joseph Marmette; also Innis, *Select Documents on Canadian Economic History*, 107-15.

[10]See "Correspondance générale, Île Royale," 1744, cccxli, cccxlii; also Governor Cosby of New York to the Council of Trade and Plantations, December 15, 1733, *Calendar of State Papers, Colonial, America and West Indies, 1733*, XL, 256; *ibid.*, 255, same to the Duke of Newcastle, December 15, 1733.

[11]J. S. McLennan, *Louisburg from Its Foundation to Its Fall, 1713-1758* (London, 1918), 121.

Two Thousand men were landed upon the Island as soon as they may be conveniently got ready . . . such a number of men, would, with the blessing of Divine Providence upon their Enterprize, be masters of the field at all events, and not only possess themselves of their two most important batteries with ease, break upon their Out Settlements, destroy their Cable and Magazines, ruine their Fishery Works, and lay the town in ruines, but might make themselves masters of the Town and Harbour.[12]

In view of English sea supremacy and the recognized weakness of the French citadel, it would be a mistake to think of Governor Shirley's proposal as "a desperate step to avert impending calamity." Unless France should win command of the sea, New England had nothing to fear from invasion, because Louisbourg the fortress had no relationship to Louisbourg as base for a fleet. Lacking a strong fleet, the fortress was impotent to threaten any enemy that lay outside the range of its guns. "A coast fortress," says Mahan, "defends the nation to which it belongs chiefly by the fleet it shelters." "What good is Louisbourg?" was the rhetorical question posed by an Acadian priest. "It would be good if France were as strong at sea as England."[13] A fortress by itself cannot control a sea route, and without a standing fleet Louisbourg was in no position to block the St. Lawrence. Such ships as found shelter in the harbour became tools of the defence rather than threatening instruments of invasion. Louisbourg never became a base for offensive operations against the enemy. Far from being a calamitous threat to the New England colonies, it was in no position to ensure the protection of its own lines of communications, subject as they were to blockade in the Mediterranean and in the Channel. The "menace of Louisbourg" was not a strategist's phrase; it was a useful political slogan to present to a colonial legislature, whose thrifty members frowned on costly expeditions, which in the past, at least, had been anything but lucrative in their returns.

The decisive elements in the Massachusetts resolve to take Louisburg were anger and greed. New England had no reason to fear invasion, and a reading of Governor Shirley's correspondence sug-

[12]This message was delivered to the Court on January 9, 1745. (See *Correspondence of William Shirley*, I, 159-60.) On January 29, he submitted to the Lords of the Admiralty a general scheme of attack, which involved a landing in Gabarus Bay, a rendezvous at Canso, and if possible a surprise attack on the harbour and fort. The force suggested was three thousand troops, supported by a naval force sufficient to blockade the port against the arrival of M. de Vivier, whose supply ships for the garrison would in all probability be accompanied by no more than two thirty- or forty-gun ships. (*Ibid.*, 175-7.)
[13]Quoted in McLennan, *Louisburg*, 331.

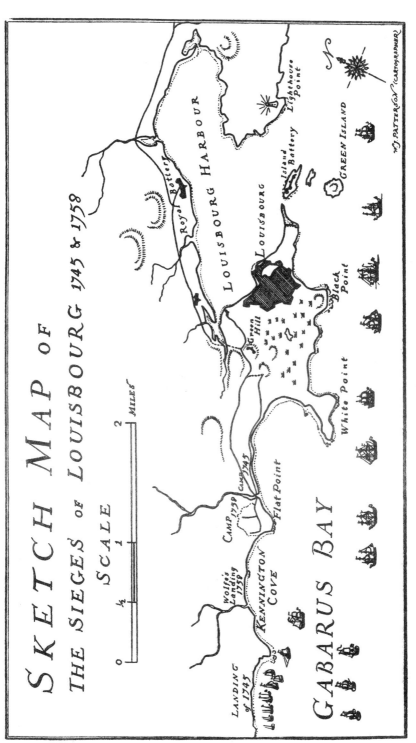

III. THE SIEGES OF LOUISBOURG

gests that the foraging activities of the Cape Breton French did eventually produce a pent-up feeling for revenge.[14] For twenty-five years, privateers and semi-pirates from Louisbourg had preyed on New England's trade and fisheries, robbing and destroying from Newfoundland to New Jersey. As compared with the gains from the Gulf and Bank fisheries, the losses may have been meagre; but constant interference meant accumulated grievances. These could be easily exploited by leaders of opinion such as Shirley, who in his own heart took a far broader view of French rivalry, and looked to the final conquest of Canada. Added to the desire for revenge was the hope of gain: for Boston merchants, the prospect of demolishing a highly competitive rival in the fisheries; for the adventurer and impoverished farmer, the prospect of good pay and substantial plunder.

On January 25, 1745, the Shirley proposal to destroy the hornets' nest (somewhat absurdly considered as "secret") was "cheerfully" adopted by the General Court. It was decided to raise 3,000 volunteers by the beginning of March; in addition to pay of twenty-five shillings a month, plus a free blanket, a generous House moved by patriotic impulse voted each recruit a half pound of ginger and a pound and a half of sugar.[15] The Court further recommended that a Committee be appointed to "procure & fit Vessels to serve as Transports," and to provide "suitable Naval Force" as convoy.[16]

Meanwhile, Shirley wrote to Sir Chaloner Ogle, in command of the Jamaica squadron, and to Commodore Peter Warren at the Leeward Islands, asking their co-operation.[17] To the Admiralty he explained that such a contribution would make it possible to block the approaches to Louisbourg by sea, and thus cut off the relief which was expected from France in the early spring. To the Duke of Newcastle, he pointed out that success would mean the preservation of Nova Scotia, and the ultimate reduction of Canada, thus securing to His Majesty the whole fur trade of the continent and the whole of the fisheries. Apart from the revenues accruing to the fishing industry, "the Nursery of able Seamen rais'd thereby for the Royal Navy would be very considerably increas'd; And it would

[14]Cf. McLennan, 133-4.

[15]*Ibid.*, 131-3 (a summary of the sessions of the House of Representatives).

[16]*Correspondence of William Shirley*, I, 169-70.

[17]See Shirley to the Duke of Newcastle, Boston, March 27, 1745, in *Colonial Office series 5* (found in the Public Record Office, London; nereinafter referred to as *C.O. 5*), vol. 900, 168. In the previous September, Warren had been made commander-in-chief of all ships in North American waters.

render the Roman Catholick States in the neighbouring Seas in some measure dependent upon his Majesty's Subjects for part of their provisions."[18]

From Ogle at Jamaica, Shirley got neither help nor encouragement, but Peter Warren, whom he hoped to see take command of the sea forces, showed plenty of initiative and even aggressiveness, once he had overcome his initial doubts about the prospect of capturing a Vauban stronghold with colonial levies. Married to a Boston woman who possessed considerable wealth in the form of western lands, Warren's new-found imperial appetite may have been stimulated by personal motives. At any rate, despite his deep respect for "a very regular fortification," he urged his Admiralty friends, of whom Anson was one, to back the proposed expedition as one means of freeing the North American colonies from the threatened danger of encirclement. From the St. Lawrence to the Mississippi, the French frontiers were on the move; if the French colonies north and south joined up in the rear of the English, westward expansion from the Atlantic coastal strip would be brought to a complete halt.[19]

Warren proposed to sail with his best ships as soon as official permission was forthcoming, leaving only a few of the lower rates on the Leeward Island station. Fearful of such impetuosity, his council of war voted against the plan and protested that a substantial French squadron was assembling at Martinique. The governor and assembly of Antigua added their own indignant criticisms; but Warren persisted on the correct assumption that the enemy's mission to Martinique could be no more than a local and passive defence of trade and territory.[20] With one fourth- and two fifth-rates, Warren sailed directly for the rendezvous at Canso, where on April 25 he joined the colonial expedition led by Sir William Pepperell, that had arrived some three weeks previously.

William Pepperell of Kittery, Maine, was a landowner, merchant, and "lumber king," a Yankee without book-learning but of sound common sense and sterling integrity. Although able to work with Warren in perfect harmony, his position was not an easy one. Discipline was practically non-existent in his volunteer army, and he had

---

[18]*Ibid.*, 152, letter of January 14, 1745; also contained in *Correspondence of William Shirley*, I, 161-5.

[19]See Richmond, *The Navy in the War of 1739-48*, II, 204.

[20]See "The Maritime Wars of the Early Eighteenth Century," *Department of Intelligence* (1936), Naval War College, Newport, R.I., U.S.A., 31.

to handle his officers and men with scrupulous tact.[21]   From the
point of view of the British regular, such an army was hardly suited
to prolonged siege operations. Under the circumstances, it may have
been fortunate that in Massachusetts the expedition was regarded
as a Puritan crusade. "Thy people shall be willing in the day of Thy
Power," was a favourite text of recruiting sermons. Parson Moody
of York, Maine, a cleric with "lungs of brass and nerves of iron,"
was appointed senior chaplain to the troops. Moody, who was in
the habit of yanking erring militiamen out of Boston bar-rooms by
their coat collars, went on board carrying his meeting-house Bible
and an axe with which to hew down "the altars of anti-Christ" at
Louisbourg.[22]   But apart from such mild hysteria, the expedition
had been soberly and efficiently planned by Shirley, and it was well
equipped. In the short time of seven weeks, 4,000 volunteers (of
whom some 3,000 belonged to Massachusetts) had been assembled,
all of them New Englanders. New York loaned ten 18-pounders
to a hopelessly inadequate "siege train." The only real failure was
the lack of secrecy, a weakness attending all previous colonial expeditions. Shirley had warned the Assembly of the need for silence,
but the destination leaked out, and accurate news of the project
reached Canada and Louisbourg. Happily, however, it was treated
with scepticism, and in Louisbourg no additional steps were taken
to guard against attack.

On March 24, 1745, some four battalions of farmers and fishermen clambered on board their bankers and lobster schooners and
cleared from Nantasket Road to besiege a fortress which (if rumours
about its strength were true) might have made Marlborough pause.
They reached Canso on April 4, three days after the New Hampshire
contingent.[23]   Warren joined them on the 23rd, and thence bore
away to blockade Louisbourg. On the early morning of April 30,

[21]Shortly after the expedition sailed, Shirley wrote Pepperell on the need for
co-operation with Warren. "It is a general observation that the land and sea
forces, when joined upon the same expedition, seldom or never agree, but I am
persuaded it will not be so between you and Commodore Warren, as any mis-
understanding between you might prove fatal to his Majesty's service in the
expedition," April 10, 1745. (*Correspondence of William Shirley*, I, 205.) Unhappily, Shirley's hopes proved vain, although serious estrangement was avoided
until the end of the siege.
[22]"The Maritime Wars of the Early Eighteenth Century," 29.
[23]The Connecticut contingent reached Canso on April 25.

the vanguard of the troops began to disembark in Gabarus Bay, less than two miles to the west of the fortress.

Commodore Warren's arrival, with three men-of-war, was timely; the capture of some twenty store-ships just short of their goal deprived the beleaguered garrison of vital supplies of food and ammunition. On May 20 two more large ships were taken—one the *Vigilant* of 64 guns and 560 men, laden with stores, cannon, and powder. On the point of entering harbour she had been attacked by a British frigate which fired a few shots and then took to flight. Instead of disregarding such small prey, the *Vigilant* turned about in pursuit and drove straight into Warren's arms.[24] During the whole course of the siege only one vessel got through, whereas the British forces were maintained throughout by convoyed transports which arrived without difficulty. Shortly after the first landing operation, the *Canterbury* and *Sunderland* of 60 guns each, and the *Chester* of 50 were added to his force, and on June 11, the squadron was further reinforced by three more ships—the *Princess Mary* of 60 guns, the *Hector* and *Lark* of 40 guns, making a total of four ships of 60 guns, one of 50, and five of 40, besides a number of smaller vessels.[25]

The task which lay before Warren and his New Englanders was formidable. The navigable entrance to the harbour was less than half a mile in width, and was under fire from Island Battery at the entrance, and from Royal Battery on the mainland; all told, these two works mounted sixty heavy pieces. On the land or western side, Louisbourg was defended by the conventional work of ditch and rampart, the ditch being eighty feet wide and from thirty to thirty-six feet deep, while the rampart of earth faced with masonry was about sixty feet in thickness. There are varying accounts of the total number of French guns, but in all probability there were no more than one hundred mounted for action. The artillery available for the attackers is no less uncertain, but a likely estimate is thirty-four cannon and mortars.[26] The few British siege batteries were of poor stuff, and later on some of them burst through overloading; the remainder, firing at long range, could hardly do much damage to

[24]See Lacour-Gayet, *La Marine militaire de la France sous le règne de Louis XV* (1st ed., Paris, 1902), 180. McLennan, *Louisburg*, 156-7.
[25]See Richmond, *The Navy in the War of 1739-48*, II, 209-10, 212, 215, 215n.; Beatson, *Naval and Military Memoirs*, III, 55-6; also "Biographical Memoir of the Late Sir Peter Warren, K.B., Vice-Admiral of the Red Squadron," *The Naval Chronicle* (London, 1805), XII, 262-4.
[26]See F. E. Whitton, *Wolfe and North America* (London, 1929), 158.

French inner defences.[27] Yet there was need for haste. The St. Lawrence was now open, and reinforcements might be expected any day from Quebec as well as from France.

The first landing, near the head of the harbour, on May 2nd, was covered by a barrage of grape. A detachment of 100 men fought a delaying action, but it was soon dispersed. Next morning the isolated Royal Battery was taken by assault; the garrison evacuated the defences in a panic, spiking the guns without firing even a single round. An attempt to retake the battery failed; the guns were drilled out by New England gunsmiths and turned upon the town. Owing to the surf, the landing of heavy guns and stores was a difficult procedure which occupied nearly two weeks. Slowly, but surely, the fortress was ringed, as batteries took positions from Green Hill on the north-west down to and around the harbour.[28] In marshy ground, the guns were dragged on sleds, improvised by a New Hampshire ship-builder. But all this took time, and as the weeks passed sickness took a heavy toll of the besiegers. The men were without tents, and subject to the discomforts of cold, damp nights and foggy days. Fortunately, the absence of strict discipline permitted them to keep in good condition by off-duty exercises such as fishing, shooting, racing, and chasing enemy cannon balls.[29]

Late in May, discouraged by the slow progress, Warren planned an attack on the Island Battery. With muffled oars, some 400 troops were rowed in dories to the harbour, but they were repulsed with the loss of nearly 200 killed, drowned or captured.[30] Meanwhile, however, a battery, equipped with French guns which had been retrieved from the beach, had been established on Lighthouse Point, and soon a devastating fire was directed on the "Island." With most of the French batteries crippled, the time was ripe for a combined assault from land and sea. But hardly had preparations been set in motion, when a flag of truce signalled the end.[31] Facing

[27]See McLennan, *Louisburg*, 155. McLennan gives a good general account of the siege based largely on ships' logs and contemporary journals.

[28]For details of the siege, see *C.O. 5*, vol. 900, 240, William Shirley to the Duke of Newcastle, Louisburg, October 28, 1745, along with enclosed account (pp. 248-55) of the proceedings from the landing at Canso to the time of the surrender; also *Narrative and Critical History of America*, ed. J. Winsor (8 vols., Boston, 1884-9), V, 410-13, 434-47; and a pamphlet by Shirley entitled *A Letter to the Duke of Newcastle with a Journal of the Siege of Louisburg* (London, 1746).

[29]Whitton, *Wolfe and North America*, 160.

[30]William Pepperrell to William Shirley, *Correspondence of William Shirley*, I, 223.

[31]See *C.O. 5*, vol. 13, 59, William Pepperrell to the Duke of Newcastle, June 28, 1745; also *Correspondence of William Shirley*, I, 241, Shirley to the Lords of Trade, July 10, 1745.

starvation and certain that Warren's reinforced fleet barred all hopes of aid from the sea, the garrison capitulated on June 16, 1745, and marched out with the honours of war. After a siege of forty-seven days, a garrison of 1300 had surrendered a fortress built according to the best engineering of the day to an amateur attacking force consisting largely of rustics and fishermen.

The news of the reduction of Louisbourg reached England during the last week of July and did much to eradicate the gloom aroused by the battle of Fontenoy.[32] So unexpected was the victory that most people were inclined to regard it as an amateur's fluke, the result of "an interposition from Above, truly uncommon and extraordinary."[33] Not only did the capture of Louisbourg mean the destruction of the French fishery, worth according to semi-official estimates, some £980,000 a year,[34] but it removed all British fears of encroachment or competition on the Banks as well as on the North American coasts. The conquest was not only a severe blow to the trade of the French, for Louisbourg was the *entrepôt* and port of call for both West Indies and East Indies traffic, but it deprived them of their main harbour in North America, and widened the door to Quebec. Furthermore, the Acadian Indians, who had regarded Louisbourg as a symbol of French overlordship, were shaken in their faith by the easy victory; while New England, freed from the ominous presence of a great naval base in adjoining waters, could balance the costs of conquest with anticipated returns from the increased trade in fish, West Indies products and Boston-distilled rum.[35] Governor Shirley added one last item to the list of victory benefits. Louisbourg, he wrote the Lords of Trade, gave Britain a strategic hold on her colonies, "if ever there should come a time when they

---

[32]The Duke of Newcastle is reported to have run panting to the King, not merely "to announce to him the acquisition of this important fortress . . . but also to give him information of a geographical discovery he had made, that Cape Breton was an island." (J. Barrow, *Life of George, Lord Anson, Admiral of the Fleet*, . . . (London, 1839), 130.) In view of the Duke's demonstrated interest in plans for the defence of Nova Scotia, this anecdote, like others of its kind, must unhappily be regarded as apocryphal.

[33]Douglass, *A Summary, . . . of the British Settlements in North America*, I, 336.

[34]C. E. Fayle, "Economic Pressure in the War of 1739-48," *Journal of the Royal United Service Institution*, LXVIII, 1923, 443.

[35]"By the Possession of Cape Breton we are become, or have it in our Power to become, entire Masters of all the Cod-fishery, which, as Charlevoix asserts, is of more value than the Mines of Peru." Anon., *The Importance and Advantage of Cape Breton truly Stated, and Impartially Considered* (London, 1746), 84.

should grow Restive and disposed to shake off their Dependency upon their Mother Country. . . ."[36]

The expedition had been planned in the colonies, and to New England must go the chief glory. None the less, the victory was a supreme example of combined operations. Had the Admiralty not supported Warren in his temporary abandonment of the Leeward Islands, and twice sent reinforcements, the outcome might have been very different. Moreover, the value of a strong covering force in home waters revealed itself clearly, for without command of the sea, Warren would have been at the mercy of any French relieving force. Had not the squadrons intended for Louisbourg been tightly blockaded by a British force off Brest, the mere possibility of their approach might have paralysed his arrangements. Certainly, the pains taken to reinforce him showed how conscious the Admiralty was of this fact. It is clear that had a superior French naval force managed to escape, Warren must either have abandoned the troops which were landed, or stayed with them in Gabarus Bay, to be besieged in turn by the garrison of Louisbourg.[37]

Meanwhile, the French garrison was returned to Brittany, there to dampen the last sparks of rejoicing which the victory at Fontenoy had kindled in the previous May. At the same time, Warren, now promoted rear-admiral, took over the vacated command as governor of the fortress and commander-in-chief of the naval forces in adjacent waters.[38] It seemed certain that the French would attempt to recover the island in the following year; indeed the governor heard rumours that a scheme was on foot in Canada to send 6,000 French and Indians for a surprise attack during the coming winter. But Warren was little disturbed; there was small chance of an expedition bringing artillery such a great distance, or acquiring the necessary transport, and he continued quietly with his plans for strengthening harbour defences, convoying the Newfoundland and West Indies

[36]*C.O. 5*, vol. 885, 153, letter of July 10, 1745; *Correspondence of William Shirley*, I, 244; *C.O. 5*, vol. 900, 197, on same subject, same date, to Duke of Newcastle.

[37]See P. H. Colomb, *Naval Warfare: Its Ruling Principles and Practice Historically Treated* (London, 1891), 355-6.

[38]Warren also received a knighthood, and this, in addition to the other honours, seems to have provoked Pepperell, who, although made a baronet, asserted with some degree of justice (and Shirley agreed with him) that at least the command of the city should have been given to the leader of the land forces. *Correspondence of William Shirley*, I, 303n.

trade, and scouting about the Gulf of St. Lawrence.[39] He had scant resources at his disposal. With the greatest difficulty a boom was secured to block the entrance of the harbour, and this was covered only by an ancient sloop hastily reconstructed as a fireship. There were no facilities for careening; indeed, at a time when the French were building ships in Canada, and the Spaniards at Havana, neither in Newfoundland nor in Nova Scotia were there dockyards for fitting or repairing any kind of ship of war.[40]

As the winter wore on, it became more and more certain that any plan of reconquest by the French would be preceded by an attack on Nova Scotia. There, apart from accessible advantages such as provisions and familiar terrain, they could count on the probable help of five or six thousand Acadians and numerous Indian auxiliaries. If the enemy secured Nova Scotia, New England settlements would once again lie open to the marauder, and William Shirley, the governor of Massachusetts, was sufficiently aroused to address a series of urgent letters to the Duke of Newcastle.

This train of Consequences from the Enemies being Masters of Nova Scotia may seem remote, My Lord, but they are not impossible, and it may be very difficult for the French to regain Louisburg at least without being Masters of Nova Scotia, and that seems under the present Circumstances of the Garrison where no recruits are yet arriv'd from England and the Inhabitants of the Country surrounding it are Enemies in their hearts, no difficult Acquisition, and to be made with a small Train of Artillery in three weeks at farthest.

Shirley was convinced that the French were bound to try for revenge "after the blow we had given 'em at Louisburg (which if they don't recover it soon by retaking Cape Breton or getting Nova Scotia will prove their Death wound in North America."[41]

Any local attempt was certain to be in association with a French expeditionary force, and both Shirley and Warren warned the government of the need during the ensuing spring and summer for constant

[39]See *Admiralty In-Letters* (London, Public Record Office, Secretary's Department; hereinafter referred to as *Ad. 1*) vol. 480, sec. I, Warren to the Secretary of the Admiralty, Hon. Thomas Corbett, October 3, 1745, and November 23, 1745. (Transcripts are to be found in the Manuscripts Division, Library of Congress, Washington, D.C. Since folio numbers of transcripts and originals do not correspond, they are omitted; date, volume, and section numbers are a sufficient guide to either source.)

[40]*Ibid.*

[41]*Correspondence of William Shirley,* I, 298-9, to the Duke of Newcastle, Boston, December 14, 1745. Shirley estimated the forces in Canada to be 500 regulars, 10,000 to 15,000 militia, and between 500 and 800 Indians. See *ibid.,* 332-5.

patrols in Cabot Strait as well as to the north of Newfoundland in the Strait of Belle Isle.[42] Of course, the whole business could be avoided, once and for all, as Shirley suggested none too hopefully, by the taking of Quebec and the conquest of Canada. As it happened, Admiral Warren (after handing over in June his sea command to Vice-Admiral Townsend and his governorship to Commodore Knowles) had barely passed the harbour mouth en route for Boston, when news arrived from England that an expedition was actually preparing for the capture of Quebec, and that he was to be given charge of the fleet. In the circumstances, he immediately put back to discuss arrangements with the officers of the squadron and the garrison.[43]

The decision of the home authorities in the early spring of 1746 to attack Quebec was not the result of long deliberation. During the months after the fall of Louisbourg the country was still suffering from the chills brought on by the Jacobite uprising, the panic of Prestonpans, and the fear of a French invasion. Not until the retreat of Prince Charlie from Derby, accompanied by the final frustration of a French landing, could the government breathe freely and consider taking advantage of the colonial success at Louisbourg. The Duke of Bedford, as First Lord of the Admiralty, had only the Paymaster of the Forces, William Pitt, to support him; neither Henry Pelham, the leader of the government, nor his brother, the Duke of Newcastle, had any stomach for the expedition which Shirley had urged in vain for so long.[44]

Now that the time for final action had come, Admiral Warren was far from optimistic about the situation. His despondency may have been partly caused by scorbutic fever which had further smitten his garrison, already reduced during the forty-seven days of the siege to little more than half of their original strength of 4,000.[45] All winter the sickness had raged, and the garrison came close to annihilation. "For tho' I thank God," wrote Warren in June, "it is now very healthy it may be otherwise next Winter.—We have buried near 2,000 Men since we have been in Possession of this place, owing greatly to the want of Necessaries."[46] The arrival of three reinforcing battalions in April gave him new courage, but he was still fearful

[42]*Ad. 1*, vol. 480, sec. I, Warren to Corbett, January 18, 1746.
[43]Richmond, *The Navy in the War of 1739-48*, III, 3.
[44]See B. Williams, *The Life of William Pitt, Earl of Chatham* (2 vols., London, 1914), I, 163-4.
[45]*C.O. 5*, vol. 13, 101-2, Warren and William Pepperell to the Duke of Newcastle, January 18, 1745.
[46]*Ibid.*, 117, Warren to the Duke of Newcastle, June 2, 1746.

that the Admiralty might underestimate the task confronting them. Respectfully, but forcefully, he warned them that the projected attack on Canada "seems to me to have been founded upon some misrepresentation of the Strength and the situation of that Colony, for if my information is right, they have Forty thousand fighting men in Canada, besides the Indians. . . ."[47] Nevertheless, in June, a few small scouting vessels were sent up the St. Lawrence "as far as they could safely go" to master the navigation, take soundings, mark rocks and shoals, and as far as possible gain intelligence of the motions of the enemy.[48]

The projected attack was to be delivered from both land and sea. From Albany colonial troops were to advance up the Lake Champlain route towards Montreal; another force led by Admiral Warren, consisting chiefly of British troops under General James St. Clair, would, after calling at Louisbourg, press up the St. Lawrence to Quebec. The first week in August, it was assumed, would be the latest date at which the expedition could proceed up the St. Lawrence with reasonable assurance of returning before the winter set in.

Early in June the troops were embarked at Portsmouth, and after a two days' delay owing to south-west gales, the expedition finally put to sea only to be held up for a week by contrary winds interspersed with calms. During this time the alarming news arrived that a French fleet under de Roye de la Rochefoucauld, Duc d'Anville, had escaped for an unknown destination, and in such strength that the accompanying escort to the expedition, under Commodore Cotes, could not hope to match it. As a consequence, on June 25, St. Clair was ordered to move to Spithead and disembark his troops. Shortly after this was done, the government suddenly decided to reinforce the escort and send the expedition after all, under command of Admiral Lestock. St. Clair was informed that the attack on Quebec would be delayed until the following spring, but it was suggested that he might attack Crown Point on the western shore of Lake Champlain and hold it as an advance base for the ultimate attack on Montreal. Meanwhile, should d'Anville's fleet show aggressive tendencies and threaten the West Indies, Lestock was left at liberty to bring him to action if that were possible.

[47]*Ad. 1*, vol. 480, sec. I, Warren to Corbett (Secretary of the Admiralty), June 6, 1746.
    [48]*Ibid.*, Vice-Admiral Townsend (Commander-in-Chief of His Majesty's Ships in North America to the northward of Carolina) to Captain Harman, June 8, 1746 (copy).

So once again the now dispirited troops were marched on board
the transports, where they waited until the second week of August
for fair winds. But when at last fortune smiled on them, the ships
were in the middle of re-victualling, a process which consumed another twenty-four hours. Happily, the wind held, and they were just
rounding the foreland when the elements renewed their sport. A
rising headwind forced the expedition to return to the Isle of Wight.[49]

For the Pelham government this was the last straw. Admittedly,
sailing fleets were always at the mercy of the winds, and only an
early start (preferably in April) and more effective preparation could
have minimized this chronic evil. As it was, even had the weather
favoured, it may be questioned whether St. Clair's force would have
been strong enough for the work, even assuming that the three battalions at Louisbourg could have been added to his original force of
ten.[50] In the end "to save appearances, that the vast charges of our
naval armament this year may not seem to have been flung away,"
the expedition was diverted to the coast of Brittany, where a landing
was made at Quimperley Bay on September 26, followed by a sloven-
ly assault on Port Lorient.[51] On October 1, the troops were re-
embarked leaving behind them four pieces of cannon and a ten-inch
mortar, along with a variety of ammunition and stores.

Meanwhile, the French fleet had sailed for its rendezvous at
Chebucto Bay (later Halifax)on the east coast of Nova Scotia. Although the British Admiralty were aware that such an expedition
was planned—the first reports had been received in March— d'Anville was able to assemble his armada at Rochefort, and finally, on
June 22, escape to sea with a squadron of ten ships of the line, three
frigates, three bomb-vessels, and some sixty transports carrying 3,500
troops. That the expedition eventually failed in its purpose was
only indirectly due to British enterprise. Short of ships and be-
wildered by lack of information, the Admiralty's scheme of blockade
broke down hopelessly. The French too lacked information, but they
gambled with incredible audacity. As Admiral Richmond has well
said, without reconnaissance or scouting of any sort, without any
knowledge of British forces that might be in the way, d'Anville

[49]J. W. Fortescue, "A Side-Show of the Eighteenth Century," *Blackwood's
Magazine*, CCXXXIII, March, 1933.
[50]*Ibid.*
[51]See Williams, *The Life of William Pitt*, I, 164. An account of the expedition
is contained in the *Chatham Papers* (*G. & D. 8*) (London, Public Record Office).

sailed into an "uncommanded sea." Had the British forces been differently disposed, he might have been smashed at the start. Had a strong squadron of ships been maintained to westward with sufficient scouting frigates to watch the ports where the fleet was assembling, the French would have escaped only with the greatest difficulty.[52]

The French plan, conceived by Maurepas, was the reconquest of Louisbourg and Port Royal, and, time permitting, the destruction of Boston and the ravaging of the New England coast. To leave Louisbourg in the hands of the enemy was, in his view, as good as the abandonment of Quebec. Acadia and Cape Breton had to be secured for the proper protection of Canada. From the very beginning, however, ill fate dogged the expedition. Delayed since April, the hulls of many ships had become fouled, and the holds, thanks to neglect and bad administration, had been left unscoured to nourish the pestilences which bad food and scurvy were to initiate. The fact that d'Anville alone knew the nature of the sealed orders roused the suspicions of officers who detested the young admiral as an intruder from the galley corps. Certainly, d'Anville lacked experience, and his officers, most of whom possessed the bare minimum of sea-time, could contribute little either to discipline or to tactics.[53]

The Atlantic crossing occupied three months. After a rough passage through the Bay of Biscay, dead calms were encountered, followed by violent storms and lightning, which in one case led to a magazine explosion, resulting in thirty killed and wounded. Several transports foundered with all on board; two ships of the line were dismasted, and a third returned to Europe.[54] Towards the middle of September, the expedition sighted Acadia, but again gales scattered the squadron and convoy; two of the smaller vessels were thrown back to mid-Atlantic, and eventually made their way to Brest, the survivors of the crews half dead from hunger. On September 17, d'Anville began to reassemble his convoy in the Bay of Chebucto, but it was not until the 27th that all the surviving transports arrived, most of them in shattered condition. His fleet was now reduced to seven ships of the line, two frigates, one fireship, one bomb-ketch, twelve privateers, and eighteen transports—in all fifty-six sail. Moreover,

[52]Richmond, *The Navy in the War of 1739-48*, III, 8-17; see also *Naval Chronicle*, XII, 265-6.
[53]See Wood, *The Great Fortress*, 86; Tramond, *Manuel d'histoire maritime*, 379-80.
[54]Beatson, *Naval and Military Memoirs*, I, 323.

the expected reinforcements from the West Indies were not there to meet him. Admiral Conflans had arrived early in September with four ships of the line, but failing to find the main body, had returned home.

Five months of heart-breaking strain had at last found d'Anville in America, but he was in no condition to undertake a major operation. Already scurvy had broken out on board; unchecked by the simplest hygienic precautions, fever and the smallpox plague carried off in a few days 800 seamen and 1,500 soldiers.[55] By October 3,000 had died and only 1,000, one tenth of the survivors, were in efficient fighting shape. Himself weakened by fever and anxiety, d'Anville died of apoplexy on the night of September 26.[56] The command then devolved upon d'Estourmelles, commander of the *Trident*, who called a council of war to consider the future. An attack on Louisbourg was regarded as impracticable considering the reduced condition of the fleet and the lateness of the season. D'Estourmelles was, however, in favour of an immediate attack on Annapolis, a plan which the majority of the council opposed until the squadron had refitted. Whether or not d'Estourmelles, who appears to have been an impetuous man, attempted suicide in consequence of the rebuff is uncertain. French historians suggest he was suffering from fever and was delirious, which seems more likely. In any event, he did succeed in stabbing himself seriously with his own sword and, while the wound did not prove mortal, the command was passed to M. de la Jonquière.[57]

During these macabre proceedings, Massachusetts had not been unmindful of "the exposed and hazardous condition of the province of Nova Scotia," and early in September the governor was given permission to withdraw troops from the projected expedition to Crown Point, and to use them for the defence of Annapolis.[58] Having won over his own legislature, Shirley immediately began the laborious task of rousing his fellow governors, urging them to accelerate the recruitment of auxiliary forces, and painting lurid pictures of imminent peril.

[55]*Ibid.*, 324; cf. Lacour-Gayet, *La Marine militaire de la France sous le règne de Louis XV*, 183.

[56]Among the crews it was rumoured that he had ended his troubles by poison. For the drama of events see F. Parkman, *A Half Century of Conflict*, chap. xxi.

[57]See *Ad. 1*, vol. 480, sec. II, Captain John Rous to Admiral Townsend. October 17, 1746; also Beatson, *Naval and Military Memoirs*, I, 324.

[58]*Correspondence of William Shirley*, I, 350, Massachusetts General Court to William Shirley. being the address passed by the House of Representatives, September 10, 1746.

The loss of his Majesty's province of Nova Scotia [he wrote Governor Wentworth of New Hampshire] would be an event so fatal to his service in every respect and to the intended expedition for the reduction of Canada (if that should proceed next year) in particular, as the enemy by means of that acquisition would augment the number of their fighting men very considerably, and besides enabling them forthwith to break up the late Province of Maine, and very probably the whole Province of New Hampshire, within which limits is comprehended all the mast country in America (from whence His Majesty draws at present the whole supply of masts, yards, &ca, for his royal navy), would greatly endanger the safety of the other English colonies upon this continent, and even of the island of Cape Breton itself, the recovery of which would be facilitated to the enemy by their possession of Nova Scotia. . . .[59]

Meanwhile, in answer to the plaintive appeals of Lieutenant-Governor Paul Mascarene at Annapolis, Shirley hurriedly despatched 1,000 men, along with ordnance stores, and prevailed upon the obdurate commander at Louisbourg, Vice-Admiral Townsend, to spare one ship and a galley for the protection of the harbour. Whether or not d'Anville's expedition was capable of undertaking invasion operations, it was reliably reported that the French in Canada were on the move, and that de Ramesay was marching from Canada with 600 troops to the head of the Bay of Fundy to join forces with Micmacs and Abenaki under the Abbé le Loutre. Both Shirley and Warren were convinced that Annapolis would be the first objective, chiefly because of the presence of a friendly population of Acadians and Indians, of whom some five or six thousand might join the fight. Mascarene himself had no confidence in the local inhabitants "who will run away and give intelligence to the enemy as soon as his force appears."[60] ". . . His Majesties said French Subjects are esteem'd to be no less than 5000 fighting Men all Roman Catholicks and . . . may be said to be intirely [sic] devoted to the Interest of France."[61]

Apart from the makeshift works recently erected by New England forces at Canso, Annapolis provided the only adequate base of operations in the whole of Nova Scotia, and even here the policy of

[59]*Ibid.*, 351.
[60]*Ad. 1*, vol. 480, sec. II, Lieutenant-Colonel Paul Mascarene to Captain Collins, August 9, 1746; *ibid.*, Warren and Shirley to Townsend, Boston, September 12, 1746.
[61]"Representation of the State of His Majesty's Province of Nova Scotia and Fort and Garrison of Annapolis Royal, Drawn up by a Committee of Council and approv'd in Council," signed "P. Mascarene," Annapolis Royal, November 8, 1745, in *Documents Relating to Currency, Exchange and Finance in Nova Scotia, with Prefatory Documents, 1675-1758*, selected by Adam Shortt, completed with an introduction by V. K. Johnston, and revised and edited by Gustav Lanctot (Ottawa, 1933), 236-7.

laissez-faire had taken its toll. In 1744, according to Mascarene, it was "little better than a heap of rubbish"; by the time of the siege of Louisbourg, it could "be reckon'd a patch'd up unfinished Place, and not able to hold long against any vigorous regular attack." Despite occasional reinforcements from New England, the garrison had steadily diminished in numbers, and those who remained were "discontented, uneasy and desirous to be dismiss'd." Nor were there any vessels to defend the harbour, a condition which left the garrison "liable to be block'd up by a very insignificant force by Sea." Mascarene admitted that the reduction of Louisbourg had greatly added to the security of Annapolis, provided British squadrons kept up a constant patrol of the adjoining waters; nevertheless, "'tis well known how much we are expos'd in the naked Condition we now are in to a Surprise by Sea should the French be so lucky as to make use of this favourable Opportunity."[62]

By September, 1746, Mascarene's worst fears seemed to be realized. For the moment, the French were "Masters of the Seas here," and Admiral Warren could only hope that Admiral Lestock was already on the way with a larger force than the enemy.

God grant he may get in time, not only to disappoint our Enemy but to destroy them.—Neither their fleet nor ours will be able to keep the Sea here after next month, nor even till then, without great hazard; and it may be very naturally supposed, the French will then go to the West Indies, and destroy some of our Islands. . . .[63]

At that time, Warren could hardly know that the Lestock expedition had dwindled into a miserable sideshow in Brittany, or that storms and disease had drawn the teeth of the French armada.[64] Not until August 30 were the French ships reported off the coast of Nova Scotia, and for the next three weeks there was speculation on where they would land.[65] By September 14, when there was no sign of them either off Louisbourg or Annapolis, it was assumed that Chebucto Harbour would be the rendezvous.[66] Not until October 4 did news of d'Anville's disaster reach Annapolis,[67] and not till a week later did it percolate to Boston.

[62]Ibid., 237.

[63]Ad. 1, vol. 480, sec. II, Warren to Corbett, Boston, September 23, 1746.

[64]Ibid. In a letter dated October 1, from Boston, Warren still hoped for Lestock's appearance.

[65]See C.O. 5, vol. 901, 45, Admiral Townsend and Governor Charles Knowles to Governor Shirley and Admiral Warren, Louisburg, September 11, 1476.

[66]Ad. 1, vol. 480, sec. II, Warren to Corbett, Boston, October 1, 1746.

[67]Ibid., Captain Spry to Townsend, October 4, 1746.

Meanwhile, so long as the objective of the French remained in doubt, New England and Cape Breton fought for shares in the available defence forces. Fairly snug at Louisbourg with his small squadron riding in the harbour under the guns of the fort, Admiral Townsend had no wish to divide his strength by sending more ships and men to Annapolis.

You seem, Gentlemen, [he wrote Warren and Shirley in answer to their appeals] to be in a good deal of pain for Annapolis Royal; and I think with You, that that Place demands your greatest attention. I wish 'twas my power to give you that Assistance my Inclination leads me to; but if You'll consider the very few Ships I have here, and how much I'm prest by my Instructions . . . to have a careful attention to Louisburg, You'll perceive that this Place was the principal Object of the Government, when my Instructions were framed. . . .[68]

Messrs. Warren and Shirley *were* "in pain" for Annapolis, as they caustically advised the Louisbourg commander, "and in very little for Louisburg at this Season." Luckily they had been reinforced on October 1 by 250 colonial troops from New England, but even then the garrison was pessimistic about holding out against a combined attack by the forces now assembled at Minas and at Chebucto.[69] But Townsend rightly refused to send a small force "to be destroyed," by superior forces thus risking Louisbourg "which place the Government have so much at heart." He tried, nevertheless, to comfort Governor Mascarene with the advice that the French would hardly attack Annapolis without cannon, and that difficulties in the way of bringing heavy guns either from Minas or Chebucto made the scheme impracticable. Assuming the French gained even a temporary command of the sea, this hardly makes sense, and Townsend may have realized this, for he concluded with words of cold comfort which reflect the sense of security provided by his own rockbound haven; should the enemy "contrary to what I have suggested, attack Annapolis, you will receive supplies of men from Boston, as Governor Shirley and Admiral Warren are thoroughly acquainted with your situation, and the Posture of the Enemy's."[70]

As a matter of fact, even before news of the French disaster had arrived, Townsend was content; work on the fortifications had been completed, and they were "now in a much better state of defence"

[68]*Ibid.*, letter of September 23, 1746.
[69]See *ibid.*, Warren and Shirley to Townsend, October 3, 1746; also *ibid.*, Captain Spry of the *Chester* to Townsend, Annapolis Royal, October 3, 1746.
[70]*Ibid.*, October 3, 1746.

than they had ever been,[71] despite the undermanning of many of his ships, and the general poor health of garrison and crews.[72] However, beyond rumours of a great disaster at sea, nothing was known of French plans or the state of their fleet.   To ease the uncertainty and ". . . that we might not be ignorant what the Enemy are doing at Chibucto," wrote Admiral Townsend, "Mr. Knowles dispatch'd a Flag of Truce to the Duke D'Enville with forty Prisoners my Cruisers have taken at times, for the better Face, and withal . . . requesting an exchange. . . . [One] may reasonably expect the Duke to be a Man of Honour."[73] Although he had seen his two predecessors succumb in curious ways and watched disease and scurvy cut a rich harvest throughout his diminishing fleet, M. de la Jonquière, the new commander, remained a French gentleman of dignity and courtesy as well as courage. With delicate irony he replied: "You will not be surpris'd, Sir, that I have been oblig'd to detain Mr. Scott till my Departure from this Coast, as his Message seems to me a little suspicious and it being likewise natural in times of War to take all necessary precaution to prevent our Enemies having Intelligence of our Transactions."[74]

As a matter of fact, La Jonquière, even had he acted as a "Man of Honour," could have given little comfort to the inquisitive Townsend. Although smallpox was still rife, a council of war decided that Annapolis should still be the goal. With four ships of war and a few transports—all that were serviceable or that had not been turned into hospital ships—he set sail on October 13.   But misfortune, which never seemed to relax its grip on the doomed expedition, struck once again. Rounding Cape Sable the ships ran into another gale. The damage was not serious, but it was sufficient to end any thought of attack. La Jonquière made for Brest followed by his limping consorts.

The voyage home must have been a nightmare to the starving and typhus-ridden crews, who consumed even the rats in the holds, and in their delirium came close to cannibalism. After disembarking

[71] *Ibid.*, Townsend to Shirley and Warren, October 13, 1746.

[72] A good deal of the responsibility for illness can be laid at the door of contractors, whose unwholesome provisions spread disease and death throughout the Royal Navy until late in Nelson's time.   "Beef in particular," wrote Townsend, "is in very bad condition, being nothing but Mud, & Dirt; and they are now employ'd in overhauling it, washing it out from the Filth & repickling it; and 'tis a Query, when they have done so, whether it will prove fit for the Men to eat." *Ibid.*, Townsend to Charles Apthorp, Louisbourg, October 17, 1746.

[73] *Ibid.*, Townsend to Shirley and Warren, October 13, 1746.

[74] *Ibid.*, Letter of October 16, 1746.

his sick and clearing the wreckage, La Jonquière made his way to Marseilles to report his failure: 8,000 men dead, including the commander-in-chief, and none of the objectives attained. To the credit of the government, it may be said that no scape-goats were demanded. "Events," Maurepas remarked to the downcast admiral, "can diminish the glory of leaders, but they can diminish neither their work nor their merits."[75]

At Annapolis, Mascarene and his slender garrison rejoiced as well they might, for the threatened siege had been averted, and Annapolis was safe. Given better weather and an earlier passage, the tale might have been very different, especially if Louisbourg, which was by no means impregnable, had fallen in the early summer. Commodore Knowles (who succeeded Townsend after it was definitely known that the d'Anville expedition had returned to France) believed that the fortress must have succumbed had the French fleet arrived in August or before.[76] Yet even had Louisbourg held, Nova Scotia would still have been in danger, for only a British naval force could have brought relief, and the methods of government as revealed in the St. Clair expedition offered little encouragement that help would have arrived in sufficient strength and in time.

As it happened, Quebec had been spared for a year at least, and the great movement which Shirley had begun in 1745, and which he hoped might have been completed in 1746, had lost momentum.[77] A French fleet had succeeded temporarily in commanding colonial waters; the blockade of the St. Lawrence had been broken and the arrival of victuallers during the summer put new life into the Canadian capital. French squadrons still sailed to the West Indies, and France still planned to retrieve her lost possessions. Newcastle and Bedford favoured another attempt on Quebec in 1747, but Admiral Warren opposed this, and his alternative suggestions show a shrewd appreciation of the strategic scene in North America. Warren suggested the establishment of civil government in Cape Breton and the promotion of Protestant settlement, the landward blockade of Canada by means of blockhouses along the principal routes and passes, the erection of a fort at Halifax with a garrison of 500 men, and the permanent organization of four regiments for duty at Louisbourg. Lastly he advised the building of a flotilla on Lake Ontario

[75]Lacour-Gayet, *La Marine militaire de la France sous le règne de Louis XV*, 184.
[76]See Richmond, *The Navy in the War of 1739-48*, III, 48-9.
[77]See Brebner, *New England's Outpost*, 116.

in order to gain the mastery of the inland lakes, and thus prevent the French from maintaining communications with the Mississippi.[78]

But Warren's plan had only long-term significance. Not until the French were driven completely out of Nova Scotia could the English build a blockhouse on the isthmus. Although de Ramesay was not aware that the projected campaign against Quebec was to be abandoned for 1747, he had not given up hope of taking Annapolis, and he might have succeeded had La Jonquière's second expedition got through. On May 3, 1747, in attempting to bring a convoy to Quebec, the newly appointed governor of Canada was intercepted off Cape Ortegal by Admiral Anson with a greatly superior force. Outnumbered and outgunned, La Jonquière's thirteen armed ships fought hard but to no avail, and of some thirty-eight ships in convoy, only sixteen reached Quebec.[79] Had the whole convoy run the gauntlet, La Jonquière might well have attempted to reverse the verdict which fate had passed upon him in 1746.[80] As it was, had Britain been able in the following year to provide the troops and supplies for overseas service, she must have succeeded in taking Canada. Despite the escape of an occasional blockade-running squadron, Quebec could not have counted on sufficient supply to withstand a siege, and for lack of food and powder alone must sooner or later have surrendered.

In view of France's vast European gains, some French historians have called the Treaty of Aix la Chapelle, signed on October 18, 1748, a stupid and disastrous settlement.[81] In a foolish peace, French diplomacy, they say, threw away the advantages won for them by the generalship of Maurice de Saxe. On the other hand, some British historians attempt to explain it as a product of the enormous dislocation of French trade and industry with its disastrous effects on French finance. Cut off in whole or in part from such important sources of financial strength as the East and West Indies trade and the Canadian fisheries, France could no longer continue to support and pay her armies.[82]

[78]See Richmond, *The Navy in the War of 1739-48*, III, 50.

[79]*Ibid.*, 80n., and 89; also Tramond, *Manuel d'histoire maritime*, 380.

[80]*Correspondence of William Shirley*, I, 401-4, The possibility of renewed attack is suggested in the Duke of Newcastle's letter to Shirley, October 3, 1747.

[81]See Lacour-Gayet, *La Marine militaire de la France sous le règne de Louis XV*, 206.

[82]See Fayle, "Economic Pressure in the War of 1739-48," 445; see also *Cambridge Modern History* (Cambridge University Press, 1902-21), VI, 249, where the author asserts that "the recovery of naval supremacy by England was making

Such speculations are tempting; France was exhausted, and the War of the Austrian Succession had ended in unhappy stalemate. But there is no evidence to suggest that the denial of overseas commerce materially altered the French position on the continent; there was no "strangulation" by English sea power. The fact that a high total of French shipping was destroyed in the war, or that a large part of the French mercantile marine was unable to leave harbour as a result of a British blockade, means little unless the importance of overseas trade is measured against the national economy as a whole.[83] Admittedly the French colonial trade was an extremely valuable asset, but the whole course of French policy indicates emphatically that it was a buttress rather than a foundation. The real strength and vigour of France lay in a continental self-sufficiency that the Seven Years' War was clearly to demonstrate. France was to prove that a rich nation with the limited help of neutrals could live without colonial trade and still fight a war effectively.[84]

The French Ministry had to count on losing the war at sea; war without command of the sea had become almost an accepted part of French strategy since La Hogue. So long as France could retain her hold on the Low Countries, or better still, possess Hanover, she could always enter the market of peace negotiations with valuable bargaining counters. That she eventually lost an empire at the peace table, and took the first opportunity to win her revenge, does not alter the fact that French ministers, mercantilist philosophies notwithstanding, did not believe that overseas trade was the backbone of national strength. And the men who helped to make public opinion agreed. "Les princes," said Montesquieu, "ne doivent pas songer à peupler de grands pays par les colonies; l'effet des colonies est d'affaiblir le pays d'où on les tire, sans peupler ceux où on les envoie."[85]

---

itself felt in France through the heavy sufferings of the French mercantile marine, which was almost swept from the seas, with disastrous results to the French finances."

[83]Details of the number of ships captured or sunk are of little importance as evidence of the effectiveness of commercial war. Indeed, the British lost approximately 3,238 ships as compared with the combined enemy total of 3,434. (See Beatson, *Naval and Military Memoirs*, I, 414; and Richmond, *The Navy in the War of 1739-48*, III, 245-6). The significant consideration is not the total of losses, but the fact that in the later stages of the war, by their inability to command the sea, France and Spain could not afford to risk the bulk of their mercantile marine on the high seas.

[84]See R. Pares, *War and Trade in the West Indies, 1739-63* (Oxford, 1936), 392-3.

[85]Quoted in Lacour-Gayet, *La Marine militaire de la France sous le règne de Louis XV*, 15.

For France the empire was an important side-show. Though parts might be lost in the war at sea, thanks to the successes of marshals like de Saxe, they could be retrieved at the peace; and enraged New Englanders might have been somewhat appeased had they known that Britain would probably have been willing to surrender Madras as well as Louisbourg in order to dislodge the hereditary enemy from the Low Countries.

The recovery of Louisbourg by France, in 1748, while it could not assure the safety of Quebec, did compel the English to settle and fortify Chebucto Bay, where the first governor, Colonel the Honourable Edward Cornwallis arrived in 1749. Within three years, Halifax, so named in honour of the president of the Board of Trade, had some 4,000 inhabitants, as many as Louisbourg had received during a period of forty years.

VIII

Prelude to Conquest
1749-1757

THE Treaty of Aix-la-Chapelle, while it ended formal hostilities, was little more than a truce. In North America irregular warfare on the frontiers and along the Acadian coastline broke out as early as 1750, thus foreshadowing the Seven Years' War that was to embroil not only Europe and America but Asia as well. It was not, however, until Pitt won control of government, that the conquest of Canada became an avowed object of British strategy, and the Seven Years' War a war for empire. Samuel Johnson once remarked that Pitt had the uncanny power of setting the state in motion. Even to Johnson it was something of a miracle how, at the touch of a master hand, the ill-adjusted machinery could move with such precision.

One prime object of Pitt's plans was the relief of the American colonies by means of the conquest of Canada. To secure the British empire in America he aimed at destroying root and branch the maritime and colonial power of France. Men of the City of London who saw the Atlantic as the future medium of a great ocean commerce were behind him; but there were still influential groups in Parliament opposed to heavy overseas commitments. During the War of the Austrian Succession, as has been noticed, the British government had shown relative indifference to the acquisition of colonies. "The partisans of the Ministry," wrote Horace Walpole as late as 1755, "damn the Plantations, and ask if we are to involve ourselves in a War for them." Only the English colonists in America showed any eagerness for conquest, as the Louisbourg expedition had demonstrated, and their agents and some of their governors continued to urge upon the mother country the benefits which would result from the expulsion of the French from Canada.

But imperial thinking was still dominated by an almost exclusive concern with economic values; and Canada promised little in the way of returns except furs that were already being liberally supplied from New York and Hudson Bay. Moreover, according to mercantilist logic, overseas commerce could be most cheaply secured by means of outposts and factories supplied and defended by men-of-war. For this reason colonial defence had little to do with territorial expansion. "It was negative, the protection of already existing colonies whence came England's treasure in trade, the holding of what England had."[1]

In the early years of the war official and unofficial correspondence bear out the view that Britons were too absorbed in their own domestic concerns to pay much attention to the prospect of French colonial acquisitions. In the interval between the War of the Austrian Succession and the Seven Years' War, a few English periodicals had stressed the dangers of French imperialism in North America, and, to some extent, these accounts of American affairs may have awakened popular interest.[2] On the whole, however, colonial incidents were but straws in the wind that blew over Europe; to most men they merely reflected the basic clash of interests on the home front. Only a few, like William Pitt, were deeply concerned about the future of British North America and Canada.

Yet even Pitt looked at North America in terms of European interests. Admittedly, the war for empire overseas was the chief object of his plan of campaign; thanks to Frederick the Great, Pitt never had to maintain a continental army sufficient to do more than slightly occupy the French. It was overseas that he sent the cream of his forces, and had he possessed a Marlborough he would almost certainly have shipped him to North America or India. Nevertheless, his plan to wrest Canada from France was part of a larger strategy, and it must not be interpreted as a revolutionary effort to divorce British strategy and British foreign policy from Europe. Pitt's far-flung assault on French possessions all over the world was stimulated chiefly by an almost fanatical zeal to destroy France in Europe.[3]

[1]S. Pargellis, *Lord Loudoun in North America* (New Haven, Conn., 1933), 3.
[2]See C. F. Mullett, "James Abercromby and French Encroachments in America," *The Canadian Historical Review*, XXVI, March, 1945, p. 53.
[3]In the beginning of his ministry, Pitt did not consider the annexation of all Canada a necessary condition of peace. He merely wished the establishment of a satisfactory military frontier, and the rest of the colony, "was no more a *sina qua non* than Louisburg with its fisheries, Goree with its command of the slave trade, or even Guadaloupe itself." Parès, *War and Trade in the West Indies, 1739-1763*, 186.

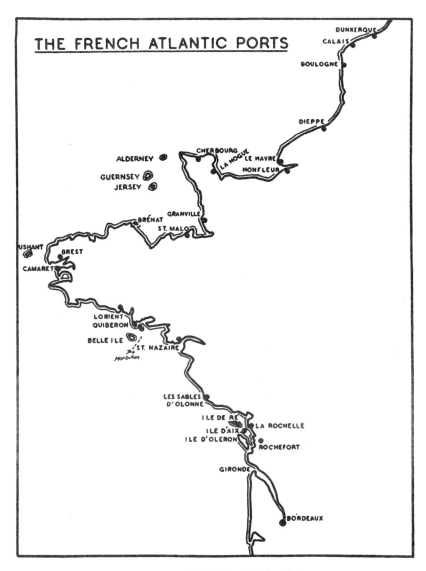

IV. THE FRENCH ATLANTIC PORTS

The sinews of Britain's strength as the mercantilists saw it, rested in trade, and Pitt believed that the key to Britain's survival as a nation lay in utilizing that strength to maintain the European balance. To achieve his purpose, he had to eliminate French maritime power, and this involved cutting off North America by sea.

Already by 1755 Britain was in a far better position to make an all-out offensive than at any time during the War of the Austrian Succession. Chastened by failure, the government allowed Admiral Anson to clean out the Augean stables of naval administration, and under his administration as First Lord the dockyards were reorganized, and the powers of corrupt vested interests cut away as far as was humanly possible.[4] Inept officers were ruthlessly weeded out, and subsequently, with Pitt's backing, Anson was responsible for the appointment of vigorous seamen to high command, admirals such as Hawke, Boscawen, Saunders, Rodney, Howe, and Keppel. The recruiting of seamen was accelerated by a system of bounties, while discipline, less happily reformed, was assured by rigorous amendments to the Articles of War, which remained essentially in force until 1865. With well over one hundred ships of the line Britain had a navy almost double that of France, and a slight superiority over Spain and France combined. By 1758, thanks to the efficiency which Anson introduced into naval administration, the projects of Pitt's churning mind were carried into rapid execution. Meanwhile, the steady development of the "Western Squadron" raised blockading to a fine art, and thus made possible the decisive actions off Lagos and Quiberon Bay.

It had long been an axiom of British policy that the Royal Navy should command the English Channel and its entrances, and that the hostile coasts of the western European promontory should be regarded strategically as the "British frontier." In other words, the seas about those coasts were to be considered as British territory which the enemy must be prevented at all costs from controlling or invading. This command could be achieved in two ways: either by destroying the main forces of the enemy, or if that was impossible by reason of his reluctance to risk decisive battle, by so disposing the fleet as to make it impossible for him to leave harbour without being brought to action by a superior British force. From this latter

[4]See W. V. Anson, *The Life of Admiral Lord Anson, The Father of the British Navy, 1697-1762* (London, 1912).

alternative derived the practice of blockade which demanded a constant predominance in western European waters. It followed obviously that dispersal to distant points was wrong if that predominance was in any way weakened.

This principle of "blockade" has been misinterpreted by some critics, who have argued that it favoured passive defence at the cost of the offensive spirit; that it involved "all the privileges of command of the sea without running the risks inseparable from battle."[5] Although "blockade" is difficult to define precisely, it was rarely, in British practice, a method of defensive warfare. Nelson pointed out its real purpose to the Lord Mayor of London, when acknowledging a vote of thanks passed by the Corporation in appreciation of his successful effort in the blockade of Toulon. "I beg to inform your Lordship, that the port of Toulon has never been blockaded by me: quite the reverse—every opportunity has been offered to the enemy to put to sea, for it is there that we hope to realize the hopes and expectations of our country, and I trust that they will not be disappointed."[6]

Sometimes, when British superiority was complete and unchallenged, orders were given for a *strict* blockade, but British fleets were seldom strong enough to maintain a prolonged "offensive" operation of this sort. Ordinarily blockade amounted to a "close watch," as Nelson explained to the Lord Mayor. To make that action effective, a fleet more efficient or numerically stronger than the enemy had to be maintained on guard. With the exception of the War of American Independence, when lack of numbers was responsible for faulty execution, all the wars subsequent to that of the Spanish Succession were conducted in the light of this doctrine. "Whatever the number of ships needed to watch those in an enemy's port," said Mahan, "they are fewer by far than those that will be required to protect the scattered interests imperilled by the enemy's escape."[7]

It is clear, however, in view of the intense strains imposed on the blockader, that the first desire of the Admiralty was to end such nerve-racking vigils by bringing the enemy to decisive engagement.

[5]An acute analysis of this issue is contained in H. Rosinski's article, "Command of the Sea," *Brassey's Naval Annual, 1939,* 89.
[6]Although "blockade" has become the common term used by Mahan, Colomb, and other naval historians, it is not strictly correct. Technically it means the prevention of ingress or egress or, in the words of an Admiralty declaration of 1756, "a detention of the enemy's strength in their ports."
[7]*Journal of the Royal United Service Institution,* "Blockade in Relation to Naval Strategy," XXXIX, November, 1895, 1061.

Unfortunately for eager British captains, French naval strategy after La Hogue had become increasingly defensive in general purpose, and more and more tied to the policy of a "fleet in being."[8] Inferiority in numbers bred an obstinate scepticism of the effectiveness of sea battle, and encouraged the husbanding of existing resources. Indeed, the more one studies French naval history, the more it becomes clear that the French problem was almost as much psychological as material. The reasons for the failure of France at sea are multiple, and most of them can be estimated; but one determining factor lies in the region of imponderables—the growth of the *defensive* spirit. In the course of many indecisive engagements, the French counted themselves victorious if they saved their ships, much in the manner of the Germans after Jutland. Seamen like Suffren occasionally rebelled, but ordinarily policy and poverty dictated caution in the presence of numerically superior forces, and elevated prudence as a virtue above audacity. By the middle of the eighteenth century the art of sparing ships had become firmly welded into French strategic doctrine.[9]

The tragedy of inflexible doctrine was that it inevitably turned potentially bold and intelligent seamen into the puppets of a system. Before his departure from Toulon in March of 1756, La Galissonnière received the following instructions.

The object that he must keep always foremost in his mind is the preservation of the forces which His Majesty has detailed for this expedition. It is with this end in view, that His Majesty wishes him to direct all operations necessary to attain the required objectives. The intention of His Majesty is that neither his squadron nor his troops should be risked against superior forces.[10]

Assuming that command of the sea by means of offensive operations was now beyond reach, such a defensive attitude is understandable, and in retrospect, it was probably wise. Had the French staked all on a decisive fleet action in the beginning of the war,

[8]See Chap. IV, pp. 62-3.
[9]Because the offensive spirit demanded offensive tactics, the *Ordonnance* of 1765 forbade specifically any suggestion of independent effort that involved risk. In the entire official act, according to Admiral Castex, there was no mention of the principle of concentration on "fragments" of the enemy, a principle in essence superior to that of simple manœuvre. "To attack 'in line,' " he wrote, ". . . is admittedly a form of naval tactics, rudimentary it is true, but still tactics. But to attack by combining total strength at one point shows inspiration . . . even though to concentrate one must, in the majority of cases, sacrifice the 'line-of-battle.' " Castex, *Les Idées militaires de la Marine*, 66.
[10]*Royal Instructions*, March 22, 1756; quoted in Castex, op. cit., 42.

Canada might have fallen two years earlier. By avoiding offensive operations which involved the risk of decisive battle and final defeat, the French were able during five North American campaigns to prolong the contest for three years, during which time they could conceivably count on territorial gains in Europe to serve as bargaining pawns at the peace.[11] Furthermore, the failure of the Royal Navy (with few exceptions) to bring the French to battle forced a policy of blockades and "close watches," and the disposition of so many ships of the line before Toulon and Brest, by consuming men and ships, obviously increased the opportunities for French raiders to inflict injury on British commerce.

In this sense, blockade was bound to place Britain on the defensive strategically. When Mahan remarked that France, despite her maritime weakness, possessed certain advantages of the offensive, he was thinking in terms of "breaking" the blockade.[12] Whereas a French squadron or fleet might escape, let us say, to North America, it was not always expedient to give chase for fear the detachment of a British force might so weaken the Home Fleet as to endanger the security of the Channel. Hence, if a substantial division of the French fleet managed to get away, it could hold the initiative in overseas theatres until tracked down by a superior British force. Moreover, since the French navy was usually redistributed at the beginning of every campaign, the British could never be quite sure whether the various squadrons would be eventually concentrated at Brest, Lorient, or Rochefort, and after that, what would be their ultimate destination overseas. If the Royal Navy divided its forces and watched all three, it might fail to deal competently with a strong concentration issuing from one. On the basis of experience the Admiralty had been inclined to put most effort into watching Brest, with the result that groups from Lorient or Rochefort were bound to get away occasionally.[13] Indeed, in the forties it became a habit for French squadrons to steal out of port and elude superior English forces; and what is impressive is not so much the fact that they got away, but rather the remarkable punctuality with which they effected their rendezvous before crossing the Atlantic.

During the War of the Austrian Succession, the system of blockade by means of squadrons based on home ports proved to be too spasmodic in application and too loose in texture to guarantee the

[11]See J. S. Corbett, *Some Principles of Maritime Strategy* (London, 1911), 211-12.
[12]Mahan, *Types of Naval Officers*, 180.
[13]See R. Castex, *Théories stratégiques* (4 vols., Paris, 1931), III, 223.

immunity of British North American possessions. Even at Brest it had been impossible to prevent the exit of reinforcing expeditions for Canada. How could Anson and his captains, with some seventy-eight ships of the line, keep a continuous guard over more than seventy in the hands of France and Spain? True, the enemy allies were split by the Bay of Biscay, and concentration was difficult. On the other hand, even the greatest economy could not provide a comprehensive blockade force constantly equal to the largest force the French could put to sea from any one port.

To maintain even a small squadron at sea in constant fighting trim demanded a high standard of repair and replacement. The English sailors were ordinarily better seasoned than the French, and despite the awful food and cramped living conditions were usually healthier than the French and better able to withstand long periods at sea. But British ships, because they saw more continuous service, were rarely in as good condition as the French. In the days before copper sheathing, bottoms fouled rapidly, with consequent loss of speed and manœuvrability. Moreover, cruising in all weathers wore out hulls and masts and played havoc with rigging. Under the circumstances, ships had to return to port frequently to be cleaned, repaired, and sometimes completely refitted, and many extra ships had to be available in order that a force superior to anything that the enemy might possibly send out could take to sea ready for action. During the winter of 1746-7 Anson brought his ships and crews to the point of exhaustion, and when the time for refitting was at last forced upon him, despite his utmost endeavours, the squadron was not ready for action until late spring.[14]

There was no division of opinion in the Admiralty as to the necessity of keeping a permanent watch on enemy ports. The real difference of opinion lay in the manner with which the watch should be conducted—by frigates alone or by frigates closely supported by ships of the line. It could be asserted that since a blockade even with vastly superior forces could not be made air-tight, it was sufficient to have small cruising squadrons on patrol. These could be reinforced in the event of any large-scale French movements; unhampered by transports they could take up the pursuit, and with any luck would reach the threatened area overseas before serious damage had been done. Furthermore—and apart from strategical considerations —any decision to weaken overseas stations in order to devote a

[14]Richmond, *The Navy in the War of 1739-48*, III, 78.

larger proportion of the best ships of the line and frigates to the wear and tear of ceaseless blockade in all weathers was bound to encounter heavy political opposition.

For these reasons, the system of a strong permanent guard over the chief enemy ports was never actually put into practice. Instead of expending large ships on close blockade, Anson and Hawke, recognizing the fundamental importance of containing the enemy within the Channel or the Mediterranean, planned a continuous distant blockade based on systematic reliefs from British ports. The new idea was publicly explained in 1756, and the writer was probably Anson:

> Our colonies are so numerous and so extensive that to keep a naval force at each equal to the united force of France would be impracticable with double our Navy. The best defence therefore for our Colonies as well as our coasts is to have such a squadron always to the Westward as may in all probability either keep the French in port or give them battle with advantage if they come out.[15]

While some naval historians put the origin of the "Western Squadron" as far back as 1739,[16] the force of that time was not strong enough either in numbers or replacements to perform the task which strategists like Anson demanded of it. During the War of the Austrian Succession, it rarely consisted of more than ten ships of the line and even when strengthened in moments of emergency was never in a position to deal with any concentration of enemy forces. French convoys still sailed to the West Indies and often returned unmolested; D'Anville took two expeditions across the Atlantic without being intercepted.

In the manner of Admiral Sir John Fisher in the early years of the twentieth century, Anson fought successfully for a concentration that should be able to deal expeditiously with the strongest enemy force in the decisive theatre, whether fleet, squadron, or convoy. Under his administration, an effective "Western Squadron" grew yearly, and the wisdom of his policy revealed itself in the last two years of the Seven Years' War, when the French convoys to Canada almost disappeared from the seas.

[15]Quoted in H. W. Richmond, *National Policy and Naval Strength* (London, 1928), 346.

[16]It is possible to find a precedent as early as 1673, when Charles II stationed cruisers to protect the trade passing through the Channel, and in the latter days of William III and during Anne's reign it was customary to earmark ships to cruise as a Western or Soundings squadron in defence of trade. See J. H. Owen, *War at Sea under Queen Anne, 1702-1708* (Cambridge University Press, 1938), 68-9.

Admittedly, within North America, France had the superior military organization—a cadre of professional soldiers under centralized authority—and some French historians have gone so far as to say that, granted a more enterprising naval policy and a more consistent colonial policy, French dominion might have been preserved.[17] But such an achievement must have depended on the ability of New France to attain security in the economic as well as in the military sense, and economic security meant primarily control of communications to the mother country. If France could for a time place overseas interests ahead of European, command of the sea was a not unreasonable possibility. Such was the point of view, not merely of visionaries, but of calculating statesmen like Choiseul.

Like Richelieu, Choiseul recognized the peculiarly potent leverage exerted by sea power, since "this it is which enables His Majesty to sustain numerous armies for the defence of his allies, as it is the maritime power of England which to-day arms so many enemies against them and against France."[18]

We must not deceive ourselves [he wrote to the ambassador at Stockholm in 1759]. The true balance of power really resides in commerce and in America. The war in Germany, even though it should be waged with better success than at present, will not prevent the evils that are to be feared from the great superiority of the English on the sea. The king will take up arms in vain. For if he does not have a care, he will see his allies forced to become, not the paid auxiliaries of England, but her tributaries, and France will need many a Richelieu and Colbert to recover, in the face of her enemies, the equality which she is in peril of losing.[19]

As a matter of fact, the French navy had already begun to make another of its periodic recoveries. French losses during the War of the Austrian Succession had been severe, but not devastating;[20]

[17]See Lacour-Gayet, La Marine militaire de la France sous le règne de Louis XV (1902), 177-8.
[18]Recueil des instructions données aux Ambassadeurs et Ministres de la France depuis les Traités de Westphalie jusqu'à la Révolution française, ed. A. Sorel (Paris, 1884), I, 386; quoted in E. S. Corwin, French Policy and the American Alliance of 1778 (Princeton, 1916), 33.
[19]Quoted in M. de Flassan, Histoire générale et raisonnée de la diplomatie française depuis la fondation de la monarchie jusqu'à la fin du règne de Louis XVI (7 vols., 2nd ed., Paris, 1811), VI, 160.
[20]French losses had been: 23 ships, 9 frigates, 6 corvettes, and 3 large store ships. In 1748, the effective force consisted of 30 ships of the line in good repair, of which 9 were at sea and 21 in port; in addition 19 light frigates and 10 ships were in course of construction. All told, there was a total of 45 to 50 ships of high rating, a number hardly less than that before the outbreak of war in 1744. Lacour-Gayet, La Marine militaire de la France sous le règne de Louis XV, 208-9.

there remained a foundation to build on. Realizing that the Treaty of Aix-la-Chapelle represented only a truce, Comte de Maurepas, the Minister of Marine, laid down a programme of reconstruction which called for 110 ships of the line and 54 frigates within ten years. Owing to the interference of Mme de Pompadour, he was disgraced and dismissed, but his successors while far from brilliant were conscientious. Between 1749 and 1754, 38 ships were built; by 1756, there were nearly 70 ships of the line ready for sea.

But morale did not keep pace with construction. Lack of pay and bad food encouraged desertions, and not infrequently pressed men had to be taken in chains to the ports of embarkation. The situation was worsened by bad discipline in the officer class. This was hardly comparable to the demoralization which followed the French Revolution; none the less, jealousies between the professional *grand corps* and the volunteer *officiers bleus* worked against efficiency, especially during operations. As a consequence, even with the resources placed at their disposal, the few great and heroic captains could accomplish little in the face of slackness and irresolution on the part of their subordinates. In 1755, 700 officers out of 900 were serving in shore establishments, which may explain certain disastrous faults of judgment that were to play into the hands of the more seasoned English captains and their crews.[21]

Hence, because France was not in a position to challenge British command of the sea, the position of French possessions overseas remained precarious. Cut off from regular home sources of supply, New France was bound sooner or later to face starvation; indeed, during the latter stages of the war, many of the French forts in Canada surrendered with hardly a shot fired. The fact that three bootless expeditions against Quebec were made in 1690, 1711, and 1746, indicates apathy on the part of British governments rather than any real ability on the part of Canada to resist. Had British governments resolved to take the colony, they might have done so at any time after 1692; but their ambitions stopped with the North American shore line, and even sea-girt Louisbourg, which the New Englanders captured in 1745, was held to be more important as a diplomatic lever to release the Netherlands from French control than as a potential key to the St. Lawrence.

In retrospect, neither revised strategy nor heightened morale could have compensated France for the preponderant weight of

²¹See Tramond, *Manuel d'histoire maritime*, 398.

British sea power. As a fight for empire, the Seven Years' War was a one-sided struggle. British command of the sea, based on numerical superiority, assured the safety of the home country while it isolated the colonies of France. As long as the French could be hemmed in their European harbours, Britain could ensure safe passage to her small armies, and carry out those combined amphibious operations which were to place Wolfe on the Plains of Abraham.

Meanwhile, the unsettled no man's land in North America—that area of wilderness which hitherto had separated French and British territories—had begun to melt away under the impetus of French expansionist policy. Forts began to spring up on every important strategic river in the Ohio Valley and to the southward, scattered thinly as far as the Gulf of Mexico. Loosely but pugnaciously the French closed in on the Thirteen Colonies in an attempt to cut them off from the traffic of the Great Lakes and the Mississippi River.

While appearances suggested an aggressive role, fundamentally, French strategy was concerned with defence. Since Champlain's day, the Canadians had overrun a territory larger than the whole of Europe; and while this pushing of the frontier west and north enabled them momentarily to outstrip the English in the fur trade, they lacked the numbers to give their claims anything but paper validity. In terms of empire, the millions of acres between the Mississippi and Ohio rivers and Hudson Bay were scarcely more than a precarious option. Furthermore, with the loss of Acadia, the colony was now almost encircled by the English. Apart from its productive value as a fishing area, Acadia had flanked the route up the St. Lawrence to Quebec. Defensively, Louisbourg remained of little more than symbolic value. Sustenance in terms of reinforcements and supplies still depended upon the ability of the mother country to maintain constant communications, a task impossible to perform in time of war without command of the sea.

Hence the object of the French in Canada was to fight for time, until the war in Europe had been settled in their favour. In this design, geography was with them. New France was well placed to resist any British effort to roll up the interior approaches to Quebec and Montreal. Access from the interior could be obtained only by two water routes—Lake Champlain and the Richelieu River, or from the Upper Ohio to Lake Ontario—and these the French could control by a series of fortified posts. From the sea, Quebec had been approached three times without success, and optimistic French leaders (Montcalm was not one of them) continued to put faith in the natural hazards of St. Lawrence River navigation.

To the eastward, in Acadia, further preparations had been made. In 1749 the Chevalier de la Corne was entrusted by the Governor of Canada, M. de la Galissonnière, with the task of building or repairing forts on both sides of the Isthmus and on the Bay of Fundy at the mouth of the St. John River. Apart from securely blocking the English within the peninsula, the new fortifications helped the French to maintain all-year communications with Louisbourg by sea, and gave them complete command of the fur and timber trade of the St. John valley.

Built on a high hill overlooking the marshy lands of the Bay of Fundy, Fort Beauséjour was a stout earthwork fort of five bastions faced with timber and surrounded by a deep ditch. The normal garrison was 80 to 100 regulars, but according to British intelligence reports the fort had recently been reinforced by some 300. Gaspereau, on the east side of the isthmus at Baie Verte, was a palisaded depot rather than a regular fort, but its strategic position on the Gulf between Louisbourg and Quebec, and the neighbouring presence of some 1400 Acadians and loyal Indians made it a post of considerable consequence.[22]

The British had built Fort Lawrence to checkmate Beauséjour, but Fort Lawrence remained essentially an outpost on the edge of a foreign land, always on the defensive and in constant danger of combined attack by French and Indians. Annapolis Royal, on the east coast of the Bay of Fundy, was in a different position. Its fate was reasonably secure so long as Britain retained command of the Bay and maintained in Europe a sufficiently close blockade to prevent a second d'Anville from bursting into the Atlantic. Land communications with Halifax, some 160 miles away, were not good, and the garrison was always seriously undermanned, but its fine harbour made it an attractive port for refitting, as well as an excellent base of operations against smugglers and interlopers in the Bay.[23]

Annapolis Royal was never intended as a rival to Louisbourg. That challenging role was given to Halifax, which had been specially

---

[22]See Beatson, *Naval and Military Memoirs*, I, 418; *Selections from the Public Documents of the Province of Nova Scotia*, ed. T. B. Akins (Halifax, 1869) hereinafter referred to as *Akins Collection*, "Remarks on the State of the Isthmus of Chignecto"; also, "Forts on the Isthmus of Chignecto" pp. 403-5.
[23]*Ibid.*, 403.

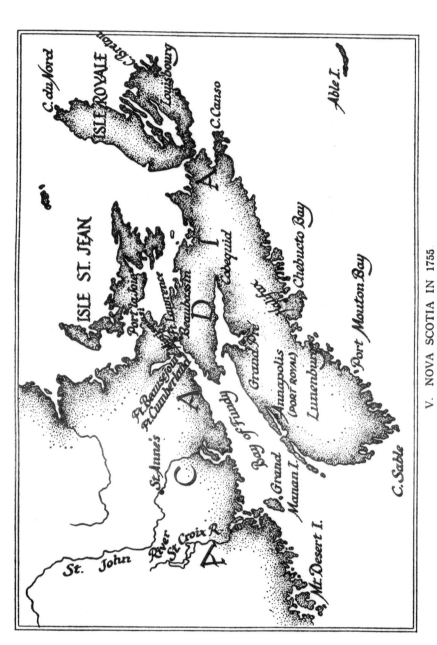

V. NOVA SCOTIA IN 1755.

designed as the guardian of the Gulf and the North Atlantic trade and fisheries.

> . . . it is easy to judge that it [the soil] did not at all enter into consideration in the establishing of this place [wrote a French visitor of legal attainments in 1793]. What determined making it the capital of Nova Scotia is the excellence of the port, placed in front of the possessions remaining to England in North America. She has there the arsenal for all the colonies and there can be seen large and splendid magazines stocked with artillery, and with all kinds of war munitions, others with masts, ropes and gear for the repair of ships. The islands of Newfoundland of Cape Breton, and Canada are all within range of obtaining there everything they need for their defence.[24]

With periodic injections of British emigrants, the settlement, following its establishment in 1749, grew quickly. But, as with St. John's in Newfoundland, local defences never kept pace with the developing strategic importance of the port.[25] By 1754 the garrison of less than 400 was well below strength, and the incompleted batteries above the harbour lacked sufficient guns.[26] Isolated by sea and land from the New England colonies to the south-west, and incapable of making more than gestures of defence, Halifax remained utterly dependent on British command of North American waters.

During the last months of armistice that preceded the opening of continuous campaigns in 1755, the small British garrisons awaited with apprehension, if not dread, the coming of the raiders from over the ocean. New England was much more concerned with the military threat from Lake Champlain region than with any attack on the Atlantic sea face. Nevertheless, the coast from Boston to Portsmouth was hardly less vulnerable than the indented shore-line

---

[24]From the "Journal of our navigation leaving from the port of Falmouth in England to that of Halifax in Nova Scotia, 12 June, 1793," by Bénigne Charles Fevret de Saint-Mesmin, *Report of the Department of Public Archives for the year 1946*, xxv.

[25]   *Halifax Stationed Ships 1755*

State and condition of Ships and Vessels under command of Richard Spry Esq., Captain of Fougueux in Halifax Harbour, December 8, 1755:

Fougueux — unrigged.
Success — leaky in upper works.
Norwich — dismantled.
Litchfield — (no note)
Centurian — unrigged.
Small vessels:
Otter — fit for sea.
Vulture — unrigged.

Apart from the *Otter*, the remainder were not reported fit for sea until July 26, 1756. (*Ad. 1*, vol. 480, sec. VI.)

[26]*Acts of the Privy Council, Colonial Series*, IV, 245-6.

from Halifax to Annapolis, and a sudden swoop into these commercially rich waters seemed, in view of recent French encroachments on land, a dramatic but not unreasonable stroke to mark the opening of formal war.

> . . . if Nova Scotia should be lost by any sudden blow, [declared Governor Shirley of Massachusetts in November, 1754] the Eastern parts of the Province of Massachusetts Bay, and the whole Province of New Hampshire (within wch. Tracts of Territory are included the Woods from whence the Royal Navy is now supply'd with Masts, yards and Bowsprits) together with the Rivers of St. John's, Pentagoet and Kennebeck, and all the Sea coast as far as Merrimack River with the whole fishery to the Westward of Newfoundland must soon fall into the possession of the French most likely in the same Spring and if they should hold these acquisitions together with Canada and Louisburg that they would then have it in their power to assemble and support a very large body of Regular Troops in these Parts (wch. they cant possibly do long at present) and by the Situation of their New Sea Coast abounding with most Commodious Harbours for the largest ships of war, perhaps be able to dispute the mastery of the Eastern part of the Atlantick Ocean wth. the British Navy.[27]

On land the lines of contact fluctuated month by month, as probing raids or scouting expeditions bent or wrinkled the frontiers and prepared the way for the final clash. In the Ohio region, the French steadily unrolled their network of forts, sometimes slashing savagely at advanced English outposts. On July 4, 1753, George Washington had abandoned Fort Necessity, leaving the Ohio Valley to the enemy, who promptly built Fort Duquesne at the junction of the Ohio and the Monongahela Rivers. To the east, there was good evidence to suggest that the French intended "to make themselves masters of the Bay of Fundy."[28] At the same time, both sides took steps to reinforce their arms in America. Early in 1755 a small squadron under Commodore Keppel set sail with a detachment of 400 men under General Braddock. To counter this move, the French organized an expeditionary force of some seventeen ships of war, under Lieutenant General du Bois de la Motte, with transports to carry 3,000 men to Canada. The regiments were embarked at Brest on April 15, 1755.

No sooner had the news of the project reached England than the British Ministry ordered the immediate preparation of a squadron "to fall upon any French ships of war that shall be attempting to

[27]*Akins Collection*, 387, Extract from a letter to Sir Thomas Robinson, November 11, 1754.

[28]See *Akins Collection*, 401, Governor Lawrence to Lords of Trade, January 12, 1755; see also, Brebner, *New England's Outpost*, 176.

land troops in Nova Scotia or to go to Cape Breton or through the St. Lawrence to Quebec."[29] The command was given to Admiral Edward Boscawen, who had seen service in all parts of the globe and had earned the high esteem of such discriminating seamen as Anson and Vernon. Boscawen managed to get a head start on the Brest fleet, and he was followed almost immediately by an additional squadron under Francis Holburne. When the two eventually joined forces, Boscawen's total amounted to fifteen ships of the line.

Formal warfare had not yet been declared; there was no thought of bringing the French to engagement in the Channel, and the French ambassador was blandly assured that Admiral Boscawen had no instructions to undertake offensive operations. As a matter of fact, Boscawen did intend to destroy the French fleet if opportunity offered; his only anxiety was that he might be unable to find the French commander, whose ultimate destination had been kept a closely guarded secret.

Although there was no certainty of French intentions, Boscawen believed that Halifax, in view of its depleted strength, was the enemy's goal.[30] However, on arrival at Halifax, further information suggested that a landing on the shores of Newfoundland, near Cape Race, was the more probable,[31] and in that area he prepared to take up station. At one time, Boscawen seems to have sighted a French fleet off the Banks, but lost it in the fog. Search proving vain (apart from the capture of two stragglers), he joined Holburne close by Louisbourg in late June. But once again his prey had eluded him. Only four ships and two frigates lay within the harbour, sufficient evidence to justify the assumption that "Mons. Bois de la Motte is gone into the Gulph of St. Lawrence."[32] While Braddock was marching to disaster in the wilderness to the south, de la Motte had landed his forces at Quebec, and then, evading not only Boscawen's squadron (which once more lay in wait for him off the St. Lawrence), but also the Western Squadron under Admiral Hawke, had returned to France. To add to British chagrin, a second expedition managed to escape from Brest, carrying with it 1000 highly trained professional soldiers led by one of the great strategists in North American history, the Marquis de Montcalm.

[29]Quoted in McLennan, *Louisburg*, 195.
[30]See *Ad. 1*, 481, sec. I, Edward Boscawen to John Clevland (Secretary to the Admiralty), November 15, 1755.
[31]*Ibid.*
[32]*Ibid.*, Boscawen to Clevland, *Torbay* off Louisbourg, June 22, 1755.

During this time, Governor Lawrence of Nova Scotia was being urged by his distant neighbour, William Shirley, to assault the French forts on the Acadian Isthmus. Shirley was a lawyer "who had long burned to exchange the pen for the sword," and his boundless energy, characterized by an uninhibited contempt for red tape, had been for many years the scourge of colonial officialdom in England. As commander-in-chief of the British forces in North America he was able to infuse his colleagues, both military and administrative, with something of his own tempestuous spirit, and until petty politics forced his resignation, he showed an appreciation of the broad strategic situation which his successors, Abercrombie, Webb, and Loudon, did not always manifest. Shirley wanted to break the Isthmus defences, and safeguard the Bay of Fundy lines of communication with New England.

Early in June 1755, Commodore Keppel was prevailed upon to supply three ships under Captain Rous, with 2,000 troops under the command of Lieutenant-Colonel Monckton to drive the French from Beauséjour. Ascending the Missaguash River to Fort Lawrence, the British troops were able to consolidate themselves with little difficulty on the Cumberland ridge above the fort, and thus sever French communications from the rear. After a brief siege, accompanied by heavy mortar bombardments, Beauséjour capitulated on June 17. Two days later, the British took Gaspereau on Baie Verte, and on the 29th the French themselves blew up their fort on the St. John, retreating some twenty-five miles up the river.[33] Monckton had accomplished with ease what Montcalm was to achieve on Lake Champlain, the control of a valuable defensive line of communications. ". . . this last acquisition," wrote Boscawen to the Admiralty, "has put us in possession of the Whole bay of Fundi, without which the Colony of Nova Scotia can never flourish."[34] By this offensive, not only had the pressure on the whole peninsula been relieved, but the links had been broken which joined the Chignecto forts with the French settlements on the St. John River as well as those between Baie Verte, Louisbourg and Quebec, whence the enemy had been

[33] *Ibid.*, Captain John Rous to Edward Boscawen, Annapolis, July 8, 1755 and Boscawen to Clevland, Halifax, July 12, 1755, also Lieutenant-Colonel Robert Monckton's "Journal of the Expedition against Beauséjour Fort," in J. C. Webster, *The Forts of Chignecto: A Study of the Eighteenth Century Conflict between France and Great Britain in Acadia* (Shediac, N.B., 1930), 110-16.
[34] *Ad. 1*, 481, sec. I, Boscawen to Clevland, July 12, 1755.

wont to draw supplies and from which points the province was most exposed to attack.[35]

Assuming that the men and the ships were available, the British were now in a position from the north side of the Isthmus to intercept the traffic which flowed between Cape Breton and Quebec. Across the neck, the captured Beauséjour, renamed Cumberland, was now unchallenged from the rear, and could serve as base for communications with the New England colonies through the Bay of Fundy.[36] The potential danger arising from the activities of some 10,000 "neutral Acadians" had been removed, temporarily at least, by their removal and distribution among American colonies in the south.

Boscawen and Holburne cruised in the Gulf until late in the autumn, and managed to collect fourteen provision ships. Owing to sickness it was difficult to keep a sufficient squadron off Louisbourg. "Those that recover of the fever," wrote Boscawen, "fall down with the scurvy."[37] However, never more than two ships of war were observed in the harbour after de la Motte's return to France, and Boscawen was able to return most of the ships (which had gathered at Halifax from all parts of the coast) to their various stations.[38] On October 19, he set sail for England, leaving a small force of five ships to winter in Halifax, with orders to proceed to the Gulf at the earliest possible moment to prevent any supplies of men or provisions from reaching Quebec.[39] Constant westerly winds prevented Holburne from joining his chief at Halifax and forced him to seek refuge in Newfoundland, whence he too returned to England with crews badly weakened by disease.[40]

It was Boscawen's design, as we have noticed, to watch Louisbourg and in the following spring to block the Gulf before the French could reach it. The probability of an attempt to retake former French holdings on the St. John River also forced the admiral to keep an eye on the Bay of Fundy, and directions were given that all stationed ships on the North American coast—chiefly frigates and

[35]See *Akins Collection*, 433, Governor Shirley to Governor Lawrence, Boston, March 13th, 1756.
[36]*Ibid.*, 433.
[37]*Ad. 1*, 481, sec. I, to Clevland, June 22, 1755.
[38]*Ibid.*, to Clevland, November 15, 1755.
[39]*Ibid.*, Boscawen to Captain Richard Spry, Commander-in-Chief of H.M. Ships in North America, October 19, 1755.
[40]*Ibid.*, Boscawen to Clevland, November 15, 1755.

sloops—should repair to Halifax in April. Commodore Spry, who took over the command after Boscawen's departure, was in no position to create more than a diversion in the face of a large fleet; he was short of complement and he lacked pilots who knew the Gulf. Nevertheless, he was ready for sea by the end of April, 1756, and prepared to cruise between Louisbourg and Cape Ray (Newfoundland), the likeliest area in which to intercept the French supply ships.[41] Beset by fogs, scurvy, and all manner of fluxes, which turned some of his ships into floating hospitals, Spry maintained his arduous vigil, and he was able to capture two men-of-war before turning over the command in June to Commodore Charles Holmes.[42]

In the meantime, several of the assembled stationed ships had been sent to cruise in the Bay of Fundy, not only as a precaution against raiders from overseas—for formal war had been declared in May, and there were rumours that a French fleet was on its way—but to impress the "neutral Acadians," whom Governor Lawrence suspected of returning from the southern colonies in great numbers.[43] Nova Scotia was ill-prepared for trouble. The colonial troops refused any close co-operation with the regular forces, and 900 New Englanders had already been withdrawn homeward.[44] Fortunately, no French fleet was able to undertake offensive operations in northern waters during the year 1756. Holmes had a brush with one small squadron—two ships of the line and two frigates—which successfully entered Louisbourg harbour; but by the end of August the danger was passed. Using the time-honoured pretence of sending an observer under a flag of truce he discovered that all French ships of war had left Louisbourg for Europe.[45]

Until November, Holmes dispersed his fleet on patrol and raiding tasks around the Gulf. The nets were well spread and included the Bay of Gaspé, the coastline of Anticosti Island and the lower reaches of the River St. Lawrence, where he hoped not only to destroy the fisheries, and capture any tardy supply ships, but "to alarm them so as to Cause their keeping a strong Garrison at Quebec."[46] Mean-

[41]*Ibid.*, 480, sec. VI, Spry to Clevland, April 18, 1756; February 16, 1756; and also Shirley to Spry, Boston, April 6, 1756.

[42]*Ibid.*, Spry to Clevland, June 19, 1756.

[43]*Ibid.*, 481, sec. II, Charles Holmes to Clevland, July 25, 1756.

[44]*Ibid.*, 480, sec. VI, Spry to Clevland, April 18, 1756; see also *ibid.*, 481, sec. II, Holmes to Admiral Sir Charles Hardy, August 27, 1756.

[45]*Ibid.*, Holmes to Spry, August 28, 1756; Major Hale to Colonel Lacelles, August, 1756; Holmes to Clevland, July 25, 1756; and *ibid.*, 480, sec. VI, Holmes to Spry, July 26, 1756.

[46]*Ibid.*, 481, sec. II, Holmes to Loudon, Commander-in-Chief of H.M. Land Forces in America, September 12, 1756.

while, a small squadron continued to parade before Louisbourg, with occasional expeditions to the coast of Newfoundland to pick up French fishermen. Early in November, however, Holmes collected his forces and sailed for England, leaving, to the governor's disgust, only one ship of sixty guns to secure the harbour of Halifax.

Governor Lawrence had good reason to feel neglected. His small garrison had already been denuded to supply reinforcements for Fort Cumberland on the Chignecto Isthmus, and further troops were required on the St. John River. Without ships, the fortifications of the harbour were quite insufficient to face even the two large frigates which the French maintained at Quebec, apart from stronger naval forces which might conceivably attack Nova Scotia before the spring reliefs arrived. But the governor's entreaties for at least two ships of the line and several frigates were to no avail. Until the following May, Halifax could claim for its security only the winter perils of the North Atlantic.[47]

Meanwhile in December, 1756, at a time when William Pitt had taken control of a badly shaken government, France, from her base at Louisbourg, was already preparing to dispute the command of waters leading to the Gulf. The Chevalier de Bauffremont, avoiding the blockading squadron, left Brest for San Domingo at the end of January 1757, arriving at Louisbourg without interference on May 23. Three weeks later, he was joined by Captain du Revest, who had left Toulon on March 18, and got safely through the Straits of Gibraltar despite Saunders's efforts to check him. On June 19, the 74-year-old du Bois de la Motte, after an equally uneventful crossing from Brest, added his small squadron to make a united force of eighteen ships of the line and three frigates. Although de la Motte sent two of his precious ships to revictual Quebec, he was, for the time being, master of Canadian waters.[48]

During this interval, the administration in Britain had pondered various schemes for the conquest of Canada. Although Pitt favoured an initial attack on Louisbourg, there was a good deal of support for a direct attack on Quebec, leaving the reduction of Louisbourg

[47]See ibid., Lawrence to Holmes, October 25, 1756, and Holmes to Loudon, November 8, 1756.
[48]See Lacour-Gayet, La Marine militaire de la France sous le règne de Louis XV, 359-60; McLennan, Louisburg, 198-9; see also Anon., "Journal of the Cruise of the Squadron of M. du Bois de la Motte in 1757, written by one of the officers of 'L'Inflexible,' " Report Concerning Canadian Archives for the Year 1905, I, Part VIII.

for a later occasion.[49] This was originally the view of the commander-in-chief, Lord Loudon, for early in 1756 he had recommended "an attack on Quebeck as the only Measure likely to be effectual; that this must be done by a strong Fleet, & Force from Home, which should be sufficient for the purpose; & at the same time a proper Strength left to protect the Frontiers."[50] But Pitt was reluctant to leave Louisbourg in the rear, and on February 4, 1757, he sent definite instructions to Lord Loudon that the Cape Breton assault must be preliminary to any plan for the conquest of Quebec.[51] Not until the following month did he consent to compromise, and leave the final decision to Lord Loudon himself. On March 13, 1757, a Cabinet Council instructed the commander-in-chief that while "the two great Objects of Offensive Operations for the ensuing campaign in America are Louisburgh and Quebec; That the Taking of Louisburgh is judged the more practicable Enterprize; Yet His Lordship is, nevertheless, to use his Discretion with regard to which of the Two above mentioned Attempts He shall judge it most advisable first to proceed."[52]

The government's decision had come none too soon. Already in February, a fleet under Vice-Admiral Holburne, consisting of fifteen ships of the line with 12,000 troops, was ready to start, but not until April 25 did fair winds allow the expedition to get under way for Nova Scotia. Holburne arrived in Halifax on July 9, one week after Admiral Hardy, whose task it had been to bring Lord Loudon and six regiments from New York. Hardy was fortunate in his arrival. Late in May he had learned of Beauffremont's withdrawal from San Domingo, and while the destination of the Frenchman was still uncertain, Hardy guessed quite correctly that Louisbourg was his goal. When the news was confirmed, with the additional information that the squadron consisted of six ships of the line, all heavily gunned, he was bound to hesitate. His own force was far inferior, and for all he knew, Beauffremont knew of Loudon's preparations and would be

[49]See "Minits in regard to a Descent propdsed to be made upon the Island of *Cape Breton* & for Attacking The Garrison of *Louisburg*, 1757," by Colonel Hopson, formerly Governor of Louisburg (1747) and Governor of Nova Scotia in 1752, quoted in S. Pargellis, *Military Affairs in North America, 1748-1765: Selected Documents from the Cumberland Papers in Windsor Castle* (New York, 1936), 302-10. The *Cumberland Papers*, according to Dr. Pargellis, contain a memorandum entitled, "Considerations offered by (?) Upon a scheme for Attacking Louisburg & Quebec, 1757." This memorandum shows the need for cutting off Canada by sea and suggests a direct attack on Quebec, thus by-passing Louisbourg.

[50]Abstract of Lord Loudoun's Instructions & Letters, 1756, *Chatham Papers* (G. & D. 8), Vol. 95.

[51]See Pargellis, *Lord Loudoun in North America*, 231-2.

[52]Minutes of March 13, 1757, in *Chatham Papers* (G. & D. 8), Vol. 95.

in a position to smash the convoy off Cape Sable.⁵³ Moreover, if
other French forces had, as he anticipated, reached Louisbourg, they
would in all probability outnumber the fleet which Holburne was
bringing from England. With the fate of the whole expedition
against Canada hanging fire, Hardy decided to gamble. With transports containing some 11,000 men, he set sail on June 20, arriving
safely in Halifax on the last day of the month.⁵⁴

Hardy had been lucky, and so was Holburne. De la Motte, after
his successful concentration at Louisbourg, might have destroyed
the New York expedition (which he knew was on its way); had he
done so, he could then have turned upon Holburne with superior
force, and with reasonable hopes of destroying him before reinforcements arrived from Britain. As it was, de la Motte, lacking the
ardour of youth, and obsessed with the century-old doctrine of passive
defence, locked himself in Louisbourg harbour, where his crews were
racked with scurvy and the plague. He had achieved his object—
the salvation of Louisbourg; now he only waited an opportunity to
return to France.

Meanwhile, Loudon and Holburne confronted the awful problem
of whether or not they should risk their ships and their men in an
attack on a stronghold which, apart from its garrison, (now well over
5,000 men) had in all probability the support of a superior fleet. In
Halifax there was no news as to the exact strength of the French
forces. Continuous dense fogs made accurate reconnaissance impossible; but rumour made the total formidable, and the commander-in-
chief, as he saw his own forces decimated by fevers—1,000 in hospital,
200 dead—felt himself between the devil and the deep sea. On the
one hand, he had his orders to take Quebec—and William Pitt liked
to have his orders carried out; on the other hand, there was the
danger of tackling an enemy whose real strength was unknown and
at a time of year unfavourable to long campaigns.

In the end, Lord Loudon called a council of war to consider two
questions: *one*, the state of Louisbourg, and *two*, whether it was "most
proper" to attack Quebec or Louisbourg? There was no difficulty
about deciding in favour of Louisbourg. Holburne informed the
Admiralty in a letter of August 4.

⁵³*Ad. 1*, vol. 481, sec. IV, Admiral Sir Charles Hardy to Clevland, June 1,
1757; also *ibid.*, sec. III, Hardy to Holburne, New York, May 28, 1757.
⁵⁴J. S. Corbett, *England in the Seven Years' War* (2nd. ed., 2 vols., London,
1918), I, 168.

We could not possibly think of leaving Such a Strength behind us in the Isle of Breton; upon this the Council was dissolved, and his Lordship have Orders for embarking the Troops immediately . . . but there is not the least prospect of being able to force the Harbour if I had double the number of Ships. . . . It would have been very happy if We had been off there in the Month of May, as we should have had a Chance of intercepting the different Squadrons of the Enemy.[55]

Faced with such gloomy prospects, sixteen regiments of British troops stood by waiting a fair wind to take them on their hazardous mission from Halifax. Fortunately for Lord Loudon's peace of mind, the indefatigable Captain Rous brought news of French numbers which confirmed his worst fears. Supported by the fleet captains he prepared to abandon the campaign and return to New York. Hardly had his fleet left harbour (August 16), when an express arrived from General Webb which must have removed any lingering doubts on the correctness of his decision. Lacking sufficient colonial assistance, the British were being steadily pressed back in the Lake Champlain area.[56] Fort William Henry with 2,000 men was as good as gone, and Fort Edward was in immediate danger. Moreover, Quebec had been reinforced with troops and supplies, many of which would be released to General Montcalm. Loudon immediately re-embarked two battalions previously intended for the Chignecto forts, leaving one battalion to garrison Fort Cumberland.

Meanwhile, Holburne prepared to sail, after directing Captain Rous to land his Lordship "as expeditiously as winds permit."[57] He made his way to Louisbourg, "looked in" and found "all the ships there, seventeen Sail of the Line and Four Frigates, A Vice & Rear Admiral & Two Chief (sic) d'Escadres," with many encampments on the beach.[58] The approach of bad weather made blockade difficult, but Holburne planned in the event of dispersal through storm (which might aid the escape of the French fleet) that his own fleet should make for Europe and join the cruising squadron west of

[55]*Ad. 1*, 481, sec. III, Holburne to Cleveland, August 4, 1757. For the proceedings of the council of war, see Pargellis, *Lord Loudon in North America*, 239-43.
[56]The capture of Oswego in 1756, which followed not long after Montcalm had reached Canada, was a purely defensive move which gave France command of the Great Lakes. Control of Lake Ontario might have saved Oswego but, thanks to military hesitations and hagglings, the British naval forces on the lake had never been brought up to the strength which Governor Shirley of Massachusetts had planned. See W. L. Grant, "The Capture of Oswego by Montcalm: A Study in Naval Power . . . ," *Transactions of the Royal Society of Canada* (Ottawa, 1914), XX, sec. 2.
[57]*Ad. 1*, 481, sec. III, Holburne to Cleveland, August 20, 1757.
[58]*Ibid.*, Holburne to Cleveland, August 20, 1757, and August 17, 1757, *ibid.*

Ushant.[59] Unhappily his design was shattered by a gale which, on September 24, so damaged his ships that he was forced to return to Halifax to refit.[60]

Haligonians were delighted at the turn of events which gave them such harbour protection. As yet, there was no conclusive information on the condition of the French squadron and even Holburne was uneasy that knowledge of his own injuries might encourage the French to attack Halifax.[61] As it happened the storm gave de la Motte the opportunity he craved. With ships in foul condition, and burdened with fever-ridden crews, he set sail for Brest. Once again, thanks to gales that drove Hawke's squadron into retirement, he made his goal.

Some French historians have been severe on de la Motte charging that he should have risked his superior fleet in battle with Holburne. Two things made this course a difficult one to carry out. One was, as we have noticed, the doctrine of passive defence, to which de la Motte subsequently referred in justifying his alleged timidity. "His Majesty, however, does not positively order him to attack the enemy. Assured as is His Majesty of his zeal, his valour and his prudence, His Majesty can only refer in this manner to what he believes ought to be done in this regard, without too greatly risking the forces committed to his care, the safe keeping of which so vitally affects the Navy."[62] The second obstacle was the condition of de la Motte's own fleet, long immured in harbour, ridden with disease and low in morale. The English had been similarly inflicted with illness; but they had stayed afloat and there can be little doubt that, had the French essayed an engagement, the sea-conditioned crews of Holburne's ships would have given short shrift to the enemy fleet. A formidable force would thus have been removed from the lists, and the task of subduing Louisbourg in the following year, made that much easier.

Meanwhile, by early December, Holburne had brought his battered fleet back to England, having left eight ships of the line under Lord Colville to winter in Halifax.[63] In preparation for the renewed assault in the following year, Colville was ordered to keep in close correspondence with Lord Loudon, as well as with the governors of

[59]*Ibid.*, Holburne to Ships re rendezvous, September 8, 1757.
[60]*Ibid.*, Holburne to Clevland, September 29, 1757.
[61]*Ibid.*, Holburne to Clevland, September 30, 1757.
[62]Quoted in McLennan, *Louisburg*, 300.
[63]*Ad. 1*, 481, sec. III, Holburne to Clevland, December 7, 1757.

the several provinces. He was instructed to give adequate protection to the New England seaboard, and more especially, "have great Regard to Safety and Defence of the Province of Nova Scotia, and more particularly of the Town & Harbour of Halifax."[64]

[64]*Ibid.*, Holburne to Rt. Hon. Lord Colvill [sic] (no date, probably November 14), enclosed with Holburne to Clevland, December 19, 1757.

IX

From Louisbourg to Quebec

THE Pitt scheme for 1758 was simple and distinct. The French were to be held in Europe by a strong Western squadron which should keep their fleets bottled up in Toulon, Rochefort, and Brest. Based on an assured command of the sea which would make possible the transport of British troops and supplies and the blockade of French reinforcements, the plan of campaign called for a threefold advance: in the east, to Louisbourg and thence to Quebec; at the centre, through the Lake Champlain region, where Crown Point and Ticonderoga guarded the way to Montreal; and in the west, against the enemy's flank as buttressed by forts Duquesne, Niagara, and Frontenac. Some failures were inevitable, for Pitt inherited a few inferior commanders, and his instinct for land warfare never equalled his genius for strategy by sea. On occasion, moreover, the French were bound to escape through rents in the blockader's net; but doggedly and untiringly Howe, Boscawen, and Hawke kept up their sweep of the western approaches, and twice, at Lagos and at Quiberon Bay, were able to smash the outgoing French fleets. Overseas, their junior colleagues, Colville, Hardy, Byron, and Durell, dominated the focal sea areas to the St. Lawrence, clearing the stage for the entry of Amherst and Wolfe.

It must have been obvious to the French that Louisbourg would be attacked again. Since 1754 there had been talk about a second attempt. It was known that men were working on the harbour and fortifications of Halifax, and that British ships cruised regularly and vigilantly in sight of the Cape Breton coast.[1] Some effort had been made to improve the position of the fortress. Under an able and

[1]See "Correspondence générale, Île Royale," XXXIV, c. 11, ccclxxvi *et seq.*, Governor Drucour to the Minister, June 2, 1755.

169

gallant governor, Drucour, the garrison had been increased to 2,500 men, with about 1,000 militia as well as Indians. In addition, a permanent squadron, normally of twelve ships, frequented the harbour, mounting some 590 guns and carrying nearly 3,500 men. Seventeen mortars and 200 cannon were scattered about the surrounding walls and outworks.

Unhappily, discipline had not improved, and the regiments of Artois and Bourgogne were no more successful in disguising their contempt for the Canadian militia than were the seamen in concealing their prejudice against the landsmen. None were very willing to submit to the authority of the governor.[2] Moreover, Drucour had no authority to add to the fortifications, which were still far from complete; and even had he possessed the power, the funds were not forthcoming. Owing to the war in Germany, the French treasury was low, and while inadequate sums had been despatched to the fortress at irregular intervals, even these pittances had been largely misspent or stolen by unscrupulous contractors.

Even more vital than bricks and mortar was the problem of subsistence. By 1757 the British blockade off Brest and Rochefort and outside the harbour of Louisbourg itself had brought the island to the verge of starvation. From 1755 onwards, Governor Drucour's letters reflect the despair which poor harvests and broken communications had inflicted on his fortress colony.[3] Hunger was the worst evil, for hunger encouraged negligence, insurbordination, desertions, and probably plague. Under the circumstances, Drucour could do little more than wait impatiently for the attack which he knew to be coming soon. If the English sent a sufficiently powerful force, the loss of Louisbourg was certain. All he could hope for was to hold the enemy long enough to prevent them from reaching Quebec before Montcalm returned from his offensive down Lake Champlain.

Meanwhile the Western squadron tightened its guard in the Bay of Biscay in an effort to break up any reinforcements intended for Louisbourg, a process already accomplished in the Mediterranean where Osborne smashed a Toulon squadron in the latter part of 1757. On March 11, 1758, Hawke, with seven sail of the line and three frigates, destroyed at Aix Roads, off Rochefort, the reliefs on which Drucour had counted so heavily. Five French ships of the line were driven on shore after jettisoning guns and stores in an effort to

---

[2]*Ibid.*, ccclxxviii, same to same, November 14, 1755.
[3]"Correspondence générale, Île Royale," 1755-7, ccclxxxiii-xxxvi.

escape destruction. Three small divisions did manage to break through with supplies from Aix and from Brest, but as fighting reinforcements they were quite insufficient to deal with the formidable armament which the English were already preparing to launch on the beleaguered fortress.[4] Without leaving the European theatre, Hawke, even more successfully than Martin in 1745, made possible the reconquest of Louisbourg.

On February 19, 1758, Admiral Boscawen set sail for Halifax, followed shortly after by a convoy which conveyed the remainder of the army including the Commander-in-Chief, Major-General Jeffrey Amherst. Boscawen's fleet comprised twenty ships of the line, eighteen frigates, and one hundred transports, carrying in all 12,000 men.

> From Christopher Columbus' time to our days, [wrote Wolfe], there perhaps has never been a more extraordinary voyage. The continued opposition of contrary winds, calms or currents baffled all our skill and wore out all our patience. A fleet of men-of-war well man'd, unincumber'd with transports, commanded by an officer of the first reputation, has been eleven weeks in its passage. We made the Madeira Islands, the Canaries, Bermudas, and lastly to crown all the Isle of Sable. Two or three of the ships are sickly, the rest are in very good condition. . . .[5]

On May 12, the fleet reached Halifax.

Meanwhile, on the North American side of the Atlantic, Lord Colville, whose scouting force consisted of a sloop and a schooner, had been out since early March, cruising in the vicinity of Louisbourg, to intercept any stray supply ships that might run the gauntlet from Europe. By the end of the month he was joined by Sir Charles Hardy, who took over the little squadron of nine sail that had wintered in Halifax. In spite of the shortage of masts and yards, all the ships were in fair condition, although damp and ice had played havoc with the caulking.[6] During the second week of May they joined the main body of Boscawen's fleet off the Nova Scotian coast, whence troops and seamen took part in simple landing exercises.[7] These drills carried on until Amherst arrived, ships and transports coming "very sickly into Halifax."

[4]Lacour-Gayet, *La Marine militaire de la France sous le règne de Louis XV*, 384-6.

[5]To Lord George Sackville, Halifax, May 12, 1758, in *Historical Manuscripts Commission Report, Sackville MSS.*, II, chap. XXI, "Canada and Nova Scotia, 1758-80," 257.

[6]*Ad. 1*, vol. 481, sec. IV, Hardy to Clevland, Halifax, March 22, 1758; also *ibid.*, sec. I, Vice-Admiral Boscawen to Clevland, Halifax, May 10, 1758.

[7]See James Cunningham to Lord George Sackville, May 30, 1758, quoted in McLennan, *Louisburg*, 239.

On May 29, after a salute of seventeen guns from the citadel, the entire fleet of 180 sail bore away for Louisbourg. In the beginning, the weather was not unfavourable, but fog engulfed them near Cape Breton Island, and Boscawen stood out from the land. On the night of June 1, French look-outs in Gabarus Bay thought they saw lights to the southward. They waited impatiently for the first morning light, but when the darkness lifted, there was dense mist. Among the inhabitants the rumour sped around that the English fleet was in the offing, and the town of Louisbourg stirred uneasily, sensing that behind the grey curtain lay the ships of the enemy. As the morning advanced, a light breeze blew in from the Atlantic; it dissipated the fog, exposing against the dark field of the Atlantic the great white crescent of sail that had been drawn with such perfection by Boscawen's navigators. And from the sea, the English seamen of the van saw the spires of the town rise up sharply through the low-lying mists as they moved slowly into Gabarus Bay, followed on June 3 by the rest of the fleet and the transports.

Although Wolfe claims to have been uneasy about the strength of the forces, his concern was hardly justified. Including land and sea units, the united forces of Britain were numerically three times the strength of the French. If efficiency in terms of morale and talent for amphibious co-operation are taken into consideration, the disparity was even greater. The British fleet mounted 1,842 guns and carried crews totalling 14,000; the army consisted of 13,142 men.[8]

Apart from disparate numbers the second siege of Louisbourg differed little in fundamentals from that of thirteen years earlier. Amherst made his landing in Gabarus Bay on June 8, and Boscawen followed Warren's tactics almost exactly. The only substantial difference lay in the character of the French defences. On this occasion, the assault forces were opposed by troops protected near the shoreline by makeshift earthworks, while at the entrance to the harbour, four vessels had been sunk as an additional safeguard against direct attack. In view of the heavy surf, and the prevalence of rocks, the defenders were in a good position to block a landing by means of heavy fire from their shore batteries. Until the stores and guns were ashore, the initial landing parties were, therefore, bound to be in a precarious situation; and had a well-directed sortie been made, they might have had difficulty in holding their ground. The French were more concerned, however, in putting the fortress in shape for a siege.

[8]McLennan, *Louisburg*, 242.

Counting vainly on help from overseas, they made a tactical mistake which was to cost them the battle.[9]

On the English side, seamen and soldiers worked like a well-drilled team; there was, according to Wolfe, the utmost co-operation.[10] Possibly the outstanding example of "commando" tactics occurred when a party of seamen and marines rowed boldly into Louisbourg harbour to cut out two French ships of the line under the guns of their own forts. Despite the terrific bombardment from land as well as sea, the remaining ships stayed in harbour to the end, although most of the crews took refuge on the land, where they joined in the defence of the fort. Against superior British forces it would have been folly to have offered battle, although one or two of the faster vessels might have escaped. On the other hand, the French, by retaining a squadron of sorts in harbour, kept the British fleet out. Boscawen had no chance of making an entrance under the combined fire of ships and forts.

On July 26 Louisbourg surrendered. Up to the last, the doomed fortress had looked vainly to Europe for help, but the blockade had held, and only a solitary frigate, the *Arethuse*, through combined luck and audacity, broke Boscawen's lines and reached the harbour to take part in the defence. Nevertheless, the French had gained the respite for which Drucour had hoped. Despite Wolfe's optimistic faith in the weather,[11] it was now too late to prepare an attack on Quebec. While most of the troops, supported by a small squadron, were left to endure the rigours of a Halifax winter, Boscawen, with the bulk of the fleet, sailed for home.

The capitulation of Louisbourg did not open the way to Canada; it merely removed a theoretical threat to communications leading to the St. Lawrence. The demolition of the fortress, completed by the end of 1760,[12] was in itself evidence that the possessor of Canada needed no north-eastern bastion to guard the Gulf. Ships, not fortresses, were the key to supremacy in the New World; as long as command of the sea was assured, the grass and the scrub might grow unmolested

[9]They were counting, too, on either a storm or an outbreak of plague or scurvy to dislodge the invaders. As it happened, the elements played fair, and the only outbreak of smallpox on board the English ships was quickly brought under control. See Whitton, *Wolfe and North America*, 285-90; also "Correspondence générale, Île Royale," cccxc-cccxciv, and cccxcvii-cccxcviii.

[10]*Sackville MSS.*, II, chap. XXI, 264.

[11]"We have suffered very little, so little that if we are carried directly to Quebec, notwithstanding the time of the year, I am persuaded we shall take it." *Ibid.*, 262.

[12]See *Ad. 1*, vol. 482, sec. II, Colville to Clevland, October 7, 1760.

over the broken walls of Louisbourg. Yet France had lost an important island stepping-stone on the way to her continental dominion, and the blow to prestige and morale was incalculable. For Britain the capture of Louisbourg was the first striking success of the war, and the fall of Quebec seemed an assured and final step, provided the mistake of 1748 were not repeated and peace were not made too soon.

Although the siege of Louisbourg had provided Quebec with an unintended year's respite, Pitt was determined that Canada should not last out the coming year, and he was prepared, at the risk of criticism at home, to send a quarter of the Royal Navy "to lay the axe at the root."

There are but two roads to get to it [wrote General Jeffrey Amherst] one up the River St. Lawrence to Quebec, and the other to Ticonderoga and Montreal, we must go both to be sure of prospering in one, and whichsoever of the two succeeds, the business is done. . . . Quebec is everything, and I am not sure, it is not the easiest as well as the greatest plan to be pursued.[13]

It had been Pitt's original idea that the finishing blow should be struck up the Lakes, but Abercrombie's costly defeat at Ticonderoga in 1758 had given the British a severe check, and Amherst's subsequent progress up the Lake Champlain route proved to be painfully slow. Consequently, as Amherst himself ruefully admitted, the decisive blow had to be struck, not in the centre, but at Quebec. Time left no alternative, but failure in the centre nearly cost Wolfe his success at Quebec.

It was a far call to the days of the first conquest when Champlain, short of munitions and men, surrendered to the Kirkes in 1629. But the same strategical consideration was dominant. The determining element in the first capture of Quebec was command of the sea. The naval action off the Saguenay in 1628 can hardly rank as a sea battle, but in defeating the four small vessels of Claude de Roquemont, the Kirkes secured eighteen transports on which Quebec depended for sustinence and safety. In miniature, this little affray contained the lesson that had become basic naval doctrine by 1759. Command of the sea meant the ability to bar the enemy's access to his own overseas possessions.

The fleet and convoy led by Admiral Saunders—counting in total 277 sail—was the greatest expedition to travel the St. Lawrence

[13]*Sackville MSS.*, II, chap. XXI, 262-7, Amherst to Lord George Sackville New York, January 19, 1759.

until the first Canadian Contingent sailed from Quebec in 1914. Had not Wolfe needed Saunders's men and ships to supply tactical mobility to his army, the ships of the line would have served a more useful purpose guarding the Atlantic approaches.   But the assault on Quebec was planned as an amphibious operation, involving far more naval assistance than would have been required for a straight-forward landing as conducted at Louisbourg.   Hence, the dispro-portion between sailors and soldiers.   Including the crews of all supply and transport vessels, there were three times as many seamen as troops.   "Wolfe's little army," declared an informed student of the campaign, "was really no more than a most efficient landing party from an overwhelming fleet."[14]   Moreover, the victory on the Plains did not secure Canada or even clinch Quebec; not until the decisive battle of Quiberon Bay in the following November was the French power of intervention finally extinguished, and the way paved for the reduction of an isolated colony.   Wolfe's victory was "glorious" because it came with all the drama of death and triumph, after a long series of set-backs and defeats; but the honour which posterity properly bestowed on a brave and talented leader has, until recent times, served to cloud the significance of Hawke's success at Quiberon Bay, and it was bound to shadow the perform-ance of the man whose skilful seamanship brought an armada up the tortuous River St. Lawrence to the heart of New France.[15]

The selection of Saunders to lead the expedition confirms Pitt's reputation as a war leader.   Outside the service, Saunders was al-most unknown, and the public might have been expected to question such an appointment when senior men like Hawke and Boscawen were about.   But Anson knew his worth, for Saunders had been his executive officer on his voyage round the world, and he did not hesi-tate to press his merits on Pitt.   Saunders had fought with distinction under Hawke, and in 1756 he had gone with Hawke as second-in-command to replace the ill-starred Byng after the failure at Minorca. Yet he had never commanded a fleet in action; and he became a

[14]W. C. H. Wood, "The Misunderstood Campaign of 1759," in *The Centenary Volume of the Literary and Historical Society of Quebec, 1824-1924*, under the general title "Unique Quebec" (Quebec, 1924), 57.

[15]"I should not do justice to the admirals, and the Naval service," wrote General Townsend to Pitt, "if I neglected this occasion of acknowledging how much we are indebted for our success to the constant assistance and support re-ceived from them. . . . It is my duty to acknowledge for that time how great a share the Navy has had in this successful campaign."   W. V. Anson, *Life of Lord Anson* (London, 1912), 173.

vice-admiral only on the day before he sailed from England. No one but a man of Pitt's incredible self-confidence would have dared to place a comparative junior in command of the greatest fleet afloat.[16]

But long before Saunders's appointment, plans for the safe conduct of the expedition had been worked out. After the capture of Louisbourg, it was essential that no enemy reinforcements should get up the river to Quebec, and at Pitt's request ten sail of the line and three frigates had been left behind, under Rear-Admiral Durell, to winter at Halifax.[17] The function of Durell's squadron was to take over and hold the entrance of the St. Lawrence as soon as the ice broke up in the spring, thus securing the passage for the British expedition as well as preventing French reinforcements or supply vessels from reaching Quebec. Even if a strong French force managed to elude Hawke, it was assumed that Durell would be in a position to damage it, or at any rate prevent it from holding up Saunders's advance.

After repairing the storehouses and harbour installations at Louisbourg, Durell conscribed all the French pilots he could find, and in late autumn set sail for Halifax.[18] There he spent the "severest winter since the place was settled." From the beginning of January until the middle of March he was completely cut off from Louisbourg, and, on account of the cold, was unable to carry out his plans for building a much needed careening wharf, and setting up jetty heads and breast works.[19] But the main consideration was the preparation for a quick start. As soon as the ice began to break up, everything depended on getting to the entrance of the river before any French relief expedition should appear. "I intend," wrote Saunders to the Admiralty secretary on March 10, 1759, "to-morrow or next Day, to send Admiral Durell, to inforce the Absolute Necessity there is for his being very early in the River St. Lawrence."[20] Whether or not Durell ever received the letter, the fact remains that he already had his orders and well understood their importance. On March 19, he wrote to the Admiralty:

[16]W. C. H. Wood, *The Fight for Canada* (London, 1904), 82; also Wood, *Logs of the Conquest of Canada*, 20.

[17]A frigate each was sent to Virginia, New York, Carolina, and Providence for "Station" service. *Ad. 1*, vol. 481, sec. I, Boscawen to Clevland, September 13, 1758, and November 1, 1758.

[18]*Ibid.*, vol. 481, sec. V, Durell to Clevland, September 30, 1758.

[19]*Ibid.*, Durell to Clevland, Halifax, March 19, 1759.

[20]*Ad. 1*, vol. 482, sec. I.

As the Gut of Canso generally is the first pass open into the Gulph of Saint Lawrence, [I] propose to send the Sutherland and Porcupine Sloop into it, as soon as it is practicable—The part they will anchor in is not above half a mile wide, so that it will effectually prevent any Vessels getting thro' that Way—I shall myself sail with the rest of the ships, and cruize off the Gulph, as soon as there is a possibility of doing it.[21]

But Durell was too cautious; he was still waiting for reports on ice conditions when Saunders appeared on the coast of Nova Scotia. Hastily, he made for the vital area, but arrived too late to catch Bougainville with three frigates and seventeen store ships which were bringing provisions, munitions, and recruits to Quebec.[22] Had it not been for this error, the task of subduing the capital of New France might have been a matter of days or weeks rather than months. Whatever may have been the extenuating circumstances— and they are difficult to estimate—Saunders seems to have borne no grudge, for he was later to write of the "great assistance" given him by Admirals Durell and Holmes.[23]

On June 6, Saunders "stood in" for the River St. Lawrence. Twenty-two ships of the line, some twenty sloops and frigates, and large numbers of transports and store-ships, prepared to follow the intricate windings of a river from which all buoys and marks had been carefully removed by the enemy.[24] As usual, the unfortunate local pilots were far from intelligent and barely trustworthy. Copies of river charts captured from the French were available, but these had to be scrupulously checked. The success of the expedition depended, therefore, on the quality of survey work which was undertaken in advance of the main fleet. For this vital service, Saunders appointed James Cook, whose later journeys and surveys were to bring him fame far beyond that of his chief.[25] It was an interesting historical coincidence that while a great English navigator, Cook, was helping Wolfe to reach Quebec, that great French circumnavigator, Bougainville, was doing his best to keep him out.

Some ten miles below Quebec the narrowing river is partially blocked by the Île d'Orléans and a number of scattered reefs and

[21] *Ibid.*, vol. 481, sec. V, Durell to Clevland, Halifax, March 19, 1759.
[22] *Ibid.*, vol. 482, sec. I, Saunders to Clevland, Sterling Castle, off Point Levi, September 5, 1759.
[23] *Ad. 1*, vol. 482, sec. I; see also A. G. Doughty and G. W. Parmelee, *The Siege of Quebec and the Battle of the Plains of Abraham* (6 vols., Quebec, 1901), VI, 121.
[24] For "Disposition of the Ships under the Command of Vice Admiral Saunders in North America, 5 September 1759," see A. G. Doughty and G. W. Parmelee, *The Siege of Quebec*, VI, 118-19.
[25] See *Naval Chronicle*, VIII, 10-13.

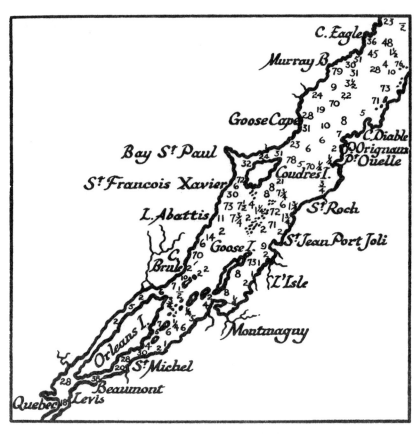

VI. THE SIEGE OF QUEBEC: A MODERN MAP
OF THE TRAVERSE

tiny islands close by its eastern extremity. At this point ships were accustomed to move from the northern side of the St. Lawrence, passing south of Île d'Orléans by the channel known as the Traverse. Competent French observers believed that without the aid of buoys and other markings (all of which had been removed) the Traverse was impassable to large ships. Obviously, it had to be re-marked. While Saunders was making his way from Halifax through the Gulf, Cook and his colleagues "with boats man'd and arm'd" were busy taking soundings and fixing buoys. His log recorded his conscientious toil and complete success; on June 11 he returned to his ship "satisfied with being acquainted with ye channel."[26]

On June 24, Saunders began the passage of the Traverse; within a week the fleet of more than two hundred vessels accompanied by sounding boats had safely negotiated its tortuous channel. How the more self-confident skippers accomplished the journey is best described in the language of Captain John Knox's *Historical Journal.* Whether or not other ships had skippers of the flavour of Old Killick, they probably shared a common audacity and a similar ability to "smell" their way to safe water.

June 25, 1759.

At 3 p.m. a French pilot was put on board of each transport, and the man who fell to the Goodwill's lot gasconaded at a most extravagant rate, and gave us to understand it was much against his inclination that he was become an English pilot. The poor fellow assumed great latitude in his conversation, said he made no doubt that some of the fleet would return to England, but they should have a dismal tale to carry with them; for Canada should be the grave of the whole army, and he expected, in a short time, to see the walls of Quebec ornamented with English scalps. Had it not been in obedience to the Admiral, who gave orders that he should not be ill used, he would certainly have been thrown overboard. At four P.M. we passed the Traverse, which is reputed a place of the greatest difficulty and danger between the entrance of St. Lawrence and Quebec: it lies between Cape Tourmente (a remarkably high, black-looking promontory) and the east end of Orleans on the starboard side, and isle de Madame on the larboard. Off Orleans we met some of our ships of war at anchor. . . . As soon as the pilot came on board today, he gave his directions for the working of the ship, but the Master would not permit him to speak; he fixed his Mate at the helm, charged him not [to] take any orders from any person except himself, and, going forward with his trumpet to the forecastle, gave the necessary instructions. All that could be said by the Commanding Officer, and the other Gentlemen on board, was to no purpose; the pilot declared we should be lost, for that no French ship ever presumed to pass there without a pilot. "Ay, ay, my dear," replied our son of Neptune, "but d——

[26]H. Carrington, *Life of Captain Cook* (London, 1939), 24.

me, I'll convince you, that an Englishman shall go where a Frenchman dare not show his nose." The Richmond frigate being close a-stern of us, the Commanding Officer called out to the Captain, and told him our case; he enquired who the Master was?—and was answered from the forecastle by the man himself, who told him "he was old Killick, and that was enough." I went forward with this experienced mariner, who pointed out the channel to me as we passed, showing me, by the ripple and colour of the water, where there was any danger; and distinguishing the places where there were ledges of rock (to me invisible) from banks of sand, mud, or gravel. He gave his orders with great unconcern, joked with the sounding-boats who lay off on each side, with different coloured flags for our guidance; and, when any of them called to him, and pointed to the deepest water, he answered "Ay, ay, my dear, chalk it down a d——d dangerous navigation,—eh, if you dont make a sputter about it, you'll get no credit for it in England, etc." After we had cleared this remarkable place, where the channel forms a complete zigzag, the Master called to his Mate to give the helm to someone else, saying, "D—— me, if there are not a thousand places in the Thames fifty times more hazardous than this; I am ashamed that Englishmen should make such a rout about it." The Frenchman asked me if the Captain had not been there before. I assured him in the negative, upon which he viewed him with great attention, lifting, at the same time, his hands and eyes to heaven with astonishment and fervency.[27]

Unlike Louisbourg, which was constructed as a fortress from well-prepared and scientific plans, Quebec was hardly more than a fortified town. When Samuel Champlain founded the settlement in 1608 he was not thinking about defence against European enemies, or principles of strategy as affected by sea power. He saw only a great fresh-water anchorage "capable of containing a hundred men of war," hardly "one hundred and twenty leagues distant from the sea," and above it, marking the junction of the St. Charles River with the St. Lawrence, a huge rocky eminence which might be defended with little difficulty against Indian attacks. Since Champlain's time, the river had gradually retreated from the Rock leaving a large space of dry land on which the narrow rows of wooden houses forming the lower town were built, and from which ascent could be made to the upper town by means of steps cut out of the rock. In 1720 Père Charlevoix had climbed that steep passage, and from the ramparts looked across the basin (filled with vessels from all over the world) towards the green meadows and hills of Île d'Orléans. To Charlevoix was granted an experience which has been shared by other travellers since that day, and which the simple Breton sailor, Jacques Cartier, who had climbed Mount Royal above Montreal in

[27]J. Knox, *An Historical Journal of the Campaigns in North America, 1757-60* (2 vols., London, 1769), I, 290.

1535, would have understood. Beyond the quays of the lower town to the valley of the St. Charles, "crowded with villages," he looked northward to the forbidding grey-brown ranges of the Laurentian hills. Close beside him rose the citadel—a rugged square fort, from whence ran narrow communication roads to join the long hilly streets with their low-roofed stone houses and handsome public buildings; and he seemed to see a new Paris rising on the banks of the St. Lawrence, a capital of New France "as flourishing as that of the Old," with "towns, castles and villas."[28]

Until Phips's attack in 1690 the outward defences had been little more than a stone wall around the fortified Chateau, with a "strong place" in the Lower Town on each side of the present Sous-le-Fort Street. In 1692 Frontenac finally succeeded in getting means and materials to build the first walls around the city, but, as at Louisbourg, official corruption and bad workmanship brought only short-lived security. From 1720 until the conquest, improvements consisted of successive patchwork efforts. The fortifications, wrote Montcalm shortly after his arrival in the country, were so bad and so "ridiculous" they were certain to fall as soon as they were assaulted. "What a country, what a country, where rogues grow rich and honest men are ruined."[29]

Admittedly, the town was naturally strong, even though it was not adequately or scientifically fortified, and it was in an excellent position to hold the upper St. Lawrence against hostile craft. On the other hand, the fact that it was the capital of New France meant that many troops were removed from the field in order to guard its offices, cathedrals, and public buildings from attack either by land or by sea. Within four years after his arrival in the colony in 1756 Montcalm had won four successive victories which might, had he not been concerned about Quebec in his rear, have taken him as far as Albany. There were good grounds for believing, according to one military critic, that had an enemy attempt on Louisbourg been followed by an immediate military advance on lines carefully prepared beforehand, and had the focus been Kingston, not Quebec, France would have had at least "the opportunity of occupying territory with which to bargain at the peace negotiations, or of protracting operations until the question of sea-power could be put up for

[28]*Journal d'un voyage fait par ordre du Roi dans l'Amérique Septentrionale, par le P. De Charlevoix, de la Compagnie de Jésus* (3 vols., Paris, 1744), III, 70-8.
[29]Quoted in Wood, "The Misunderstood Campaign of 1759," 51.

contest once again."[30] But Montcalm himself held no such hopes. He was sceptical, even after success, about the chances of holding Canada. The Commander-in-Chief was not a free agent; whatever his plans, they had to be adjusted to the exigencies of governmental policy at Quebec. Only too willingly would he have exchanged the American forests for the plains of Germany, where a professional soldier could at least conduct his campaigns scientifically and without the uninformed interference of governors like M. de Vaudreuil.

Montcalm had at first proposed to encamp the army on the Plains of Abraham and along the St. Charles, making that river his line of defence. He changed his plans, however, and eventually posted the bulk of his force (which consisted of about 14,000 men, including Indians and raw militia) on the St. Lawrence below the city, with his right resting on the St. Charles and his left on the Montmorency.[31] These two rivers were linked by stout barriers of entrenchments, which prevented all access to the city from the Beauport shore. At one time, Montcalm seems to have intended stationing strong detachments of infantry and artillery at Pointe de Lévy, which would have obstructed the upper courses of the river to Saunders, and considerably restricted those diversionary movements so essential in disguising a surprise attack. Such a blockade would, moreover, have enabled the French to bring in supplies from Montreal by the easier water route. But the general was apparently overruled by the governor; Vaudreuil preferred to place his total strength on the north shore, and as a consequence, the French defenders lost an opportunity of controlling a strategic point which might have given them command of the waters above the city.[32]

As it was, Saunders, shortly after his arrival, became dissatisfied with his exposed position in a very crowded anchorage, and immediately after Monckton subdued Pointe de Lévy he moved to the South Channel, a sort of "reach" between Pointe d'Orléans and the mainland. The British fleet now occupied a strong strategic position, watching both approaches. The French with a numerically superior

[30]Whitton, *Wolfe and North America*, 130.

[31]In this chapter no pretence is made of examining the progress of the siege in detail. For a narrative of the campaign, see J. S. Corbett, *England in the Seven Years' War*, I, chaps. XVII and XVIII. (Corbett has drawn heavily on Doughty and Parmelee, *The Siege of Quebec*, especially vols. IV-VI.) Also "Journal of Happenings at Quebec by an Officer of Royal Americans, endorsed May 24, 1760," in Pargellis, *Military Affairs in North America*, 439-46.

[32]See Lord Keyes, *Amphibious Warfare and Combined Operations* (2nd ed., Cambridge University Press, 1943), 13 and 17.

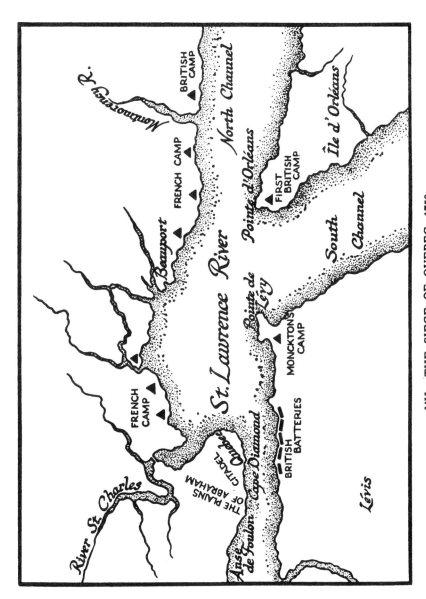

VII. THE SIEGE OF QUEBEC, 1759

force had to stay on the defensive, unless, of course, Amherst should break through below Montreal.

In these circumstances, Wolfe's object was clearly to entice Montcalm from behind his defences; and, after some preliminary experimenting, he turned finally to the method, which was to remain his favourite to the last. By seizing the heights on the eastern side of the river above Montmorency Falls, he believed he could dominate Montcalm's left, and, by the threat of his position, force the French to attack and try to dislodge him. His army was now divided between Lévis and Pointe d'Orléans, and although this meant another wide separation of forces, he counted on the fleet to hold his scattered units together. The manœuvre was successfully carried out, but the strategy failed of its objective. Despite the vehement protestations of the townsfolk, Montcalm kept his head. "Drive them thence," he said, "and they will give us more trouble. So long as they stay there, they cannot hurt us. Let them amuse themselves."

Meanwhile, by July 12, the land batteries on the Lévis heights were completed, and in the evening they opened fire on the Lower Town. Although Wolfe's aim was principally to weaken French-Canadian morale by a rain of cannon balls, the advantage of the bombardment as a form of barrage resolved Saunders to chance the second major exploit of the siege. Under cover of fire, he planned to pass the town and make a landing on the north shore above Quebec. The pitch-black night of July 18 lent itself to his plans, and a new field was opened for siege operations.

It is probable that Wolfe at one time intended to make a landing between Quebec and Cap Rouge; but he seems to have concluded that the attempt would mean too great a dissipation of his forces. Hence, on July 30, he resumed his former strategy. Two days after the French had made a last desperate attempt to destroy the English fleet by fireships, he attacked in force above Montmorency Falls. But Montcalm was ready, and in a blinding rainstorm the British grenadiers were hurled down the slippery slopes of the redoubts, leaving 800 of their dead behind them.[33]

For the French the success was timely. From the west came the news that Prideaux, on Amherst's orders, had seized Niagara. Canada was now open on all three lines of communication, and as a result Vaudreuil felt forced to weaken the garrison in order to send aid to

[33]See Corbett, *England in the Seven Years' War*, I, 440-2.

Montreal. Another cause of anxiety was the dissatisfaction of Canadians and Indians with Montcalm's defensive policy; desertions had become increasingly frequent.

On August 8, by way of diversion, Murray attacked the French camp at Pointe-aux-Trembles. But Bougainville was too alert and he was beaten back with a loss of eighty men. Five days later, however, a secret attack resulted in the destruction of the magazines at Deschambault twenty miles further up. On account of shoals, Murray had failed to reach the French supply ships, but the confusing effect of his actions on French headquarters was undoubted. The attack confirmed Montcalm in his belief that no genuine assault would be made above the town.[34]

Wolfe was now almost prostrate with an illness which had been threatening ever since the siege commenced. None the less, he managed to put his views on paper, and ordered a council of the brigadiers to confer, along with Saunders, on the problem of assault. He presented three alternative methods of reaching Montcalm, each involving attacks on, or adjacent to, Beauport. Wolfe had still no real faith in the virtue of operating above the town. However, the brigadiers rejected all the Lower Town plans with the entire approval of Saunders and Holmes, and Wolfe, although still unconvinced, was forced to acquiesce. The brigadiers urged that an attempt should be made to gain a footing on the north shore above the town, thus placing the army between Montcalm and his base of supply, and forcing him to fight or surrender. This plan meant the abandonment of Wolfe's cherished position at Montmorency; but his regrets may have vanished when it became clear that the movements of Saunders's ships up the river were adding daily to the confusion and bewilderment of the French command. The exasperated Vaudreuil was giving orders and counter-orders; he was sending troops to Pointe-aux-Trembles, then to Quebec, and back again. For the French troops there was no rest, and for Montcalm no peace of mind. The British movements, he wrote to Bougainville, were "as embarrassing as they were equivocal."[35]

From the day that Wolfe broke camp at Montmorency on Sep-

[34]Doughty and Parmelee, *The Siege of Quebec*, V, 177-81.
[35]Corbett, *England in the Seven Years' War*, I, 460. Cf. Guy Frégault, *Le Grand Marquis: Pierre de Rigaud de Vaudreuil et la Louisiane* (Montreal, 1952) 43 fn. The author quotes a letter of July 29, 1759, from Montcalm to Vaudreuil, discouraging special precautions at the Foulon—a rather dubious authority for events that were to take place more than six weeks later.

tember 3 until the final day of battle, Montcalm could not count on any reliable information as to his enemy's plans. Behind the screen of the British fleet, Wolfe's army manœuvred at will up the whole thirty miles of river from Montmorency to Pointe-aux-Trembles. Saunders's technique provided a supreme example of the value of diversionary movements to conceal an intended landing spot. The enemy had no opportunity to learn whether a real attack was coming or merely a feint; even if troops were landed they could not be sure that such a demonstration was not intended to cover the main attack elsewhere. As it happened, the French, in an effort to guard their flanks, were bound to weaken their middle defences by overstretching. Two important landing places, Anse des Mères and Anse de Foulon, were left with only a militia guard.

Realizing that the French troops were being thus drawn to the two flanks, Wolfe at last conceived the plan of thrusting his whole force at the centre, which he assumed would be the vulnerable area. After careful reconnaissance he chose Anse de Foulon as the likeliest landing-place. The plateau above the cove was guarded by small patrols, and there was no path or track to permit even a two-abreast charge up to the top. Nevertheless, he believed his troops could quickly scale a scrubby slope some two hundred yards to the right, and with any luck assemble in force before substantial French forces could be mustered to repel them.

Baffled as he might well have been by the intricate covering movements of Saunders's squadron, Montcalm seems to have guessed Wolfe's plan. On September 12, he ordered a battalion of French regulars to take up station at the Anse de Foulon. He was not commander-in-chief, however, and Vaudreuil blocked his design by issuing counter-orders, along with the alleged pronouncement: "Those English have not got wings—I'll see about it to-morrow."

Meanwhile, in order to weaken further the centre, Wolfe planned two feints to be carried out simultaneously with his attempted landing at the Foulon. Below the town Saunders prepared to make a massed attack with his marines against Beauport, while the fleet above was to sail further up, as if intending to land upon the north shore, and then at ebb tide withdraw quietly and quickly. As a result, Montcalm and Bougainville were held firmly to their positions until the last moment.

Under Holmes's direction, the initial night landings were conducted with clock-like punctuality, and the enemy gained no suspicion of what was going on. The French look-outs were expecting the arrival of provision boats, and two challenges were satisfactorily answered. British light infantry scaled the cliff and overpowered the guard. Sheer good luck quite as much as skill and courage had placed Wolfe in an open field where Montcalm had to fight, if he would save his communications.

The operations which culminated on the Plains of Abraham on September 13, 1759, were a tribute to what Saunders called "a perfect good understanding between the Army & Navy," and the Lords of the Admiralty were gratified to record their pleasure "that the fleet contributed so much to success."[37] The battle of the Plains meant the capture of Quebec, but it did not mean the conquest of the colony; and military experts are almost entirely agreed that had Wolfe feinted at or near Quebec and then landed some twenty miles up river, he might well have cut off the whole French army, thus forcing the complete surrender of New France.[38]

Wolfe's plan was only a second best. The brigadiers had suggested a landing near Pointe-aux-Trembles, twenty-two miles above Quebec, and their reasons were simple. To the east and south, the French army was cut off by the British fleet; to prevent Montcalm's forces from escaping, it was necessary to cut the upper road which led towards Montreal and joined the St. Charles Valley road leading to Quebec. Had this been done, and the French army trapped, New France must have fallen shortly. Such was doubtless the argument of the brigadiers, and it is the opinion of many naval historians, soldiers, and admirals. "Wolfe," declared Lord Wolseley somewhat harshly, "was a first-rate Commanding officer of a Battalion; but, in the only campaign he ever conducted, he did not, according to my views of men who have conducted campaigns, display any originality or any great genius for war."[39]

Since Wolfe's capture of Quebec was not decisive, his success was to be quickly challenged. The French army had moved around the British left and made its way to Montreal. Moreover, three French frigates, accompanied by several merchant ships, had retired up the

[37]*Ad. 1*, vol. 482, sec. I, Charles Saunders to the Secretary of the Admiralty, Quebec, September 21, 1759.
[38]See *The Centenary Volume of the Literary and Historical Society of Quebec*, 65-7, for the views of Colonel William Wood, Sir Julian Corbett, Sir John Fortescue, Admiral of the Fleet Sir Edward Seymour, Admiral of the Fleet Lord Jellicoe, Lord Roberts, and Lord French, contained in William Wood's "Unique Quebec."
[39]*Ibid.*, 67

river, and Saunders had found it impossible to get at them. The task might have been accomplished by boats, but at some risk. Amherst was still far away from Montreal, and by November ice might quickly immobilize the fleet and lock it in the St. Lawrence.[40] As a consequence Saunders prepared to sail home, leaving behind him at Quebec a small force under Captain Spry to watch the French as long as the season would permit.[41]

Meanwhile, badly housed, insufficiently clothed, and beset by scurvy, the English troops under General Murray suffered the worst rigours of a Quebec winter. During this time the enemy frigates lay up the St. Lawrence waiting for the ice to melt. By mid-April with the appearance of patches of clear water, they got under way, and doggedly gnawed their way down river to the Rock, where they prepared to join the Chevalier de Lévis's troops in the second siege of Quebec. Stung by the defeat of the previous year and emboldened by the news that the defenders were short of food and decimated by illness, the French made ready to take the fort by storm. Against de Lévis's 7,000, Murray could muster scarcely 3,000 sick and undernourished men. Yet, on April 28, he led the "poor pitiful handful of half-starved scorbutic skeletons" against the enemy in the second Battle of the Plains, and only after suffering more than 1,000 casualties did he take refuge once more within the walls. Provided the survivors could hold back the coming assaults, the fate of the city now depended upon whether the first reinforcements from the Gulf should be British or French.

There was not long to wait. On the morning of May 9, the first flecks of white sail were sighted, and anxious watchers on the ramparts and along the banks gazed eastward as a frigate came slowly up the river. A tiny bundle ascended slowly to the masthead, hung motionless for a moment, and then broke out into the white ensign. It was the *Lowestoft*, heralding the approach of a squadron under Captain Swanton, with stores and men. In the circumstances there was nothing for de Lévis to do but break camp and retreat to Montreal, to await the arrival of General Amherst who was pressing steadily northward.

[40]By December 5, the river was entirely frozen over. See *Ad. 1*, vol. 482, sec. II, Colville to Philip Stephens, October 14, 1763.
[41]Corbett, *England in the Seven Years' War*, I, 474. "There is no Place near Quebec," wrote Lord Colville to Philip Stephens, "where ships can lye afloat in the Winter, on account of the Ice and rapidity of the Tides" (*Ad. 1*, vol. 482, sec. II, October 14, 1763). During this winter of 1759-60, two sloops were left at the wharf, but by spring one of them was almost a complete wreck.

Montreal fell to Amherst on September 8, 1760, and the conquest of Canada was at last complete. Its ultimate fall was inevitable; yet it is interesting to speculate on what might have happened had the first Quebec reinforcements been French, for only the want of supplies had prevented de Lévis from taking the enfeebled fortress by storm. In other words, Quebec must have fallen to the French in May, had Colville and his scouting force in the neighbourhood of the Gulf repeated in the spring of 1760 the mistake made by Durell in the spring of 1759. On this occasion, however, Lord Colville, who had wintered with his small squadron at Halifax, was restless to make an early start. As a result, he not only kept his rendezvous with Swanton's squadron from England, but managed to pick up the first French supply ships off Gaspé. It was fitting that the Admiralty should subsequently congratulate him on the "expedition he has used in getting up to Quebec, and of seasonable relief the Garrison received from the appearance of the ships under his Lordship's and Cap. Swanton's commands."[42] But Colville had been able to count on safe sea communitions between Quebec and Europe. That he and Swanton were able to enter the St. Lawrence with hardly more than a scratch relief force was owing directly to Admiral Hawke's persistance and audacity in home waters. By the use of blockade and battle Hawke had ensured British control of Atlantic sea routes for the last campaign.

On November 14, 1759, Admiral de Conflans, taking advantage of a gale which held Hawke at Torbay, had cleared from Brest to pick up a corps of troops in the Morbihan which were to be used, it was hoped, for a landing in Cornwall. On the 19th he arrived with twenty-one ships off Quiberon, chasing away a small English patrol which retired to break the news to Hawke. On the 20th Hawke arrived on the scene with twenty-three ships.[43] Conflans was no coward, but he was old and ill, and the fleet under his command, largely manned by inexperienced crews, was hardly one to inspire confidence.[44] The Morbihan was his goal, and he immediately prepared to enter into the wilderness of shoals and islets which extend between Houat, Hoedic, and the coast, assuming that the English would not dare to follow.

But Hawke was intent on reaching his prey. "Where the enemy

[42]*Ad. 1*, vol. 482, sec. II, Colville to Clevland, September 12, 1760, *ibid.*, and October 26, 1760.
[43]See map, p. 145.
[44]Tramond, *Manuel d'histoire maritime*, 413.

can go, I can go," and late in the afternoon, as the French line stretched out to pass the *Travers des Cardineaux*, he fell upon the rear. By that time, the wind had freshened into a westerly gale; there was no hope of entering the Morbihan, and Conflans turned to engage his full force. In the appalling confusion which saw French and English vessels hopelessly mixed, the demoralized French fleet was either driven on the rocks, or scattered out to sea, a few of them making Rochefort. With one stroke, Hawke had certified the fall of Quebec and sealed the conquest of Canada.

In December, 1760, General Murray had news that the enemy planned to send various small armed vessels into the Gulf and the St. Lawrence River to prey on English commerce. The notorious M. Cadet was presumed to be organizing this privateering project, and the winnings from British merchantmen were to be sent to the French colonies in the West Indies.[45] The raids did not materialize, but not from lack of opportunity. After the fall of Montreal, there was a substantial diminution in the quality and numbers of the local naval force. By December 1761, there was not a single British *stationed* ship of the line left on the North American coast, and privateers from as far away as the West Indies had become an actual threat to New England ports.[46] Under the circumstances, when the Chevalier de Ternay, with two "74's," one "64," a frigate of 36 guns, and a smaller vessel of 28, escaped from Brest in a thick fog on May 8, 1762, he had little opposition to face once he had arrived at Newfoundland.[47]

This expedition—the last shot in the locker—was conceived by the Duc de Choiseul, who had temporarily vacated the Ministry of Foreign Affairs in 1761 to take over the departments of Marine and Army. Following the break-down of peace negotiations, Britain had declared war on Spain in January, 1762. With Spanish support (which he vastly over-estimated), Choiseul apparently believed that the issue of naval and colonial supremacy might yet

[45]See *Ad. 1*, vol. 482, sec. II, Colville to Clevland, Halifax, December 8, 1760.
[46]*Ad. 1*, vol. 482, sec. II, Colville to Clevland, Halifax, December 1, 1761. "My whole Force for the protection of all the American Colonies and the River Saint Lawrence and Newfoundland," wrote Captain Spry at the end of 1762, "consist in the Mars, Enterprize and Weazle, and that [sic] I can have no dependence, on any Ships from the West Indies." At the time Spry commanded all His Majesty's ships to the northward of Florida. *Ad. 1*, vol. 480, sec. VI, Spry to Clevland, December 24, 1762.
[47]See *ibid.*, vol. 482, sec. II, Colville to Clevland, August 16, 1762.

be decided in his country's favour. In any event, he obviously hoped to win one substantial bargaining counter by a surprise occupation of Newfoundland.

Ternay reached his destination on June 24. Three days later d'Haussonville in command of some 870 grenadiers and marines disembarked in Bay Bulls and marched against St. John's to the northward. Even without the disadvantage of surprise, the garrison of Fort William, the chief harbour bastion, had no chance against a force so much superior. The English surrendered at the first summons "without coming to Action or obtaining a Capitulation."[48]

Not until the beginning of July did the commander of the North American squadron at Halifax, Lord Colville, learn of the raid, and more than two weeks elapsed before he got news of the capture of St. John's. On both occasions he seems to have submitted somewhat uneasily to the pleadings of the local administration, who urged him to consider "the defenceless condition of the Province."[49] "I would have sailed for Newfoundland immediately on receiving this Intelligence," he wrote to the Admiralty on July 24, "but was again prevented by a serious Remonstrance from the Governor and Council, intreating me in the strongest Terms to continue with them."[50] Meanwhile, General Sir Jeffrey Amherst at New York had been informed that the keys of Canada were in the hands of the enemy,[51] and he acted immediately. On September 8, Colville, now at sea, was rejoiced to learn that Amherst was preparing "to muster up all the Troops he could," from New York, Halifax, and Louisbourg.[52]

Colville with three ships had already set sail on August 10, joining a small detachment under Captain Graves at Placentia. Thence the combined forces made for St. John's, arriving on August 23. While the port was thus blocked from the sea by a squadron inferior to the French, Amherst, after scouring the garrisons from New York to Halifax, had at last despatched about 800 men, chiefly Highlanders and provincial light infantry under the command of his brother. This contingent joined Colville on September 11. A day's sail took

[48]Ibid., Colville to Clevland, July 24, 1762. Cf. Beatson, Naval and Military Memoirs, II, 575-80; Anspach, A History of the Island of Newfoundland, 157-64; and Lacour-Gayet, La Marine militaire de la France sous le règne de Louis XV, 364-5.

[49]Ad. 1, vol. 482, sec. II, Colville to Clevland, Halifax, July 2, 1762.

[50]Ibid.

[51]See C.O. 194, vol. 15, Captain Graves (at Placentia) to the Board of Trade, August 18, 1762.

[52]Ad. 1, vol. 482, sec. II, Colville to Clevland, September 20, 1762.

them to Torbay, about seven miles north of St. John's, where they were able to land despite a heavy fire from the beaches.[53] The light infantry then drove through rough, wooded country subject to sniping until they were able to occupy the hills overlooking the town. Even then the fate of the French was hardly settled. Within the harbour there were still the two "74's" and the "64." Ships' crews and troops must have totalled some 1,500 men and there were corresponding quantities of artillery and stores. The French had had sufficient time to enlarge and strengthen the fortifications, and although they were tactically at a disadvantage, their superior numbers in men and ships offered reasonable opportunities for a renewed offensive.

As it happened, however, the situation was solved for the British with very little fighting. Taking advantage of a violent storm which had driven Admiral Colville's squadron some distance from the coast, Ternay, on the night of September 15, slipped his cables and made his escape under cover of a dense fog, avoiding by a second stroke of luck Captain Palliser's squadron which had been sent as an additional relief.[54] "Thus," reported Colville to the Admiralty, "after being blocked up in the St. John's Harbour for three weeks, by a Squadron of equal Number, but smaller ships with fewer Guns and Men, did Monsieur Ternay make his Escape in the Night by a shameful Flight."[55]

Abandoned by the fleet, the French troops ceased their fire against the surrounding British batteries and surrendered on September 18. With the colonial empire almost annihilated and his navy in ruins, Choiseul's last hope of repairing disaster once more depended on the skill and resourcefulness of French diplomacy.

[53]See *ibid.*, Colville to Clevland, September 20, for narrative of attack.
[54]*Ibid.* The topmasts of four ships were seen by Colville's squadron in the early morning of the 16th about seven leagues from St. John's, but no one believed they could be the enemy.
[55]*Ibid.*

X

The Break-Up of the First Atlantic Empire, 1775-1782

IN APRIL 1775 British troops detailed to destroy stores at Concord, Massachusetts, were fired upon by colonial troops; within a year, Britain found herself engaged in major operations at a serious geographical disadvantage.[1] She was committed to a struggle far from her own shores, and against enemies who could draw plentiful subsistence from within or adjacent to their own territories. None of the loyal territories on the continent of North America could be relied upon for much help. Even Canada, which had been expected to provide at least bread and pease, found itself within a short time facing the prospect of famine.[2]

Not that the loyal colonies lacked strategic importance. The dockyard at Halifax was a convenient rendezvous for refitting and victualling, and for a brief period it served as a base of operations against New England. But it was rarely of more than secondary

[1]The best narrative of operations is contained in Admiral A. T. Mahan's *The Major Operations of the Navies in the War of American Independence* (London, 1913). Apart from the naval campaign on the Lakes, no attention is given to the part played by British North America and Newfoundland on the border lines of the struggle. A useful study is that of Admiral W. M. James, *The British Navy in Adversity* (London, 1926). For a good summary of phases of the war, see J. K. Laughton's introduction in volume one of *Letters and Papers of Charles, Lord Barham, 1758-1813* (London, Navy Records Society, XXXII, 1907); also the several introductions by the editors to *The Private Papers of John, Earl of Sandwich, First Lord of the Admiralty, 1771-1782*, ed. by G. R. Barnes and J. H. Owen (London, Navy Records Society, 1932-8; hereinafter referred to as the *Sandwich Papers*), LXIX, LXXI, LXXV, LXXVIII. Parts of this chapter are based on a paper published in the *Bulletin of the Institute of Historical Research*, vol. XXII, No. 65 (London, May, 1949) under the title "Considerations on the War of American Independence."

[2]See *Ad. 1*, vol. 485, sec. II, Admiral Graves to Philip Stevens (Secretary of the Admiralty), Boston, September 22, 1775, and Alex. Brymer to Graves, August 16, 1775.

significance. Predominant on the sea until the later stages of the war, and able, therefore, to base her armies on ports such as New York, Boston, or Charleston, Britain had no need to rely consistently on distant colonial bases. The prime function of the fleet was that of protecting and supplying British armies along the coast, and of maintaining connections between such forces. In other words, the main channels of communication ran straight from Great Britain to the battle lines.

As long as the government insisted on putting down the rebellion, British forces were compelled to conduct major campaigns on colonial territory, since the American colonies were self-sufficient in food supplies, and only in part dependent on Europe for munitions and money. Even a successful blockade of the French ports could not have ended the struggle.

The full extent of this colonial self-sufficiency was not at first appreciated in Britain. It was not realized that serious land operations would be necessary to achieve victory. In December 1774, the Secretary at War, Lord Barrington, urged that military action, if inevitable, should be confined to a naval blockade of Boston. "A conquest by land," he wrote, "is unnecessary when the country can be reduced first to distress, and then to obedience, by our Marine totally interrupting all commerce and fishery and even seizing all the ships in the ports with very little expense and bloodshed."[3] But Barrington failed to see that a well-organized rebellious minority was not going to submit merely because American overseas trade was stifled. The Thirteen Colonies had become practically self-sustaining; the main roots of their strength lay within the North American continent beyond the reach of British sea power.

Had an energetic policy been pursued in the very beginning, the rebellion might have been snuffed out before France entered the war. More effective use might have been made of an unchallenged supremacy at sea. Troops and supplies might have been poured in, and the disaffected areas tightly blockaded and quarantined. Immediate energetic action could have swamped the original opposition. As it happened the British government hesitated to use against kinsfolk the preventive measures it would have taken at once against an ordinary enemy. When the first British squadron arrived on the North American coast after the outbreak of hostilities, the commander-in-chief was instructed not to molest colonial ships, despite

[3] Quoted in Richmond, *National Policy and Naval Strength*, 34.

the fact that American privateers had already begun to run amuck in British shipping lanes.[4] This order was maintained for six months. Similarly, the troops at Boston were prevented from taking the offensive beyond the city, an inept prohibition of which the revolutionaries took full advantage.

More important still was the failure to exploit colonial military weakness during the spring and summer of 1776. On the advice of the Canadian governor, Guy Carleton, a well-equipped British army of some ten thousand men had been sent, *not* to the heart of the strategic theatre, but to the northern periphery at Quebec.[5] Had these troops, which arrived in early May, been disembarked at Boston, the Revolution might well have been crushed before it gathered headway. Political errors may lose a battle or even a war. When the British government finally decided to resort to force, it was a blunder of the first magnitude not to have applied that force directly on land and sea in overwhelming strength.

Shuffling between policies of punishment and appeasement, the government was in no position to take decisive action. Ministers were divided on the policy to be pursued, and even George III's personal leadership failed to cement all the differences. Such confusion was not unprecedented. As a consequence of party cleavages and personal animosities, there had been a similarly erratic treatment of military affairs during the war of Queen Anne. None the less, there is a conspicuous distinction between the two periods, and it is possible to say that a new phase in the history of English politics had begun with the outbreak of the American Revolution. Administrations under George III were a great deal more susceptible to the pressures of public opinion than in Anne's or Walpole's time, a tendency which was undoubtedly accelerated by the publication of parliamentary debates. It was not merely the bitter opposition of the Whig factions, but the fresh and incalculable compulsions of partisan opinion that hampered the formation of a strong American policy.

The intervention of France in March of 1778, and of Spain in the following year, while not unexpected, changed the whole picture. It turned a distant colonial war into a fight for existence. The nightmare which had so often in the past haunted British statesmen became a reality. Britain had now to contend against the combined

[4]See G. A. Ballard, *America and the Atlantic* (London, 1923), 215.
[5]See A. L. Burt, *The Old Province of Quebec* (Minneapolis, 1933), 220, 233.

forces of the Bourbons, while the utmost efforts of her diplomacy could not secure her a single continental ally. It was thus inevitable that she should be outmatched at sea. Lord Sandwich put the situation in a nut-shell:

It will be asked why, when we have as great if not a greater force than ever we had, the enemy are superior to us. To this it is to be answered that England till this time was never engaged in a sea war with the House of Bourbon thoroughly united, their naval force unbroken, and having no other war or object to draw off their attention and resources. . . . We have no one friend or ally to assist us, on the contrary, all those who ought to be our allies except Portugal act against us in supplying our enemies with the means of equipping their fleets.[6]

Faced with so painful a dilemma, a less resolute government might have pocketed its pride, cut its losses, and concentrated completely on the struggle with the hereditary enemy. But the North ministry was loth to make an outright release. To concede the surrender of a North American empire would have been a painful decision at any time; in 1778 it could be (and eventually was) politically disastrous to the court party.

George III was quite as insistent as Chatham that the abandonment of America for fear of a French invasion would be not only unnecessary but cowardly.[7] Whatever the manner or wisdom of the decision, once the war in North America became a matter of party policy, naval strategy was inevitably bent to conform with party necessity, and this sometimes meant taking grave risks.

For example, increasing commitments overseas necessitated periodic diminutions of strength in home waters, and after March 1778, made it impossible for the Grand Fleet to take the offensive and ensure unchallenged command of the Channel. Ordinarily such withdrawals should not have overtaxed fleet resources. The Admiralty liked to count on a two-power standard, with a total strength nearly equal to the combined navies of France and Spain. Even after the break with the Thirteen Colonies (which meant the loss of almost a third of her merchant shipping and an estimated 18,000 seamen),[8] Britain retained a delusive "two-power" supremacy on paper. Official figures for 1777 gave a total of 102 ships of the line,[9] but

[6]*Sandwich Papers*, III, 170.
[7]Regarding George III's determination to fight on, see Williams, *The Life of William Pitt*, II, 318 and 328; also B. Tunstall, *William Pitt, Earl of Chatham* (London, 1938), 470.
[8]*Annual Register* (London, 1778), 201.
[9]*Sandwich Papers*, App. A, 422, Abstract of the Royal Navy on January 1, 1778.

actually only about forty were fit for sea.[10] Some sixty frigates were available but these were divided between the North American and Newfoundland coasts, the East and West Indies, the Mediterranean, and the coast of Africa. As a consequence, Britain could muster in European waters a cruiser force of only some twenty sloops and other small craft, which meant that the squadron to protect the trade in home waters and to prevent enemy supplies from reaching America consisted almost entirely of line-of-battle ships.[11]

Had the fleet been up to strength, and its crews seasoned and disciplined by constant exercise at sea, political purpose and naval strategy could have been integrated smoothly and securely; command of the Channel would never have been in doubt. Indeed, a large part of the French navy might have been destroyed in one battle, that of Ushant in July 1778. But Admiral Keppel had superiority in neither numbers nor skill; the engagement was indecisive, and there remained a French "fleet in being" capable, as George Washington put it, of delivering "the casting vote in the present conflict." "If . . . our equipment had begun sooner," the First Lord of the Admiralty informed the Cabinet, and had an effectual blow been struck against the French fleet before they were joined by Spain, we should probably still have been triumphant everywhere."[12] As it was, Great Britain did not possess the ships to conduct successful war across the Atlantic as well as in the Channel, the North Sea, and the Indian Ocean.

Notwithstanding, a desperate attempt was made to hold everything. When d'Estaing captured St. Vincent and Grenada, and attacked St. Lucia, and also when de Grasse made clear his designs on Tobago and St. Eustatius, British forces were diverted from the Channel area. The diversions were never on a great scale, although they were sufficient to save Jamaica; but in view of Britain's tenuous hold on the Channel, such expedients did seem to threaten the security of the British Isles.

"Our [West Indian] Islands," wrote George III in September 1779, "must be defended even at the risk of an invasion of this Island. If we lose our Sugar Islands it will be impossible to raise

[10]See *Parliamentary History*, XIX, 728-30, 818-34, 874-95; XX, 204-38, 372, Debate on the Naval Estimates, February 13, 1777. See also N. Wraxall, *Historical Memoirs* (London, 1818), 498.

[11]In this information I am indebted to the careful investigations of Commander J. H. Owen, R.N.

[12]Memorandum to the Cabinet, September, 1779, in *Sandwich Papers*, III, 171.

money to continue the War. . . ."[13] And Sandwich advised Lord North:

> Not only the West Indies ought to be immediately strengthened, but on the first suspicion of any evil intention on the part of France, it is obligatory on us instantly to send very considerable reinforcements to Lord Howe. Should Monsieur Du Chaffault have orders to go to New York with his thirteen ships, he might give such a blow to the English fleet that it would be difficult ever to recover. The loss of America would in such an event be by far the inferior consideration.[14]

In the opinion of the Secretary of State for the Colonies, Lord George Germain, the loss of the Thirteen Colonies could mean the ultimate subjugation of Canada, and conceivably the loss of Newfoundland and the West Indies.[15]

As it happened, the greater part of the empire was retained, and Britain was not invaded, but this result was owing rather to enemy errors than to British strength at sea. "The unpardonable fault," says Admiral Richmond, ". . . lay in the neglect of the navy during many years since 1763, and the condition of impotence to which it had been reduced which made it impossible to fit out effective ships, or when fitted, to man them."[16]

Until recent years, it has been customary to place the major share of responsibility for this naval weakness on the administrative negligence and political intrigues of the First Lord of the Admiralty, the Earl of Sandwich. Certainly there was plenty of contemporary evidence on which to build a strong case. When Edmund Burke, wearied of the disclosures of unreadiness and incompetence, hurled the book of Navy Estimates at the Treasury Bench, he was giving expression to an indignation that infected a large section of the House of Commons. Even naval officers joined in the Whig attack. They were embittered by frustrations which they attributed to Admiralty carelessness or favouritism, and a few of them followed Charles James Fox into outright opposition. Admiral Keppel, for example, had refused to serve against the Americans, and only when war with

[13]*The Correspondence of King George the Third from 1760 to December 1783*, ed. J. Fortescue (6 vols., London, 1927-8), IV, no. 2773, to Lord Sandwich, September 13, 1779.

[14]*Sandwich Papers*, I, 237.

[15]*Historical Manuscripts Commission Report, Papers Relating to the American War, 1775-1782*, contained in *Report on the Manuscripts of Mrs. Stopford-Sackville of Drayton House, Northamptonshire* (hereinafter referred to as *Stopford-Sackville MSS.*), II (1910), 218, Memoir of Lord George Germain (probably 1780).

[16]H. Richmond, *Statesmen and Sea Power* (Oxford, 1946), 149.

France became inevitable was he persuaded to take command of the Western squadron.[17]

The publication by Sir John Fortescue of *The Correspondence of King George III from 1760 to December 1783* began the gradual reversal of a generally accepted verdict; and the publication of the *Sandwich Papers* under the scrupulous editorship of Mr. G. R. Barnes and Commander J. H. Owen has provided new materials which compel a reassessment. A study of these *Papers* offers good evidence that Sandwich's administration was no less efficient and no more corrupt than that of any other in eighteenth-century Britain. Sandwich himself was not incompetent, and he opposed the economies in naval expenditure which he claimed were forced on him by the Cabinet. His abilities justify the tribute of Horace Walpole: "No man in the Administration was so much master of business, so quick, or so shrewd, and no man had so many public enemies who had so few private."[18] Moreover, he was served by able men. The brilliant Charles Middleton (later Lord Barham), who never hesitated to speak his mind, began his long tenure as Comptroller in 1778;[19] and a man of real capacity, Vice-Admiral Sir Hugh Palliser, acted as principal sea officer at the Admiralty from April 1775 to the spring of 1779.

Admittedly there was corruption in high as well as low places. Ships of the line rotted to pieces in harbour, while money for repairs was wasted in unessentials or plain jobbery.[20] In March 1778 when Admiral Keppel (who had been promised thirty-five ships) arrived at Portsmouth to take over the Western squadron, he found only "six ships fit to meet a seaman's eye."[21] But this wretched state of affairs cannot be laid entirely at the doors of Admiralty misgovern-

[17] *The Barrington Papers: Selected from the Letters and Papers of Admiral the Hon. Samuel Barrington*, ed. by D. Bonner-Smith (London, Navy Records Society, 1941, vol. LXXXI), II (1941), 339-40, provide evidence of continued political bitterness; see a memorandum, "Conversation between Lord Sandwich and Admiral Barrington, May 1780."

[18] *Memoirs of the Reign of King George III*, ed. by G. F. Russell Barker (London, 1894), 170.

[19] Regarding Lord Sandwich, Middleton remarked: "He was called a jobber, but they are all equally so, and indeed more so than ever I found him to be, though more secret in their manner. In short, where there is no religion, there can be no public principle." *Sandwich Papers*, IV, 367.

[20] "...unless a new plan is adopted," wrote Charles Middleton to Sandwich in 1779, "and your lordship gives your whole time to the business of the admiralty, the misapplication of the fleet will bring ruin upon this country." Laughton, *Letters and Papers of Charles, Lord Barham*, II (1910), 3.

[21] See *Parliamentary History*, XIX, 479-80; XX, 184.

ment.[22] Peace-time economies were heavily responsible for reducing the efficiency as well as the numbers of the Royal Navy. Between 1766 and 1769, the estimates were cut by about one half. Fear of costs held back repairs, construction, and commissioning even during the three years preceding the declaration of war with France. Such negligence was not unique. There had been the same lethargy and short-sightedness during the years 1754-56, and it was to become apparent again in 1793 at the outbreak of the war of the French Revolution.

In the second place, as a result of the rebellion, Britain had been cut off from her chief source of masts which, with other naval stores, New England had provided since Cromwell's day.[23] Even the Baltic forests could not supply satisfactory substitutes for the New England pines. The problem of timber shortage had always been serious, but after 1775 the main difficulty was one of quality rather than of quantity. Ships tended to develop dry rot, especially if they had been hurriedly built of unseasoned oak. "I should be exceedingly happy," wrote a well-known ship-builder, William Wells to Lord Sandwich "if by any information I could furnish to your Lordship I could contribute towards preventing for the future that rapid decay of his Majesty's ships which we at this time most severely experience; the sole cause of which in my opinion, is their being built in a hurry with green materials. . . ."[24] It was estimated that by April 1780 the Home fleet would, at the utmost, total fifty-eight serviceable ships.[25]

Even then Britain might have been spared some of her worst humiliations had it not been for the spectacular recovery of France. For the first time since La Hogue (1692) the French navy was in a

[22]Fortescue, *The Correspondence of King George the Third*, IV, 441. See "Thoughts upon Naval measures to be taken Sept. 14, 1779, with an account of the then State of the English Fleet"; also *ibid.*, V, 342, 351, "Sandwich's Defence of His Administration of the Navy."

[23]Albion, *Forests and Sea Power*, 282. See also G. Adler, *Englands Versorgung mit Schiffsbaumaterialien aus englischen und amerikanischen Quellen* (Stuttgart, 1937).

[24]February 20, 1771, in *Sandwich Papers*, I, 14; see also "Essay on Timber Preservation," by Captain Robert Tomlinson, R.N. (about 1775), in *Tomlinson Papers*, ed. J. G. Bullocke (London, Navy Records Society, LXXIV, 1935), 203-72.

[25]*Sandwich Papers*, III, 169-70, memorandum of Lord Sandwich, September, 1779. See also *List Books* in *Admiralty Records* (*Ad. 8*) (London, Public Records Office; nos. 51-8 cover the period 1775-82). Fortescue, *The Correspondence of King George the Third*, IV, 439; and *Letters and Papers of Admiral of the Fleet, Sir Thomas Byam Martin*, ed. R. V. Hamilton (London, Navy Records Society, XIX, 1900), III, 379.

position to challenge British superiority, and actually to win command of the sea. The disasters of the Seven Years' War had not been forgotten in France. Almost immediately after the peace of 1763, according to the French historian Henri Doniol, who edited the relevant documents of the French Foreign Office in five great quarto volumes, the French government sought to take advantage of colonial restlessness in order to reap vengeance on England. "L'intérêt qu'avait la France à surveiller les dissensions de l'Angleterre, afin d'en tirer profit le jour opportun, ne faisait guère doute à Versailles."[26]

The times were auspicious. The new king, Louis XVI, was unique among French monarchs because he took a direct interest in things of the sea, and, unlike Louis XIV, made a point of visiting the ports and inspecting the ships.[27] His choice for the headship of the Ministry of Marine, Gabriel de Sartine, was a happy one. Sartine knew next to nothing about ships, but he was well aware of his own failings, and had the wisdom to surround himself with advisers who did know. Moreover, with the help of the foreign minister, the Comte de Vergennes, he took pains to make the country interested, with the result that donations flowed in from every province for the construction of new ships. Sartine deliberately prepared for war, and under his driving leadership the navy had a revival, in quality as well as quantity, hardly paralleled since the days of Colbert. Whereas the normal budget in 1776 was 35 million livres, after 1777 it went up rapidly until in 1780 it totalled 169 millions, and by 1782 had reached the 200 million mark. By 1778, France possessed some sixty ships of the line; by 1780, the number was seventy-nine, which gave her something like equality with Britain. In conjunction with Spain, however, she had a numerical advantage of about thirty.[28]

The weapon had been forged, and, equally important, men had been equipped to handle it. Together with a building programme had gone systematic training in naval science. In the new art of signalling, the Frenchman was well up with his rivals, and he was capable, as he had always been, of handling fleets as well as ships. In practical seamanship, the Briton still held the advantage, but there

[26]H. Doniol, *Histoire de la participation de la France à l'établissement des États-Unis d'Amérique: Correspondence diplomatique et documents* (5 vols., Paris, 1886-99), I, 240, 241-9.

[27]Tramond, *Manuel d'histoire maritime*, 448.

[28]See *Sandwich Papers*, I, App. C; and Lacour-Gayet, *La Marine militaire de la France sous le règne de Louis XVI* (Paris, 1905), 476-8, 629-30, 636-7, 639-40. Cf. Tramond, *Manuel d'histoire maritime*, 450; and M. le Comte de Lapeyrouse Bonfils, *Histoire de la Marine française* (3 vols., Paris, 1845), I, 78-9.

was little else, apart from numbers and pugnacity, to balance his inferiority in the field of theory and techniques. At the Académie de Marine, mathematics, hydrography, astronomy, navigation, instrument construction, naval architecture, medicine, botany, agriculture, and philosophy found a place on the curriculum.[29] The average British officer's training suffered far less diversion. In 1773 Admiral Sir Thomas Pye offered to Lord Sandwich the apologies of a self-made man.

> Give me leave my Lord to make one Observation More and I have Don— and that is When You peruse Admiral Pyes Letters you will please not to Scrutinize too Close either to the speling or the Grammatical Part as I allow my Self to be no proficient in either. I had the Mortification to be neglected in my education, went to sea at 14 without any, and a Man of War was my University.[30]

According to Mahan, only two British admirals of this period, Rodney and Howe, had the same mental and professional qualifications as their French opponents.[31] But Mahan's dictum, examined in the light of battle experience, is far from satisfying. Suffren belonged to the heights: he was certainly the greatest admiral France ever possessed; on the other hand, Kempenfelt, Hood, Palliser, Edward Hughes, Darby, and possibly Thomas Graves, were fully equal in capacity to the other good French admirals— Grasse, La Motte-Picquet, Vaudreuil, and Guichen. The best French seamen were fine tacticians in so far as their system allowed, but unorthodox strokes in the face of an emergency were rarely in evidence.[32] The French inclination to follow a scheme through according to the academic book bred caution; it encouraged adherence to orthodox patterns at times when circumstances did not favour standard dispositions.

The French naval revival was closely paralleled by a similar resurgence of activity in Spain. Like France, Spain had lost heavily during the Seven Years' War. But an energetic building programme quickly changed the situation, and by 1779, Spain possessed forty-nine ships of the line.[33] Moreover, every effort was put forth to

[29]See Castex, *Les Idées militaires de la Marine*, 99-102.
[30]*Sandwich Papers*, I, 36.   [31]*Types of Naval Officers*, 195.   [32]See pp. 148-9.
[33]See C. F. Duro, *Armada Española desde la Union de los Reinos Castilla y de Aragón* (9 vols., Madrid, 1895), VII, 231-2, 236, 239-40, 242-3, 251, 253, and 263n. Cf. G. Desdevizes du Dezert, "Histoire de la Marine au XVIIIᵉ Siècle," being Chapter VII of "Les Institutions de l'Espagne au XVIIIᵉ Siècle," *Revue Hispanique*, LXX (Paris, 1927) 443; and *Sandwich Papers*, I, App. C, which give higher figures, but such totals probably include ships that were not fit for service.

modernize the three great ports of Cartagena, Cadiz, and Ferrol and add to the number of refitting ports both at home and in the Caribbean. The best testimony to the resurrection of Spanish morale and material was afforded in 1779 when thirty-two ships, combined with an equal number of French, cruised in the English Channel and for nearly two months of the summer kept the British fleet in port.

From the Thirteen Colonies, obviously little could be expected beyond hastily organized "nuisance" forces. At varying intervals American cruisers were a scourge to British commerce, but from the beginning of the war their usefulness was marred by divided counsels. The rebels' Marine Committee had the main responsibility for conducting naval operations, but two other committees of Congress, the Committee of Foreign Affairs and the Committee of Commerce, interfered continuously, and even went so far as to fit out armed vessels on their own responsibility.[34] Then there were a variety of 'state' navies, insignificant in strength and parochial in loyalty. Washington, for example, was forced to fit out one fleet in New England, and another in New York, while Arnold organized still another on the Lakes.[35]

In view of the number of extemporized naval craft—probably two-thirds were converted merchantmen—and the gaps in central organization, it is impossible to estimate with any accuracy the strength of the American fleet. Apart from small local craft used for raiding parties, the naval forces at the beginning of the struggle certainly did not total more than twenty-seven ships, with an average of twenty guns, and few of these ships were adequately manned. The number of seamen or marines at any time during the war rarely exceeded three thousand.[36]

Until the end of 1779 the forces at the disposal of the North American station were never strong enough to patrol properly the long seacoast. With most of the larger ships congregated in the neighbourhood of Boston to support the army, there were few available to stem the activities of privateers manned by colonial merchant seamen whom the interruption of trade had forced into more exciting pursuits. Such vessels as did remain at their stations performed, in the words of their commander, a year-round work which was "un-

[34]C. O. Paullin, *The Navy of the American Revolution* (Chicago, 1906), 160.
[35]See *ibid.*, chapter entitled, "The State Navies," 493-505.
[36]*Ibid.*, 158.

precedented and incredible."[37]   By the end of 1775, some thirty-four vessels of varying sizes, only two of which were rated 50-gun, covered the coast at varying intervals from Boston harbour to the Bahamas. With the opening of hostilities, Halifax had only two stationed ships, the *Cerberus* of 28 guns, and a sloop, the *Savage*, of 8; Liverpool, further down the coast, had the old *Senegal* of 14 guns; Annapolis had the *Merlin* of 16; and Quebec the sixth-rate *Lizard* and the sloop *Hunter* of 20 and 10 guns respectively.[38] These ships and others of the North American squadron carried supplies to isolated bastions of British power, reinforced garrisons, and embarked civilians; at one time there was even the possibility that they would be used for transporting Cape Breton coal to the chilled and fuelless "regulars" of Massachusetts.[39]

By the winter of 1775, American armed schooners were in the Gulf of St. Lawrence and off Canso, but not one British ship could be spared to cruise in either area. As a consequence, these privateers were able to attack local shipping with impunity, capping their exploits with a plundering raid on Prince Edward Island.[40] The presence of just one frigate, as had been customary, would have prevented the depredations, but frigates were scarce even for fleet use. As a consequence Nova Scotia lacked sufficient craft for its own local defence.[41] The commander of the North American station could only assign "what exigencies allow" and express regrets "that the Rebels enjoy so flourishing a trade along the Eastern Coast."[42]

Meanwhile, General Sir William Howe, the commander-in-chief, faced starvation in Boston.[43] By the summer of 1775 the southern states under Congressional intimidation had ceased to fulfil their contracts, and the army was left dependent almost solely on Great

[37]*Ad. 1*, vol. 484, sec. II, Vice-Admiral Shuldham to Stephens, February 26, 1776.

[38]*Ibid.*, Disposition of Ships, January 27, 1776; also Beatson, *Naval and Military Memoirs*, VI, 43.

[39]*Historical Manuscripts Commission, American Manuscripts in the Royal Institution of Great Britain* (hereinafter referred to as *Am. MSS.*), I (1904), 251 and 265; also *ibid., The Manuscripts of the Earl of Dartmouth* (hereinafter referred to as *Dartmouth MSS.*), II (1895), 583-602.

[40]*Report of the Canadian Archives for 1895*, 15-16, Calendar of Papers relating to Prince Edward Island; and Paullin, *Navy of the American Revolution*, 66.

[41]See *Ad. 1*, vol. 484, sec. II, Vice-Admiral Shuldham to Stephens, April 16, 1776; and *The Despatches of Molyneux Shuldham* (New York, Naval History Society, III, 1913), 167 and 249. See also *Ad. 1*, vol. 484, sec. II, Shuldham to Stephens, May 10, 1776, and *The Despatches of Molyneux Shuldham*, 211.

[42]*Ad. 1*, vol. 484, sec. II, Shuldham to Callbeck, Boston, February 6, 1776.

[43]A brother of Richard, Viscount (later Earl) Howe, the admiral, Sir William commanded all the forces from Nova Scotia to West Florida.

Britain. But the British victuallers either did not sail or, failing to run the gauntlet, fell one by one into the hands of privateers. In consequence, Howe was forced to send his transports under convoy to forage for grain and cattle around the shores of the Bay of Fundy.[44] During the winter the position of his force steadily deteriorated. Endangered by growing rebel strength on the heights of Dorchester, he prepared to evacuate the town and harbour and retreat to Halifax, "the nearest and most likely place of refuge for our Army under such necessitous and Singular Circumstances."[45]

On March 17, 1776, the army was embarked and a few days later some 160 ships, under the protection of Vice-Admiral Shuldham's squadron, sailed for Halifax. There Howe planned to await reinforcements which should enable him to attack and hold New York.[46] But the reinforcements did not come. Once again, privateers picked up the victuallers and transports which were bringing supplies to Boston, while at home a vacillating ministry sent their first contingents under Commodore Sir Peter Parker to attack Charleston, an episode which ended in calamity and did as much to encourage southern secessionism as the military subjugation of New England would have discouraged it.[47]

Meanwhile, the army lay cold and helpless at Halifax, waiting for the supplies which never came.[48] As luck would have it, the winter had been exceptionally severe, and "the haven of refuge" became, for General Howe at least, "that nook of penury and cold."[49] None the less, he worked on the defences of the dockyard, counting on the guns of the *Cerberus* and *Savage* to hold the harbour against stray marauders. There was little time to strengthen the fortifications on Citadel Hill or to build the blockhouses which he had planned as a means of protecting the isthmus leading to the town.[50] In the middle of June, escorted by Vice-Admiral Shuldham, Howe sailed for New

[44]*Ad. 1*, vol. 485, sec. II, Graves to Stephens, Boston, August 19, 1775.
[45]*Ibid.*, vol. 484, sec. II, Shuldham to Stephens, Boston, March 8, 1776.
[46]*The Despatches of Molyneux Shuldham*, xxx.
[47]*Sandwich Papers*, I, 43-4.
[48]*The Despatches of Molyneux Shuldham*, xxxii.
[49]According to the journal of a visiting naval officer, "the severity of the frost was such at this time in Halifax that the meat which was served to the ship's company was always sawed in pieces with a cross-cut saw, as no other instrument could penetrate it; and innumerable shoals of fish of a peculiar fine taste were daily to be picked up on the surface of the ice, frozen to death." *Journal of Rear-Admiral Bartholomew James, 1752-1828*, ed. J. K. Laughton (London, Navy Records Society, VI, 1896), 23.
[50]*Am. MSS.*, I, 22, Major-General William Howe to Brigadier-General Massey, December 19, 1775.

York, and his forces landed unopposed on Staten Island, one day before the signing of the Declaration of Independence. By the end of September, New York was invested. In December, Rhode Island was seized, and a first-rate base provided for an attack on Boston and the contemplated isolation of New England.[51]

During this time, Halifax remained in constant danger of sporadic enemy raids; and there were rumours that, once Quebec had fallen before the renewed assaults of avenging Americans, Nova Scotia would be subject to a full-dress invasion.[52] Despite General Howes' short-lived exertions, Halifax faced the prospect of being overrun from the land approaches as well as from the sea.[53] According to an official report made at the end of the war, £100,000 had been expended on the citadel, but it was in no shape to hold out forty-eight hours against a "regular approach."[54] At the beginning of 1776 the total garrison consisted of some 500 men, many of whom were inexperienced recruits from the Newfoundland fishery; and like any other northern garrison, this one was constantly ridden with scurvy and the plague.

Moreover, the problem of defence was complicated by the presence of numerous American-born, whose "hearts and good wishes" went out unblushingly to New England. An invasion from New Hampshire, in the opinion of Admiral Graves, "would be sure of Assistance not only from the Town and Country people but even from the Artificers of the Yard who I am told are mostly of this province— It is indeed a very serious Consideration that those employed in the King's Yard are so intimately connected with the Rebels that barely by not working they might throw us into many difficulties. . . ."[55] Without troops to command the heights above the Yard, and short of loyal labour to construct batteries and entrenchments, the Com-

[51]*Sandwich Papers*, I, 45, 281.

[52]See *Ad. 1*, vol. 484, Lieutenant Governor Legge to Shuldham, Halifax, February 25, 1776.

[53]*Sandwich Papers*, I, 116-17, Mariot Arbuthnot (Commissioner at Halifax) to Lord Sandwich, January 14, 1776. Admiral Graves managed to add to the garrison a lieutenant and thirty marines: but without additional support from ships in harbour, he held out scant hopes that the port could withstand a siege, and recommended accordingly that all stores in the Yard should be put on board such transports as could be found, and sent to a place of security. *Ad. 1*, vol. 484, Arbuthnot to Shuldham, Halifax, February 15, 1776; also contained in *The Despatches of Molyneux Shuldham*, 145-6; see also *Sandwich Papers*, I, 231, William Eden to Lord Sandwich, July 20, 1777, regarding the threat from New England.

[54]See *Am. MSS.*, IV (1909), 144, Major-General James Patterson to Governor, Sir Guy Carleton, Halifax, June 11, 1783.

[55]*Ad. 1*, vol. 485, Graves to Stephens, Boston, October 3, 1775.

missioner of the Halifax Yard, Mariot Arbuthnot, regarded his headquarters as doomed.[56]

During this first interval of sporadic warfare, Washington's miscellaneous high seas navy, in keeping with British practice, had been held back from unrestricted warfare on enemy commerce; the same ruling applied to the first so-called "Continental" fleet which sailed from Delaware in February 1776. Even the privateers of Massachusetts which were provided with local *letters of marque* by the General Court in November 1775, were limited, by instructions at least, to operations against merchantmen giving succour to the beleaguered port of Boston.[57]   Not until March 23, 1776, did the Continental Congress, with a growing sense of confidence, authorize a vigorous offensive against British commerce and possessions.[58]

As soon as the decision had been taken, American strategy envisaged an all-out attack on vulnerable shipping lanes, such as the West Indies' sugar route, the Newfoundland and Nova Scotia fishing areas, and Hudson Bay. During the late autumn of 1776, privateering squadrons swooped upon Nova Scotia, destroying the fishery at Canso and stripping the harbours of small craft from Chester to Yarmouth. A small expedition of some three or four hundred besieged Fort Cumberland, and Judge Charles Morris of Halifax believed the capital would be next to fall. "We are threatened with a total destruction by the other Colonies, who look upon this place as a magazine of stores for the Army and Navy and have come to a determination to make an entire conquest of it this winter."[59]   Only the capture of the Americans' fastest frigate, the *Hancock*, served to

[56]*Ibid.*, vol. 484, Arbuthnot to Graves, Halifax, January 15, 1776.
[57]W. B. Clarke, "American Naval Policy, 1775-6," *The American Neptune*, vol. I, No. I, January, 1941, 26. Since the little armed American fishing vessels known as "pirates" were no great menace, Admiral Howe preferred they remain unmolested. As he explained, they captured New England coastal craft which British ships-of-war took over from them almost as rapidly. *Am. MSS.*, I, 177, Major-General Eyre Massey to General Sir William Howe, January 10, 1778.
[58]It was obvious that the infant American fleet was helpless to protect the continental coastline, and eventually the Marine Committee sought relief in a spectacular invasion of enemy home waters. It was by no means a mad decision. In the Channel and North Sea they could use French ports as naval bases whenever they wished to raid the British coasts. As a consequence, the famed expeditions of John Paul Jones were initiated, not with any idea of inflicting really grievous damage, but for the sake of nuisance value, as a faint means of encouraging the recall of British forces overseas. See Paullin, *The Navy of the American Revolution*, 169-70, 175-6.
[59]*Dartmouth MSS.*, I, 414-15, Judge Morris to Lieutenant Governor Legge, Halifax, November 18, 1776, and November 24, 1776.

lighten the gloom, a feat which was exuberantly greeted by the local traders, whose ships "were adorn'd with flags and colors at their mastheads, and at night most of the houses were illuminated."[60]

Not until mid-winter did the long-feared invasion come. It was not a sustained operation like the invasion of Canada in 1775, for it lacked Congressional support; yet the little expeditionary force of enthusiasts from New England did get within distant reach of Halifax before retreating in the face of the elements rather than enemy-gun-fire.[61]

In neighbouring waters, the Newfoundland fishery suffered the same kind of ravaging expeditions, stimulated by orders from Congress "to Take, Burn, Sink or destroy every English Vessel they should find Fishing on the Banks."[62] With only two 20-gun vessels and one sloop at his disposal, the governor, Vice-Admiral Montagu, could do little, until reinforced in the summer of 1777 with the 50-gun *Romney*, the 64-gun *Bienfaisant* and seven smaller craft.[63] Until then, with the exception of St. John's, every harbour from Cap Rouge to Bonavista was open to the enemy.[64]

St. John's was the only port in any condition to stave off the attacks of the privateers. As a result of careful surveys in 1765-6, it had been decided to dismantle the works at Placentia, and to concentrate on the defence of the old Avalon settlement.[65] During the summer of 1772, part of the garrison of Fort Frederick (Placentia) was removed to St. John's, where a new structure was begun under the name of Fort Townsend; the battery at the entrance to the harbour was finished and a new barracks prepared for 300 men.[66] As it happened, however, voluntary enlistments for service at New

[60]*Stopford-Sackville MSS.*, II, 69.

[61]W. B. Kerr, "The American Invasion of Nova Scotia, 1776-7," *Canadian Defence Quarterly*, XIII, July, 1936, 433-45.

[62]*C.O. 194*, vol. 33, Vice-Admiral Montagu to Lord George Germain, June 11, 1777; see also *Stopford-Sackville MSS.*, II, 69.

[63]In 1778, the Newfoundland station was again reinforced from John Byron's squadron by the addition of a "74" and a 28-gun frigate, which had put into St. John's as the result of a gale. *Sandwich Papers*, II, 287. Cf. Beatson, *Naval and Military Memoirs*, VI, 87.

[64]*C.O. 194*, vol. 32, Robert Pringle, Commanding Engineer, to Lord Dartmouth, October 20, 1775; also G. O. Rothney, *The History of Newfoundland and Labrador, 1754-1783* (a thesis submitted for the M.A. degree at the University of London, 1934), 237.

[65]See *Dartmouth MSS.*, II, 68, Cabinet Minutes, May 31, 1769; also 559 and 582.

[66]For details of the defences of St. John's, see G. S. Graham, "Britain's Defence of Newfoundland," *The Canadian Historical Review*, XXIII, September, 1942, 276-7

York and Halifax soon reduced the effective troops to thirty-three, and the morale of these survivors was hardly improved by lack of bedding, fuel, and provisions.

The rest of the island had no land defences at all, and in the out-lying ports the depredations continued unabated. In May of 1778, Placentia was attacked, and shipping in the harbour destroyed or damaged;[67] next, Bay Bulls, Ferryland, and St. Mary's were plundered with a loss of twenty-two fishing vessels. Most of the settlements on Labrador suffered a similar fate at the hands of Captain Grimes of the *Minerva*.[68] Admiral Montagu complained bitterly of Admiralty neglect; but even had there been more ships, hide-and-go-seek tactics were bound to fail in the fog-bound waters of Newfoundland.[69]

The outbreak of war with France eased the situation in one way, for it made possible the capture of two nests of privateers. Both St. Pierre and Miquelon surrendered on September 14, and the victors began their accustomed task of destroying harbour installations, houses, stages, and fishing rooms.[70] By the end of 1779, the privateers had all but disappeared, the Gulf and Banks were patrolled, two sloops-of-war watched the Labrador coast, and three new batteries guarded the entrance to the harbour of St. John's.[71]

In the meantime, Saratoga had set the seal on Carleton's fateful blunder of 1776. The news of General Burgoyne's surrender determined the moment of French intervention. On February 6, 1778, two treaties were signed with the United States—one of "friendship and commerce" and the other of "alliance." At the same time the commanders at Brest and Toulon were ordered to prepare their ships for active service. On March 13 the British government was officially informed of the first treaty, and a declaration of war followed. A month later, Admiral the Comte d'Estaing left Toulon for North America with eleven ships of the line and one 50-gun ship.

Despite Burgoyne's disastrous collapse, the British government was still unprepared to admit that the colonial revolt could not be suppressed. Canada and the Maritime Provinces were intact; the army held New York, with a detachment at Rhode Island where a

[67]*C.O. 194*, vol. 34, Pringle to Germain, June 6, 1778.
[68]*Ibid.*, Vice-Admiral Montagu to Germain, October 5, 1778.
[69]*Ad. 1*, vol. 471, Montagu to Stephens, May 5 and 19, 1778.
[70]*C.O. 194*, vol. 34, Montagu to Germain, October 5, 1778, with three enclosures; also *ibid*, same to same, October 16 and November 19, 1778; see also Beatson, *Naval and Military Memoirs*, IV, 380.
[71]G. O. Rothney, *The History of Newfoundland and Labrador*, 250-1.

British squadron rode serenely at anchor in Narragansett Bay, the finest strategic harbour on the whole seaboard.[72] The Howe brothers had occupied Philadelphia in September 1777, and there was a small contingent of troops in Florida. Indeed, on March 8, 1778, the Cabinet issued bold and optimistic instructions for the forthcoming campaign.

Two weeks later, however, news of the Franco-American treaty caused an alteration of plans. "The object of the war being now changed," read additional instructions of 22 March to Admiral Howe, "and the contest in America being a secondary consideration, the principal object must be the distressing of France and defending and securing H.M. own possessions. . . ."[73] As a consequence, the army was instructed to give up Philadelphia; St. Lucia was to be seized as a vital base for the defence of the West Indies; Florida was to be reinforced; while the remainder of the British forces were to retire to New York to await "the issue of the Treaty which we have authorized our Commissioners to propose."[74] If the peace proposals failed, even New York might have to be abandoned.

The military outlook in America was unanimously recognized as sombre. Britain's capacity to carry on campaigns on the North American continent now depended entirely upon whether or not the French had the wisdom and the enterprise to use their superior forces to break British sea communications. It is clear that had the French immediately secured American bases, as well they might have done, and concentrated on interrupting British lines of communication, the British commander-in-chief must have withdrawn from want of supplies. But from the beginning France preferred to concentrate her forces in the Caribbean and collect West Indian islands, with the consequence that, for the better part of two years, British transports and victualling ships made their way to New York with comparatively little interference.

It might seem possible to offer an explanation of this "phoney" war at sea in terms of French naval doctrine and territorial ac-

[72]Admiral Rodney's estimate, in Mahan, *The Major Operations of the Navies in the War of American Independence*, 48.

[73]*Admiralty Out-Letters* (hereinafter referred to as *Ad. 2*), vol. 1334, Letters from the Secretary of State and Secret Orders and Instructions, signed by Lord Sandwich, Admiral Palliser, and Captain Lord Mulgrave. The idea and even the words were Amherst's; see copy of a note (original in Amherst's handwriting), in *Sandwich Papers*, I, 365.

[74]The Carlisle Commission which was sent out with instructions dated April 12, to try to arrange terms with the colonies. See *Historical Manuscripts Commission Report, Carlisle MSS.* (London, 1897).

quisitiveness. Traditional caution certainly played a part in Admiral d'Estaing's decision to follow Fabian tactics on the Atlantic coast; his reluctance to risk his superior force in battle drove Washington nearly frantic, and elicited the criticism of Suffren.[75] But doctrines of *passive defence* were not the only considerations influencing d'Estaing's behaviour. Politics and diplomacy, which had so deeply influenced the administration and movements of the Royal Navy, had now begun to play a part in shaping French naval strategy.

At the beginning of 1778, the French Foreign Office had reached the conclusion that in order to preserve the proper balance of power in North America, Canada and Nova Scotia must be left to Great Britain.[76] In July of the same year, Spain gave unqualified assent.[77] The Treaty of Alliance concluded at Paris on February 6, 1778, confirmed the French decision to renounce further schemes of North American conquest; but it did not, however, guarantee continued British occupation of Canada. By Article VI, France renounced forever the possession of the "islands of Bermudas," as well as "any part of the continent of North America which before the treaty of Paris in 1763, or in virtue of that treaty, were acknowledged to belong to the Crown of Great Britain, or to the United States, heretofore called British Colonies, or which are at this time, or have lately been under the power of the King and Crown of Great Britain." But Article V formally recorded the agreement that if the United States "should think fit to attempt the reduction of the British power remaining in the northern parts of America, or the islands of Bermudas, those countries or islands, in case of success, shall be confederated with or dependent upon the said United States."[78]

From the outset the French foreign minister, the Comte de Vergennes, aimed at neutralizing this latter claim. He had no wish to see the new republic consolidating its strength after a quick victory, and becoming independent of French influence. Gérard de Rayneval's instructions as first plenipotentiary to the United States stated with unusual directness that the retention of Canada by England would

[75]Lacour-Gayet, *La Marine militaire de la France sous le règne de Louis XVI,* 129.

[76]Doniol, *Histoire de la participation de la France à l'établissement des États Unis* III, 153-7, Gérard de Rayneval's Instructions, March 29, 1778.

[77]In July, 1778, Florida Blanca remarked, "Seeds of division and jealousy must be sown between the new republic and its former mother country, to which end the latter must be left Canada and Acadia." *Ibid.*, 556-9, Montmorin to Vergennes, October 15 and 19, 1778.

[78]Text contained in E. S. Corwin, *French Policy and the American Alliance of 1778* (Princeton, 1916), App. I.

be a valuable source of uneasiness and vigilance to the Americans; it would make them feel the need of the French partnership and it was not in the French interest to destroy that feeling. Furthermore, no small part of England's strength and care would be permanently diverted from the European balance to the maintenance of a minor balance in the Western Hemisphere.[79]

Although Benjamin Franklin at the behest of Congress continued to urge on Vergennes the wisdom of reducing Halifax and Newfoundland, no instructions were ever issued from Versailles.[80] Vergennes was anxious to avoid any encouragement to an American invasion of Canada. D'Estaing's instructions did, indeed, admit the possibility of an attack on Newfoundland but responsible ministers in France recognized that if St. John's were attacked by a French squadron, Congress would almost certainly demand an assault on Canada in order to remove the threat which Vergennes, for good reasons, was anxious that the Americans should continue to bear. A British Canada was a safeguard of American good-will and of American weakness. Nothing else explains satisfactorily d'Estaing's failure to attack Halifax and St. John's (which he had originally proposed to do in the summer of 1778), or the unusually pressing instructions from home to concentrate on acquisitions in the West Indies.[81]

Nevertheless, so long as d'Estaing's destination was uncertain, Halifax seemed a likely target for French guns, a British conjecture which intercepted despatches seemed to confirm.[82] Moreover, the decision to erect fortifications on the Penobscot River below the Bay of Fundy meant heavy demands on ships, men and materials, and left Halifax for a greater part of the summer practically at the mercy

[79]Doniol, *Histoire de la participation de la France à l'établissement des États Unis*, III, 156-8, 557; IV, 74. Corwin, *French Policy and the American Alliance of 1778*, 22. See also Gérard to Vergennes, Philadelphia, July 9, 1779: "No person during the course of the present negotiation has proposed to demand Canada even on the supposition of the indefinite continuance of the war," in Abstracts of Political Correspondence relating to the United States, 1778-80 in the Ministry of Foreign Affairs, France, in *Report of the Canadian Archives for 1912*, App. L, 198. Governor Haldimand did not appreciate his unique security until Germain wrote him secretly in October, 1781, that the French Court were opposing in every way the attempts of Congress to take Canada. *C.O. 42*, vol. 42, Haldimand to Germain, Quebec, October 23, 1781, acknowledging receipt.

[80]See G. O. Rothney, *British Policy in the North American Cod-Fisheries, with Special Reference to Foreign Competition, 1775-1819* (a thesis submitted for the Ph.D. degree of the University of London, 1939), 116.

[81]See in this connection Lacour-Gayet, *La Marine militaire de la France sous le règne de Louis XVI*, 174-5.

[82]*Am. MSS.*, II (1906), 51, Clinton to McLean, New York, October 20, 1779.

of any visiting American forces.[83] Even Penobscot was a temptation to the potential invader, since its small garrison of 400 men could hardly have coped with a serious attack. General McLean, who was organizing the defences, showed little enthusiasm for his new task; indeed, for the sake of Halifax he recommended a complete withdrawal from the posts on the St. John River and at Cumberland. However, as the autumn drew on and no French squadron appeared, it seemed likely that d'Estaing would once more seek his tropical retreat, leaving the initiative to New England skippers and captains who had spent the late summer busily fitting out an armament at Boston.[84]

But the governors of Newfoundland, Nova Scotia, and Canada continued to act on the assumption that the "principal effort" would be directed against their own respective domains. As a consequence, Newfoundland rushed the formation of a local regiment of volunteers, on the pattern of the American "provincials."[85] At Halifax, batteries were repaired, new entrenchments dug on Citadel Hill, and bomb-proof magazines sunk,[86] while Haldimand at Quebec prepared to destroy all the stores at Bic and intern all the French pilots should the enemy put in an appearance in the Gulf.[87] Neither at Halifax nor Quebec were there sufficient men adequately to defend the existing works, and Haldimand faced the additional problem of finding skilled seamen to man the ships on the Lakes.[88] Well for his peace of mind had he known that diplomatic rivalries adequately protected his realm. Congress still talked boisterously about the projected invasion of Newfoundland and Nova Scotia, but French diplomacy gingerly shunned all such temptations.[89]

[83]See *Am. MSS.*, II, 18-19, Sir George Collier to General Sir Henry Clinton, August 24, 1779; also *ibid.*, I, 381, Clinton to McLean, February 11, 1779; *ibid.*, 458 and 459, McLean to Clinton, June 26, 1779; and *ibid.*, 461 and 462, Captain Andrew Berkley to Clinton, June 27, 1779. See also *ibid.*, I, 452 and 453 regarding the precarious situation of Nova Scotia.

[84]*Ibid.*, II, 50, Clinton to McLean, October 15, 1779; also *ibid.*, 51, same to same, October 20; and *ibid.*, 52, McLean to Clinton, October 20, 1779; see also *ibid.*, 55, Clinton to McLean, October 28, 1779. Further correspondence in *ibid.*, 66, 67, and 121.

[85]G. O. Rothney, *The History of Newfoundland and Labrador, 1754-1783*, 252-3.

[86]*Am. MSS.*, II, 180, McLean to Clinton, September 14, 1780.

[87]*Calendar of Haldimand Collection, II, Report of the Canadian Archives for 1887* (Ottawa, 1888), 474, Haldimand to Captain Young, June 6, 1780.

[88]*Ibid.*, 477, same to same, April 24, 1781; also *ibid.*, 479, Captain Pringle to Haldimand, September 29, 1781.

[89]The French attack on the Hudson Bay posts in 1782 was a nuisance raid, and was not concerned with conquest. See Appendix C.

On the European side of the Atlantic the situation continued to deteriorate for Britain as a result of Spain's entrance into the war in April 1779. Until illness crippled it, a combined French and Spanish fleet threatened to gain command of the English Channel. In these circumstances, British Ministers were forced to recognize that if they could not, in the near future, bring Washington to decisive action, they would have to relinquish any hope of carrying on further offensive operations on land. In consequence, the commander-in-chief, General Sir Henry Clinton, made his final effort—a detached landing operation in the southern states.[90] After capturing Charleston on May 12, 1780, Clinton returned to New York leaving Lord Cornwallis in command. With the object of diverting Washington from New York, and counting, fruitlessly as it turned out, on Loyalist aid, Cornwallis with some 7,700 men (about half Clinton's army) decided to advance into North Carolina, thus separating himself from his naval base at Charleston. The country south of the James River was wild and difficult, offering many traps for a small army in an alien land; but so long as Cornwallis could keep in contact with the coast he could continue to draw supplies, or in an emergency embark his troops on board the fleet. Everything, therefore, depended on maintaining the supremacy in North American waters at a time when the only British hope of security, not to speak of success, lay in maintaining sea communications. Yet at the very time that Cornwallis had begun his sweeping operation in the south, Rhode Island was occupied and held by the French, who were thus in an excellent position to operate against New York.[91] The British were no longer favourably placed to assume the offensive on the North American coast, and the fate of the Thirteen Colonies now depended on the extent to which beckoning opportunity would generate an offensive spirit in the French, whose strategy had hitherto been remarkable for its restraint.

In August 1781, when Washington, after frantic appeals, at long last secured the necessary support of a large French fleet, the British

---

[90]For the naval side of operations, and short bibliography, see *The Keith Papers: Selected from the Letters and Papers of Admiral Viscount Keith*, ed. by W. G. Perrin (London, Navy Records Society, vol. XLII), I (1927), part II, sec. III, *passim*.

[91]The lack of co-operation between British sea and land forces is urged by W. B. Willcox as one reason why Rhode Island was not regained by assault, or neutralized by blockade. See his excellent article, "Rhode Island in British Strategy, 1780-81," *The Journal of Modern History*, XVII, December, 1945, 304-31.

army on the continent found itself in gravest jeopardy. Assuming that New York was the objective of Admiral de Grasse, Clinton refused to reinforce Cornwallis, leaving the latter with little more than 7,000 men all told. Having penetrated well into Virginia, it was impossible for Cornwallis, in the face of growing enemy resistance, to fight his way back to his base at Charleston. Hence, he marched to the coast, and on August 22 took up position at Yorktown on a tongue of land between the James and the York Rivers. There he hoped to be in a position to hold out until rescued by British ships from New York.

The ensuing indeterminate action of Chesapeake Bay that led to the surrender of Cornwallis on October 19, 1781, is part of a large and complicated story which Mahan has told well, but which needs revision in the light of new evidence.[92] Whether or not the traditional strictures against Rear-Admiral Graves's conduct of the battle have any justice, one fundamental fact emerges above the mass of technical and sometimes contradictory data: France and Spain had gained superiority in American and West Indies waters.

While arguing that "the arrangements for the protection of America . . . failed from accidents that could not be foreseen or guarded against by the Government," Lord Sandwich unhesitatingly acknowledged that "if we had had a superior fleet in America, Lord Cornwallis would have been saved."[93] This concentration in American waters was impossible because, in the year 1781, France and Spain and Holland outnumbered Great Britain at sea. At the time when Graves faced French superiority off the North American coast, and Vice-Admiral Peter Parker confronted numerically greater Spanish forces in the neighbourhood of Jamaica, a sadly weakened Grand Fleet in home waters was preparing desperately to defend itself against a French-Spanish fleet, nearly twice its strength.[94]

Chesapeake Bay was a trifling engagement as battles go, but because of its immense consequences, it served to demonstrate in chilling fashion that British naval superiority was not the relatively certain thing it had been for three quarters of a century after La Hogue. Without allied support on the Continent to divert French energies, the Royal Navy had not been strong enough to ensure con-

[92]This evidence consists partly of letters from Graves and Hood, published in the *Sandwich Papers*, IV.
[93]See *ibid.*, 351, Notes for a Speech. The debate took place on March 6, 1782; see also *ibid.*, 125-7, Introduction.
[94]See *Sandwich Papers*, IV, 9-14.

tinuous command of North American waters. Against a hostile coalition such as the American War had produced, with the constant danger of Baltic neutrals like Russia adding to the numbers of the enemy, Great Britain was threatened with defeat in European waters, and was fighting for survival.

Even had there been no Yorktown, it is most unlikely that the mother country could have quashed the rebellion. As long as British troops were regularly supplied from home, they might have kept their footholds in New York or Charleston; but the occupation of a few strategic segments on a long coastline did not necessarily mean the subjugation of a vast territory that was largely in a position to support its own forces. To suggest that only French intervention in North American waters could have won independence for the United States is an over-simplification. In one sense, of course, the argument is a truism, since the achievement of local command at Chesapeake Bay was decisive. It sealed independence. But even if the French had not intervened in the North American theatre, it is difficult to believe that Great Britain, bereft of allies and occupied with three powerful enemies in other parts of the globe, could have found the resources and the men to subdue a quarter of a continent, three thousand miles away.

It was not merely administrative failure, nor was it military and naval ineptitude that was accountable for this condition. The dominating factor was political isolation. The failure of diplomacy, hastened by the unprecedented intrusion of politics on strategy, was responsible, in the final issue, for bringing down the first British Empire.

XI

The Outskirts of War, 1793-1812

DURING the wars precipitated by the outbreak of the French revolution, British possessions in North America were in no real danger of invasion so long as Britain retained command of the sea and the United States remained neutral. This aloofness from the main stream of events is reflected in most of the official correspondence. There is sometimes a note of urgency and sometimes of bitterness in the letters from the Halifax station; but by and large the little ships which tossed in the Bay of Fundy or poked their way into the Gulf of St. Lawrence in search of privateers seem very far away from the roars and confusion of the European struggle. Spies and agents report plots of invasion and tamperings with the British Indians; there are long memoranda on the state of fortifications and the equipment of the troops and numerous letters regarding the convoy of wheat and masts to Britain; but direct references to the titanic struggle being waged overseas are almost entirely absent. People submerged in the problems of pioneer settlement, trade, and fishing, gave little thought to Europe unless called upon officially to celebrate a victory of "the Nile" or a "Cape St. Vincent."

For the first few years after 1793, France was rarely in a position to carry organized warfare overseas. The French revolution had dealt a blow to the navy which only years could repair. After the fall of the Bastille, most of the officer class was driven from the service as neo-aristocrats, and while many of the new men proved to be good and zealous seamen, the essential experience and discipline were lacking. In addition, the dockyards had suffered a dislocation which even Napoleon was unable to repair; the British blockade severely limited the import of naval stores, and many of the hundreds of hastily built ships began to disintegrate as soon as they were launched. It is not unfair to say that the French fleets, which Howe, Nelson, and Collingwood defeated cannot be compared in quality with the fleets that sailed the seas under d'Estaing, de Grasse, and Suffren during the War of the American Revolution.

So complete an initial supremacy undoubtedly suggested and facilitated the various expeditions overseas, chiefly in the West Indies, which historians have generally described as costly "sideshows." Theoretically, Pitt's object was to sap French commerce by occupying French bases. Yet in terms both of material and strategic advantage the operations were unnecessary. As the war progressed, the French merchant marine, never very strong, lost steadily in manpower and ships, and the trade cut off by such operations had only a trifling effect on the stability of French war finance.[1] Moreover, the strategic situation had changed since Chatham's day. France was no longer a power in North America, and apart from ridding the Caribbean of privateering nests, these extravagant amphibious expeditions had no real relation to the task of defeating her.[2]

The British position in the West Indies and in North America depended, as always, on the ability of the Royal Navy to control and command the seas in the European theatre of operations. What happened elsewhere could have no lasting effect on the conduct or result of the war. As it happened, St. Vincent, the Nile, Camperdown, and Trafalgar extinguished any new claims either France or Spain might have made in the New World, and at the same time, guaranteed the integrity not only of British North American possessions but of the United States as well. Strategically, the colonies were still weak, since they were not yet self-supporting; but unless the French won a battle as decisive as Trafalgar, their captains had no chance in the world of emulating Saunders's example and ascending the St. Lawrence to storm Quebec.

The weakness of the French navy at the beginning of the war naturally simplified the problem of blockade; at the same time, the successful application of blockade by superior British forces sapped the efficiency of the existing French fleet still further by preventing

---

[1]Departures and entries to and from French ports indicate a trade about half that of England, but only 29 per cent was under the French flag. Tramond, *Manuel d'histoire maritime*, 536; and H. W. Richmond, *Amphibious Warfare in British History* (Exeter, 1941), 6.

[2]Pitt, unlike his father, had little knowledge of local conditions; disease swept off the British soldiers, and within three years, some 40,000 died, a number which Mr. Arthur Bryant has suggested was roughly equal to the number which Wellington used in six years to drive Napoleon's troops out of Spain.

it from exercising in open waters. "The pavements of the great ports," wrote a French naval historian, Jurien de la Gravière, "are fatal to discipline. . . . Let us clearly understand that the English owed their triumph neither to the number of their ships, their plentiful seafaring population, the strength of their Board of Admiralty, nor to the clever tactics of their great admirals. They defeated us because their ships' companies were better trained, their fleets better disciplined than our own."[3] This statement is borne out by the remarks of courageous and devoted French captains, who fought, in addition to the enemy, jealousies, ignorance, sickness, and mutiny.

With the ports of Brest and Toulon scrupulously guarded by the Western and Mediterranean squadrons, there was little need, therefore, to detach ships for overseas duty. Apart from the obligation to provide convoys for the trade routes, the abbreviated British Atlantic coast line, including Newfoundland, required hardly more than two or three fifty-gun ships in addition to a few frigates. The bulk of the Royal Navy continued as formerly to watch the enemy ports, "only sending abroad such force as we are certain they may have sent, in order to re-inforce the commander-in-chief upon the station upon which an attack is intended. For more effectually performing such service when required, a certain proportion of the Channel Fleet may always be kept stored and victualled for foreign service."[4] In 1800, while the stations at Jamaica and Leeward Islands were assigned six first-class ships of the line, one fifty-gun, forty-five frigates, and forty-three sloops, Halifax had to be content with four frigates and two sloops, while Newfoundland had two frigates and four sloops.[5]

It was certain, nevertheless, that the French would use their island possessions as bases for flying squadrons to interrupt British North American trade. The Newfoundland fisheries had always been a principal object of attack by privateers; interceptions near the Gulf of St. Lawrence were expected to injure the Quebec trade, as well as the export traffic of Nova Scotia and New Brunswick, consisting chiefly of naval stores, timber, and masts.[6]

[3]*Guerres maritimes sous le Republique et l'Empire* (2nd ed., Paris, 1853), 223.
[4]Laughton, *Letters and Papers of Charles Lord Barham*, II, 395, Captain Philip Patton to Sir Charles Middleton, June, 1794.   [5]*Naval Chronicle*, 1801, V, 552.
[6]See Laughton, *Letters and Papers of Charles Lord Barham*, II, 366, 398, Memorandum of October, 1793; also G. F. G. Stanley, "The Defence of the Maritime Provinces during the Wars of the French Revolution," *Canadian Defence Quarterly*, XIV, July, 1937, 437-47.

There was no doubt where American sympathies lay; French influences were strong south of the St. Lawrence and almost daily came rumours of pending invasion.[7] Moreover the governors felt they could not count on the loyalty of the French Canadians; and while official fears were exaggerated, there was an apparent "spirit of disobedience" which French agents from the United States were reputed to have nourished, and a "marked satisfaction" among certain elements in Montreal whenever rumours of the approach of a French squadron went the rounds.[8] Assuming, of course, that an expedition managed to escape the attentions of the Western squadron, the invasion of Canada by the St. Lawrence was a possibility. Quebec was not an impregnable fortress; if it were captured, Montreal, still more weakly defended, was bound to fall quickly, and with the aid of native Canadians, the enemy would, in the opinion of local authorities, be in a position to make a nuisance of themselves on land whether or not they retained mastery of the seas.[9]

But such dangers were purely speculative. The main threat to the North American colonies lay in attacks on shipping by chance raiders from such rendezvous as St. Pierre and Miquelon. Since the most effectual way to protect trade was to occupy the ports from which the raiders sailed, a small expedition was hastily organized in 1793. The subsequent reduction of both islands in May, and the return to France of the weary inhabitants, was carried out with a speed and efficiency which showed the benefits of previous practice. Once more, subsequent to the Peace of Amiens, the islands were re-occupied,[10] but from 1816 onwards they remained in the possession of France.

In August 1793, news reached Halifax that a French squadron had arrived at New York and that, "from the Quantity of warm Clothing laid in," an attack on either Halifax or Newfoundland might be pending.[11] In the following year, the squadron commanders

[7]See *Canadian Archives, Q Series*, vol. 67, 191; vol. 68, 162, Dorchester Correspondence.

[8]See *ibid.*, vol. 78, 7, Prescott to Portland, October 24, 1796.

[9]See *ibid.*, vol. 282, 599, Simcoe to Portland, December 11, 1796.

[10]See *Ad. 1*, vol. 475, Admiral James Gambier to Evan Nepean, May 24, 1803, acknowledging Admiralty orders.

[11]*Ad. 1*, vol. 492, Commodore Rupert George to Philip Stephens, Halifax, August 27, 1793. In October 1793, reports had reached Canada that a French fleet consisting of two "74's," two frigates, a sloop, and two armed brigs with 2,500 soldiers, had sailed from Sandy Hook (New York) for the St. Lawrence. *Canadian Archives, Q Series*, vol. 66, 250, Minutes of Council, Quebec, October 25, 1793.

were "positively assured" that an expedition consisting of six ships of the line had sailed from France with the intention of intercepting trade off the southern end of the Newfoundland Banks.[12] To make matters worse, numerous French privateers were fitting out at Charleston and Baltimore, with obvious American support and encouragement; indeed, it was suspected that many of the ships were manned by American volunteers.[13]

For the moment, Halifax remained unperturbed. "We are here perfectly at ease respecting an attack upon us," wrote the commodore in charge of the station, "having between forty and fifty heavy Cannon (32 & 24 Pound[rs]) mounted on the different Batteries, one 13 inch Mortar and two 8 inch Howitzers, with Furnaces for heating Shot." The regular troops, including artillery and the governor's corps, amounted to less than 600, but to this total could be added two battalions of local militia, as well as the crews of the merchant vessels and war-ships in the harbour. As an extra precaution, Lieutenant-Governor Wentworth called in 1,200 of the "Country militia" thus providing, it was assumed, sufficient strength to resist any attack from the sea.[14]

The defences of Halifax were, however, no protection against invasion by the St. Lawrence, or against privateering attacks on local trade routes. Accordingly, the Admiralty took steps to reinforce the North Atlantic station. In May of 1794 a squadron which included one ship of the line was placed under the command of Rear-Admiral George Murray, and directed to take responsibility "for the protection of the North American Provinces."[15] Murray had a dual task, that of protecting the long coast-line of the Maritime Provinces, the Bay of Fundy, and the Gulf of St. Lawrence against French privateers and American interlopers, and secondly, of patrolling the southern Atlantic coast as far as, and sometimes beyond, the Chesa-

---

[12]*Ad. 1*, vol. 492, Captain Alex. F. Cochrane to Rear Admiral George Murray, New York, November 14, 1794.

[13]See *ibid.*, Admiral Murray to the Earl of Chatham, Halifax, December 16, 1794, and same to Philip Stephens, December 7, 1794.

[14]*Ibid.*, Commodore Rupert George to Philip Stephens, August 27, 1793.

[15]*Canadian Archives, Q Series*, vol. 67, 68, Dundas to Dorchester, Whitehall, May 9, 1794. Until 1810, when French squadrons were finally expelled from the West Indies, British ships based on Jamaica and the Leeward Islands were usually more than four times the strength of the Halifax and Newfoundland squadrons combined. See *Correspondence, Despatches and Other Papers of Viscount Castlereagh*, ed. by his brother, C. W. Vane, Marquess of Londonderry (London, 1851), VIII, 296.

peake, to intercept enemy supply ships en route to or returning from the West Indies or the southern ports of the United States.[16] In addition, he was called upon to break the traffic in naval stores, masts, horses, and provisions between New England and the French West Indies, whence convoys assembled to take the articles to France.[17]

In view of the smallness of his squadron, the commander-in-chief was always loth to split it up; on the other hand, some of the smaller vessels had to be left in the north to watch for French privateers based on New England ports.[18] But even when the squadron was substantially intact, it was never adequate to cope with any large French force, and in times of emergency he could only hope that the West Indies squadron might speedily reinforce him "should the French ships escape them."[19] As a matter of fact, the Halifax

[16]As commander-in-chief of the Halifax station, Murray's command embraced "His Majesty's Ships and Vessels employed & to be employed in the River St. Lawrence, along the coast of Nova Scotia, the Island of St. John & Cape Breton, in the bay of Fundy & the Islands of Bermuda." Not until 1809 was the boundary between the Halifax station and that of the Leeward Islands accurately defined. See *Ad. 2*, vol. 932, W. W. Pole to Vice-Admiral Sir J. B. Warren, May 1, 1809.

[17]*Ad. 1*, vol. 493, Murray to Evan Nepean, July 15, 1796.

[18]List and Disposition of His Majesty's Ships and Vessels under the command of Vice Admiral Murray, Commander in Chief, etc., 19th July 1796.

	Guns	Men	
Resolution	74	612	
Assistance	50	343	
Topaze	38	254	
Raison	28	195	Refitting at Halifax
Esperance	16	121	
Bermuda	16	80	
Spencer	16	80	
Thetis	38	284	
Privoyante	38	284	Cruising off the Carolines and Georgia
Thisbe	28	195	
Bonitta	16	121	
Lynx	16	121	Gone to Martinique with a Mast Ship. On her return to join the Thisbe.
Cleopatra	32	215	Gone to Bermuda with stores and to cruise S.E. off it.
Hussar	28	195	Gone for a Mast Ship to New Brunswick and under orders for England.
Rover	—	—	Fitting out at Bermuda.
Hunter	—	—	

(Sgnd) G. MURRAY (*Ad. 1*, vol. 493).

[19]*Ad. 1*, vol. 493, Murray to Evan Nepean, July 15, 1796.

squadron was never intended to engage superior forces. If, in the course of cruising, the British ships found themselves outnumbered, they were firmly instructed not to run the risk of being shut up in American ports "whereby the Function of His Majesty's Ships may be impeded, but immediately to proceed to Halifax."[20]

As might be expected, there were frequent complaints from Governor Dorchester at Quebec, and from the provincial authorities in Nova Scotia and New Brunswick, on the lack of adequate protection for shipping in the Gulf of St. Lawrence and along the coasts of the Maritime Provinces. Whatever the measures taken, the coastal fisheries were bound to suffer from marauding privateers; but it was the West Indies trade that felt the war most severely. At the end of four years, Liverpool (Nova Scotia) out of her original total of sixty decked vessels had only one ship fit to send to the Sugar islands.[21] Other ports had similar tales of grievance which, even allowing for distortion, bore tribute to the zeal of enemy raiders.

It seems certain that Admiral Murray dispersed his scanty force with as much efficiency and ingenuity as resources and authority allowed. Furthermore, from all the evidence it would appear that most of the losses were sustained midway on the Halifax or Saint John route to the West Indies. The area around Chesapeake Bay continued to be the favourite rendezvous of French ships of war as well as merchantmen. "I am sorry to say," wrote Admiral Murray to the Secretary of the Admiralty, "that the trade of New Brunswick has suffered severely by the War, Yet that I do not apprehend, it has been owing to captures made near their own coast, or that any predatory excursions have been attempted."[22]

But apart from patrol activities, the most important task of the Halifax squadron was the convoying of the mast ships from Saint John or other Bay of Fundy ports to Halifax, and sometimes as far as St. John's, Newfoundland, where ordinarily they fell in with one of the fishing convoys which sailed at irregular intervals for Great Britain. Not infrequently Halifax harbour was practically denuded to ensure a safe start to the mast ships. The War of the American Revolution had demonstrated that success could be jeopardized for lack of strong pine masts; and the commanders on the Halifax station had had the lesson well dinned into their ears. When re-

[20]*Ibid.*, vol. 494, Vice-Admiral Vandeput to Captain Mowat, May 5, 1797.
[21]See *ibid.*, vol. 495, Memorial of Joseph Freeman of Liverpool, on behalf of himself and others, November, 1799.
[22]*Ibid.*, vol. 493, to Evan Nepean, November 17, 1796.

quests for convoys came through, there was never any hesitation. "Another Frigate must of course be sent as an Escort to the Mast Ships and Trade of this Province," wrote Admiral Sir William Parker to the Admiralty, although the withdrawal left the station with only one frigate and two sloops.[23]   Convoy had been granted, wrote Admiral Vandeput, with the forced cheerfulness of a man who does his painful duty, "in consideration of how great advantage the safe arrival of such valuable & necessary Stores must be to His Majesty's Service."[24]

Meanwhile, the work of patrolling the Gulf of St. Lawrence was made more efficient by careful definition of the routes to be followed and the rendezvous to be visited.   In the summer of 1798 one frigate was assigned the task of cruising in the Gulf of St. Lawrence "for the protection of the Trade of Canada, and the Fisheries carried on by His Majesty's Subjects in that Quarter." In addition arrangements were made to attach a frigate to the homeward-bound convoy on its journey from Quebec as far as the Banks, and similarly to accompany return convoys from Anticosti to Quebec.[25]

Bermuda was the southern rendezvous of the Halifax command. Unfortunately, although its port of St. George provided a useful anchorage for watering and taking stores, the island lacked a naval yard fit for the careening and repairing of ships of war, and all such tasks had to be performed at Halifax.   Partly for this reason, and partly because of the appeals of the Commander-in-Chief, Prince Edward, Duke of Kent, some of the ships spent the winter months, from November to April, at Halifax.[26] Obviously, however, Bermuda was the best outpost for watching the Chesapeake. The garrison was badly undermanned, and the gun defences were weak, but Admiral Murray recognized the compensating advantages, "as from thence ships can sail at all times of the year. . . ."[27]   His captains could cruise to the southward until the beginning of April, "& at such other places as may seem best from the Intelligence . . . keeping the Ships more or less collected, according to the probable force of the Enemy."[28]

[23]Ibid., vol. 495, to Nepean, April 26, 1801.
[24]Ibid., vol. 494, to Nepean, July 8, 1799.
[25]See ibid., Admiral Vandeput to Nepean, June 12, 1798; and July 15, 1799.
[26]See ibid., vol. 493, Murray to Evan Nepean, Halifax, August 26, 1795; and April 8, 1796; Captain H. Mowat to Nepean, Halifax, November 16, 1796.
[27]Ibid., Murray to Evan Nepean, October 1, 1796.
[28]Ibid., Admiral Murray to Captain Mowat, November 1, 1796.   The Naval Establishment at Bermuda was temporarily broken up following the peace of

The difficulties of patrolling the Bermuda area were considerably enhanced as a result of American collaboration with the enemy, and the resolute refusal of the American authorities to permit the right of "chase" through inshore waters, where French merchantmen found convenient asylum. Of more serious consequence, the Americans refused to co-operate in the search for and detention of British deserters. Despite instructions to the commanders of the Halifax station "to observe that it is the wish of the Government at home, to cultivate the friendship of the United States by all honourable and conciliating methods," periodic desertions followed not unnaturally by frequent impressments led to increasing friction.[29] Within the next few years, despite barbaric punishments, desertions came close to paralysing the activities of cruising squadrons.

Although the state of discipline was the cause of constant anxiety,[30] the mutinies of Spithead and the Nore had few repercussions in North America. In August 1797, the foretopmen of a ship in St. John's harbour refused to go aloft, and subsequent evidence indicated that mutiny had been discussed "under the Fish flake near the sign of the Romney Sunday last between the hour of one and three o'clock."[31] In Halifax the admiral in command of the station prepared to take "the most vigorous measures for Counteracting any attempt that may be made by ill designing Persons to excite a spirit of Mutiny amongst the Crews of His Majesty's Ships."[32] But at neither base was there really active discontent, and such anxiety as did exist was soon dispelled by the "joyful tidings of Parker's execution, and the Mutiny in the Fleet, in consequence, being entirely quell'd in England."[33] The Irish rebellion excited a certain amount of agitation among the numerous Irish settlers in Newfoundland, but there was no resort to arms. Racial and religious issues raised their heads for the first time, but

Amiens, the stores being sent to Halifax for the use of the squadron on that station. See *ibid.*, vol. 495, Admiral Sir Andrew Mitchell to Evan Nepean, Halifax, October 19, 1802; same to same, December 31, 1802, refers to the discharge of personnel.

[29]See *ibid.*, vol. 493, Instructions of Admiral Murray to Captain Mowat, November 1, 1796.

[30]Subsequently the Admiralty were to protest against the severity of punishments on shipboard, and to "show alarm" at the state of discipline. See *Ad. 2*, vol. 933, Sir John Barrow to Admiral Sir John Warren, November 4, 1813.

[31]*Ad. 1*, vol. 473, Admiral Waldegrave to the Duke of Portland, August 14, 1797.

[32]*Ibid.*, vol. 494, Admiral Vandeput to Evan Nepean, July 6, 1797.

[33]*Ibid.*, vol. 473, Admiral Waldegrave to Duke of Portland, August 14, 1797.

the governor was little concerned. "I have no apprehension," he wrote to the Duke of Portland, "of any important disturbance at Newfoundland, whilst Ireland is in subjection. . . ."[34]

Meanwhile, the fishing and sack ships[35] from Poole and Dartmouth and London continued to sail unmolested for St. John's, sometimes in company with the Quebec convoy. The main concern of the merchants was the possibility in early spring of enemy depredations on the out-ports before the convoys arrived from England. St. John's harbour was reasonably defended with eight twenty-four-pounders, so situated, wrote the military commander, "to give us confidence in defending it against the fire of any Frigate which may attempt to enter it."[36] But apart from the value of the property involved, there was no great strategic importance in holding the town, even if it could have been defended against serious attack. "The Town here,"continued Major Thorne, "being of no Importance constructed of Wood, the Destroying it is of no Consideration and the Island being freed of Works and Buildings of all kinds, not anything would be left to Harbour an Enemy, and it consequently could be taken Possession of again as a Spring and Summer Settlement for the Fishery."[37]

As it happened, France made only one serious attack on the island. In August 1796, both the Canadas and Nova Scotia were stirred by the news that Admiral Richery had escaped the blockade off Cadiz, and was proceeding to Newfoundland with seven sail of the line and several frigates.[38] Against this force Vice-Admiral Wallace at St. John's could only oppose the old *Romney* of 50 guns, two "32's" and two "16's." Subsequent reports increased alarm on the mainland by telling of French landings in Conception Bay, and a subsequent march on the capital itself. In France, indeed, the public were informed that Richery had forced the surrender of St. John's, captured large quantities of shipping and sent more than a thousand sailors as prisoners to San Domingo.[39]

[34]*Ibid.*, vol. 474, Admiral Charles Pole to Portland, October 25, 1800.
[35]Supply ships for the fishery.
[36]*Ad. 1*, vol. 473, Peregrine F. Thorne, Major Commanding, to Admiral Commanding His Majesty's Ships, August 3, 1793; see also, *ibid.*, Memorial of the merchants of Dartmouth to the Privy Council and the Admiralty.
[37]*Ibid.*, Thorne to Admiral commanding His Majesty's Ships, August 3, 1793.
[38]Five "74's" and two "84's."
[39]Anspach, *A History of the Island of Newfoundland*, 225-7; see also *Canadian Archives*, Q Series, vol. 78, 3, Prescott to Portland, October 24, 1796.

Not until October did authentic information reach England, when it was learned that the French admiral after destroying a few houses, ships, and stores at Bay Bulls, had given up the larger plan of an assault on St. John's and had left the coast on September 29.[40] Two days previously, Admiral Murray had arrived at Halifax from Bermuda. Although the accounts presented to him were still confused, the apparent lack of transports and troops indicated that the expedition was a raid rather than a serious attempt to take Newfoundland. But whatever the object, Murray's force was no match for seven ships of the line; discretion was obviously the better part of valour. It would be highly imprudent, he wrote the Admiralty's secretary, "to leave this place without a Naval force, while such a superior Squadron is so near."[41]

From 1796 to 1811 Newfoundland remained untouched by the war. Occasionally a French ship was sighted off the Banks, but there were no more raids, and trade from the out-ports to St. John's was carried on without convoy. In 1806 there were rumours that a force under Jerome Bonaparte, was approaching the coast. In view of the fact that the Newfoundland command then consisted of one 50-gun ship and two small frigates, the governor's anxiety was justified. But no more than his predecessors was he able to convince a hard-beset Admiralty that his flag ship should be a "74," that sloops were impotent craft for coastal defence, and that frigates on convoy duty should be at least "30-guns."[42]

As regards base defences, it was accepted that St. John's could be defended against raiding expeditions, but in case of an attack from a superior army, which might land at any of the neighbouring bays and harbours and take the town in the rear, no effectual defence was provided nor intended. In the event of an invasion, it was planned that the garrison should retire to Signal Hill, overlooking the entrance to the harbour, and, aided by natural defences, attempt to hold out until reinforced from Britain. "The plan of Military Defence for Newfoundland being . . . confined to the preservation of Signal Hill," wrote Admiral Gower, "and thereby commanding the Entrance of the Harbour of St. John's, the effectual defence of the Trade and

[40]See *Ad. 1*, vol. 473, Admiral James Wallace to Commanding Officer at Halifax, September 5, 1796.
[41]*Ibid.*, vol. 493, Murray to Evan Nepean, October 1, 1796.
[42]See *ibid.*, vol. 476, Admiral Erasmus Gower to Rt. Hon. Thomas Grenville, March 14, 1807.

Fishery in general throughout the Island, must depend wholly on the Naval Force employed on that station."[43]

The local defence of Newfoundland, therefore, continued to be provided in two ways. The Admiral, who after 1729 had held the additional authority of governor, left England usually about the middle of May, and from his base at St. John's controlled the movements of the convoys to and from Britain, Portugal, and the West Indies. His was the task of allocating frigates between various outgoing convoys and possibly holding a few for local fisheries' defence. As a nucleus defence force, he possessed his *stationed* squadron, made up of a flagship, two or three frigates, and one or two sloops, which were ordinarily assigned to patrol particular localities, but instructed to join up in the event of a serious threat to St. John's or any other station. Except in periods of emergency, as for example when Richery escaped into the Atlantic, the Admiralty held that no substantial naval force was required to safeguard the island and the Banks.[44] Continued exploitation of the fisheries remained, as hitherto, dependent on British command of the sea; hence the island's unique aloofness from general strategical considerations.

In the gentle language of official understatement, St. John's remained content, with a "respectable state of defence." The fisheries were rarely interrupted by hostilities, although the markets suffered from recurrent booms and slumps. The chief menace to the British fishery lay in the growing aggressiveness of American competition. Not content with "green" fishing off the Banks, the Americans made use of the innumerable small bays and creeks to dry and cure their fish, sometimes under the noses of British men-of-war which could not follow them. Moreover, virtue did not always bring its own reward. They did not scruple, said an outraged captain, "to break on the Sabbath, whereas the former [British] never do, [and] consequently have the mortification of seeing a great quantity of Fish caught before their eyes, without being partakers of the spoil."[45]

With the imposition of the Jefferson embargoes, the illicit trade with the United States grew apace, and more and more American fishing schooners bartered provisions, tea, and textiles, for furs and

[43]*Ibid.*
[44]See G. S. Graham, "Britain's Defence of Newfoundland," *The Canadian Historical Review*, XXIII, September, 1942, 274; also Graham, "Newfoundland in British Strategy," in *Newfoundland: Economic, Diplomatic and Strategic Studies*, ed. R. A. MacKay (Toronto, 1946), 261.
[45]*Ad. 1*, vol. 475, Captain Northey to Admiral Sir Erasmus Gower, St. John's, September 8, 1805.

salmon, along the inlets of the south and west coasts. But apart from the "prejudice to British navigation," this traffic facilitated wholesale emigrations of fishermen and seamen to Boston and other New England ports.[46] Indeed, by 1804 the newly formed Newfoundland Regiment was so badly weakened by the drain in manpower, that the governor was compelled to forbid recruiting by agents of the Nova Scotia and New Brunswick Fencibles.[47]

Meanwhile, ignoring the decline of their own powers and parliamentary influence, fishing interests in Dartmouth, Poole, and London continued to implore the Admiralty to add another ship-of-the-line to the Newfoundland squadron, and to increase the strength of the convoy escorts to Portugal and Britain. But the government rightly refused to be diverted from its main tasks in the Channel and Mediterranean.[48] In any event, Newfoundland had now ceased to be "a great English ship moored near the banks" for the breeding and nourishing of English seamen; and Cabinets had come to recognize that the famous "nursery" was no more. The rapid growth of settlement had broken the monopoly of Poole and Dartmouth. By the turn of the century, the fishery was carried on almost exclusively by a resident population whose male members were expected to combine the work of fishing and civil defence.

In Lower Canada, as in the Upper Province, the United States, not France, was regarded as the greatest potential danger to security. The news of Richery's return to France in the autumn of 1796 was greeted, officially at least, with "emotions of exultation and gratitude that arise from the care and vigilance of our Mother Country, from the superiority of the British Navy and the external security derived therefrom."[49] The failure of Richery to extend his foray as far as the Gulf was certainly a relief, but Canadian governors were much more concerned with plots and rumours of plots within and outside their own borders than with a straightforward invasion from the sea. Ira Allen's dealings with the Directory in France have since been proven, and both Allen in Vermont and a German-American fur

[46]*Ibid.*, vol. 474, see Admiral Charles Pole to Duke of Portland, October 25, 1800.
[47]*C.O. 194*, vol. 44, Governor Gower to Lord Camden, November 19, 1804.
[48]See *Ad. 1*, vol. 474, Committee of the Newfoundland Trade representing the Ports of Dartmouth and Exon., January 24, 1798; also Admiral Waldegrave to Evan Nepean, January 31, 1798.
[49]*Canadian Archives, Q Series*, vol. 79-2, 278; Council Minutes, January 26, 1797.

trader, Jacob Astor, from New York, were engaged in gun-running.[50] Information on the work of French emissaries in the United States still trickled in, and the colonial authorities still lived in fear of a renewed French attempt to regain the country with the connivance of the United States.[51]

The American government, however, was still unwilling to see a French occupation of the colonies to the north. The withdrawal of British forces from the western fur posts in 1796, as a consequence of Jay's Treaty, had eased diplomatic strains between the two powers; and once the official pendulum began to swing backwards again, an accompanying change in the climate of American public opinion contributed substantially to the security and tranquility of the British provinces.[52] "I am confident," wrote Governor Prescott from Quebec to the British Minister in Washington, "that no Representations will be wanting on your part" to show the Americans "how ultimately their safety is connected with ours, for nothing can be more obvious and certain that their Independence would be at an end, were this country to fall into the hands of the French."[53]

Governor Prescott's advice was unnecessary. A projected conquest of Canada, Nova Scotia, or even Newfoundland, could not have been a matter of indifference to the American government. The new republic had little affection for Great Britain, but it was still without a navy fit to meet any one of the first-class powers of Europe. Thirty years before the promulgation of the Monroe doctrine, wise Americans like Washington and Jefferson realized that the overturn of British sea power would complicate their situation unbearably. The transfer of Canada or the West Indies to an alien power was no more favoured by either president than the cession of Louisiana to France. Had Canada rather than Louisiana been at stake, Jefferson would have written to Livingstone, the United States minister in Paris, in much the same language as he used in his famous despatch of April 1802.

The cession of Louisiana and the Floridas by Spain to France, works most sorely on the United States. . . . The day that France takes possession of New Orleans fixes the sentence which is to retain her forever within her low-

[50]See A. L. Burt, *The United States, Great Britain and British North America* (New Haven and Toronto, 1940), 171-3. Governor Prescott expressed his suspicions to the Duke of Portland on September 6, 1797; see *Canadian Archives*, Q Series, vol. 79-1, 212-15.

[51]*Ibid.*, vol. 81-1, 21, Prescott to Portland, October 1, 1798.

[52]See *ibid.*, vol. 80-1, 180, Prescott to Liston, Quebec, May 14, 1798.

[53]*Ibid.*, 182.

water mark. It seals the union of two nations who, in conjunction, can maintain exclusive possession of the ocean. From that moment we must marry ourselves to the British fleet and nation. . . . This is not a state of things we seek or desire. It is one which this measure, if adopted by France, forces on us as necessarily as any other cause, by the laws of nature, brings on its necessary effect.

Thanks to British sea power, Napoleon was forced to release Louisiana to the United States. Napoleon realized, as Jefferson realized, that France could not effectively control a North American dominion without command of sea communications. The threat of an American Alliance with Great Britain was sufficient of itself to pave the way for the sale of a territory which more than doubled the area of the original Union.

During this time, despite the chronic complaints of London merchants, colonial trade with the mother country gained by the exclusion of European competition. This was made possible as a consequence of the progressive reorganization of the convoy system. By orders-in-council of February and March, 1793, outward-bound merchant vessels were allowed to sail independently with arms and ammunition for their own defence; but unarmed ocean traders were prevented by a general embargo from sailing "until the Naval preparations now carrying on shall be sufficiently advanced to afford them adequate protection."[54] These safeguards were soon forthcoming. The ban was lifted, and under the protection of hired escorts known as "Standing Convoys," the unarmed ships made their way to the various convoy assembly points, after giving bail as a guarantee of obedience to Admiralty convoy instructions.

For the first and most dangerous part of the voyage from the Kingdom, they were accompanied, as had been customary in previous wars, by ships of the line; after leaving the heavy escort the convoy broke up into its component parts, and each part, under small escort, proceeded independently to its destination. Similarly, on the return voyage, arrangements were usually made for a naval reinforcement to meet them near the Channel approaches, where not infrequently substantial proportions of the crews were impressed for service with the fleet. The strength of the initial escort varied according to circumstances of the time.[55] In August 1793, Howe

[54]*Ad. 1*, vols. 5179 and 5197. I am indebted to Lieutenant Commander D. W. Waters, R.N., for allowing me to see various of his notes based on sources in the Public Record Office and the Admiralty Library.   [55]See Appendix D.

took his whole fleet from Torbay in order to shepherd the Newfoundland ships out of the Channel, and to meet the West Indies fleet on
its journey home.   In May of 1794, he directed thirty-four ships
of the line, besides frigates, to start the East and West Indies and the
Newfoundland convoys on their way. Off Falmouth, this temporary
escort was cut down to six of the line and two frigates, and not until
the latitude of Cape Finisterre had been reached were the merchant
ships entrusted to their share of the permanent escort.

In 1795, owing to a critical shortage of seamen, a second general
embargo was imposed in order that the Royal Navy might comb the
harbour-bound merchant ships for recruits. It was, however, only a
temporary expedient. In June 1798, the Compulsory Convoy Act
was passed,[56] and it continued in force until the Peace of Amiens.
Under its terms, a duty on the merchandise carried, as well as a tax
on the ships themselves, was assessed to cover the cost of convoy
organization.[57] It was understood, moreover, that if a ship were
captured while sailing independently the owners should not recover
insurance on policies where the warrant read: "to sail with convoy."[58]

As in 1914-15, so in Napoleonic days, the whole question of the
expediency of convoys was repeatedly discussed, and the arguments
pro and *con* were practically the same as in the days of steam.
Critics emphasized the delay in collecting great fleets of merchant
ships, and the fact, familiar to many escort commodores in 1939-45,
that the whole assemblage had to travel at the pace of the slowest
hulk. Moreover, there were limits to the amount of protection that
could be provided. Ships might be captured on their way to the
rendezvous; gales combined with fog and mist could scatter them;
and there was always the risk that a superior enemy force might fall
upon so cumbersome a body, and capture or destroy the whole at
one blow. In 1793, for example, a French squadron put to sea to
intercept the West Indies convoy, but met instead the Newfoundland fishing fleet, and captured seventeen sail.   In 1794, another
French squadron of four ships of the line and six frigates happened
upon the Newfoundland convoy on its way out, and captured
fourteen ships as well as the escort.

[56]38 Geo. III, cap. 76.
[57]See G. A. Rose, *A Brief Examination into the Commerce, Revenue, and Manufactures of Gt. Britain from 1792 to 1799* (London, 1799), 33.
[58]According to law, onvoy was legally protected only when the escort was
duly appointed by a co..petent authority, which in the colonies was either the
admiral or the commander-in-chief on the station. See P. H. Colomb, "Convoys:
Are They Any Longer Possible?" *Journal of the Royal United Service Institution*,
XXXI, 1887, 297.

With the renewal of war in 1803, following a brief embargo on all ships in British ports, a new Compulsory Convoy Act was passed.[59] On the basis of almost ten years' experiment, this measure introduced a highly regulated system of convoys, supplemented by cruiser patrols in home waters, which was to last until the end of the war. All ships, including armed merchantmen, were now compelled to sail in convoy, and heavy penalties were exacted for failure to abide by the law.[60] Unlike the Act of 1798, however, that of 1803 contained no provision for taxing individual ships to pay the costs of convoy operation.

Meanwhile, the danger of invasion from France strained British shipping resources to the uttermost. In addition to the task of protecting trade, the Admiralty was forced to organize a complicated system of "Advanced Squadrons" of frigates and small craft to watch Napoleon's preparations across the Channel. As a consequence, a great many hired armed merchantmen were taken for convoy duty to release regular war vessels for the "Advanced Squadrons," and these were able to provide an effective convoy service not only in the Channel and the North Sea but as far as the Baltic.[61]

The Battle of Trafalgar banished the possibility of invasion, but enhanced rather than diminished the importance of strong convoys. A French fleet still existed after 1805; but its prestige had been destroyed in the minds of the French administration as it had been after La Hogue. Certain that he could achieve no decision at sea, Napoleon returned to the old strategy of *guerre de course*. From then on, his main naval efforts were directed against British trade.

In order to ensure that enemy ships should be tied up in European waters, he built some 150 ships of the line which he stationed in various ports from Hamburg to Venice. While British squadrons were thus employed in watching these potential threats to communications, he despatched light squadrons and privateers to assault British commerce in every sea. As a consequence, on the coasts of Newfoundland and Nova Scotia, and in the Gulf of St. Lawrence, dozens of frigates, sloops and gunbrigs were now needed to face the clouds of privateers which came from France and the surviving French islands in the West Indies. Between 1805 and the War of

[59]43 Geo. III, cap. 57.
[60]A penalty of £1000 was payable for sailing without convoy, and this was increased to £1500 if the vessel carried government stores. Moreover, all insurance was forfeited.
[61]See *Ad. 1*, vol. 540, Correspondence of Lord Keith, especially February and March, 1804.

1812 there was little actual fighting, but much dreary watching and arduous patrol work, which incapacitated ships almost as rapidly as gun-fire. The rise in insurance rates, the intensification of the blockade, the growing concern of the Admiralty over convoys, and the fears and anxieties expressed in the letters of the admirals, all suggest that the protection of trade had become more than ever a dominant feature of British strategy.[62]

In consequence of this intensified *guerre de course*, the Admiralty was forced further to strengthen the permanent escorts, and to make up annual time-tables which the merchant-owners might consult before arranging their shipping schedules.[63] The chronic difficulty was that of concealing the dates of sailing from the enemy. When passages were arranged so long in advance leakages were bound to take place, and this risk was never satisfactorily overcome. In Nova Scotia at least, convoy sailings were publicly advertised during the greater part of the war, an incredible instance of naïveté which brought no remonstrances from Halifax merchants until 1813.[64]

The sudden growth of a British North America–West Indies trade, as a direct result of American legislative attempts to starve the Sugar islands by banning intercourse with the southern states, called for new action. Prior to 1806, Nova Scotian and Quebec trade to the West Indies had steadily declined, and escort arrangements for the remnant had been helter-skelter. Consequently, many crews had fallen into the hands of Spanish or French privateers and languished in crowded West Indian gaols. According to the Nova Scotia Council Minutes of 1805, there were barely enough seamen in the colony to provide half the complement of a sloop of war.[65] The West Indies trade alone required, in the opinion of the merchants, four convoys a year; but the colonial authorities made it quite clear that only the mother country could supply the escorts.

This the Admiralty prepared to do, and by 1809 a complete schedule had been drawn up, covering the North American trade to

[62]See in this connection K. G. B. Dewar, "Influence of Overseas Commerce on the Operations of War," *Journal of the Royal United Service Institution*, 1913, LVII, 449.

[63]See Laughton, *Letters and Papers of Charles Lord Barham*, III (1911), 86. The memorandum which bears Lord Barham's signature has no date, but was probably written in 1805, addressed to the Heads of the Committees for the East Indies and for managing the affairs of the Foreign Trade. See also suggestions of Lord Sheffield, *Strictures* (London, 1806), 187-8n.

[64]See *Provincial Archives of Nova Scotia*, vol. 226, no. 75, William Sabatier (for Halifax merchants) to Sir John Sherbrooke; also "Advertisement of Convoy for Europe," *The Weekly Chronicle*, Halifax, May 22, 1807.

[65]May 18, 1805; in *Provincial Archives of Nova Scotia*, vol. 214, 153.

and from the United Kingdom, and to and from the British West Indies. Six convoys were appointed to sail annually from Spithead between March and August to Nova Scotia, New Brunswick, and Quebec, the Maritime Provinces' group parting company with the Canadian group at the south end of the Green Bank off Newfoundland. Between June and November six convoys were to sail from Quebec for England, and between April and November, eight from Nova Scotia and New Brunswick. Sixteen annual convoys were provided for the out-going West Indies voyage from Britain, and ten for the return trip.[66]

Lying almost on the direct route from Halifax, Quebec, and the West Indies, St. John's became the North American pivot of the convoy system. With convoys and their escorts concentrating on Newfoundland from the east, west, and south-west, the tiny *stationed* squadron became now a negligible factor in the defence of the harbour, and hence occupied itself more and more in hunting "the Americans." The new system worked with almost clock-like regularity. For example, at the request of the Admiralty, colonial trading concerns were notified that convoys bound for the West Indies would sail "on the first day of each month from May to December from Saint Johns Newfoundland."[67] Subsequently, to facilitate the New Brunswick trade, especially in masts, convoys sailing from Saint John made a six hours' stop off Head Harbour to enable the ships from St. Andrews to join.[68] Neither in Britain nor in America were delays permitted; if ships were not ready to sail, they had to wait until the next convoy, whether or not, as was sometimes the case in Jamaica or Barbadoes, their cargoes were perishable.[69]

The declaration of war by the United States meant an increasing demand for the protection of shipping, and severely tested the resources of the North Atlantic command. Captures helped to balance losses, but the Prize Court at Halifax seems to have been deliberate in its undertakings, and large quantities of enemy shipping which were urgently required for patrol work and trading, simply stayed in harbour awaiting condemnation. In the long run, however, in

[66]See *Minutes of the Board of Trade, Series 1* (London, Public Record Office), vol. 45, W. W. Pole (Secretary of the Admiralty), to Messrs. Inglis, Ellice & Co., Admiralty Office, March 2, 1809.

[67]See *Ad. 1*, vol. 496, Captain John P. Beresford (acting commodore and commander-in-chief) to William Marsdene, Halifax, May 19, 1806.

[68]*Ibid.*, vol. 500, Admiral J. B. Warren to W. W. Pole, November 28, 1809.

[69]See *Minutes of the Board of Trade, Series 1*, vol. 45, W. W. Pole to Messrs. Inglis, Ellice & Co., Admiralty Office, March 2, 1809.

terms of shipping tonnage, the colonies probably won more than they lost. During the last years of the war Nova Scotian privateers alone brought into port at least two hundred prizes, exclusive of recaptures.[70]

But in 1812 such successes may have appeared small compensation to the strained commander-in-chief of the Halifax station as he read of the American privateers—some 318 it was estimated—that were being fitted out in neighbouring Atlantic ports. For Admiral Warren, gazing sadly over the harbour at his small and motley collection of sloops and frigates, the war had, indeed, assumed "a new, as well as more active, and inveterate aspect than heretofore."[71]

[70]G. E. E. Nichols, "Notes on Nova Scotian Privateers," *Collections of the Nova Scotia Historical Society*, 1908, XIII, 124.
[71]*Ad. 1*, vol. 502, J. W. Croker, October 5, 1812.

XII

The American Adventure of 1812

ALMOST simultaneously with the renewal of war in Europe in 1803, British relations with the United States began to worsen.[1] International rules for the determination of the rights of neutral or belligerent have never sufficed to meet the demands of either, once a conflict has arisen, and during the course of the Napoleonic War, neither Britain nor France hesitated to deal vigorously with the privileges and claims of neutrals. A short naval struggle between France and the United States at the end of the century was ended by a promise from Napoleon to reform his conduct towards non-belligerents; but after the collapse of the Peace of Amiens, both Britain and France began to adopt new and more rigorous policies of trade restriction which were certain to affect American commerce.

As it happened, command of the sea gave Britain's restrictive decrees far greater effectiveness than was possible for Napoleon to achieve. By its very completeness the British blockade led to rigorous and indiscriminate search of American ships, and, what was much more vexatious, the impressment of English-speaking sailors without much regard to national identification. The United States government admitted the belligerent right to declare and enforce actual blockade, to stop and search neutral vessels to determine their nationality and destination, and even to seize recognized contraband, but it strenuously denied the right of search for any other purpose.

There is no lack of evidence to show how keenly the American government, as well as the American public, felt about impressment.

[1]For the best analysis of the causes of the War of 1812 see Burt, *The United States, Great Britain and British North America*, chapters XI-XIII, which questions certain conclusions in J. W. Pratt's excellent study, *Expansionists of 1812* (New York, 1925).

During the first decade of the nineteenth century it took precedence over every other claim or grievance. Without a settlement of the impressment issue, there was no chance of successfully negotiating any other matter of disagreement. To achieve peace, wrote the President of the United States, shortly after the outbreak of war,

> . . . it is necessary that the interest of impressment be satisfactorily arranged. He [the President] is willing that Great Britain should be secured against the evils of which she complains. He seeks, on the other hand, that the Citizens of the United States should be protected against a practice, which while it degrades the Nation, deprives them of their rights as Freemen, takes them by force from their families and their Country, into a foreign service, to fight the Battles of a foreign power, perhaps against their own kindred and Country.[2]

Impressment had become an acute issue shortly after the outbreak of war with France in 1793, and remained a chronic one as a result of the constant flow of naval deserters to the United States. Service on the North American station required frequent calls at American ports for water and victuals. Almost every visit meant a loss of seamen, with the consequence that British captains, even when threatened by violent weather, hesitated to avail themselves of the shelter of American harbours. Anchorage within sight of land encouraged the bolder spirits to try for safety by swimming, or by stealthily removing a ship's boat. Courts martial, executions, and floggings make up a chilling and uninterrupted narrative in the official correspondence of successive commanders who sought to check the practice. The Halifax squadron suffered most, because the facilities for escape by land from Nova Scotia and New Brunswick were obviously greater, and the temptations of a comfortable life with higher wages more generally publicized. At times, the squadron was too weakened in manpower to put to sea.[3] In the circumstances, hard-pressed captains were inclined to "press" indiscriminately, in an effort to balance the losses through desertions; and in so doing they fought strenuously against the efforts of British diplomacy to ameliorate or stop the practice.

The British minister at Philadelphia, Robert Liston, watched the rising temper of American opinion with growing apprehension. His

---

[2]*Ad. 1*, vol. 502, James Monroe to the commander-in-chief of the North American station, Vice-Admiral Sir J. B. Warren, October 27, 1812.

[3]See *ibid.*, vol. 495, Captain Robert Murray to His Excellency, Robert Liston, July 22, 1800; vol. 499, correspondence of Vice-Admiral J. B. Warren for the year 1809.

office was inundated with complaints and threats, not from "the Vulgar only," but from "persons of superior station," and "the most respectable members of the Government of the United States."[4] In Liston's opinion, "a fair & equitable mercantile & political friendship" was possible. Only one obstacle stood in the way, and that, he wrote to Commodore Henry Mowat, "it is much in your power to remove—I mean the impressment & ill-treatment of American seamen—While complaints on this subject are frequent and spacious, no real harmony and conciliation can take place; whereas if they come to cease I see no bar to any degree of intimacy & union that we ought to wish."[5] Mowat's reply expressed the jaundiced view of every suffering commander on the North American station.[6] ". . . it is my duty to keep my Ship manned, & I will do so wherever I find men that speak the same language with me, & not a small part of them British subjects, & that too producing certificates as being American Citizens [.] at the same time I tell you, Sir, that I have not got an American subject on board, but I will not say how long it will be so."[7]

In 1800, the United States proffered the suggestion that an additional article be added to Jay's Treaty of 1794, to the effect that a deserter should not be demanded after the lapse of two years, and that the British should renounce the right of taking seamen "of any description" from the vessels of the United States on the high seas.[8] But the commanders on the station continued to oppose any such stipulation, and provided they confined their energies to conscribing ostensibly British seamen, they had the support of the Admiralty at home. "The only compensation which the squadron have received for the continual desertion to the United States," wrote the acting commander-in-chief to Liston, "is the power they have exercised in taking British Seamen out of American Vessels . . . and the cautious and moderate use of this power has produced such benefit to His Majesty's Service that I am clearly of opinion the advantage to be derived from the other points of the convention would not be equivalent to the loss we should sustain by relinquishing this power."[9]

[4] *Ibid.*, vol. 493, to Vice-Admiral George Murray, September 4, 1796.
[5] *Ibid.*, vol. 494 Philadelphia, March 6, 1797.
[6] See, for example, *ibid.*, vol. 493, Admiral Murray to Liston, November 5, 1796.
[7] *Ibid.*, vol. 494, letter of March 27, 1797.
[8] See *ibid.*, vol. 495, Liston to Captain Robert Murray, July 5, 1800. The project of a new convention forbidding impressment was submitted again in 1804, *cf.* Burt, *The United States, Great Britain and British North America*, 227-8.
[9] *Ad. 1*, vol. 495, July 22, 1800.

". . . if the question of Search is conceded in the smallest degree," read a memorial of the Nova Scotia merchants, "a mortal blow will be struck at the vitals of English commerce, and at our own Country's surest and best defence—the Naval Power and Dignity of Britain."[10]

The rhetorical boldness of the merchants' recommendations was precipitated not so much by the long-term needs of provincial trade as by the excitement of impending war with the United States. In June of 1807, the British frigate *Leopard*, while searching for deserters, had her famous encounter with the American *Chesapeake*. War feeling in the republic immediately rose to a fever heat, and the Yankee officer who fired a gun with the aid of a live coal in his fingers became a national hero. Mob agitations broke out in many of the seaboard towns, and steps were taken to fortify some of the principal American harbours.

The situation looked ominous for British North America. In the opinion of Vice-Admiral George Berkeley, then in command of the North American station, the United States was only waiting for the right moment to strike a blow at the British provinces, and in all probability it could count again on aid from France.[11] To avoid the apparently inevitable attack on Canada and Nova Scotia, Berkeley talked wildly of "Copenhagening" New York and other important ports while the United States was yet unprepared, "cutting up the sinews of their maritime strength, which will otherwise be employed against our trade in the most hurtful way. . . ." As it happened, there was no such simple means of forestalling the Americans. Berkeley had too few ships even to "show the flag" before New York. Part of his force was engaged in blockading a French squadron up the Chesapeake, leaving Halifax open to a *coup de main* unless frigates and brigs were provided in time.[12] Indeed, the position of the British provinces seemed so precarious that the Secretary for War and Colonies momentarily contemplated the removal of all

[10]*Ibid.*, Andrew Belcher, Chairman, to Vice-Admiral George Berkeley, October 7, 1807.

[11]Berkeley to Lord Bathurst, Halifax, August 13, 1807, in *Historical Manuscripts Commission Report, Bathurst MSS.*, 1923, 63-4; *Ad. 1*, vol. 497, Berkeley to Lord Commissioners of the Admiralty, August 17, 1807; see also G. S. Graham, "Lord Castlereagh and the Defence of British North America," *Canadian Defence Quarterly*, January, 1939, vol. XVI; see also *Canadian Archives, Q Series*, vol. 310, 5, Berkeley's letter of August 17, 1807; also vol. 107, 261, Sir James Craig to D. M. Erskine, May 13, 1808, on the possibilities of a Napoleonic invasion.

[12]*Ad. 1*, vol. 497, Berkeley to Lords Commissioners of the Admiralty, August 17, 1807.

British forces from the mainland in order to concentrate on the retention of Newfoundland. Castlereagh's pessimism was based on the
assumption that without strong reinforcements of troops, British
North America lacked the trained manpower to defend itself against
serious attack by land. He was anxious that militia forces should be
organized as quickly as possible in both the Canadas and Nova
Scotia, but if an emergency arose, and the mother country found it
impossible to supplement the militias with 10,000 or 12,000 regulars,
"the most prudent course we could pursue would perhaps be to
withdraw our forces in time and to confine ourselves to the protection of Newfoundland."[13]

As it happened, however, the clouds of war suddenly evaporated
with the Presidential announcement that respect for the American
flag would be enforced by peaceful means. At a time when the
United States still profited from a huge neutral trade, Thomas
Jefferson prepared to punish the belligerents by inflicting a blockade
on his own countrymen. Between December 1807 and March 1808,
laws were applied which were intended to prohibit all trade in
American ships with foreign ports. Although the Royal Navy feared
for their New England spars and timber,[14] the immediate effect of
the embargo was to encourage a brisk overland and coastal trade
with the British provinces. Halifax, Montreal, and Quebec hummed
with activity, and were soon handling more shipping than the whole
of the Atlantic seaboard.[15] American lumber, flour, and other provisions flowed steadily through Halifax and other ports to the Sugar
islands, as Nova Scotia and New Brunswick became the centres of a
vast business in contraband. The result in the United States was a
mounting resentment, and riots broke out in several seaboard cities.
When a revolution in Spain during the late summer of 1808 opened

---

[13]*Correspondence, . . . of Viscount Castlereagh*, VIII, 104, letter to Earl of
Chatham, December 31, 1807. Other considerations led him to modify this original counsel of despair. ". . . considering the value of those provinces in point of
naval resources, as well as their importance as a means of supply to the West
Indies, and recollecting also the feeling which exists in this country towards them,
their ultimate influence upon the security of Newfoundland, and the protection
the Crown owes to the Loyalists who formerly adhered to it, and now compose a
large proportion of the population of those dependencies, I hardly see the possibility of deliberately directing their evacuation without a struggle; and if not, it
seems desirable to throw the conflict, as far as we can, upon the local force, in
which we risk nothing but the expense, without exposing a large British army."
Ibid., 105.

[14]*Ad. 1*, vol. 498, Vice-Admiral J. B. Warren to W. W. Pole, Halifax, May 31,
1808.

[15]See G. S. Graham, *Seapower and British North America, 1783-1820* (Cambridge. Mass., 1941), 201.

up new South American outlets for trade, the clamour for release from the Jeffersonian strait-jacket grew louder than ever.

In the circumstances, a change in American policy was inevitable. The Non-Intercourse Act passed on March 1, 1809, repealed the embargo as a form of self-blockade but created a new embargo which was to apply more strictly than before to the two belligerents, Great Britain and France. Trade with those two countries was still forbidden; but in order to make the barrier watertight, all British and French vessels, all goods shipped from Great Britain and France, and all goods produced by them, were forbidden to enter American ports from May 20, 1809. One year later, a new law withdrew the restrictions for a period of ten months; during that time, if one of the two belligerents should rescind its regulations and the other not follow suit within three months, the President was empowered to enforce the provisions of the Non-Intercourse Act against the defaulting country. Since Napoleon was unable to enforce his Milan and Berlin decrees with any great degree of success, his offer to revoke them was little more than a ruse. He had little to lose and a great deal to gain. For, as a consequence of this tactical move, the United States in the spring of 1811 had no alternative but to apply against Great Britain the trade penalties which she had threatened against a defaulter.

At a time when the strain of European responsibilities was becoming increasingly difficult to bear, it must be obvious that Great Britain was not anxious to fight the United States. Yet, despite the warning of 1807, which followed the crisis over impressment, she had stubbornly maintained the orders-in-council until it was too late. Spurred on by the warmongers, President Madison was gradually drawn into a policy of bravado and belligerence which, scorning further negotiation as shameful to prestige, left no alternative to armed conflict.

On June 18, 1812, the President of the United States signed the declaration of war, and the republic found itself engaged in a struggle for which it was utterly unprepared. The acquisition of Canada, Thomas Jefferson had remarked, was not likely to be more than a matter of marching, but off the Atlantic coast a different situation prevailed. With little beyond a scratch force of fighting ships, Americans were to experience all the humiliations which defensive warfare invites, and which only the brilliant performance of individual commanders was able to relieve.

For this awful weakness at sea, Jefferson was himself largely responsible. During the "Quasi-Naval War" with France (1798-1801) the administration, in an effort to chastise the assailants of American shipping, built up a small force of frigates and cutters.[16] In addition, over a thousand merchant vessels were refitted and armed, and provision was made for the construction of six ships of the line. But in the ten years after 1801, the fruits of this fine growth were tossed away. Jefferson forsook the strategy of the offensive with its requirements of frigates and ships of the line, and substituted two hundred gun-boats which were quite unfit to operate in the high seas. In so doing he wedded the nation to a defensive policy of continental isolationism.[17] The United States renounced any hope of contesting command of the sea in conjunction with the French, and staked its future on coastal defence. For offensive operation it counted on a policy of commerce raiding by fast privateers; guerilla attacks on hostile merchant shipping would, it was assumed, bring a rich harvest of prizes, and at the same time might so cripple the enemy's trade as to force a peace.[18]

In 1812 the American navy, apart from gun-boats, consisted of nineteen ships, of which only some fourteen were fit for sea, and eight of these were sloops or brigs carrying less than twenty guns.[19] For this small force, there were sufficient officers (men who had won their spurs in the war with France or against the Barbary pirates) but there were not enough trained seamen, a deficiency that persisted throughout the war, as a result of tempting opportunities offered by the merchant service and the growing fleet of privateers. Moreover, in unhappy contrast to Britain, which had good dockyard facilities at Halifax and in the West Indies, the Americans, as a consequence of ten years of neglect, had no navy yard worthy of the name. "The United States," wrote the Secretary of the Navy, Paul Hamilton, in 1811, "does not own a dock. To repair our vessels we are compelled to heave them down—a process attended with great labour, considerable risk and loss of time. . . ."[20]

[16]See D. W. Knox, *Naval Documents related to the Quasi-War between the United States and France, 1797-9* (7 vols., Washington, 1935-39).

[17]A. T. Mahan, *Sea Power in Its Relation to the War of 1812* (2 vols., London, 1905), I, 291, 295.

[18]H. and M. Sprout, *The Rise of American Naval Power, 1776-1918* (Princeton, 1939), 71.

[19]*Ibid.*, 76.

[20]Quoted in E. S. Maclay, *A History of the United States Navy from 1775 to 1894* (2 vols., New York, 1897), I, 319.

Since the force was a small one, the United States had no need of a large fleet organization. Apart from temporary commodores in charge of squadrons, the highest rank was that of captain, and ordinarily each ship was responsible directly to the Navy Department rather than to a commander of a fleet.[21] But the Navy department had no clear-cut plan of operations, and vacillated between a strategy of single-ship commerce raiding and passive defence in the neighbourhood of the coasts. When war finally came, the ships put to sea without receiving any definite instructions.[22]

In the circumstances, the so-called American navy was fortunate to achieve as much as it did. Had not the Royal Navy, consisting of some hundred ships of the line,[23] been preoccupied with Napoleon

[21]Mahan, *Sea Power in Its Relations to the War of 1812*, II, 315-16.
[22]Sprout, *The Rise of American Naval Power*, 77; H. Adams, *History of the United States of America* (9 vols., New York, 1891), VI, 363-8.
[23]The British Navy in 1812 was roughly:

100 of the line	150 sloops
150 frigates	100 gun-brigs and other small craft.

The backbone of the United States Navy consisted of 6 frigates:

Constitution	
United States }	44 (nominal) 24-pdrs.
President	c. 1500 tons
Chesapeake	
Congress }	38 (nominal) 18-pdrs.
Constellation	c. 1100 tons

List of U.S. Navy as laid before Congress by the Secretary of the Navy in December, 1810. (Enclosed in *Ad. 1*, vol. 502, Vice-Admiral Sawyer to J. W. Croker, April 7, 1812.)

		Stations	
Frigate	President	New York	
	Constellation	Newcastle (Delaware) }	Under Commodore Rogers
Brig	Argus	Boston	
Schooner	Revenge	New Port (R.I.)	
Frigate	United States	Hampton Roads	
	Essex	" "	Under Commodore Decatur
Brig	Hornet	" "	—Essex has gone to Europe
	Nautilus	" "	—Hornet is repairing.
Corvette	John Adams	Charleston & Savannah	
Ship	Wasp	" "	
Brig	Siren		
	Viper	} New Orleans	
	27-gun-boats		
Brig	Oneida	Sacketts Harbour	
	Vixen	Navy Yard, Washington	

In Ordinary.

Frigate	Chesapeake	Boston	
	Congress		
	Constellation		
	New York	} Navy Yard, Washington.	
	Adams		
	Boston		

Various Gun Boats [some 150]

in Europe, the initial exploits of individual American captains could never have been accomplished.

That the British did suffer several reverses during the first twelve months of the war has occasionally led to the assumption that the Royal Navy had gone stale after Trafalgar. In view of the long weary years of blockading with little fighting, it would have been almost curious had there not been some sort of relapse. Gunnery was bound to decline for want of action, and there was, in the beginning, a tendency to underestimate the capabilities of a numerically weak but ingenious enemy. The *Constitution*, the *President*, and the *United States* were called 44-gun frigates (c. 1,500 tons), but in workmanship, sailing qualities, timbered strength, and gun-power, they were far ahead of the normal frigate like U.S.S. *Chesapeake* or H.M.S. *Shannon* of 38 guns, or the numerous "36's" of 950 tons, such as H.M.S. *Belvidera*. It has sometimes been said that the three "44's" were "more like line-of-battle ships," and certainly they were equal to the old British "64's" of 1,350-1,400 tons, carrying twenty-four pounders. But very few "64's" were in existence at this time; the only one in North American waters, the *Africa* (built in 1781), returned home in the autumn of 1812. Hence, to counter this disparity in power, Britain was forced to use ships of the line ("74's") to back up the weaker frigates. In July 1813, eighteen-pounder frigates were forbidden to engage American "44's" except in couples.[24] Finally a number of old "74's"—*Majestic, Goliath,* and *Saturn*—were cut down to 56 guns,[25] and two new ships, *Leander* and *Newcastle*, were built with the object of matching the "44's."

Although outnumbered, the Americans had the initial advantage of strategic position close to their own bases and alongside British trade routes; at the beginning of the war the few British ships were scattered among several North American stations. Not till 1813 were any considerable numbers of ships of the line employed across the Atlantic, when a reduction in the North Sea squadron was partial-

[24]In January, 1814, Stephen Decatur challenged two British frigates to meet the U.S.S. *United States* and *Macedonian* in a duel. The commander-in-chief, Vice-Admiral Warren, forbade the engagement, regarding it as "extremely improper that private feeling should interfere in such points with the public service, and be the means of affording the Enemy an opportunity to advance his small force upon an equality with ours in its present great superiority." See *Ad. 1,* vol. 505, Decatur to Commodore Sir Thos. M. Hardy, January 19, 1814, and Warren to J. W. Croker, Bermuda, February 2, 1814.

[25]See *Ad. 1,* vol. 503, Vice-Admiral Warren to Admiralty, December 29, 1812 and *Ad. 2*, vol. 1375, Admiralty to Warren, February 10, 1813.

ly compensated by the addition of some Russian ships.[26] Meanwhile, Halifax and Bermuda between them had only one ship of the line, six frigates, and sixteen smaller vessels; all told, including the two squadrons in the West Indies and one based on Newfoundland, there were in July, 1812, three line-of-battle ships, twenty-three frigates, and some fifty-three sloops, brigs, and schooners. It was a small force, but one which carried almost seven times the armament of the American navy. In the following year the North American squadron was built up to some ten ships of the line, in addition to four at Jamaica and the Leeward Islands and one at Newfoundland.[27] In

[26]British "commitments" in ships of the line in 1812 were roughly:

Channel Fleet	15	(watching Brest and Rochefort)
North Sea	25	(watching Flushing and the Texel)
Baltic	12	(helping Sweden and Russia, protecting the Baltic trade and convoying arms, troop horses, etc. to Sweden and Russia)
Mediterranean	30	(including a squadron in the Adriatic to watch French ships built and fitted at Venice)

Jamaica, Leeward Islands, S. America, E. Indies, Cape of Good Hope } 1 or 2 each

For these statistics, based on Admiralty sources, I am indebted to Commander J. H. Owen, R.N.

[27]LIST BOOK STRENGTHS IN SHIPS OF THE LINE (*Ad. 8*, vol. 100)

	July 1812	*July 1813*
East Indies	1	2 (1 about to go home)
Cape	1	1
S. America	2 (1 of them going to relieve the other)	1
Leeward Islands	1	2
Jamaica	1	2
N. America	1 (Africa)	11
Newfoundland	—	1
Mediterranean	29	29
Portugal	6 (one ordered home)	1
Baltic	10	8
Channel W.S.	14	16
Portsmouth	4 (for Cherbourg)	2
North Sea	27	12 plus 4 or 5 Russians
Convoys &c.	—	4 incl. 2 cruising c. 40°N, 45°W.
Unappropriated	6	10
	103	102

TOTAL STRENGTHS FOR STATIONS IN W. ATLANTIC (*Ad. 8*, vol. 100)

	July 1812	*July 1813*
S. America	1 Line	1 Line
	1 Frigate	8 Frigate
	1 Small	5 Sloop & smaller
Leeward Islands	1 Line	2 Line
	5 Frigate	1 IV-rate(?) *Goliath* razé or a "50"

part, this was a precautionary move to guard against the possible intervention of France, which the Americans, indeed, anticipated; and for the same reason the Royal Navy continued to watch French ports, line-of-battle ships remaining, as in the time of the American Revolution, the backbone of the Western squadron. Moreover, special cruising squadrons—a further commitment in line-of-battle ships—took stations in the Atlantic, off Madeira and the Azores, to protect the trade against the large American frigates.[28]

As early as May 1812, the British government was aware that growing American irritation against its orders-in-council might lead to hostilities, possibly in combination with France. Consequently both Newfoundland and Halifax stations were warned to be on their guard.[29] By the end of July it was known that war had, in fact, been declared by the United States government and, while urgent affairs in Europe prevented the sending of immediate reinforcements, the first steps were taken to meet the new crisis. British merchant vessels were forbidden to sail without convoy to any part of North America or the West Indies, and an embargo was laid on all American shipping in British ports. No general blockade was authorized, and enemy ships possessing British licenses were to be immune from capture.[30]

This latter concession was born of material and political necessity. The Maritime Provinces could ill afford to break their trade ties with New England, and Great Britain had every reason to encourage a section of the country which from the beginning showed so much opposition to the war. Diplomacy has always been a major

	21 Small	10 Frigate
		26 Small
Jamaica	1 Line	2 Line
	8 Frigate	6 Frigate
	9 Small	8 Small
N. America	1 Line	11 Line (includes *Majestic* razé, which was
	6 Frigate	afterwards a IV-rate)
	16 Small	18 Frigate
		28 Small
Newfoundland	1 "50"	1 Line (*Bellerophon* "74")
	4 Frigate	6 Frigate
	7 Small	5 Small

[28]See *Ad. 2*, vols. 1375-78, Admiralty Secret Orders, and Captains' Letters containing reports of the cruises.

[29]See *Ad. 1*, vol. 501, Vice-Admiral Sawyer to J. W. Croker, April 7, 1812; also Mahan, *Sea Power in Its Relations to the War of 1812*, I, 385.

[30]*Naval Chronicle*, XXVIII, 1812, p. 73; Mahan, *Sea Power in Its Relations to the War of 1812*, I, 388.

constituent of naval strategy, and not infrequently its fruits have won more than could have been obtained by a dozen battles. In the case of New England it can be safely affirmed that the neutrality of this wealthy ship-building and trading area saved British North America. In the long run Nova Scotia and Prince Edward Island were likely to stand secure, for they were entirely accessible to the sea which Britain was able to command. But New Brunswick and the lower banks of the St. Lawrence were not so defensible, and in times past the ranger militia to the southward had not found the woods of Maine an impenetrable jungle. The exemption of New England from the worst effects of the early blockades, helped, therefore, to consolidate a buffer which protected New Brunswick as effectually as British arms, and, as time was to show, it paid both partners rich dividends in trade.

Now the obvious strategy of the British high command was to close as tightly as possible the Atlantic coast-line of the United States in an effort to prevent American commerce destroyers from sallying forth. A complete commercial blockade—one which would have cut off the republic from all trade, neutral as well as coastal— was out of the question in 1812; there were not, as we have seen, enough British ships to make the attempt feasible. An ordinary close watch of American ports, which would confine their shipping within harbour and make possible the interception of blockade-runners, was a simpler project, and although strong divisions were not available to scan every port, the stationed squadrons of Halifax and the West Indies were combed of all warships not needed to hunt privateers in the Bay of Fundy and the waters between Nova Scotia and Newfoundland.[31]

Not until November, however, was the commander-in-chief of the North American station ordered to "forthwith institute a strict & rigorous blockade of Chesapeake Bay and the Delaware";[32] and not until the end of the year did reinforcements make possible its effective application.[33] By the spring of 1813, with the arrival of further ships of the line, arrangements were made to extend the blockade to include New York, Charleston, Port Royal, Savannah, and the Mississippi.[34]

[31]Mahan, *Sea Power in Its Relations to the War of 1812*, II, 14.
[32]*Ad. 1*, vol. 4223, Bathurst to Admiralty, November 21, 1812; and *Ad. 2*, vol. 1375, Admiralty to Vice-Admiral Warren, November 27, 1812.
[33]See *Ad. 1*, vol. 4223, Bathurst to Admiralty, December 25, 1812.
[34]*Ibid.*, vol. 4224, Bathurst to Admiralty, March 25, 1813.

None the less, Newfoundland, New Brunswick, and Nova Scotia were in a peculiarly open position for sporadic attack by American privateers. Many former merchant captains were well acquainted with the coasts, knew the meagreness of the defences, and, it was generally assumed, would make the most of very tempting advantages. With the exception of the raid by the French admiral, Richery, in 1796, the British colonies had so far escaped the slightest depredations of war. No enemy ships had appeared off their coasts; the fisheries had been as undisturbed and secure as in peacetime, and the coastal trade had passed along the shores and about the Gulf without convoy. As a consequence of long immunity, the batteries at St. John's and Halifax had been either dismantled or corrupted by decay; the out-harbours in the Bay of Fundy and on the east and south shores of settled Newfoundland were practically defenceless. The *stationea* ships had been stripped to the bone, and in the Bay of Fundy only a single gun-brig remained to protect the coast.[35] A flood of rumours spread about rapidly, tales of the size and gun-power of the new American frigates and the number and speed of the privateers which, according to report, were swarming out from American ports like locusts.

Halifax was first to hear of the war, when the frigate *Belvidera* commanded by Captain Richard Byron arrived with the news that on June 24 she had been fired upon by an American squadron while cruising off Sandy Hook. Admiral Sawyer immediately sent a sloop with a flag of truce to ask for an explanation, and began to assemble all available ships on the Halifax station.[36] Merchant vessels were forbidden to sail without convoy, and steps were taken to ensure coordination between the West Indies and the Halifax squadrons, subsequently combined in August under the command of Vice-Admiral Sir John Warren.[37] Meanwhile, American privateers filtered into the Bay of Fundy, threatening Saint John and St. Andrews; others cruised off Cape Sable or combed the area from Mount Desert eastward as far as Digby.[38]

---

[35] *Ibid.*, vol. 502, undated and unsigned note apparently addressed to Admiral Warren (1812).

[36] *Naval Chronicle*, XXVIII, 1812, p. 73.

[37] The Admiralty decision to unite the hitherto separate commands of Halifax, Jamaica, and Leeward Islands was forwarded to the Foreign Office on August 3, 1812 (see *Ad. 2*, vol. 1375). In November 1813, the North American and West Indian stations were once again separated (see *Ad. 2*, vol. 1378, Admiralty to Warren, November 4, 1813.

[38] *Ad. 1*, vol. 502, unsigned note to Warren.

In view of the demand for convoy escorts, Warren's position was a difficult one, and the Admiral was himself convinced "of the impossibility of our trade navigating these seas unless a very extensive squadron is employed to scour the vicinity." Without strong reinforcements he saw no hope of applying a blockade or repressing "the disorder and pillage which actually exist to a very alarming degree, both on the coast of British America and in the West Indies. . . ."[39] Since his forces were barely sufficient to undertake concentrations against the chief American ports, it was clearly impossible to cover the entire Atlantic seaboard; and not until the middle of 1814 could the Admiralty count on an effective all-year blockade of the chief American harbours, in addition to maintaining the close watch on French ports.[40] Meanwhile, they were happy to intensify the "separatism" of New England by further encouraging an illicit trade with the Maritime Provinces in American ships under neutral flags. Until April of 1814, New England ports, through a liberal licensing system, enjoyed all the privileges of trade to British possessions which were available to the ships of neutral nations.

The United States replied to the British blockade in the only way possible—by sending out, in divisions or singly, a host of cruisers and privateers. In and about the focal trade areas, this minor strategy, while it could never be decisive, did win some immediate results. As long as ships could run the blockade, guerilla warfare against British trade was possible; indeed it was the one offensive operation that the United States could undertake. But these forays failed to provide even local command of the seas, and before the end of 1813 American frigates found the greatest difficulty in getting clear of their own ports. No form of local operations by frigates in combination could break the cordon, once it was supported by ships of the line. Unable to dispute British supremacy and open her own lanes of ocean commerce, the United States was thrown on the defensive —backed up against her own coastline.

Nevertheless, the American privateers won a rich harvest— well over two hundred merchant or fishing ships—before the close-blockade was organized, and probably three quarters of these were seized in the Bay of Fundy or in the neighbouring waters between

[39]Quoted in Mahan, *Sea Power in Its Relations to the War of 1812*, I, 402.
[40]See *Ad. 1*, vol. 507, Vice-Admiral Alex. Cochrane to J. W. Croker, Halifax, October 5, 1814.

Nova Scotia and Newfoundland. In this area, the trade lanes from the British West Indies to New Brunswick, Nova Scotia, and the Gulf of St. Lawrence, crossed the routes from the British Isles to the same ports, and there, between the eastern edge of the Grand Banks and the waters adjoining Halifax, rovers like Rodgers and Barney found their principal source of profit and glory.[41] Gradually, however, the fruits of guerilla warfare began to thin, as the British reinforced their escorts and enforced their Convoy Law with strict penalties. In one of his last great sweeps of the western Atlantic, Commodore Rodgers captured only two merchant ships; during the entire month of December 1812, which he spent on the Halifax-Bermuda trade route, he did not even sight a British ship out of convoy.

As a consequence, American ships withdrew from the Atlantic coast-line. Some, like Rodgers's squadron, went overseas, and from bases in France intercepted British coastal commerce; others, chiefly as single units, took up positions off the Gulf of St. Lawrence, forcing the temporary diversion of British blockading strength. But the strengthening of the blockade after the spring of 1813 made it increasingly difficult for other than light-draft ships to run the gauntlet, and those that succeeded were hard put to to avoid capture. The safest resort for the American raiders during the later stages of the war lay in European waters, and any successes they obtained were disconcerting rather than distressing in so far as their effect on the war was concerned. In the language of an Admiralty communiqué, "the weight of the enemy's force was employed at a distance from the North American station."[42]

During this time, the Bluenoses of Nova Scotia responded as effectively as available ships and men allowed. All told, less than fifty *letters of marque* were issued to skippers by the Vice-Admiralty Court at Halifax, but before the end of hostilities, the privateers so authorized had produced a bag of some two hundred American ships. By the end of 1813, apart from the licensed and neutral trade from New England, enemy merchantmen were hard to find. At the end of a four months' cruise between the Newfoundland Banks and Bermuda, a small British force returned to its base at Halifax with only one American prize.[43] The coasting trade by small craft could

[41]See Mahan, *Sea Power in Its Relations to the War of 1812*, I, 392-6.
[42]Quoted *ibid.*, 406.
[43]Mahan, *Sea Power in Its Relations to the War of 1812*, II, 20.

not be entirely eliminated; and, as we have noticed, the coast above New York was not included in the general blockade which Admiral Warren applied with ever increasing vigour after April of 1813. Strengthened by ten ships of the line, the British squadrons continued to draw the constricting net ever tighter, and by the end of the year, apart from the clandestine New England trade which was deliberately encouraged, American sea traffic had been practically annihilated.

Meanwhile, the rich stream of colonial trade continued to flow undiminished. Owing to its position as *entrepôt* for the illicit trade with New England, the prosperity of Halifax grew by leaps and bounds. Patriotic New Yorkers angrily watched their ships mouldering in harbour while their neighbours to the north of Newport enjoyed a treasonous commerce, which incidentally drained the rest of the country of specie, besides enriching the enemy. Without New England flour, which arrived in Halifax from Boston under Swedish or Spanish flags, the British forces in Canada could hardly have kept the field. Overland smuggling practices, first tried during the period of the embargo of 1808-9, were revived; and Quebec and Montreal shared in the activity which was making Halifax a boom town. At the same time, the withdrawal of some 1000 sail of American vessels from the Gulf and Labrador fisheries provided an incentive to coastal populations who more than doubled their activity in an industry hitherto pursued somewhat casually from the shore.

Until the late autumn of 1813, the British government purposely avoided blockading the coast of new England, leaving to Yankee merchants a practical monopoly of the existing import trade in British manufactured goods; and not until Admiral Sir Alexander Cochrane succeeded Warren as commander-in-chief in March 1814, was it definitely decided to seal up the whole Atlantic coast from New Brunswick to Florida.[44] This extended and rigorous blockade was not officially announced until peace had been arranged with France in May, but its initial and unofficial application some six months earlier aroused a storm in Maritime trading circles. The Halifax merchants, especially, had not calculated on such an interruption to their profitable *entrepôt* trade, and had either accumulated or ordered large stocks of British merchandise for American sale, of which they had now no means of disposing. As a consequence, petitions and complaints came pouring in to the home government

[44] See *Ad. 1*, vol. 505, Warren's and Cochrane's dispatches.

urging the restoration of licensed trade in the interests of national commerce.[45] The reply of the Secretary for War and Colonies, Lord Bathurst, was a gem of mingled apology and irony. "I have only to express my regret that a measure which operates so severely against the enemy should in any degree affect the interests of any of His Majesty's subjects."[46] Happily for the colonial merchants, the British forces soon after occupied the territory between the Bay of Passamaquoddy and the Penobscot River. A provisional government was set up, and a proclamation of September 21, 1814 opened the country to trade through the port of Castine. By the end of the war Sherbrooke estimated that goods to the value of a million pounds sterling had passed through Nova Scotia to the United States.[47]

In Newfoundland the last two years of the war were prosperous. During the first five months some losses were sustained by ships on the way to market, but generally speaking, the shore fisheries remained free from the ravages of the privateer.[48] With the conditioning of the St. John's defences and the erection of temporary batteries in the out-harbours, nervousness on the part of inhabitants and fishermen disappeared, and the cod soon replaced the Yankee as the object of interest and pursuit. As a result of the almost exclusive use of the Gulf, Labrador, and Bank fisheries, the catches of 1813 and 1814 exceeded those of any previous year,[49] while the merchants enjoyed a monopoly of the markets of Spain, Portugal, and the West Indies, not to mention an increased trade with the British Isles in provisions and manufactured goods.[50]

On land the United States had its greatest opportunity; because it failed, and because colonial militia were associated with professional soldiers in defending the country, Canadians, rightly proud of local achievements, have paid far greater attention to the inland war than to the war at sea. Yet the element which decided the outcome was the British blockade, and blockade at sea influenced the

[45]See Graham, *Sea Power and British North America*, 214.
[46]*Provincial Archives of Nova Scotia*, vol. 62, no. 121, Bathurst to Sherbrooke July 15, 1814.
[47]*Ibid.*, vol. 111, no. 33, Sherbrooke to Bathurst, January 6, 1815; also W. R. Copp, "Nova Scotian Trade during the War of 1812," *The Canadian Historical Review*, XVIII, June, 1937, p. 146.
[48]See *C.O. 194*, vol. 55, Governor Admiral Sir Richard Keats to Lord Bathurst, December 29, 1814.
[49]See *ibid.*, Memorial of the London merchants, April 25, 1814; and *Original Correspondence of the Board of Trade, Series 1*, vol. 91, Memorial of the merchants of July 29, 1814.
[50]See *C.O. 194*, vol. 54, Keats to Bathurst, December 18, 1813.

course of hostilities ashore. By the end of 1813 it had already begun to make itself felt in the seaport and industrial towns, and before the defeat of Napoleon released ships and men for North American combat duty, the effect of dwindling commerce, combined with the drain of specie to New England, was already hamstringing the American war effort on land.

The naval operations on the Great Lakes had no relation to the war at sea, and were subordinate to the purely military operations, but they deserve at least mention in any study of sea power. In the beginning, the fresh-water forces were insignificant compared with those on the ocean. One ship of the line could have fired more guns than the combined American and British navies on the Lakes in June 1812. The British fleet which had grown up during the American Revolution had gone to seed. Placed under the quarter-master general's department of the army, it had gradually degenerated into a branch of the transport service, with an effective establishment of only 132 men, the majority of whom were either over age or lacking in experience.[51] Eventually, however, both sides built small flotillas, and two Lilliputian engagements, one on Lake Erie and the other on Lake Champlain, were to have a compelling effect on the course of the war.

The acquisition of Canada, Jefferson had said, was a mere matter of marching. But the strategic position of the St. Lawrence–Great Lakes chain made successful invasion depend not so much on marching as on control of water communications. Invasion on foot meant weeks of weary slogging for both men and transport along the rough-hewn tracks through wilderness country. The command of the lakes offered to the high command of either army the possibility of moving troops and supplies quickly and secretly; it gave them the advantage of interior lines and it strengthened the strategic weapon of surprise. Command of Lakes Erie and Ontario meant control of almost a thousand miles of vital military communications between east and west. Victory for the British on Lake Erie could neutralize Detroit as a base of operations for the north-west country, and pave the way for the invasion of the Mississippi Valley. American command of Lake Ontario could place the whole of Upper Canada west of Kingston in enemy hands, while similar control over Lake Champlain would inevitably put Montreal within easy reach

[51] See W. Wood, *The War with the United States: A Chronicle of 1812* (Toronto, 1915), 34; also a good general narrative, C. P. Lucas, *The Canadian War of 1812* (Oxford, 1906).

of invading forces. Should the communication between Montreal and Kingston be cut off, wrote General Brock, "the fate of the troops in this part of the province will be decided."

In short, command of the inland lakes was bound to be the determining element in deciding at least the temporary fate of Canada. Unlike Nova Scotia, which was almost an island, and therefore open to the protection of British sea power, the Canadas, and especially Upper Canada, were bound to be the first object of invasion because they were beyond the reach of ships of the line. The Great Lakes were a self-contained area of operations, isolated from the decisive theatre of war in the Atlantic. In freshwater the enormous superiority of the British navy could not manifest itself; success had to depend on local enterprise—on the skill and energy of ship-builders who could achieve superiority by building either more or bigger ships than the enemy.[52]   "Defective as it is," wrote Sir James Craig, the governor-in-chief of the Canadas, "Quebec is the only post that can be considered tenable for a moment. If the Americans should turn their attention to Upper Canada, which is most probable, I have no hopes that the forces here can accomplish more than to check them for a short time. They will eventually be compelled to take refuge in Quebec, and operations must terminate in a siege."[53]

The struggle for the lakes began as a frontier skirmish, and then became, because both sides started almost at scratch, a ship-builder's war. On the Canadian side barges and scows were pulled up the St. Lawrence rapids to supply cannon, cable, anchors, and tackle for the busy ship-yards at Kingston, while seamen of the Royal Navy were marched on snow-shoes overland from St. John, New Brunswick.[54]   Americans with somewhat less difficulty carried their supplies, their crews, their shipwrights, and their riggers up the Mohawk River, portaging to Lake Oneida, and thence down the Oswego River to Lake Ontario, where a rising American flotilla was soon to threaten the British base at Kingston from the neighbouring port of Sackett's Harbour.

In the beginning neither fleet was of any size, and the addition of a single ship could mean the loss or gain of the command of the

[52]C. Winton-Clare, "A Shipbuilder's War," *The Mariner's Mirror*, XXIX, July, 1943, 139.
[53]"State Papers, Lower Canada," *Report on Canadian Archives, 1893*, 1. Quoted in Mahan, *Sea Power in Its Relations to the War of 1812*, I, 304.
[54]See *Ad. 1*, vol. 505, extract of a letter from Rear Admiral Edward Griffith, Halifax, January 11, 1814, and Rear Admiral Griffith to J. W. Croker, January 19, 1814.

lake. Hence, the commanders on both sides were inclined "to look on their encounters in the spirit of chess players and to consider the game lost, if the enemy achieved by any means a superiority of a single piece." On Lake Ontario the British forces seemed to have the initial advantage. They had two ships—the *Royal George* and the *Charwell*, and four schooners, *Prince Regent*, *Duke of Gloucester*, *Seneca* and *Simcoe*.[55] But even in the early days it was difficult to maintain proper complements, and until the end of the war, the commander-in-chief at Halifax was almost constantly pressed for additional seamen.[56] By the end of 1813, under pressure from the governor-in-chief, Sir George Prevost, four vessels from the Halifax squadron were laid up, in order that their crews should be available for duty on the lakes.[57]

The Americans under Commodore Isaac Chauncey (who subsequently took command of all forces on the lakes) started with only the brig *Oneida* of 243 tons and 16 guns; the acquisition of ten schooners by the beginning of the winter season gave them a numerical superiority; but even with powerful guns they never became effective war-ships. The fate of Lake Ontario was to depend chiefly on new construction. After the failure of a Canadian expedition against Sackett's Harbour in July, and an attack on the fortifications of Kingston by Chauncey in November 1812, both sides settled down to the building race which was to decide the command of the inland waters.

When the war began, British command of Lake Erie led inevitably to the fall of Detroit, and the United States naturally sought to restore the balance. On September 10, 1813, this was accomplished by Commodore Oliver Perry whose victory forced the retirement of the British forces from the Detroit area. In the face of treble the manpower and double the weight of metal, "the honour of the British flag" was undoubtedly maintained by Perry's opponent, Captain Barclay; but the Battle of Lake Erie should never have taken place.

At the end of July, the American fleet was still locked in Erie Harbour, where it was being watched by a squadron under Barclay's command. To bring the larger vessels over the bar which blocked

[55]Some of the Lake Ontario ships listed in 1813 were re-rigged and re-named by Admiralty Order of January 22, 1814.

[56]See *Ad. 1*, vol. 504, Governor Sir George Prevost to Admiral J. B. Warren, Kingston, June 24, 1813, and Thos. Everard to same, Quebec, July, 21, 1813.

[57]*Ibid.*, vol. 505, Rear-Admiral Griffith (in the absence of the commander-in-chief) to J. W. Croker, January 19, 1814.

the entrance to Lake Erie, it was necessary first to lighten them by removing their guns, and then lift them further by means of floats. The distance to be traversed from deep water to deep water was about a mile. During this process, despite the protection afforded by three 12-pounder long guns on the beach, the ships were almost helpless, and faced destruction in the event of a vigorous British attack. As it happened, however, Barclay, for reasons which are still not clear, lifted his blockade on July 30, and left the neighbourhood. When he reappeared on August 4, the American ships were safely over the bar, and Perry by reason of fire power and numbers held command of Lake Erie.[58]

Barclay had heretofore been co-operating with Major-General Proctor, whose army, based on Amherstburg, depended almost entirely for provisions and stores on water communications with Long Point. This was now an impossible task, since the superior American squadron had broken the connection. None the less, although desperately short of officers and seamen, Barclay informed Commodore Sir James Yeo[59] on September 6 that unless reinforcements were on the way, he would delay no longer, but try to remedy the situation by risking battle.[60] Three days later, without waiting for the reinforcements which were being sent from Kingston, he weighed anchor and prepared to challenge Perry's command of the lake.

The ensuing battle was one-sided, but its issue was not settled until Barclay's little squadron became unmanageable owing to the loss by death or wounds of most of the officers,[61] "I am of opinion," wrote Yeo to Admiral Warren one month later, "that under the conviction he was of his own weakness, and the great superiority of the enemy; that officer was not justified in seeking a contest the result of which he foresaw would prove disastrous."[62]

Perry had won an important tactical victory; yet the American plan of seeking command of Lake Erie, while it may have been politically wise for the sake of restoring confidence in the west, was strategically catastrophic in its effects on the campaign as a whole.

[58]See Mahan, *Sea Power in Its Relations to the War of 1812*, II, 70-3.
[59]On March 19, 1813, Captain Sir James Yeo had been appointed to command all vessels on the Lakes, although he served personally only on Lake Ontario. See Admiralty Order, as above dated, *Ad. 2*, vol. 1376.   [60]*Ad. 1*, vol. 505.
[61]See *ibid.*, Yeo to Warren, October 10, 1813.
[62]*Ad. 1*, vol. 505, Kingston, November 14, 1813; see also vol. 504, Governor Prevost to Warren, September 26, 1813 and cf. "State Papers, Lower Canada," in *Report on Canadian Archives, 1896*, 133.

The naval key to Canada was Lake Ontario; indisputable control of this lake would not only have broken communications with the nerve centre of the country at Montreal, but automatically have placed Lake Erie at the mercy of the victors.   In view of the limited number of ships, American strategy should have concentrated on the pivot of total operations at Kingston; by dividing their efforts, the Americans deprived themselves of sufficient strength in a theatre, where a decisive victory would have given them control of the upper St. Lawrence and the whole of the Great Lakes.[63]

During the course of these events, the building race for Lake Ontario had got well under way.   The Americans completed the *Madison*, nearly twice the size of the *Royal George*, while two British 24-gun ships were still under construction, one at Kingston and the other at York.   Taking full advantage of his superiority, Chauncey attacked York not long after the ice opened (April 27, 1813), burned the ship in building, and captured the brig *Gloucester*. One month later, Fort George at the mouth of the Niagara River was carried by assault from the lake.

Meanwhile, Commodore Sir James Yeo who had arrived at Kingston in May to take command of the British lake forces, was able to launch the *Wolfe*, which he assumed would give him superiority over the *Madison* and her mixed brood of schooners.   Time was precious, however, for the completion of another American ship, the *General Pike*, still on the stocks in Sackett's Harbour, was bound to put the British on the defensive again.   Hence Yeo, at the moment when Chauncey was absorbed in his attack on Fort George, made a rush attack on Sackett's Harbour with the object of burning the vessel which would lift the balance in the American favour. The attack of May 29 failed in its main purpose, although the captured *Gloucester* was put out of business by the assaulting troops.

One month later the *General Pike* was launched—the most powerful ship on the lakes—875 tons with twenty-eight long 24-pounders. The tables were now turned on Yeo, who had to witness the second invasion of York on July 30.   The two little fleets met at Niagara on August 7, but apart from the loss of two American schooners by storms, little damage seems to have been inflicted by either side, and during the next few weeks Yeo and Chauncey engaged in a game of hide-and-seek about Lake Ontario.   Late in September 1813 the

[63]Cf. Burt, *The United States, Great Britain and British North America*, 325-7, 331-2.

first real engagement took place at the western extremity of the lake. The British losses were chiefly in masts, but they were sufficiently serious to force a withdrawal to Burlington Bay, and afterwards to Kingston, where Yeo, still short of seamen, found himself blockaded until the winter weather put an end to operations.[64]

From the spring of 1814 until the end of the war, it was a game of "Cox and Box"; the inferior fleet stayed in harbour until the ship-builders created superiority and then proceeded to chase its opponents to cover. Command of the lake was a matter of weeks or even days. Until June of 1814, while Chauncey drove his workmen to complete the frigate *Superior* of 1580 tons and sixty-two guns,[65] Yeo with his additions, the new *Prince Regent*, of 1294 tons and fifty-eight guns and the *Princess Charlotte* of 756 tons and forty-two guns, could, in Dutch fashion, put a broom at his masthead and "sweep" the lake. Early in May he raided Oswego[66] and temporarily blockaded Sackett's Harbour. By June the *Superior* was in service, and during the next three months Chauncey was able to take the offensive and to blockade the British forces in Kingston. On the completion of the British three-decker *St. Lawrence* of 2305 tons and 112 guns, it was Chauncey's turn to retire to harbour, and there he remained for the last few weeks of the war. There is much to be said for the dry comment of the naval historian, William James, that had the war not ended when it did, there would have been no room left on Lake Ontario to manœuvre.

Meanwhile, on September 1, 1814, a reinforced British army of 7,000 men under Governor Prevost had begun an invasion of the United States, which petered out as a result of a decisive American naval victory over the co-operating British flotilla on Lake Champlain.[67] Although the disparity between the land forces was enormous --roughly two to one in favour of the British—the opposing flotillas of small craft were relatively equal in tonnage, and in point of weight of metal there was no substantial difference, although the British *Confiance* had enough long guns to cope with an entire American squadron on the open lake.[68] In Thomas Macdonough, however, the Americans possessed a naval commander of the first rank. With

[64]See *Ad. 1*, vol. 505, Yeo to Vice-Admiral Warren, December 6, 1813.
[65]See *ibid.*, vol. 506, "Information of the Enemy's Movements at Sackets [sic] Harbour," February 26, 1814.
[66]See *ibid.*, Prevost to Rear Admiral Griffith, May 11, 1814.
[67]See D. W. Knox, *A History of the United States Navy* (New York, 1936), 82.
[68]For details of the battle, see Mahan, *Sea Power in Its Relations to the War of 1812*, II, 371-82.

superb tactical skill he drew the British force into Plattsburg Bay, where at close quarters he was able to bring his carronades to bear with devastating effect. After watching the destruction of his ships from the near-by shore, Prevost withdrew his troops to Canada. His actions were later the subject of judicial enquiry and, while much evidence exists pro and con, a certain amount of mystery still surrounds this curious campaign. But whatever the explanation of the misfortune, it provided the British with one more substantial motive for terminating the war.[69]

In contrast to American successes on the Lakes, a series of drastic humiliations on the eastern seaboard undermined the prestige of the United States government and stimulated pacific counsels of despair. Freed from responsibilities in Europe, Britain began a series of amphibious attempts against various coastal cities. Supported by strong squadrons, British troops gained a foothold in Maryland and occupied Baltimore. On August 24, 1814, 4,000 of Wellington's regulars revenged the destruction of Upper Canada's capital at York by sweeping aside the slender forces guarding the approaches to Washington, and burning the Capitol and other administrative buildings.

Meanwhile, all the American-claimed and occupied islands in Passamaquoddy Bay had been taken, and the governor of Nova Scotia, Lieutenant-General Sir John Sherbrooke, prepared to exercise his newly arrived reinforcements of ships and men from the Mediterranean by invading Maine. On September 1, at the moment when Prevost was beginning his ill-fated march to Lake Champlain, Sherbrooke, with 2,500 troops and nine men-of-war under Rear-Admiral Edward Griffith, entered the mouth of the Penobscot River and occupied Castine.[70] Shortly afterwards, a naval detachment under Captain Hyde Parker aided in the reduction of Machias and its neighbouring forts.[71] But the commanders preferred not to press their invasion further south or westward: "the Ports . . . being situated in a populous Country, and from all the information we have been able to collect, their defences of too formidable a description to be attacked with so small a force. . . ."[72] Nevertheless, with

[69]See Burt, *The United States, Great Britain and British North America*, 343.
[70]See *Ad. 1*, vol. 508, Griffith to Vice-Admiral Sir Alexander Cochrane, *Endymion*, off Castine, September 9, 1814, and other letters.
[71]See *ibid.*, correspondence of Brig. General Brewer and Lt. Colonel Andrew Pilkington (commanding land forces) and Captain Hyde Parker, Machias, September 13, 1814.
[72]*Ibid.*, vol. 506, Griffith to J. W. Croker, Halifax, August 25, 1814.

barely a casualty, Britain had lopped off the huge salient of Maine between the Penobscot River and Passamaquoddy Bay.

It was obvious that the United States had nothing to gain by continuing the struggle. All the glory had departed, and a war of expansion turned into a defensive fight for existing boundaries. For the United States, the War of 1812 was an adventure that had come to grief. At sea, American raiders had won a few surprising successes, but they had failed to dent the British convoy system, and had not once jeopardized British command of the sea. The results showed once again the folly of a defensive naval policy, even when bolstered with an offensive strategy of *guerre de course*. Only a battle fleet could secure North American coasts against attack by a naval power. Only ships of the line could ensure command of the sea even in local waters, and only by commanding the sea could coastal commerce be properly protected.

As a consequence of British superiority at sea, American commerce had been whittled away, with devastating effects on the economic life and military resources of the Republic. Apart from the south, the country as a whole had not supported the war, and New England had zealously opposed it. Lacking in unity, short of troops, with incompetent generals and misdirected strategy, the United States was fortunate in recovering her own frontiers. Had Britain possessed the determination to continue the war, she might, despite the fiasco at New Orleans,[73] have used her overwhelming sea power to revise the biased Treaty of 1783 by enforcing boundary adjustments in the interests of New Brunswick as well as Canada. But Great Britain, like the Republic, was weary of the struggle. Except for the brief respite of the Peace of Amiens, she had been continuously at war since 1793. The obnoxious orders-in-council had long been repealed; the bitter question of impressment was gently ignored, and two weary countries were happy to bring an end to bruising misfortunes by the Peace of Ghent on December 24, 1814.

[73]The last phase of operations, two weeks after peace had been concluded, ended disastrously, when a reorganized army under Andrew Jackson repulsed with heavy losses a British force at New Orleans.

XIII

The Age of Iron and Steam

At the close of the Napoleonic Wars, Britain remained the predominant, indeed the only great, naval power, and the position of the British Empire was not merely unassailable—it was unchallenged. While Europe had been torn by twenty-two years of surging war, Britain had fought no enemy on her own soil. While the weary continent faced years of reconstruction, Britain was in a position to take full advantage of the Industrial Revolution. The fruits of the factory age were almost exclusively hers, and to every corner of the earth her ships were ready to carry, and defend *en route*, the manufactures of Lancashire and Birmingham. The empire had become a world-wide business concern, whose long and shifting maritime connections have yet to be thoroughly investigated.

The Napoleonic Wars had transformed an organization whose main centre had been the North Atlantic into one that now extended in broad and intricate pattern from Canada in the west, to India and the Pacific islands of the east. More suggestively, in the words of Sir Halford Mackinder:

> When the Napoleonic War was over, British sea-power encompassed almost without competition, that great world-promontory which stands forward to the Cape of Good Hope from between Britain and Japan. British merchant ships on the sea were part of the British Empire; British capital ventured abroad in foreign countries was a part of British resources, controlled from the city of London and available for the maintenance of power on and over the seas.

By the end of the war, the total of British colonies had increased from twenty-six to forty-three. The acquisition of these new territories had come as the casual and inevitable consequence of complete superiority at sea—a portentous fact which by itself explains the amazing growth of the second empire. Yet there had been little agitation in Great Britain for expansion—rather the contrary. Like Pitt, Lord Castlereagh, the foreign minister, was more interested in building a stable Europe than in riveting the ascendency of the British Empire over the rest of the world.[1] Against the demands of British merchants, the Dutch East Indies and most of the French West Indies were restored. With the exception of a few islands of strategic importance, France and Holland were left with the bulk of their overseas possessions. No conquered colonial territory was retained because of its natural wealth. "They [the British]" said Castlereagh, "do not desire to retain any of these Colonies for their mere commercial value—too happy if by their restoration they can give other states an additional motive to cultivate the arts of peace. The only objects to which they desire to adhere are those which affect essentially the engagement and security of their own dominion."[2]

Castlereagh saw the dangerous implications of a world hegemony based on sea power; and he would have agreed fully with Sir Eyre Crowe's famous memorandum of 1907, in which was written:

Sea power is more potent than land power, because it is as pervading as the element in which it moves and has its being. Its formidable character makes itself felt the more directly that a maritime State, is, in the literal sense of the word, the neighbour of every country accessible by sea. It would, therefore, be but natural that the power of a State supreme at sea should inspire universal jealousy and fear, and be ever exposed to the danger of being overwhelmed by a combination of the world. Against such a combination no single nation could in the long run stand, least of all a small island kingdom not possessed of the military strength of a people trained to arms, and dependent for its food on overseas commerce. This danger can in practice only be averted—and history shows that it has been so averted—on condition that the national policy of the insular and naval State is so directed as to harmonize with the general desires and ideals common to all mankind, and more particularly that it is closely identified with the primary and vital interests of a majority, or as many as possible, of the other nations.[3]

Perhaps the general European hostility that had made itself painfully felt during the War of the American Revolution taught British statesmen that a monopoly of colonial power was unwise.

[1] C. K. Webster, *The Foreign Policy of Castlereagh, 1812-1815* (London, 1931), 272-3, 491.
[2] *Ibid.*, 195, Memorandum on the Maritime Peace; and by the same author, *British Diplomacy, 1813-1815* (London, 1921), 127.
[3] Memorandum of January 1, 1907, by the Permanent Under Secretary of State for Foreign Affairs, in *British Documents on the Origins of the War, 1898-1914*, ed. by G. P. Gooch and H. Temperley (London, 1927-9), III, 402-3.

In any event, the Cabinet, like the Admiralty, was much more concerned with bases than with colonies of supply; and in Malta, the Cape, Mauritius, Tobago, and St. Lucia, it believed it had obtained the required strategic positions not only in the Mediterranean, but over the long route to India and in the Caribbean Sea. Indeed, Great Britain now possessed a convenient base in every ocean of the world. To the north she had Heligoland,[4] flanking the entrance to the Baltic and the mouths of the Elbe and Weser. In the Mediterranean, in addition to Gibraltar, she held Malta and the Ionian Isles. The Cape, along with Mauritius, the Seychelles, and Ceylon, gave her security in the Indian Ocean and marked an alternative route to India. Farther east, Singapore, acquired by Sir Stamford Raffles in 1819, commanded the straits of Malacca, one of the principal entrances to the China Seas. Britain's Caribbean possessions now included two former French islands, as well as portions of Dutch Guiana (Demerara, Essequibo, and Berbice). In the south Pacific, Captain Cook's discovery was beginning to bear strange fruit, as transports brought the victims of England's drastic penal laws to New South Wales. At the same time, Canada, living precariously on the borders of a striving republic, was growing more British, as Scottish and English colonists, and subsequently Irish, followed the Loyalists to the Maritime Provinces and Upper Canada.

As for France, most of the work of her eighteenth-century administrators and sailors had been wiped out. Of her old empire, in 1815 there were left of importance only Senegal, Martinique, Guadaloupe, Guiana, Réunion, and a few establishments in India. Bereft of so many of her overseas possessions, her merchant service in decline, her navy almost annihilated by treaty seizures or by deterioration, and its personnel demoralized and disorganized,[5] France had little to cherish and little to hope for. Perhaps Britain's most obvious gain from the war was the fact that her former enemy and chief rival seemed to accept British maritime predominance as final and irremediable.

Looking backward on more than a century of struggle, sacrifice, and bloodshed, the fight for empire seemed to French cynics of the

[4]Actually Heligoland was never used as a British base except by fishermen. Only after its transfer to Germany was it developed as an outpost of defence.

[5]Thanks to Royalist thirst for vengeance, 400 officers were put on half pay and these were replaced by officers who had emigrated at the time of the revolution. J.. Tramond and A. Reussner, Eléments d'histoire maritime et coloniale contemporaine, 1815-1914 (Paris, 1947), 1. Cf. D. Greer, The Incidence of the Emigration during the French Revolution (Cambridge, Mass., 1951), Table VIII.

nineteenth century an enormous folly. So much that Colbert, Suffren, and Dupleix had striven for had vanished, and it was natural, perhaps, that Frenchmen should succumb to the same kind of fatalism which had infected the nation after La Hogue: that the defeat of France at sea was a "law of nature," and that destiny had made the French a continental people. If there were to be new adventures, let them be directed towards the Rhine or neighbouring North Africa rather than across the seas to Canada and the Indies. France, said the pessimists, was essentially an agricultural land; she should devote herself to agrarian development and home markets rather than to will-o'-the-wisps like overseas trade, with their expensive accoutrements in the shape of colonies, merchant marine, and navy. In 1822 a petition with substantial backing was sent to the Chamber of Deputies urging the government to cease further subsidizing of overseas trade.[6]

As a consequence, French expenditures on the navy dropped rapidly. In 1814 there were seventy-one ships of the line and forty-one frigates; in 1822 the number had been reduced to thirty-one and twenty-nine respectively. A few years later it was as much as the government could do to commission two ships of the line and eight or nine frigates for a few months' exercises. "The existence of a navy compromises the defence of our coasts," was the ambiguous remark of one deputy of the Right. Until well into the reign of Louis Philippe, France renounced all attempts to make a "come-back" at sea. The glories of the First Empire were by no means dead, and the longing to erase the shame of 1814-15 eventually expressed itself in North African adventures, and in support of Mehemet Ali in Egypt. But not until after the middle of the century did an aggressive naval and colonial policy under Napoleon III constitute an actual threat to British security.

Similarly, the chief Baltic power offered no serious competition. In natural resources, such as wood, flax, and naval stores, Russia was in a particularly favoured position to create a navy. With Dutch, British, and American assistance, a good beginning was made under Catherine II, but as technologies advanced Russia failed to hold her own; with the introduction of steam and the ironclad, her navy fell well behind those of other powers.[7] Moreover, as a result of the treaty which concluded the Crimean War, Russia could main-

[6]Tramond, *Manuel d'histoire maritime*, 874.
[7]See R. J. Kerner, "Russian Naval Aims," *Foreign Affairs*, XXIV, January, 1946, 291.

tain no warships, naval bases, or arsenals in the Black Sea. Even when this restriction had been removed in 1871, the Straits of Bosphorus and Dardanelles remained closed by international agreement, with the result that numerous ships in the Russian navy could not be moved outside the Black Sea. As for the United States, the War of 1812 had scotched the doctrine of passive defence and paved the way for a high seas fleet; but not until the slavery question had been settled by civil war was America in any position to begin her career as a great naval power.[8]

Lacking competition on the seas for either colonies or commerce, Britain was, therefore, for the first time in a position of "splendid isolation." As a sea power she stood alone—master of all she surveyed. The vast realms over which the sun never set occupied almost a quarter of the earth's surface, and no jealous disputants sought to curb Britain's growing prosperity. There was no need for ostentatious assertion of maritime rights, when no other power seemed to be specially concerned. As long as her own security was not threatened, there was no reason for heavy expenditures on a navy which was needed only for colonial protection against pirates and smugglers and for the occasional colonial war. This may be an over-simplification; a complete explanation of British naval policy after Waterloo awaits fuller investigation. Suffice it to say, the effective strength of the British fleet was pared down from 230 ships in 1814, to 49 in 1820 and then slightly raised in 1838 to 54. In 1814, 99 ships of the line were in commission; by 1838 only 23.[9] The budget estimates were reduced by more than half. An age of neglect set in, not altogether unlike that which followed the surrender of the German fleet in 1919. But in the half century after Trafalgar, as compared with the quarter century after Versailles, there was no enemy to threaten the national existence.

Although troubles brewed and were broached in India, the Near East, and Canada, armies, not navies, were to furnish the drama for the coming empire of Kipling. For half a century after Trafalgar,

[8]See Sprout, *The Rise of American Naval Power*, 73, 84; and A. T. Mahan, *Naval Strategy, Compared and Contrasted with the Principles and Practice of Military Operations on Land* (Boston, 1911), 84.

	1814		1820		1838	
	In commission	In ordinary	In comm.	In ord.	In comm.	In ord.
Ships of the line	99	19	14	91	23	57
50's, etc.	10	2	3	6	5	14
Frigates	121	11	32	75	26	55

the exciting achievements of British arms occurred on land—in India or on the Crimea. The bombardment of pirate haunts at Algiers and the sinking of a Turkish-Egyptian fleet at Navarino were episodes on which no grave national issues hung. Indeed, not a few prophets in Whitehall predicted that the days of great naval contests were numbered.[10] Sea Lords, as their vigour ebbed with the rising tide of free trade, lost weight in Cabinet councils. "Boards of Admiralty go by coach," wrote Sir Charles Napier to *The Times* in 1838, "when all the world are going by railroad."[11]

Yet in spite of the dislike of most British statesmen for "unproductive expenditures," in spite of strong pacifist elements in the Liberal-Whig party, no government ever argued against what might be termed vitally necessary sacrifices. Obviously Britain had to have a fleet, and as a matter of fact she did without undue financial effort keep a fleet numerically equal to the combined fleets of the world. The established superiority of the British navy discouraged competition, and under the *Pax Britannica* there was a general naval disarmament. "It has been well said," wrote Eyre Crowe in the memorandum previously quoted, "that every country, if it had the option, would, of course, prefer itself to hold the power of supremacy at sea, but that, this choice being excluded, it would rather see England hold that power than any other State."[12]

It should be remembered, too, that statesmen like Palmerston understood the meaning of sea power, and never forgot that the existence of British trade depended on the unrestricted use of ocean communications sometimes thousands of miles from the home land. It was also recognized that, by going over to free trade, the country surrendered the tariff as an instrument of bargaining. The only remaining weapon was the navy; and Britain did on occasion, when anxious to maintain some vital market, make use of the threat of sea power. The policy of supporting Latin-American independence had been based primarily on the need for keeping South American markets, and the "open door" in China was not obtained without resort to the kind of force which sea power enabled Britain to exercise in that distant theatre. Even Cobden in his later days seemed to realize the value of *Pax Britannica*, in a world where

[10]See C. Bridge, "The Share of the Fleet in the Defence of the Empire," *Brassey's Naval Annual, 1908*, chap. IX, 143-4.
[11]*The Times*, November 6, 1838.
[12]Memorandum of January 1, 1907, in *British Documents on the Origins of the War, 1898-1914*, III, 406.

British industry stood supreme, where travel on the seas was safe for all men, and where only foreign tariffs could check the outward flow of British manufactures.

On the other hand, the growth of the free trade ideal—which ultimately possessed the imagination of the country as grimly as had mercantilism in generations past—did challenge the old concept of colonies as sources of maritime power. In a world of free and equal commerce, colonies conferred no special benefits; it was obvious, remarked a colonial secretary, that "the leading motives which induced our ancestors to found and maintain a Colonial Empire no longer existed." In the eighteenth century, one fundamental motive had been the encouragement of merchant shipping, the desire for a reserve or nursery for the Royal Navy. The traditional argument had been that the old colonial system nourished the mercantile marine in numbers and efficiency; that by encouraging and protecting the colonial carrying trades and ship-building, the system indirectly supported the Royal Navy.

Yet the Industrial Revolution had already begun to upset traditional theory and practice. In the making of a sailor there was still no alternative to long experience at sea, but the advent of iron which led eventually to the building of elaborate vessels of war compelled the introduction of specialized forms of training; this, in turn, meant that less reliance was placed on the colonial carrying trades as protected breeding grounds for seamen. Moreover, as statistical analyses seemed to prove, foreign trades opened up even broader fields of maritime exploitation than the colonial empire of the eighteenth century. In urging the Spanish government, as early as 1812, to free the trade of its South American colonies, Lord Castlereagh remarked that "Great Britain had derived more real commercial advantage from North America since the separation [of the United States] than she did when that country was subjected to her dominion and part of her colonial system."[13]

Indeed, British policy after Waterloo was far less concerned with the exploitation of the British North American colonies than with forwarding trade to the United States, "for, of all the powers on the face of the earth," declared the British prime minister, Lord Liverpool, "America is the one whose increasing population and immense

[13]Webster, *The Foreign Policy of Castlereagh*, 69-70.

territory furnish the best prospect of a ready market for British produce and manufactures."[14] It was a shrewd observation. In subsequent years, the importance of the American market diminished little. Between 1830 and 1849 the United States took 15.7 per cent of the British exports, and from 1850 to 1884 the percentage went down only slightly to 12.6.[15]

None the less, colonial trade continued to expand, and colonial tariffs, when they came, offered small check to the rising tide of imports from free-trade Britain.[16] Admittedly, in terms of cash returns, the foreign customer offered better value, since he cost the taxpayer nothing in the way of administration or defence; but this obvious fact hardly justified the constant denunciation of the colonies as financial millstones. Whether or not they were bad investments is still open to question, since there was no accurate accounting. No precise attempt at estimating the over-all expense of overseas possessions was ever made. There were quantities of variegated estimates, but no direct accounts were laid before Parliament, and no one had undertaken the laborious task of adding up the different items from the Ordnance, Commissariat, and Naval ledgers, in addition to the returns of civil and military expenses from the colonies themselves, and comparing them with total trade returns. Not until 1834 was a select parliamentary committee appointed "to inquire into the Military Establishment and Expenditure in the Colonies and Dependencies of the Crown." This Committee reported that the total cost of all military and maritime stations, plantations, and settlements was slightly over £2,000,000; and that the net cost was approximately £1,700,000.[17]

Meanwhile, however, the most alarmist information had been propagated. According to the radical *Edinburgh Review*, the North American colonies alone had already cost the country between £60,000,000 and £70,000,000; "and not contented with what we have done, we still continue to lay three or four times the duty on the timber of the North of Europe, that we lay on timber imported from Canada and Nova Scotia. We are astonished that

---

[14]*Hansard* (N.S.), I, 575, Lords' Debate of May 26, 1820.

[15]J. H. Clapham, *An Economic History of Modern Britain*. Vol. II: *Free Trade and Steel, 1850-1886* (3 vols., Cambridge University Press, 1926-38), 229-30.

[16]*Ibid.*

[17]See Report from Select Committee *On the Colonial Military Expenditure*, vol. VI, No. 570, 1834, pp. 112-3.

Messrs Robinson and Huskisson should tolerate such a system."[18] Undoubtedly Canadian timber and naval stores were valuable assets, but the high artificial price based on heavy preferences struck the free-traders as an unwarranted penalty, a kind of tribute paid to a colony which in any event would ultimately leave the empire. "And for whom," asked the *Edinburgh Review*, "is this sacrifice really made? For whom are the people of Britain made to pay a high price for inferior timber? The answer is obvious. Every man of sense, whether in the Cabinet or out of it, knows, that Canada must, at no distant period, be merged in the American republic. And certainly John Bull discovers no very great impatience of taxation, when he quietly allows his pockets to be drained, in order to clear and fertilize a province for the use of his rival Jonathan."[19]

[18]*Edinburgh Review*, XLII, No. 84, April-August 1825, "Art. I.—Substance of two Speeches delivered in the House of Commons on the 21st and 25th March, 1825, by the Right Honourable William Huskisson, respecting the Colonial Policy and Foreign Commerce of the Country," pp. 291-2.

[19]*Ibid.*, p. 192. As a result of the substantial timber preferences, the trade by sea from the St. Lawrence was now employing more than 100,000 tons of shipping yearly. In 1818 the exports, chiefly timber and other raw materials, amounted to nearly a million and a half pounds a year (Cosgrave to Goulburn, January 18, 1819, *Canadian Archives, Series Q*, vol. 153, pp. 81 and 472), while by the same year the British North American colonies were consuming more than a million and a half pounds of British manufactures.

DECLARED VALUE OF PRODUCE AND MANUFACTURES EXPORTED TO BRITISH NORTH AMERICA FROM UNITED KINGDOM OF GREAT BRITAIN AND IRELAND (in £ sterling)

Year	Value
1814	£4,399,753
1815	3,461,742
1816	2,471,326
1817	1,515,317
1818	1,768,153
1819	2,020,061
1820	1,599,104

(The years 1814-15 were exceptional as a result of the large re-export trade in the United States)

OFFICIAL VALUE OF MERCHANDISE IMPORTED

1814	£322,899
1815	368,873
1816	493,025
1817	694,011
1818	787,996
1819	889,793
1820	949,655

(J. Marshall, *Digest of Accounts* (London, 1833), 120-1.)

See also, Official Value of Goods Exported from Great Britain to the British Colonies in North America 1799-1819, in *British Accounts and Papers*, Session 21 April to 23 November 1820, vol. 12. The figures are almost exactly the same as those contained in Marshall's *Digest of Accounts*.

None the less, it was appreciated that the loss of the mainland provinces could mean a substantial accession of power to the United States.[20] Fear of American intentions in the coming age of "manifest destiny" was sufficient to outlaw for fifty years any suggestion of dropping the North American burden. Even Castlereagh modified his earlier verdict in the light of political considerations, having acquired, as he put it, "a very increased notion of the value of our North American possessions to us as a naval power."[21] In terms of comparative trade values, these colonies still ranked below the East and West Indies, but their security was still associated with the preservation of the West Indies, as well as with the control of the Newfoundland and Gulf fisheries. It was probable, wrote the learned Surveyor-General of Lower Canada in 1832, ". . . that if the North American colonies were ever wrested from Great Britain, England would at once be bereft of her West Indian plantations and her immense and valuable fisheries, and thus would her 'wooden walls' be weakened to a degree commensurate with the magnitude of her present colonial trade to the west."[22]

Consequently, the mother country continued to keep up her garrisons in the Canadas, the Maritime Provinces, and in Newfoundland. The total number of troops was not large; in 1819 it was a little less than 6,000,[23] although even this small number was not far from equalling the regular army of the United States. The main outlay was in fortifications and maintenance, and for some years forts and their occupiers cost the mother country more than the colonies themselves raised in taxes for their own administrative needs.[24] In 1819 the Duke of Wellington had prepared a memo-

[20]To many people the British North American colonies were simply a kind of "receptacle for the superabundant but industrious population of these Kingdoms, (thereby preventing the high tide of Emigration flowing to the United States) and as settling a Hardy, brave and laborious people on the frontiers of these States ready to oppose any unjust usurpation of British Rights when the period arrives that these nations may be unhappily involved in War." Cosgrave to Goulburn, January 18, 1819, *Canadian Archives, Series Q*, vol. 153, 81.
[21]To Earl Bathurst, October 4, 1814, *Historical Manuscripts Commission, Bathurst MSS.* (London, 1923), 296.
[22]J. Bouchette, *The British Dominions in North America* (London, 1832), II, 242.
[23]C. P. Stacey, *Canada and the British Army, 1846-1871* (London, 1936), 13.
[24]During the decade from 1841 to 1851 the provincial revenue of united Canada varied from $1,500,000 to $2,000,000, while Great Britain was spending some £500,000 a year. Of this amount, civil disbursements came to only £20,889 and naval costs to £897; net military expenditure was £474,789. In the Maritime Provinces and Newfoundland, the total expenditure was £184,656, and the net military expenditure was £170,464. In other words, the cost of military defence

randum on the problem of inland defence, and his recommendations advised not only the development of strategic inland waterways independent of the St. Lawrence, but the construction of fortifications at vital points. As a result, within the next few years, the British government, at tremendous cost, established citadels at Quebec and Halifax, laid down fortifications at Kingston, and Île aux Noix on the Richelieu, and completed the Rideau canal from Kingston to Ottawa.[25]

Compared with army expenditure, the cost of the local squadron on the North American station was trifling. At the end of the War of 1812 Halifax had been given one 50-gun ship, three frigates and three sloops. Newfoundland received three small frigates and two sloops.[26] These ships were used chiefly for revenue work. No attempt was made to estimate their separate expense, but it was rightly assumed by colonials that most of the money provided by Great Britain for trade protection would have been spent even if the colonies had become self-supporting or independent.

Although it is extremely doubtful if any British government would have resisted a voluntary union of Canada with the United States, there was no denying that the continued expansion of the American colossus was regarded with uneasiness, a condition of mind which helps to account for Palmerston's policy at the beginning of the American Civil War and the subsequent efforts to promote Canadian federation at its conclusion. Ever since the American Revolution, plans for the defence of the colonies had been based solely on the prospect of a war with the United States. There was a widely-held concept that the chief value of British North American territories to the mother country lay in their physical position athwart the St. Lawrence, the Great Lakes, and the western plains; they represented at least a legal barrier against American expansion northward.

Even the failure of the provinces to take some of the responsibility for their own defence, while it provoked bitter reaction in Britain,[27] could not make the authorities entirely indifferent to

---

was approximately nine-tenths of the total cost. (See Stacey, *Canada and the British Army*, 42.) The naval charges may seem small as compared with the army, but it must be remembered that these took into account only shore establishments and not ships.   [25]*Ibid.*, 14-15.

[26]Viscount Melville to Earl Bathurst, August 11, 1817, *Bathurst MSS.*, p. 438.
[27]On March 4, 1862, a Select Committee on Colonial Military Expenditure presented a resolution to the House of Commons: "That this House (while fully recognizing the claims of all portions of the British Empire for aid in their protection against perils arising from the consequences of Imperial Policy) is of

American imperialism, symbolized in press and on platform by "manifest destiny." In the end it was colonial defence requirements which swung the balance of British political opinion in favour of confederation. The foundations for a united Dominion were laid primarily as a measure of defence against the aggressive designs of the neighbour to the south.

After 1867 the imperial government still accepted the responsibility of defending to the utmost an empire which now included a self-governing nation, but such a commitment did not deter the British authorities from starting a policy of military withdrawal which culminated in 1871 when Quebec fortress with its 181 guns and three new forts at Lévis was handed over to the Canadian government.[28]

The distinction between military and naval protection was, however, a substantial one. The mother country continued to take responsibility for the protection of trade and shipping in the neighbourhood of Canadian coasts. This she prepared to do by providing on paper at least a sufficient cruiser force which should be able to prevent raiding squadrons or filibustering expeditions from playing havoc with coastal towns and focal sea-trade areas. Consequently, the Dominion government was relieved of what might be termed its proper share of the expense of maintaining the Royal Navy. Canada undertook to pay a proportion of the costs of the Lake gun-boats, but her expenditure on defence—some $1,500,000— was only about a fifth of the total which Great Britain contributed each year.[29]

But already the scientists had begun to revolutionize the whole method of imperial defence. By the middle of the nineteenth century, revolutions in naval architecture had wrought greater changes than had taken place since the introduction of Henry VIII's famous cannon. Between 1859 and 1862 the ironclad took the place of the

---

opinion that Colonies exercising the rights of self-government ought to undertake the main responsibility of providing for their own internal security." (*Hansard*, 3rd series, CLXV, col. 1044.) This vague resolution was agreed to, with the addition of the words, "and ought to assist in their own external defence." (*Ibid.*, CLXV, col. 1060.) In this connection, see J. M. Hitsman, *Canadian Naval Policy* (a thesis submitted for the degree of M.A., at Queen's University, Kingston, Ontario, 1940), 1.

[28]Stacey, *Canada and the British Army*, 252. About 2,000 men were left at the Halifax shore establishment. Not until 1894 did regular imperial troops arrive at Esquimalt, and there they remained until 1906 when the newly formed permanent-force units of Canada took charge of the base. See F. V. Longstaff, *Esquimalt Naval Base: A History of Its Work and Its Defences* (Victoria, B.C., 1941), 39, 49.   [29]Stacey, *Canada and the British Army*, 202-3.

old man-of-war as the standard capital ship of the chief European nations. Henri Paixhans's determined promotion of the shell gun as a practical weapon meant the end of the wooden ship. At Sinope in November 1853, the momentous fact was not the defeat of a Turkish squadron by greatly superior Russian forces, but the destruction of a Turkish squadron by Russian shells. In Britain the significance of the event was accepted with some reluctance, and only the continued and effective use of heavy shell guns by France and Russia during the Crimean War compelled the hesitant Admiralty to hasten their own experiments with armour plate.[30]

None the less, the shell gun seemed to have upset the balance between offence and defence in favour of the weaker power. Indeed, optimistic Frenchmen like Paixhans prophesied the end of Britain's superiority at sea. Highly mechanized artillery, along with steam power, erased the heavy premium that seamanship had given to the British navy. Once again, as in mediaeval times, skilled artificers and soldiers-at-sea would take the place of sailors. In the new mechanized age, Paixhans argued, the naval power of a state would become more proportionate to total population than to its seafaring population alone.[31]

The advent of steam propulsion was, however, a revolution fraught with more immediate peril for Britain. By making warships less dependent on winds and tides, steam power was to remove an element of chance from naval warfare, making tactical planning a matter of hours and minutes rather than days or even weeks. Steamships, it was urged, could now leave a blockaded area when the opportunity suited them; they could strike at commerce and communications as man, and not the elements, dictated.

To many anxious contemporaries, the introduction of steam transport seemed to spell disaster to the British islands. Steam propulsion, wrote the Duke of Wellington impulsively in 1847, had made Britain "assailable" at all times from the sea. "If it be true that the exertions of the fleet are not sufficient to provide for our defence, we are not safe for a week after the declaration of War."[32] From Dover to Portsmouth, he continued, there was no part of the coast, except that under the fire of Dover Castle, "on which infantry might not be thrown on shore at any time of tide, with any wind,

[30]See J. P. Baxter, *The Introduction of the Ironclad Warship* (Cambridge, Mass., 1933), 17, 69.

[31]*Nouvelle force maritime* (Paris, 1822), vii, xiv, 236, 340-2, 345.

[32]Temperley and Penson, *Foundations of British Foreign Policy*, 288-9.

and in any weather."[33]   The English Channel, echoed Lord Palmerston, was no longer a barrier, but "a river passable by a steam bridge," across which France could throw 20,000 to 30,000 men in one night.[34] However exaggerated these fears, it was clear that the country had reached a turning-point in its history as final and as momentous as any since the defeat of the Spanish Armada in 1588.

In 1849 the French government had proposed a naval building armistice, but the *coup d'état* of Louis Napoleon in December of 1851 upset any possibility of an understanding, and swept Britain into a state of nerves which even partnership in the Crimean War some four years later failed to allay entirely. Wellington's warning on the revolution in strategy had been given enormous attention in the press, and fears for the safety of the "moat" continued to agitate public opinion in moments of international stress.

Official anxiety, however, was based on information that the steam fleet of France was growing almost as rapidly as Britain's. In 1859 the total British fleet was 95 sail of the line to 51 French, and 96 frigates to 97 French, but many of the British capital ships were obsolete.   Moreover, the French were vigorously pursuing their experiments with armour-plated ships, and in 1858 laid down the first sea-going ironclad warship, the frigate *Gloire.* Britain followed in 1859 with the ironclad *Warrior,*[35] but not until France initiated her great ironclad programme of 1860 did a cautious Admiralty finally surrender to the industrial age, and suspend construction of the wooden ship of the line that had remained unchanged for more than two centuries.[36]   An accelerated programme was then laid down, but for the moment there was no question of maintaining a two-power standard.[37]

While scare-mongers raised the spectre of invasion, Cabinets discussed the building of coastal defences and the reorganization of the militia. In 1860, a Royal Commission report added to the confusion by suggesting that in the event of the absence or temporary disablement of the fleet, an invading force could land in two or three

[33]This, of course, is an opinion that no sailor would countenance. It suggests, indeed, that the Duke had little acquaintance with elementary seamanship. The landings of Allied forces in Normandy in 1944 show that even today due regard must be paid to wind and tide and weather.

[34]Baxter, *The Introduction of the Ironclad Warship*, 66-7.

[35]*Ibid.*, 111-12, 131-2.

[36]*Ibid.*, 4, 165, 314-17.

[37]For classified summaries of the Royal Navy and the French navy to April, 1859, see H. Busk, *The Navies of the World: Their Present State and Future Capabilities* (London, 1859), App., 51 and 60.

hours.[38] The War Office immediately prepared to meet this frightful contingency by organizing a system of "Churchillian" house and hedgerow defences in the English shires, while Palmerston's government voted huge sums to ring the island with sea-coast forts.

It was a weird period of alarms which will repay further scrutiny. With no very apparent opposition from the Admiralty, age-old principles of strategy were thrown out the window in response to public demand for local protection.   It was a far call to the days of Elizabethan England when Sea Lords in defiance of the very principle which history had dictated as essential to English security—the role of the offensive in the open sea—could order the construction of ship after ship designed solely for coast defence. Occupied with the Indian Mutiny, the Chinese imbroglio, and subsequently the American Civil War, and partly paralysed by the mixture of Palmerston's mailed-fist diplomacy and the pacifist doctrines of the free trade school, British governments seemed to forget that command of the sea was the key not only to home defence but to the safety of overseas commerce and empire. More than ever before in history, the nation depended for sustenance, not merely on holding the Channel but on control of overseas communications.

Admittedly, fixed local defences had their uses, especially in the colonies. Fuel requirements limited the active radius of steamships, and well-protected coaling bases in all parts of the world were assets of incalculable value to any imperial power; but it was folly to forget, as some Admiralty members did, that distant bases were safe only so long as communications were intact.   Fixed local defences were never designed to be other than subordinate to maintained lines of communication.   That any kind of static fixed defences were a real substitute for command of the sea, said Rear-Admiral Colomb, was a misreading of English history.[39]

Meanwhile, the advent of steam had served not only "to bridge the Channel" but to span the empire. Almost magically, the electric telegraph and the steamship were to cut down the old conceptions

[38]See H. D'Egville, *Imperial Defence and Closer Union: A Short Record of the Life Work of Sir John Colomb* (London, 1913), 11.

[39]See his article on "Imperial Defence" in *Brassey's Naval Annual, 1888-9*.   A brother of the Admiral, Sir John Colomb, first took up the cudgels in 1867 with a paper entitled "Protection of Commerce in War."   Much of his work laid the ground for Admiral Mahan's subsequent studies; see also J. Colomb, "Britain's Defence, 1800-1900," *Journal of the Royal Colonial Institute*, XXXI, April 10, 1900; also H. Rundle, "The Principles of Imperial Naval Defence," *Brassey's Naval and Shipping Annual, 1923*, 156-7.

of time and space. Rapid communication was to make a political slogan like "the integrity of the empire" a doctrine of more than sentimental application. In 1820 it sometimes required six weeks to make a voyage from London to Halifax. Scarcely a generation later, ships from Liverpool were touching at Australia in less than eight weeks. "There is no limit to the effects of steam power," wrote a learned enthusiast, "which will work more changes in society than either the [magnetic] needle, gunpowder, or the art of printing."[40] In the fifties, commercial steamships were still used chiefly for passengers and mail; there were few steam cargo vessels, and the bulk of sea-borne commerce was still carried in wooden sailing-ships. The transition was gradual, but by the eighties the whole structure of industrial England became gradually geared to the punctual movement and increased volume of overseas trade. By largely eliminating considerations of wind and weather, by multiplying the number of voyages that could be made in a given time, and by allowing the duration of a voyage to be fixed with reasonable certainty, steam not only accelerated the growth of industrial populations, but made them completely dependent for sustenance on constant clock-like deliveries.[41] The sailing-ship could take only two freights a year or five in two years, whereas the steamer engaged in foreign trade was able to deliver ten or twelve a year. Moreover, ships' tonnage had begun to climb. In 1875 the average sailing-ship tonnage was 586; in 1885 it was 815,[42] as compared with steamships' average of 1,132 tons. The transition was neither so rapid nor dramatic as in the case of the war vessel, but the revolution was none the less significant. Within ten years after 1875, the number of sailing-ships had fallen from 5,327 to 3,180.[43] Slowly and surely another relic of the picturesque past shrank away before the onslaught of modern science.

As it happened, the decline of sail coincided with an enormous expansion of the British carrying trade; indeed, the growth of British shipping during the final three decades was one of the remarkable features of the nineteenth century. In 1870 the mercantile marine

[40] Asiatic Journal, 3rd series, I, 567, quoted in H. L. Hoskins, British Routes to India (New York, 1928), 265.

[41] See C. E. Fayle, "Economic Pressure in the War of 1739-48," Journal of the Royal United Service Institution, LXVIII, 1923, 434.

[42] The average tonnage of vessels engaged in foreign trade in 1792 was less than 150 tons.

[43] P. H. Colomb, "Convoys: Are They Any Longer Possible?" Journal of the Royal United Service Institution, XXXI, 1887, 303 and 307.

tonnage of the British Empire almost equalled that of all non-British countries, and by 1880 it exceeded it. Empire steam tonnage in 1880 amounted to 2,949,282 tons, more than double that of all other countries.[44] This expansion was not a consequence of the repeal of the Navigation Laws. It was due rather to the fact that the revolution in the science of marine architecture and engineering was exactly suited to British natural resources. Just as coal and iron had given Britain commercial ascendancy in the "factory age," so the application of iron to ship-building confirmed that leadership on the seas. With the coming of the "iron age" in ship-building, it became much easier for Britain to maintain her supremacy as an ocean trader.

On the other hand, the pre-eminence that the British mercantile marine enjoyed could hardly have been reached had not the most formidable competitor been forced temporarily out of the running by the American Civil War;[45] and after 1865, Americans were less interested in the sea than in conquering the western prairies. Until the opening of the twentieth century neither the United States nor any other maritime nation was in a position to challenge Britain's maritime supremacy. No other power had sufficiently developed its shipping resources to offer serious rivalry in the carrying trades. Coal and iron and other basic materials of production were available within the British Isles, and British manpower was sufficient to exploit them. For practical trading purposes on a world scale the country was self-contained and self-sufficient.

Yet such a tremendous superiority in merchant shipping placed a new and heavy responsibility on the Royal Navy; and in the seventies a strong reaction had already developed against the so-called "abandonment of the sea lanes of empire," which confused doctrines of "local defence" had hitherto encouraged. Disraeli, pointing the golden road to Samarkand, foreshadowed the new approach of government to empire; but the Russian war scare of 1878 probably marked the turning of the tide in terms of Admiralty policies. That alarm served to advertise the increased dangers to which trade routes were now exposed as a result of the introduction of the shell gun and steam.

[44]*Proceedings of the Colonial Conference, 1887, Vol. II (Appendix)*. (C. 5091-1). Section VII, D, No. 89: *Extracts from Reports of the Royal Commission on the Defence of British Possessions and Commerce Abroad. First Report*, p. 306 (London, 1887).

[45]See J. H. Clapham, "Last Years of the Navigation Laws," *English Historical Review*, XXV, October, 1910, 705-7.

The revived function of the Royal Navy in time of war was enunciated by a Royal Commission, under the chairmanship of Lord Carnarvon, which sat from 1879 to 1882 "to enquire into the defence of the British possessions and commerce abroad." Restored to its pre-Trafalgar status, the fleet was given the old mandate to destroy the enemy's trade, attack his possessions, and engage his ships at sea. The Royal Commission issued three reports. The first summarized the trade of the United Kingdom with British possessions and foreign countries as well as the whole trade of the empire; the second dealt with coal supplies, the protection of colonial and commercial interests by the fleet, and in particular with the defence of the Australian colonies; the third report, to be referred to subsequently in its Canadian aspects, concerned the great imperial trade routes and the nature of the commerce they embraced, the value of the trade, and the terminal ports requiring military defences.[46]

Moreover, the British government had begun already to estimate, for the purpose of colonial conference argument, the proportional interest of each British overseas community in this vast ocean trade, and the amount which each community was contributing to its defence. In the first report of September 3, 1881, the entire trade of the British overseas possessions was given as £367,000,000, of which about one half was conducted by the colonies with the United Kingdom, the other half among themselves and with foreign states. In this latter category, it was pointed out, the United Kingdom had no financial interest. All told, the amount of property at stake in

[46]A few years earlier, when war with Russia appeared imminent, a Colonial Defence Committee had been appointed to advise as to the immediate measures necessary for defending the most important colonial ports. When "immediate pressure of fear of war" had passed the Committee was dissolved, but the Disraeli government was determined to see the work completed. In September 1879, a Royal Commission was appointed, and in October a circular despatch was sent to the colonies informing them of the nature of the Commission's tasks. A paragraph was added to the copies sent to Canada, New South Wales, Victoria, South Australia, Queensland, Tasmania, and New Zealand to the effect that it was "not the intention of Her Majesty's Government . . . to interfere in any way with the measures already taken in the Colony under your Government for providing an adequate system of defence." See Minute sheet of June 1, 1880, Public Record Office, Colonial Office General, 1882, series 323, vol. 356. See also Minute of May 18, 1882 on the First and Second Reports (C.O. 323, vol. 353, and a Minute by Lord Kimberley of August 16, 1882 on the need for keeping under "lock and key" the highly confidential Third Report which had been forwarded to the Under Secretary of State for Colonies on July 24 (*ibid.*).

A copy of the complete Third and Final Report is contained among the papers of Henry Howard Molyneux, fourth Earl of Carnarvon, which were presented to the Public Record Office in 1926, and are now open freely to public inspection (see G. & D. 6, vol. 126.)

this imperial sea-borne commerce was estimated at not less than £900,000,000, of which £144,000,000 was afloat at any given time.[47]

Yet the mother country bore the entire burden of expense. Only one colony—Victoria—had so far availed itself of the authority provided by the Colonial Naval Defence Act, and even the one ship acquired by that colony had been converted for harbour defence. "What have we arrived at?" said Jan Hofmeyr at the first Colonial Conference in 1887. "Simply this: that the Australian group of Colonies will pay a certain amount annually towards the support of a few ships in their own waters. But what has the rest of the Colonial Empire done towards the maintenance of the Imperial Navy? Nothing at all. The Cape has not agreed to do anything; Canada has not agreed to do anything, for reasons which I think are weighty, and which the Conference will not overrule."[48] Almost alone among colonial statesmen, this great Afrikander understood the meaning of "command of the sea" in the history of his country. His own suggestion was an imperial customs tariff, "the revenue derived from such a tariff to be devoted to the general defence of the Empire."

As a matter of fact an attempt was already being made to crystallize this and other new conceptions. In 1884 the Imperial Federation League was organized, and not long afterwards various branches were established in Canada. The aim of the movement was not only to resist any tendency towards carelessness and indifference in the imperial connection, but to strengthen the imperial foundations by discussion of a systematic plan of empire-union which would not interfere with autonomy in local affairs. The problem of providing protection for the empire's interests, (read the fourth article of the Declaration of the Imperial Federation League) could only be met by combining the total resources of the empire in a

[47]See *Proceedings of the Colonial Conference of 1887*, *Vol. II (Appendix)*, *First Report*, p. 312, and *Second Report*, p. 313.

[48]In a speech to the Canadian House of Commons, December 5, 1912, the Prime Minister, R. L. Borden, recalled the burden which the British government had been called upon to shoulder. "So far as official estimates are available, the expenditure of Great Britain in naval and military defence for the provinces which now constitute Canada, during the nineteenth century was not less than $400,000,000. Even since the inception of our confederation, and since Canada has attained the status of a great Dominion, the amount so extended by Great Britain for the naval and military defence of Canada vastly exceeds the sum which we are now asking Parliament to appropriate. From 1870 to 1890 the proportionate costs of North Atlantic squadrons which guarded our coasts was from $125,000,000 to $150,000,000. From 1853 to 1903 Great Britain's expenditure on military defence in Canada runs closely up to one hundred million dollars." *Selected Speeches and Documents on British Colonial Policy, 1763-1917*, ed. A. B. Keith (2 vols., Oxford, 1918), II, 333-4.

comprehensive system "for the maintenance of common interests and the organized defence of common rights." In the opinion of its leaders, military and naval defence had to be the keystone of such a federation.

This concept of imperial unity, based primarily on a pooling of resources, obviously held deep strategical implications. Free trade was still a basic principle of domestic economics, but other nations had failed to accept Cobden's postulate as one of eternal value, and had already begun to raise up barriers to British trade. British industry, as we have noticed, depended more and more upon the regular importation of raw materials from all over the globe. From the beginning of the nineteenth century, the country had to count on outside sources of supply for food, and by the middle of the century, though the total of home-raised food of all kinds was still greater than the amount imported, for the most vital of all, bread cereals, dependence on outside sources was becoming absolute. In 1850 it is probable that some 25 per cent of the bread cereal consumption was imported; by 1880 the percentage had risen to more than 60.[49] In 1851 only about one fortieth of the imported wheat, wheat-meal, and flour came from British possessions abroad. Happily, however, the scale of imperial imports began to rise between 1880 and 1885; and, although the United States was soon supplying more than half the United Kingdom requirements, the proportion of wheat and flour imports from British possessions gradually rose to nearly one fourth.

For a country which was now getting two loaves out of three from overseas, the protection of the sea lanes to the colonial food-producing areas was a matter of military concern. Hence, by the beginning of the eighteen-eighties, when the wheat lands of the Canadian interior were suddenly recognized as an invaluable imperial asset, ocean communications to Canada took on a unique significance. Although India, in the decade after 1877, supplied more than two and a half times as much wheat as Canada, already men were looking towards the newly opened country in the region of the Red River and beyond. There in the far distance lay millions of virgin acres of fertile soil, that could be tapped by rail, and perhaps by sea from Churchill harbour on Hudson Bay.[50] (From Liverpool to Churchill harbour was 2,926 miles, and to the edge of the wheat district, 3,280; to Montreal from Liverpool the distance, via

[49]Clapham, *An Economic History of Modern Britain*, II, 218.
[50]See C. H. Nugent, "Imperial Defence: Part II, Abroad," *Journal of the Royal United Service Institution*, XXVIII, 1884, 463.

Cape Race, was 2,990 miles, and to the edge of the wheat district, 4,290.) Admittedly, a Hudson Bay route was a distant prospect, and a limited one at that—for the Bay was rarely open to traffic for more than six weeks in the year—but steel rail had already begun to penetrate the rock and forest barriers of the Laurentian Shield.

"The Empire's answer to a 'blocked' Suez Canal has been given by Canada," remarked a learned advocate of imperial defence, Sir John Colomb. "The influence which the 'Canadian Pacific' can exercise on our naval and military position in the Far East is immense."[51] In the event of the Mediterranean route being closed, or, for one reason or another, the Indian wheat shipments stopped, the new Canadian transcontinental rail line which tapped the prairie grain lands could save the country from starvation. It offered, moreover, a safe alternative means of reinforcing India. The route from Britain to the Atlantic terminus of the Canadian Pacific Railway offered advantages of security, and possibly of time, that even the Cape route could not equal in time of war. Whether by the Cape or by Suez, ships had to pass close to "the Atlantic sea-face of Europe"; to cross the Bay of Biscay or to travel from Gibraltar to Port Said was obviously a more risky exploit in time of war than an Atlantic journey from Liverpool or Galway to Halifax. In short, the new trans-Canada route performed a dual purpose, commercial and military. Although it was primarily a bond of federated Canada, the C.P.R. automatically became an imperial communication and a strategic supply line. Furthermore, according to sound naval doctrine the importance of the C.P.R. terminals was bound to influence the future disposition of cruiser forces in the north Atlantic.

The defence of trade routes and focal sea areas such as the Gulf of St. Lawrence remained, as before, the task of the Royal Navy; at the same time, the quality and efficiency of any cruising squadron depended heavily, as we have seen, on the establishment of base facilities for operations as well as coaling, docking, and refitting. Furthermore, such ports had to be capable of denying anchorage to the enemy, and of standing siege until reinforcements from the home land were in a position to engage the marauding squadron. Under the circumstances, it was considered vital that the British government retain full control over at least one strategically situated port and trade terminal on each coast.

[51]J. C. R. Colomb, "Imperial Federation—Naval and Military," *ibid.*, XXX, 1886, 857.

Such considerations were based solely on the possibility of American aggression by sea. A war between Britain and the United States, read the *Third Report* of the Royal Commission appointed in 1879 would be mainly one of naval operations "in which case the fortified ports of Halifax and Bermuda would be of first importance . . . as coaling stations and to merchant ships as harbours of refuge." "The Imperial Government by undertaking to keep up a fleet and maintain the fortresses of Halifax and Bermuda affords so large a measure of protection, that the defences of the purely mercantile ports need not be of a very extensive character."[52]

Bermuda had already been well equipped defensively, while of the West Indies, Jamaica and Antigua had been, or were in process of being, fortified. The historical position of Halifax as a trade depot, its status as a rail terminus, and its unequalled harbour facilities had made it the obvious choice of the eastern ports. Yet this important terminal for land and sea communications was in no position to defend itself independently against any ravaging squadron that might appear from the south. Apart from the fact that it was open to attack by land, the port possessed no dry-dock capable of accommodating a ship-of-war, until one was completed with the joint support of the Admiralty and the Canadian government in 1889. No attempt had been made to supply torpedo protection for the harbour, or to organize local naval reserves from material provided by the fishing industry and the coastal merchant marine. Only with the addition of submarine mines and possibly torpedo boats, and the construction of forts with six-inch guns to command the anchorage, could Halifax properly fulfil its function as a naval base.[53]

On the west coast, where the north Pacific ocean had slumbered for generations almost untouched by European competition for empire, plans for the establishment of a modern base had just been arranged. Since 1837 Valparaiso had been the headquarters of the eastern squadron, and not till 1847 did H.M.S. *Pandora* cruise north to survey the harbours of the newly established town of Victoria and the adjoining settlement of Esquimalt. In 1865 Esquimalt was made the headquarters of the Pacific station, and in 1887, two years after the completion of the transcontinental C.P.R., the Admiralty decided to reconstruct this primitive base, provide a dry-dock, and

[52]*Proceedings of the Colonial Conference, 1887, Vol. II (Appendix). Extracts from the Third and Final Report of the Royal Commissioners appointed to inquire into the Defence of British Possessions and Commerce abroad*, p. 335.
[53]See C. Key, "Naval Defence of the Colonies," *The Nineteenth Century*, XX, August, 1886, p. 287.

lay down "a powerful arsenal," that should command the coastal waters about Vancouver, and form a strategic link with British possessions in the Antipodes.[54] Thirteen days from Plymouth—eight by ocean and five by rail—Esquimalt was some thousand miles nearer to Sydney than Panama. It also marked the shortest route to China. Finally, apart from their value as bases for repair and refit, both Esquimalt and Vancouver could be terminals for the distribution of reinforcements by fast steamer to Hong Kong, Sydney, or other Australasian ports.

British control of Halifax and subsequently, Esquimalt, was based, as has been stated, on the assumption that the protection of trade was an imperial responsibility. There was no thought of asking Canada to provide sea-going ships in the shape of ironclads or cruisers. Similarly, it was taken for granted that the ships which used the imperial ports should not be under the authority of the colonial government. Questions of offensive or defensive strategy were for the admirals of the North American and West Indies stations alone to decide. On the other hand, it seemed proper that the self-governing colonies or dominions should undertake some of the burden of providing mines, gun-boats, torpedo-boats, and perhaps a small flotilla, for port or coastal defence and patrol work. No great pressure was applied, but the invitation remained a standing one. In the course of four colonial conferences between 1887 and 1902, the British government, while accepting full responsibility for defending all the territories of the empire and guarding all overseas communications, made it abundantly clear that any naval assistance that might voluntarily be rendered by the colonies towards their own local defence would be warmly welcomed.

There seemed no doubt that eventually all the colonies would participate; the only difficulty was uniformity. In terms of British policy the matter boiled down to a question of whether there could be distant colonial units in terms of men and small ships, or whether

[54]See Hitsman, *Canadian Naval Policy*, 18. While Canada assumed responsibility for the defensive works, the Imperial government, according to Edward Stanhope, the secretary of war, undertook to supply "a very effective armament of breech-loading guns and machine guns." For "Correspondence and Reports" on the defence of Vancouver Island, see *Third and Final Report of the Royal Commissioners appointed to inquire into the Defence of British Possessions and Commerce Abroad* (1882); Carnarvon Papers, G. & D. 6, vol. 126, appendix No. 4, pp. 419-56. See also, *Memorandum on the defences of Esquimalt*, October 8, 1880; *ibid.*, vol. 125. Miscellaneous material including confidential "Prints" on the work of the Colonial Defence Commission and on Colonial Expenditure is to be found in the same collection, vol. 131.

—and preferably—the first step towards joint imperial defence should not take the form of contributions to a federal fleet, which would be less expensive to the colony and more useful to the empire as a whole.

There were two serious obstacles in the way of a local navy; one was the political difficulty of adapting any colonial sea force to the needs of imperial strategy without surrendering a share of precious national autonomy; the other was the expense and time involved in its organization. Obviously an efficient naval unit could not be created in short order. The making of a seaman was a matter of long apprenticeship, of rigorous training in every branch of a service which was steadily expanding its domain in the fields of steam machinery, electricity and magnetism, navigation and ordnance. Moreover, frequent exercise at sea, where alone command of men as well as ships might be learned, was vitally necessary if the local force was to count as an imperial unit in actual warfare.

That there was an abundance of good naval reserve material in Canada, no one could deny; and attempts had already been made to exploit it.[55] In a report to the first Lord of the Admiralty in 1898, the Hon. William Mulock, the Postmaster General of Canada, gave the number of men engaged in deep sea and inland fisheries as 75,000—most of them good material for man-of-war training.[56] As early as 1885, the Canadian Minister of Militia, Sir Adolphe Caron, estimated that 40,000 potential seamen could be found scattered about Nova Scotia, New Brunswick, and Prince Edward Island. To utilize this material there was clearly a need to tighten the connection between the Canadian government and the private interests engaged in the mercantile marine and fisheries. But if the organization of such a reserve was to be a purely Canadian concern (even though subject to British instruction and supervision), it was

[55]In 1868 an Act had been passed "respecting the Militia and Defence of the Dominion of Canada." (31 Victoria cap. 40; *Statutes of Canada*, 1868.) It provided for the recruiting of a marine militia, as part of the active militia, to be composed of "seamen, sailors, and persons whose usual occupation is upon any steam or sailing craft, navigating the waters of the Dominion." Service involved a two-year period in peacetime, not exceeding the annual sixteen-day training period and not less than eight days.

As a consequence, a Naval Brigade was formed in Halifax and arrangements were made to provide instructors from the Royal Navy. Unfortunately, this unit of 11 officers and 205 men decreased by 1869-70 to 5 officers and 167 non-commissioned officers and men. (*Canada, Sessional Papers*, 1870, no. 7; Hitsman, *Canadian Naval Policy*, 7.) In the following year, it was disbanded, and thus ended the only effort to establish a marine militia under the terms of the Act of 1868. In all probability, the general improvement in Anglo-American relations was partly responsible for the lack of interest that eventually killed the scheme.

[56]T. A. Brassey, *The Royal Naval Reserve* (London, 1882-3), 19.

questionable whether the dominion could undertake the expense. It was estimated that it would cost at least £8,000 a year to train 1,500 men annually. Poverty, unfortunately, went hand in hand with loyalty, and in a period of vast spending on internal developments, cautious men doubted whether the country could afford the money for purposes that were not felt to be pressing.

As for outright contributions to the Royal Navy, growing national consciousness was beginning to play havoc with the plans of the military federationists. Whereas the Admiralty, in the interests of imperial defence, naturally resisted any division of naval control even in time of peace, Canadian statesmen were affected by political complications which made a precise policy unattainable. The constitutional position of the country was still unsettled; time alone could tell whether its destiny lay within the empire or in close collaboration with the United States, which under the Monroe doctrine already took certain theoretical responsibilities for the security of Canada as a North American state. Moreover, the French-Canadian dread of British imperialism made even a request for naval subsidies seem a subtle threat to racial autonomy. Under the circumstances, the question of Canada's naval policy could only be solved as Canada's own constitutional position in the empire became clearer.[57]

In 1885, the considerate gesture of Australia and Canada in providing men for the Sudan campaign had seemed to offer hope that the framework of a unified defensive organization might be hammered into shape while the iron of loyalty was hot. Indeed, the Colonial Conference of 1887 was called for that specific purpose; but as far as defence matters were concerned it had amounted to little more than a forum for Australia and South Africa. Canada took practically no part in the discussions. Relying on the British government's undertaking to defend the country, the Canadian delegation assumed that the North American squadron provided them with as much security as was possible for a small continental colony to obtain.

Sir Alexander Campbell, who, with Sandford Fleming, represented Canada, declared that the British government had agreed, at the time of Confederation, to undertake the defence of Canada. In any event, geography required that British squadrons must, for the sake of imperial communications, take stations in the north Pacific and the north Atlantic.

[57]See R. Jebb, *The Imperial Conference: A History and Study* (2 vols., London, 1911), I, 54.

They [the British government] maintain for Imperial purposes, as for other purposes, the North American Squadron, and so long as that Squadron is at our doors, Canada does not need any other naval defence. Since that agreement was made by Her Majesty's Government the Colony of British Columbia has been added to the Dominion, and therefore there is a coast of Canada now on the Pacific Ocean. That coast is defended for the present by Her Majesty's North Pacific Squadron, which goes to Esquimalt once a year, and is more or less there all the time, as the North American Squadron is more or less at Halifax all the time.[58]

This cold and unsentimental analysis was, however, bolstered by the argument that the Canadian Pacific, Grand Trunk, and Inter-colonial Railways should be regarded as auxiliary contributions to imperial defence. "The last rail [of the C.P.R.] had not been laid many days," said Sandford Fleming, "when a consignment of naval stores passed through to the station of the North Pacific Fleet from Halifax. The time occupied on the then unfinished railway was seven days and a few hours from tide water of the Atlantic to Esquimalt. Without the railway it would have taken some three months to have sent the same stores in a British bottom." In other words, Canada announced a policy of non-participation, either in local or imperial schemes of naval defence; and this policy of the *status quo*, strengthened as it was in the next few years by the arguments of national autonomy, was inflexibly maintained until the year of crisis, 1909.

The only substantial outcome of this, the first colonial conference, had been the Australian decision to form an additional force of five fast cruisers and two torpedo gun-boats to be employed for the protection of trade in Australian waters. The first costs were to be borne by the British government; the Australian colonies were required only to pay interest on the capital cost at a rate of 5 per cent, but not exceeding £35,000, and to bear the peacetime charges for maintaining the ships, some of which would be commissioned and others kept in reserve.

Though slight in comparison with the total expenditures on the fleet, the Australian contribution is noteworthy as marking the first actual acceptance of the principle of "sharing the burden." In the sphere of military strategy too, it symbolized the death of separatist influences, which had hitherto affected not only statesmen but admirals. Nevertheless, the British government was still concerned about expense, and the Navy estimates for 1888-89 were reduced to a point approximately £1,000,000 below those of 1860-61. "Twice

[58]*Proceedings of the Colonial Conference, 1887* (C.-5091), Vol. I, p. 275.

during my political life," wrote Lord George Hamilton, "once in 1868 and again in 1880, has the political party with which I am associated met with a crushing defeat at the polls; in each case their expenditure on national defence largely contributed to the success of their opponents." This fear of injuring party prospects may have been responsible for Mahan's pessimism with regard to Britain's future supremacy at sea.[59] In 1889, he wrote:

> Whether a democratic government will have the foresight, the keen sensitiveness to national position and credit, the willingness to insure its prosperity by adequate outpouring of money in times of peace, all of which are necessary for military preparation, is yet an open question. Popular governments are not generally favourable to military expenditure, however necessary, and there are signs that England tends to drop behind.[60]

The Colonial Conference of 1894, which was held in Ottawa, was concerned chiefly with cable communications, mails, and commercial relations.[61] For the time being, imperial defence was pigeon-holed. Nevertheless, the momentary threat to Anglo-American relations as a result of the Venezuelan boundary dispute did shatter the tranquillity of many Canadians who had taken the insurances of *Pax Britannica* for granted. The war scare was responsible for the declaration by Parliament on February 5, 1896, of its "loyalty and firm determination to maintain unimpaired the integrity of the Empire."[62] But within ten years national self-consciousness and geographical immunity were to reflect the enormous gulf between well-intentioned parliamentary rhetoric and the requirements of imperial strategy.

[59]This has been suggested by Admiral Sir Herbert Richmond.
[60]A. T. Mahan, *Influence of Sea Power upon History, 1660-1783* (London, 1890), 66-7.
[61]See *Report by the Right Hon. The Earl of Jersey on the Colonial Conference at Ottawa* (C. 7553), London, 1894.
[62]*Canada, House of Commons Debates,* 1896, I, cols. 1186-7.

XIV

The End of *Pax Britannica*

F ROM 1805 until the opening of the twentieth century, Britain had been in a very real sense mistress of the seas. Her command of the sea immediately after Trafalgar rested on an "active military situation," and for a century she had held, despite temporary set-backs, a positive superiority in naval strength over any other power or combination of powers. No other maritime nation was in a position to challenge this supremacy, and with respect to industries and essential war resources, she was for all practical purposes self-contained and self-sufficient. Although her overseas possessions were without strong garrisons or fortifications, they were secure from attack; the Royal Navy was easily sufficient to safeguard the empire in three great oceans.

In 1890, the British fleet was less powerful than in 1914, but its relative superiority to other powers was far greater, and the submarine had not as yet arrived to shake the predominance of the "big ships." The German fleet in 1890 offered no threat in the North Sea, and acted only occasionally as a symbol of imperial dreams in waters overseas. The warships of Japan were a mixed contribution of foreign shipyards. The idea of Japan as a first-class sea power was beyond the range of human imagination. As for the United States, while the nation had grown steadily in power, wealth, and population, the navy had been almost completely neglected. A "War of 1812" assortment of monitors and light cruisers was in no position to challenge Chile's ironclads, despite the Navy Act of 1890 which boldly authorized the building of three "sea going, coast-line" battleships to defend the country at the three-mile limit.[1] On the

[1]F. Davis, *The Atlantic System: The Story of Anglo-American Control of the Seas* (London, 1943), 16.

basis of existing realities, it was difficult to conceive a future in which, even under the stimulus of Admiral Mahan's teachings, Germany, Japan, and the United States should pursue the "trident of Neptune" and find "the power to strike as well as to shield."

The most important factor governing this imperial security was the self-sufficiency of Britain's war economy. This in itself is an immense and complicated field of study where generalization may be hazardous. It is safe to say, however, that in 1890 no other power had sufficiently developed its industrial resources to offer serious competition. The coal, iron, and other basic materials necessary for war production, were available within the British Isles, and British manpower was sufficient to exploit them. France had the next strongest navy, but French shipyards could not hope to match Britain in a building race. Japanese ships were still being built in England and in other overseas dockyards. Germany and the United States were only beginning to turn to ship-building as a war industry. Russian shipyards were comparatively unimportant, and in any event, since the Turkish Straits were closed by international agreement, a large part of the Russian navy could not be used outside the Black Sea.[2] No one at the end of the nineteenth century could have foretold that within little more than a decade Middle East and East Indies oil and American steel and machine tools were to become vital to any British war effort.

In these circumstances, imperial naval strategy was immensely simplified. During three of the colonial conferences, between 1887 and 1902, British statesmen, while welcoming any assistance which might voluntarily be rendered by the colonies towards their own local defence, were, nevertheless, able to accept full responsibility for guarding all the territories of the empire and all overseas communications. In 1902, the Admiralty issued a memorandum which embodied this doctrine of responsibility. Requirements of naval strategy, it declared, necessitated a force elastic enough to conduct, immediately on the outbreak of war, a vigorous offensive all over the world, and strong enough to permit concentrations in those areas where decisive battles seemed most likely to take place.

It is the battle-ships chiefly which will have to be concentrated for the decisive battle, and arrangements with this object must be made during peace.

[2] During the war of 1914-18 the effective tonnage of the Russian navy was only 540,000, a total which placed her eighth among the powers, Italy and Austria-Hungary exceeding her in naval strength.

The geographical conditions and the varied interests of the maritime powers prevent such complete concentration in modern times as was practicable in the past. Thus Russia divides her battle-ships between the Baltic and Pacific; the United States between the Atlantic and Pacific; both Germany and France have concentrated in European waters, where also the greater part of the British battle-ships are massed. Our possible enemies are fully aware of the necessity of concentrating on the decisive points. They will endeavour to prevent this by threatening our detached squadrons and trade in different quarters, and thus obliging us to make further detachments from the main fleets. All these operations will be of secondary importance, but it will be necessary that we should have sufficient power available to carry on a vigorous offensive against the hostile outlying squadrons without unduly weakening the force concentrated for the decisive battle, whether in Europe or elsewhere.[3]

In short, British offensive strategy involved a two-hemisphere role, and at the beginning of the twentieth century the maintenance of this traditional role was still practicable.[4] Without aggressively straining for dominion, Britain's unique predominance as mistress of the seas remained intact. Requests from the Australian premiers that a squadron of imperial ships should be set apart for the defence of their own coasts were granted almost as a matter of course. The South African War had been successfully concluded; and the popular mind was fired with the idea of imperial unity and loyalty. The Cobdenite opponents of empire had vanished from the political arena, and Chamberlain was about to proceed with his great crusade for an imperial union based on free trade within the empire. Both Australia and Canada had furnished contingents for overseas service, and the Admiralty and the War Office were confident that this established a precedent for subsequent co-operation within an imperial organization.

But the course of British destiny was to suffer rude reverse within the decade. Four hundred miles across the North Sea, a German

[3]Memorandum on Imperial Defence, presented to the Colonial Conference of 1902, The Admiralty, June, 1902 (revised April, 1903), in Keith, *Selected Speeches and Documents on British Colonial Policy, 1763-1917*, II, 232.

[4]The memorandum pointed out somewhat casuistically that the "traditional role" was not that of the defensive. The word *defence* is specifically omitted "because the primary object of the British Navy is not to defend anything, but to attack the fleets of the enemy, and by defeating them, to afford protection to British Dominions, shipping and commerce." At the same time, the memorandum is a clear and definite renunciation of the tentative policy of the early eighteen-sixties which saw a departure from "traditional policy." "To use the word *defence* would be misleading, because the word carries with it the idea of a thing to be defended, which would force attention to local defence instead of fixing it on the force from which attack is to be expected." *Ibid.*, 233.

fleet was taking shape, and by the time of Edward VII's death it was strong enough to threaten the security of the British Isles. Already by 1905, the British Admiralty had come to realize that the German Fleet Bill of 1900 was not, like earlier predecessors, to remain in a pigeon-hole, but under the galvanizing influence of Admiral von Tirpitz was rapidly transforming itself into iron and steel. The German navy was beginning to reach the "risk" stage foretold in the preamble of the Bill: "Germany must have a battle fleet of such a strength that even for the most powerful naval adversary a war would involve such risks as to make that Power's own supremacy doubtful. For this purpose it is not absolutely necessary that the German fleet should be as strong as that of the greatest naval power, because, as a rule, a great naval power will not be in a position to concentrate all its forces against us." By 1908, the year of the third German Navy Bill, that "risk" stage had been reached, and passed, and steadily from then on the clouds of suspicion began to gather over Britain.

Moreover, the balance of industrial as well as political power continued to move dangerously in favour of Germany. By 1907 France had been overtaken by the Reich as a naval power, and Russia, like France in 1904, turned to Britain for additional security. Of the cataclysmic nature of the shift, the general public remained in ignorance, but to Lansdowne and Balfour, and after them, Grey, the new policy of "Alliance" was the inevitable outcome of a drastic upset to the European equilibrium. In the Far East, with remarkable resource, Japan was fast becoming a naval power, and the Admiralty was no longer in a position to maintain the *Pax Britannica* in all three great oceans. The development of Japanese industry and naval strength was already beginning to alter the whole balance of power in the Pacific; indeed, the Japanese Alliance of 1902 had been the first recognition of the fact that Britain could no longer carry on in "splendid isolation."

Realignment of the powers compelled a drastic redisposition of British naval strength. As he saw the German naval programme change from a thing of paper and statistics to one of men and ships, the volcanic Admiral Fisher began calling home the big ships from Eastern and Mediterranean stations. The new policy of contraction and concentration was summed up by the First Lord on December 6, 1904, when he announced that a new stage had been reached in the thirty years' evolution of the modern steam navy:

... that stage is marked not only by changes in the material of the British navy itself, but also by changes in the strategical position all over the world arising out of the development of foreign navies. .... The principles, on which the present peace distribution of His Majesty's ships and the arrangement of their stations are based, date from a period when the electric telegraph did not exist and when wind was the motive power....[5]

Britain was still stronger than any two powers in the world, but she could no longer distribute her naval forces so as to maintain the two-power standard in every part of the world.[6] Hence, the radical decision in 1904 to abolish the squadrons in the Pacific, South Atlantic and North American stations, and to establish three large fleets in Home waters: the Channel fleet, the Atlantic fleet, and the Home fleet. In practice, this meant that three quarters of Britain's battleships were now facing Germany in or about the North Sea.[7] By 1912 this concentration was increased when the defence of the Mediterranean by heavy ships was turned over to the French. The withdrawal of every first-class battle ship from the Pacific indicated the importance of the Japanese alliance, as well as reflecting improved relations with Russia, a new *entente cordiale* that was facilitated by the disappearance of the Russian fleet. At the same time, arrangements were made to transfer the Halifax and Esquimalt naval bases to the Canadian government. The Halifax dockyard was taken over in January 1907, and that of Esquimalt in November 1910,[8] on condition that the Royal Navy should continue to u_⸝ the bases for fueling, refitting, or such other purposes as facilities allowed.

Meanwhile, the protection of overseas trade routes had become increasingly important to the existence of the Royal Navy. During the first decade of the century ships were still predominantly coal-

[5]"Distribution and Mobilization of the Fleet," *Parliamentary Papers*, 1905, LXVIII, 177.

[6]Distribution of First-Class Battleships in 1907:

British		*Two next powers*	
Home waters, Baltic and Atlantic	45	40	(Germany and U.S.A.)
Mediterranean	7	27	(France and Italy)
Pacific	—	14	(Japan and U.S.A.)
Total	52	81	

In 1904, the total of first class foreign battleships was 79. (Sir George Aston, *Sea, Land and Air Strategy* (London, 1914), 7-8.)

[7]A. Marder, "Admiral Fisher: A Re-Appraisal," *United States Naval Institute Proceedings*, March, 1942, 322.

[8]In 1909 the Naval Establishments in British Possessions Act was passed, under which authority two imperial orders-in-council effected the legal transfer: for Halifax on October 13, 1910; for Esquimalt, on May 4, 1911.

burning and coaling ports scattered all over the world were far more precious than all the gold mines of the Rand. Possessing a monopoly of the best steam coal in the world, the Admiralty were naturally reluctant to discard this article for oil. Indeed, as late as 1917 oil was used in most capital ships only as an auxiliary to coal, to obviate the drop in speed caused by the periodical cleaning of coal-fired furnaces.[9] But by 1913 all the signs pointed to oil as the fuel of the modern warship, and British fleets in home waters which hitherto had filled their bunkers from domestic production were soon to rely upon a fuel brought from Persia or the United States.

Similarly, and apart from food, raw materials on which the country depended for its existence had to be carried far across the ocean. Rubber, for example, had already become essential for war production, thereby adding to the importance of eastern trade routes. But, even granted a constant supply of such materials, the industries of Great Britain were barely adequate to meet the output required by the new scale of competitive armaments. In the event of war, the manufactured produce of other nations, especially the United States, might be the vital requisite of victory. As a consequence, Britain, the arsenal of a widely extended empire, depended more than ever before upon unbroken ocean communications, in a period when the prospect of blockade by submarine was already beginning to affect existing ratios of strength based on surface craft.

The revolution in the character of the empire was no less significant. At a time when economic and industrial changes forced Great Britain to rely more and more on overseas sources of supply, the general tendency of the British dominions was towards greater local autonomy. During the first decade of the twentieth century, the feeling of separate "nationalities" within the empire had grown by leaps and bounds, and even in its earlier stages this sentiment was antagonistic to any scheme of imperial federation, or even a coherent plan of imperial defence. New Zealand and South Africa were just emerging from colonial status; Canada and Australia had become semi-autonomous nations. Generally speaking, all were more, not less, reluctant to suffer any diminution of their nationalist aspirations. Already national self-consciousness had begun to confuse the traditional impulse of imperial colonial loyalty.[10]

[9]In 1915 *Queen Elizabeth* class ships were the envy of the battle fleet. Because their furnaces were oil fired, the men were spared the weekly hard labour of coaling ship.
[10]Jebb, *The Imperial Conference,* I, 350.

Until the Imperial Conference of 1907, the Admiralty had assumed a condition not far removed from colonial dependence—a relationship which might broaden, ultimately perhaps, into a unified federation. With this in mind, the system of cash contributions to a central naval fund seemed the logical and simple procedure; it upheld the original principle of imperial strategy: "One sea, one navy, one control."

In this regard, Canada had not kept in stride with her sister associates. Beginning with the Conference of 1902, Cape Colony, Natal, Australia, New Zealand, and Newfoundland, had increased their contributions for the Royal Navy, while Canada steadfastly persisted in her refusal. The government admitted an obligation to defend Canadian shores and inland territory; a local naval force was contemplated, but neither ships nor troops could be earmarked for overseas service. Canada, said Sir Wilfrid Laurier, had a greater domain than she could possibly develop in a century; she was impelled by the newness of the country and by the lack of natural unity to spend vast sums on internal development, especially on her communications, just as Britain by her situation was called upon to spend vast sums to keep open her sea-ways.[11] "The establishment of special forces," in the words of a joint Canadian-Australian memorandum of 1902, "set apart for general imperial service, and practically under the absolute control of the imperial government, was objectionable in principle, as derogating from the powers of self-government enjoyed by them, and would be calculated to impede the general improvement in training and organization of their defence forces."[12] "As far as Canada is concerned," the Minister of Marine and Fisheries, Mr. Brodeur, told the Conference of 1907, "one of the first duties we shall have to look after is our protection in connection with the Great Lakes. I say that the wars we have had since 1763, when Canada had become part of the British Empire, came from the United States."

The British government was not impressed with the American peril, but it did appreciate the impulse of local autonomy which lay behind it. So long as unified direction of command was maintained, it was ready to consider a modification of the existing arrangements to meet the views of the various dominions. While the distribution of the fleet must be determined by strategical requirements, of which the Admiralty had to be the judge, none the

[11]O. D. Skelton, *Life and Letters of Sir Wilfrid Laurier* (2 vols., Toronto, 1921), II, 298.   [12]*Ibid.*, 297.

less, His Majesty's Government welcomed such ships as the colonial governments might provide for local service in imperial squadrons, or for co-operation with the British fleet. In brief, the British government was still prepared to accept responsibility for empire defence; it merely asked that the new Dominions should help shoulder the burden by contributing coastal craft and dockyard facilities, if not money.

But all the arts of discreet understatement were dropped in the face of the naval scare of 1909. Germany, declared Sir Edward Grey to a disturbed House of Commons, was creating a fleet, larger than had ever existed before. While Great Britain still undertook as formerly to defend the empire on every sea, it was clear, as Mr. Asquith admitted, that she might not be able to accomplish it.

Now if the problem of imperial naval defence could have been considered simply as a problem of naval strategy, it was obvious that the greatest output of strength for a given expenditure was obtained by the maintenance of a single navy. The principle was axiomatic. In the days before 1942 when autonomous organizations, British and American, co-operated with efficiency, no one ever suggested that separate navies under separate and distinct governments could approach the effectiveness of one single navy under a central control. At the Imperial Conference of July and August, 1909,[13] the British Admiralty enunciated this principle of central command, but immediately qualified it to the extent of offering the Dominions the choice of forming their own separate services, or of paying towards the upkeep of the British Navy.

It has, however, long been recognized that in defining the conditions under which the Naval forces of the Empire should be developed, other considerations than those of strategy alone must be taken into account. The various circumstances of the oversea Dominions have to be borne in mind. Though all have in them the seeds of a great advance in population, wealth and power, they have at the present time attained to different stages in their growth. Their geographical position has subjected them to internal and external strains, varying in kind and intensity. Their history and physical environment have given rise to individual national sentiment, for the expression of which room must be found . . . a Dominion Government desirous of creating a navy should aim at forming a distinct Fleet unit; and the smallest unit is one which, while manageable in time of peace, is capable of being used in its component parts in time of war.

[13]*Correspondence and Papers relating to a Conference with Representatives of the Self-Governing Dominions on the Naval and Military Defence of the Empire, 1909* (Cd. 4948), London, 1909, p. 21. This subsidiary conference was called specially to deal with the subject of imperial defence, in pursuance of a resolution adopted during the Conference of 1907.

Finally, the Admiralty told the delegates that the British navy could look after the Atlantic, but that conditions virtually compelled it to abandon the Pacific, an ocean in which Canada was concerned only to a lesser degree than Australia and New Zealand. To fill the gap they proposed that all three Dominions and the mother country unite in establishing an imperial Pacific fleet, based on their own national naval forces. Canada and Australia, for example, should each contribute a fleet unit, while the United Kingdom and New Zealand should co-operate in providing two more. All told, the four units would amount to a fleet of four battle cruisers, twelve light cruisers, twenty-four large destroyers, and twelve submarines. Hong Kong was regarded as a likely base for this Pacific command, although no definite decision was taken.

According to the official report, the Canadian representatives, Sir F. W. Borden and Mr. Brodeur, took the stand that: "While, on naval strategical considerations, it was thought that a Fleet Unit on the Pacific as outlined by the Admiralty might in the future form an acceptable system of naval defence, it was recognized that Canada's double sea-board rendered the provision of such a Fleet Unit unsuitable for the present."[14] In rejecting the proposal, the two delegates asked the Admiralty to design two specifically Canadian programmes, one, for an annual expenditure of £600,000, and the other for an annual expenditure of £400,000.

In accepting this alternative, the British government, against the opinion of their experts, was reluctantly bowing before the urgent and uncompromising mood of dominion national feeling. The Admiralty's surrender of the principle of a single navy was a recognition of the strategy of local defence in the interest of political expediency. New Zealand alone maintained her policy of annual contributions—on this occasion she agreed to furnish one battle cruiser. Australia accepted the idea of a fleet unit but both she and Canada were set on raising local naval forces as symbols of their hard-won nationhood. In a purely promissory manner, therefore, Canada prepared to separate her own defensive requirements from those of the empire as a whole, and announced, first by implication and subsequently in the course of Parliamentary discussion, that her naval forces would be available for common defence only with Parliamentary approval.

Admiral Cyprian Bridge has remarked: "The greatest foe of armed efficiency is political expediency. In time of peace it is thought

[14] *Ibid.*, 23.

better to conciliate voters than to prepare to meet the enemy. If
local defence is thought to be pleasing to an inexpert electorate, it is
only too likely to be provided no matter how ineffectual and how
costly in reality it will be."[15]   It should be remembered, however,
that the political aspect can never be eliminated from any broad
discussion of defence matters.   The debate of January 1910 on the
Naval Service Bill revealed, as the biographer of Sir Wilfrid Laurier
so shrewdly observed, "how ambiguous was Canada's international
situation, how uncertain it was where nation ended and Empire
began." Laurier himself wrote an old friend who attacked his policy:

> Our existence as a nation is the most anomalous that has yet existed. We
> are British subjects, but we are an autonomous nation; we are divided into
> races, and out of these confused elements the man at the head of affairs has
> to sail the ship onwards, and to do this safely it is not always the ideal policy
> from the point of view of pure idealism which ought to prevail, but the policy
> which can appeal on the whole to all sections of the community.[16]

As a matter of fact, both the Prime Minister and the leader of
the opposition, Mr. R. L. Borden, were embarrassed by the presence
of irreconcilable elements within their own followings, whose resentment might easily bring political disaster. Both would probably
have been relieved had they been able to postpone an issue holding
such ominous consequences for the unity of country as well as party.[17]

For Laurier, the situation was especially complicated by reason
of the large French-speaking population of Quebec, on which he
leaned heavily for political support. French-Canadian antipathy to
imperial measures would have made any scheme of British control
of defence out of the question.   Indeed, in Quebec any policy of
armed preparation, whether strictly Canadian or imperial, was likely
to be denounced as militarism, and only the fear of antagonizing a
large section of his English-Canadian supporters in Ontario forced
Sir Wilfrid to take some practical step towards Canadian participation in naval defence. To his mind there was little danger of a
sudden war with Germany. Moreover, he felt that the United States
was gradually changing from threatening foe to friend; and although
the fears of "manifest destiny" had not yet fully abated, one of his
Cabinet colleagues could assert that it was unnecessary for Canada

[15]C. Bridge, "The Share of the Fleet in the Defence of the Empire," *Brassey's
Naval Annual, 1908*, 150-1.
[16]Skelton, *Life and Letters of Sir Wilfrid Laurier*, II, 331.
[17]See *Robert Laird Borden: His Memoirs*, ed. H. Borden (2 vols., London,
1938), I, 267.

to support the imperial fleet since she was protected by the Monroe doctrine, behind which "were the guns and war ships of the United States."

The Naval Service Bill, as introduced by the Prime Minister in January 1910, provided for naval personnel in the shape of a permanent corps, a reserve, and a volunteer force, in which, unlike the militia, service would be wholly voluntary.[18] Under its terms a naval college would be established, and a naval board set up to advise the Department of Marine and Fisheries.[19] For the moment, it was planned to build one third-class and four second-class cruisers and six destroyers, which should be distributed between the two coasts. This force was to be under the control of the Canadian government, but the governor-general in council might in emergency place any or all of it at the disposal of Great Britain, subject to the immediate summoning of Parliament if not in session. The cost was estimated at £11,000,000; the annual upkeep at £3,000,000. It was hoped, rather vaguely, to have the ships built in Canada, although such a scheme seemed likely to increase costs by a third.

Despite the criticism of the opposition to the effect that the plan would give no immediate or effective aid to the empire, and "no adequate or satisfactory results in Canada," the measure was passed by a majority of forty-one, and became law.[20] Supporters of the bill vigorously maintained that government policy was entirely in accord with the wishes and suggestions of the Admiralty; but it is difficult to believe that the reservations to the governor in council of the power to release or withhold the local force was in keeping with original Admiralty designs for meeting a possible emergency.

From a reading of the debates it seems probable that Mr. Borden, unlike Sir Wilfrid Laurier, seriously accepted the imminence of the German peril; but it seems equally certain that both the Prime Minister and the opposition leader were still perplexed about the problem of adjusting imperial and local defence needs with the claims of a self-governing state. Indeed, the navy issue was deeply involved with the question of Canada's share of responsibility for British foreign policy. A plan of contributions in terms of cash or ships suggested responsibility for the design and execution of Britain's imperial programmes, whereas a permanent Canadian policy—that

[18]Under the terms of the Militia Act, the whole male population from seventeen to sixty years was liable to service in case of need.
[19]Not until thirty years later was such a naval board established.
[20]*Statutes of Canada*, 1910, cap. 43.

of a local navy for home defence which should, with Parliamentary approval, be handed over to the British government in time of emergency—left the Dominion's hands free. Neither statesman was very anxious that the Naval Service Bill of 1910 should be submitted to the mandate of the people, although the opposition naturally took the stand that no permanent policy involving large future expenditures should be adopted until it had been submitted to the country and had received its approval.[21] The subject was indeed raised during the general election of 1911, but with studied vagueness. The election of September 1911 settled the fate of the reciprocity agreement with the United States, but it left the navy question still undecided.

The Conservative government assumed office in October and, while it did not repeal the Naval Service Act, it did cancel all tenders for the construction of the projected war-ships. Following the prorogation of Parliament in the spring of 1912, Borden went to Britain, and there consulted with members of the Cabinet and Admiralty on both the political and technical aspects of imperial defence. In view of his statements in opposition, he was practically pledged, in the event of undertaking a *permanent* Canadian naval policy, to seek the mandate of the people.[22] On the other hand, if he was satisfied that conditions of emergency had risen, he felt free to appeal to Parliament for immediate aid. There can be little doubt that he was deeply impressed by the figures on the recent and prospective growth of the German navy which the First Lord of the Admiralty, Mr. Winston Churchill, provided. Unlike Laurier, the new Prime Minister was influenced by a sense of urgency, quite apart from the historic claims of his party to maintain the integrity and glory of the empire. The Admiralty memorandum which he submitted to the House of Commons on December 5, 1912, concluded as follows:

Whatever may be the decision of Canada at the present juncture, Great Britain will not in any circumstances fail in her duty to the Overseas Dominions of the Crown.

She has before now successfully made head alone and unaided against the most formidable combinations, and she has not lost her capacity by a wise policy and strenuous exertions to watch over and preserve the vital interests of the Empire.

The Admiralty are assured that his Majesty's Government will not hesitate to ask the House of Commons for whatever provision the circumstances

[21] *Borden Memoirs*, I, 280.
[22] *Ibid.*, 405.

of each year may require. But the aid which Canada could give at the present time is not to be measured only in ships or money. Any action on the part of Canada to increase the power and mobility of the Imperial Navy, and thus widen the margin of our common safety, would be recognized everywhere as a most significant witness to the united strength of the Empire, and to the renewed resolve of the Overseas Dominions to take their part in maintaining its integrity.

The Prime Minister of the Dominion having inquired in what form any immediate aid that Canada might give would be most effective, we have no hesitation in answering after a prolonged consideration of all the circumstances that it is desirable that such aid should include the provision of a certain number of the largest and strongest ships of war which science can build or money supply.[23]

In the light of this disturbing information, the enunciation of a permanent Canadian naval policy was temporarily abandoned; instead, the Prime Minister asked for an immediate grant of $35,000,000, "for the purpose of immediately increasing the effective naval forces of the Empire." The grant represented the cost of three battleships, which were to be controlled and maintained as part of the Royal Navy. On the other hand, if in the future "it should be the will of the Canadian people to establish a Canadian unit of the British Navy these vessels can be recalled by the Canadian Government to form part of that navy." With regard to the building up of a permanent naval organization in Canada, the Prime Minister stressed the enormous delays that must ensue, especially if Canada undertook her own construction. "Is there," he continued, "any need that we should undertake the hazardous and costly experiment of building up a naval organization especially restricted to this Dominion, when upon just and self-respecting terms we can take such part as we desire in naval defence through the existing naval organization of the Empire, and in that way fully and effectively avail ourselves of

[23]Sir Robert Borden's speech is contained in Keith's *Selected Speeches and Documents on British Colonial Policy*, II, 308-37. Sir Robert drew heavily on the Admiralty memorandum which has been quoted and which gave full details of the ominous growth of the German navy since the original German Fleet Bill of 1898. This *publishable* memorandum was based on a secret memorandum, of which ten printed copies were sent to the Prime Minister. One of these was loaned to Sir Wilfrid Laurier with the permission to reveal its contents to those of his supporters who were privy councillors. For an excellent article which draws largely on Borden's private papers, see G. N. Tucker, "The Naval Policy of Sir Robert Borden, 1912-14," *The Canadian Historical Review*, XXVIII, March, 1947, pp. 1-30. It is interesting to compare the concluding passages of the secret memorandum with those read by Sir Robert to the House of Commons. The secret document, unlike the publishable, emphasizes the compelling moral effect of Canadian aid— "a moral value out of all proportion to the material assistance afforded." See Tucker, "The Naval Policy of Sir Robert Borden," 16.

the men and the resources at the command of Canada?''[24] At the end of the Prime Minister's address, the House and galleries sang *God Save the King*, a precedent that was followed with almost equal gusto at the conclusion of Sir Wilfrid Laurier's reply.

In the resumed debate of December 12, Sir Wilfrid boldly took the bull by the horns, and on the basis of Admiralty information, both secret and publishable, with which Borden had provided him, dexterously proceeded to demonstrate that there was no naval emergency. It was a political *tour de force* which played havoc with strategic principles as well as logic. In essence it was an appeal for the acceptance of the doctrine of local defence. Laurier admitted that the rise of German power had necessitated a British concentration in the North Sea but, in his opinion, such a policy made it imperative for the Dominions to guard their local waters.

In our humble opinion the remedy is this, that wherever, in the distant seas or in the distant countries,—in Australia, Canada or elsewhere,—a British ship has been removed to allow of concentration in European waters, that ship should be replaced by a ship built, maintained, equipped and manned by the young nation immediately concerned. If the young nations of the Empire take hold of the equipment and manning of ships to look after the distant seas, concentration can easily take place in the waters of Europe, and the British Admiralty knows what zones it has to defend. This is the Australian policy; this ought to be the Canadian policy. I insist once more upon what is stated in the memorandum. There is no emergency, there is no immediate danger, there is no prospective danger. If there were an emergency, if England were in danger— no, I will not use that expression; I will not say if England were in danger, but simply if England were on trial with one or two or more of the great powers of Europe, my right honourable friend might come and ask, not $35,000,000, but twice, three times, four times $35,000,000. We would put at the disposal of England all the resources of Canada; there would not be a single dissentient voice.[25]

On political grounds, it is quite obvious that Sir Wilfred had a good case for his plan of a *permanent* Canadian naval force. In making this case, however, he was forced to ignore or rather deliberately to underestimate the character of the emergency which less ebullient persons than Mr. Churchill had described in official memoranda. Moreover, he neglected the fundamental tenet of naval strategy throughout the ages, namely, that victory is won or security preserved by successful action in the decisive theatre. Even had

[24]*Borden Memoirs*, I, 407; *Canada, House of Commons Debates*, December 9, 1912.

[25]Skelton, *Life and Letters of Sir Wilfrid Laurier*, II, 399-405.

Canada been able to provide two dreadnoughts on each coast, they would have been useless the moment Britain's Home Fleet was defeated in the North Sea.

The debates were prolonged and bitter, and eventually the Prime Minister felt obliged to use powers of closure. Generally speaking the divergencies did not arise from interpretations of strategic needs, but rather from attitudes regarding foreign policy. The Nationalists, chiefly from French-speaking Canada, adopted the ground that since Canada had no vote in imperial policy, she should do nothing in the matter of imperial defence; the Liberals, under Laurier's lead, held the view that Canada should decide her own policy in imperial and foreign affairs, and therefore make and control her own defence policy.[26] The Conservatives maintained that an immediate contribution was necessary, and that a permanent Canadian naval policy could await the day when the relationship between mother country and Dominion in the field of foreign affairs had crystallized.

The Borden Bill passed the Commons by a vote of 101 to 68, but was crushed in the senate by a Liberal majority, despite last-minute efforts at compromise.[27] Preferring not to go to the country, Borden prepared to bide his time and perhaps await the moment when the death of aging Liberals should swing the balance of the senate in his favour.[28] Meanwhile, he announced that the government planned eventually to pay for and take over the three ships which Great Britain was laying down in substitution for the three provided for under the Bill.

In all probability the proposed battleships which the senate rejected would have been of the *Queen Elizabeth* class and, grouped with the *Malaya*, the gift of the Federated Malay States, would have formed part of an Imperial squadron based on Gibraltar. Certainly the First Lord still contemplated such a plan,[29] and Borden had not lost hope. But it was not to be. In November 1913, the German Naval Attaché in London, with admirable perspicacity, wrote to his superiors:

[26]*Ibid.*, 407.
[27]*Borden Memoirs*, I, chap. XXI.
[28]On the matter of enlarging the Senate by amending the British North America Act, see E. Forsey and G. Tucker, "Correspondence: The Naval Policy of Sir Robert Borden," *The Canadian Historical Review*, XXVIII, June, 1947, 241-2.
[29]See speech by the Right Hon. Winston Churchill on the creation of an imperial squadron, *House of Commons Debates*, March 17, 1914. At this time, Mr. Churchill, on the basis of information provided by Borden, believed there were "good prospects that the unfortunate deadlock which has arisen in Canada upon

It is doubtful whether there will be any more gifts like the *Malaya*. The naval policy of the self-governing colonies tends . . . more and more in the direction of small national fleets under local control. This development is a very gradual one which takes place, moreover, outside European waters; hence, in comparing England's naval strength in Europe with that of Germany it may be ignored.[30]

During the months that preceded the first World War, the British Admiralty no longer held to its comprehensive strategy of "the offensive" in all theatres. With the surrender of the two-power standard in favour of a sixteen-to-ten superiority over Germany in capital ships, there was a reversion to eighteenth-century practice. This meant holding the enemy in check in distant seas until the main decision had been obtained in the decisive area. In one respect, therefore, the foundations of *Pax Britannica* had been seriously shaken. At the beginning of the century the Royal Navy had been predominant in every ocean of the world, and along the shores of every continent. By 1913 it was predominant only in the North Sea. "In 1902," Borden reminded the Canadian House of Commons,

. . . there were fifty-five British warships on the Mediterranean station; today there are nineteen. There were fourteen on the North American and West Indies station; today there are three. There were three on the south-east coast of South Africa; today there is one. There were sixteen on the Cape of Good Hope Station; today there are three. There were eight on the Pacific station; today there are two. . . . Or, to sum up, in 1902 there were one hundred and sixty ships on foreign and colonial stations against seventy-six today.[31]

In Britain, the leader of the Opposition used much the same language: "Ten years ago we not only had the command of the sea, but we had the command of every sea. We have the command of no sea in the world except the North Sea at this moment."

It is well to remember, however, that the requirements of true strategy are determined in peace by the known strength and location of potentially hostile states; strategic disposition consists, not simply

---

this Navy question will be relieved, and that in one way or another, or by one joint party or other, or best of all, by the joint action of both parties, Canada will be able to take some share in her own naval defence and in the common defence of the Empire."

[30]*Die Grosse Politik der Europaeischen Kabinette*, report of Captain von Mueller, November 30, 1913, vol. XXXIX, p. 65. This and other German re-actions to Canadian policy are cited by G. N. Tucker, "The Naval Policy of Sir Robert Borden, 1912-14," *The Canadian Historical Review*, XXVIII, March, 1947, pp. 18-19.

[31]*Canada, House of Commons Debates*, December 5, 1912.

in placing ships in every sea, whether or not there is any actual need for them, but in providing adequate force at the decisive point.[32] Moreover, as previous chapters have shown, it never had been an invariable condition that British sea power could by itself retain command of all ocean communications. At various moments in her history, Britain had welcomed the collaboration of allies, not only on the continent, but at sea. Ordinarily, no nation expects to have to fight the whole world, and no nation has ever made budgetary provision for such a contingency. The most that governments can hope to do is to adjust their peace-time naval policy in the light of estimated dangers to their security. "The measure of naval strength required by any State," declared an eminent writer on naval affairs, James R. Thursfield, "is determined mainly by the naval strength of its possible adversaries in the event of war, and only in a secondary degree by the volume of the maritime interests which it has to defend."[33]

In 1913, there was no British battle squadron in the Mediterranean, but France had become virtually an ally, and Italy, while nominally a member of the Triple Alliance, was known to be antagonistic to Austria, and, therefore, a potential ally. Furthermore, the British battle cruiser squadron that had been left in the Mediterranean was two or three times as strong as the German force, consisting of the *Goeben* and *Breslau*. Admittedly, the China squadron had been drastically reduced, but Japan had become an ally. Even without Japan the British force was still adequate to deal with the potential enemy in those seas in the shape of Graf Spee's squadron. In the West Indies, the Fourth Cruiser squadron, although based at home, actually provided a consistently stronger force than had the former North American and West Indies squadron. In other words, the British Navy remained predominant in every sea over the only prospective enemy—Germany. In essentials, the strategic pattern was much the same as it had always been.

Meanwhile, although every effort was made prior to 1914 to ensure a certain degree of imperial uniformity in matériel and training (in all the services, joint staff work was still in the embryonic stage), the Canadian government had done nothing to carry into

---

[32]As early as 1906 Admiral Fisher had withdrawn from many foreign stations numerous small and obsolete sloops and corvettes with which the seas were then sprinkled, on the ground that "showing the flag" could be more effectively accomplished by cruising squadrons of modern ships sent on periodic trips from home.
[33]*Naval Warfare* (Cambridge University Press, 1913), 129.

effect the provisions of the Naval Service Act of 1910. In 1911, as a concession to Canadian public opinion, two outworn cruisers, the *Niobe* and the *Rainbow*, had been recognized by the Admiralty as the Royal Canadian Navy, but both vessels had been purchased simply as training ships for new entries and not for active service duties. Partly because of desertions, the complement of the *Rainbow* —273 officers and ratings—was only completed in July 1914, and this was accomplished by including the nucleus crew of the *Niobe* and a few semi-trained Naval Volunteer Reservists.[34]

In the circumstances, Canada made no substantial contribution to the Allied naval effort. Details of the war at sea form no part of this study; suffice it to say, although at time the scales seemed to balance precariously, Britain's "home fleets" were just sufficient to overcome successive threats to Atlantic communications. But, as after events were to prove, the narrowness of the safety margin was not fully appreciated. Indeed, the sudden collapse of Germany, followed by the humiliating surrender of her navy, helped to blind public opinion to the fundamental economic changes that continued after the war to whittle away Britain's supremacy on the oceans.

Although the destruction of the German fleet removed an immediate challenge to the British Empire, it did not diminish in the least the capacity of German industry to forge another dangerous weapon. For half a century before 1900, British power had rested on the incomparable development of British industry. During the first two decades of the twentieth century (and allowing for the temporary set-back of war), that lead had been overtaken by Germany, as well as by the United States and Japan. Errors of administration, mistakes of policy, wilful illusions on the part of the public, all these made the balance of naval and military power more unfavourable than it need have been; but no course of British policy

---

[34]The Canadian Naval Service can hardly be said to have blossomed into a real navy before 1938, when the addition of modern destroyers and mine-sweepers brought the total establishment up to 117 officers and 1,222 ratings. Until strong and efficient enough to undertake convoy and coast defence duties, the Canadian Naval Service was a training organization—a school for the officers and ratings who took charge of the expanding navy of 1939-46. (See in this connection, Longstaff, *Esquimalt Naval Base*; also G. N. Tucker, "The Career of H.M.C.S. 'Rainbow,' " *British Columbia Historical Quarterly*, VII, January, 1943, 1-30. For a fascinating account of Canada's two submarines, originally built in Seattle for the Chilean government and precipitately acquired by the Prime Minister of British Columbia on the outbreak of war, see G. N. Tucker, "Canada's First Submarines, CC1 and CC2: An Episode of the Naval War in the Pacific," *British Columbia Historical Quarterly*, VII, January, 1943, 147-70.

could have taken from Germany and Japan the industrial and technical resources and capacity which formed the solid basis of their power. The technical advances in the tank, airplane, and the submarine, which were subsequently to place both the Commonwealth and the United States in deadly peril, would have come about whether or not there had been a Hitler or a Tojo.

In other words, the immense increase in German and Japanese productive capacity became the basic factor in the strategical pattern of the post-war world. The nineteenth-century industrial revolution had expanded to embrace the whole earth, and in the military sphere the result was new and unstable equilibrium. At the time when both Germany and Japan began to re-arm on a large scale, their industries had developed to a point which made it comparatively simple for them to gain a head start over their lethargic rivals. Well before 1934 Japan was producing all her own weapons. By 1939, Britain by herself had neither the industrial capacity, nor the raw materials, nor the man-power to outbid Germany and Japan. Even a joint Anglo-French effort in war-production would have been partly dependent, as the war of 1914-18 had revealed, upon the resources of the United States. As it happened, British public opinion would not have accepted a closely integrated union with France, either in foreign policy or for defence, and by 1937 the United States had adopted the Neutrality Law.

In these circumstances, not even the most unstinted co-operation on the part of the British Dominions could have counterbalanced the vast increase in the resources of Germany and Japan. The lack of such co-operation—the refusal of public opinion to face obvious facts—merely added further complications to the task of protecting the empire. In the years after 1918, Canada stepped forth as an independent, self-governing nation without making any serious effort towards becoming self-defending. After the armistice of 1918, along with Australia, she promptly discarded her new war industries with the consequence that she became almost as dependent upon Great Britain for supply as Gambia or Sierra Leone.

In August 1918, in reply to an Admiralty memorandum on the naval defence of the British Empire, Sir Robert Borden, with the full accord of the other Dominion prime ministers, prepared a statement of principles which firmly rejected the idea of a single imperial navy towards which the individual member states of the Empire might contribute proportionately. In the future, perhaps, it was conceivable that "some supreme naval authority upon which each of the Dominions would be adequately represented" might be needed.[35] Meanwhile, despite Admiral of the Fleet Lord Jellicoe's advice (which had been sought) on separate defence needs, Canada, like the other Dominions, was reluctant to undertake the heavy expense of any long-range naval building programme.[36]

In 1923 and 1926, Imperial Conferences affirmed the principle that each part of the empire was primarily responsible for its own local defence, and the rather paradoxical recommendation was made that maritime communications should be adequately safeguarded. Yet, by 1925, with the exception of Australia, none of the Dominions was buying or building war vessels to ensure the protection of even its own sea lanes.[37] Not until 1928 did the Canadian government arrange for the loan of two destroyers from the British Admiralty, and sanction the purchase of two new ones to be delivered in 1931. By 1939, the Canadian navy consisted of six destroyers, four minesweepers, and various smaller craft.

Nonetheless, after 1931, as a consequence of the Statute of Westminster, the "naval issue" ceased to be involved with the question of national status. With the legal recognition of "independence" within the Commonwealth, a *permanent* naval policy became the obvious concomitant of political sovereignty. Thenceforward, "Canada, the nation" tended to become an accepted creed rather than the slogan of frustrated nationalism. At the same time, it was clear that problems of naval policy while divorced from any intimate European association, could not be isolated from matters of external relations. The growth of industrial and military power, both in Europe and in the Far East, was bound to make the United States increasingly aware of the vulnerability of Canada's long coast-lines; and it was natural that American policy should favour joint precautionary efforts to ensure the security of the North American continent.

As a consequence, the compelling need to safeguard Canadian national autonomy once again became entwined with the problem of national defence—but in reverse fashion. Whereas in the past, the demands for complete self-government on the part of a highly self-conscious and sensitive Dominion served to cripple and retard the

[35]Memorandum of Dominion ministers in reply to the Admiralty memorandum of May 17, 1918, in *Speeches and Documents on the British Dominions, 1918-1931,* ed. by A. B. Keith (London, 1932), 11; *The Development of Dominion Status, 1900-1936,* ed. R. M. Dawson (London, 1937), 177.
[36]See G. M. Carter, *The British Commonwealth and International Security: The Role of the Dominions, 1919-1939* (Toronto, 1947), 38-9.
[37]*Brassey's Naval and Shipping Annual, 1925,* 1-2.

development of a naval policy, now the needs of common North American defence stimulated military exertion in the interests of preserving Canadian identity against even benevolent interference by a considerate but security-minded Good Neighbour. Such adjustments, by attaching Canadian interests to the foreign policy of another state, did involve a common-law "marriage" to the American fleet and nation,[38] but they involved no renunciation of Commonwealth ties.

Fortunately for Canada, the World War had helped to cement a cardinal principle of British policy, namely, that the United States should never again be considered a potential hostile power.[39] For this reason, and because the war had eliminated the German fleet and all German overseas bases, the western hemisphere hardly entered into British strategical considerations.

In the Pacific, however, the situation had altered for the worse. The war left Japan the dominant naval power in eastern Asia; the Washington Treaty of 1922 had the practical effect of confirming that supremacy. The agreed fleet ratios left Japan inferior to Britain in total tonnage, but the absolute reduction in the British as well as the American fleets left neither power strong enough singly to carry on a war in Eastern waters. Moreover, the *status quo* provision regarding fortifications made it impossible for either power to provide the necessary bases, even if it had had the ships. In the original draft treaty, there had been no mention of bases; but Japan refused to consider a reduction in ships unless bases were taken into account. As a solution there was evolved the clause maintaining the *status quo* east of longitude 110 degrees. By this Britain retained the right to fortify Singapore, but not Hong Kong. The United States could strengthen Hawaii, but surrendered the right to develop the bases at Guam and Manilla.

Since the defence and retention of overseas bases depends ultimately on command of the neighbouring seas, and since it was impossible for Britain to seek command of the Pacific, the *status quo* of 1922 was not unsatisfactory in itself. Its weakness lay in the fact that the British position in the East was now dependent upon Japanese goodwill, goodwill which the British and American governments, for ten years after 1926, tried anxiously to cultivate.[40] The

[38]In 1802, Jefferson made the dramatic assertion: "We must marry ourselves to the British fleet and nation."

[39]Cf. Carter, *The British Commonwealth and International Security*, 40-1.

[40]It was assumed that fear of Russia would compel Anglo-Japanese cooperation in the interests of both.

navies of the Commonwealth of Nations were not strong enough to protect the colonies in the eastern seas, or even the territory of Australia. True, the United States offered a remote buffer; but apart from the binding limits then imposed by American national policy, British strategy had never been able to reckon on the American Pacific fleet as a sufficient make-weight in any struggle with Japan. American sea power had never reached far west of Hawaii. Manilla was never made a naval base; Guam and Midway remained unfortified. As a consequence the American fleet had no means of exerting its strength in waters distant from the Hawaiian outpost.

Looking backward it would seem that miscalculations on the new foundation as well as on the old function of sea power had blurred over and obscured a fundamental shift in the balance of power, a shift which had taken place irrespective of ideological banners. In 1890, when there was practically no American battle fleet, British possessions in the Far East were far more secure than in 1939 when the American fleet had risen to the first rank. In 1890, the British Empire was not seriously threatened by any power; by 1939, it faced highly industrialized powers east and west without being able to derive any corresponding strength from the colonies or Dominions. In 1890 Britain had the resources and manpower to stand alone with fair security against any prospective opponent, or even against any reasonable combination of enemies. By 1904 this was no longer the case. "Commitments" not "splendid isolation" became the essential basis of foreign policy. In 1939-45 as in 1914-18 France was the necessary ally, and both France and Britain needed the support of North American resources.

In one sense this dependence of western Europe on North America represented a definite reversal of historical process. The survival of the two mother countries depended on the maintenance of communications with their former colonies. The new world of self-governing and independent states had been called in to preserve the security of the original colonizing powers. Once again the curious unity of western Europe and North America revealed itself, a unity based on the indivisibility of a great ocean that has remained constant from the days of the Cabots to the new era of the long-distance bomber. Just as command of the Atlantic in the seventeenth and eighteenth centuries was responsible for the ultimate predominance of Anglo-Saxon stock, so in our own times command of the Atlantic made possible the survival in western Europe of the Anglo-Saxon civilization which ships and immigrants long ago transported to the New World. For nearly four centuries the sea provided the common frontier of two continents, an unguarded and unbounded frontier that gave enormous mobility to the power that controlled and used it as a highway for its own purposes of conquest and government.

The sea still provides vital links between North America and Europe, but it is no longer the only fact in their unity. The new age of air power has taken us, in many respects, back to the age of Ptolemy, to a shrunken world, not of oceans containing huge island continents, but of great stretches of land divided by gigantic lakes. Today, as Sir Halford Mackinder once predicted, Europe, Asia, and Africa are becoming one continent, not three, and the unity of the land is already a vital element in what is so often termed "global strategy."

In the past, a nation that held command of the sea could hardly avoid the growth of its possessions. Indeed, the pieces that went to make up the incongruous mosaic called the British Commonwealth and Empire were as often the casual products of naval supremacy as the consequences of deliberate national policy. At the end of the nineteenth century Admiral Mahan could still assert that command of the surface of the sea was identical with world power. To-day, however, imperial dominance based on control of the sea by ships of war alone is no longer possible. When Alcock and Brown flew their fragile aircraft across the Atlantic in 1919 the world suddenly began to shrink in time and space, and the dictum of Mahan—which had stood the test of experience since Sir Walter Raleigh's day—had lost its unconditional validity. The battle ships and frigates which had carved out Canada's destiny were no longer sufficient of themselves to maintain command of the seas.

Today, control of ocean communications involves new and varied instruments—ships that go under the waters and ships that fly above them—as the campaigns in North Africa, Sicily, and Normandy demonstrated during the second World War. With the coming of the atom bomb and the rocket, naval tactics have been profoundly affected, and they must continue to change in pace with further technological advances. Nevertheless, even though air-borne weapons become more potent than ship-borne, armies and air forces will still depend on sea transport. There is as yet no adequate substitute for ships as the means of carrying the world's resources, whether military or economic, from their place of origin to their destination; and the only method of safeguarding such transport is by controlling the routes, whatever the weapons appropriate to their seizure and maintenance. As long as oceans remain common highways of communication between states, national strategy in time of war must still be directed towards closing those highways to enemy powers, and such control will still hinge upon command of the sea. So far as one can look ahead, command of the sea in time of war will remain for any great state an indispensable adjunct of security and offensive strength. As long as there is salt water there will be such a thing as sea power. But looking backwards from our own times, the past four centuries may be recorded as one clear-cut epoch of history, when the exercise of sea power by the ship of war was the determining influence on the shaping of a North Atlantic Empire.

Appendices

APPENDIX A

UNTIL the sixteenth century, sea warfare had been confined to inshore waters, and the instrument was the galley. This vessel, propelled by oars, with mast and sail as auxiliary aid, was still used as a fighting craft in the Mediterranean; but it was too long and narrow to be a serviceable cargo carrier. For commercial purposes, most European states had long employed a heavy, tub-like vessel which the French called a "round-ship" and the English, a "cog." It had a length of only twice its breadth, and could carry bulky cargoes over long routes and through heavy seas. In such a vessel, St. Paul sailed for Malta, and using a similar type, Columbus set out for the Indies.[1] The "cog" was admirably suited to stormy Channel and Atlantic waters, and in times of crisis, with temporary "castles" erected at the bow and stern (in order to give missiles the benefit of gravity) it played the part of an unwieldy fortress as well as trader.[2]

The transition from this clumsy hulk to the fighting galleon of Elizabeth's day was not the work of Spain; indeed, Spain was the last of the Atlantic powers to adopt the galleon, the Venetians and Italians of the fifteenth century being probably the first. But while the Mediterranean peoples still continued to use the galley for battle, and the improved "round-ship" for commerce, the English under Henry VIII began to transform their "cog" into a galleon which served the purposes of both war and peace. Oars were eliminated altogether, the high sides were cut down, and the keel lengthened to three times the beam. In the end, they turned out what Sir Julian Corbett has called, "the immediate parent of the ship of the line."[3]

[1] See M. Lewis, *British Ships and British Seamen* (London, 1940), 18; also by same, *England's Sea Officers* (London, 1939), chap. I, *passim*. For an excellent critical analysis of the construction and equipping of early ocean-going ships, along with details of rigging and estimates of sailing performance, see S. E. Morison *Christopher Columbus, Admiral of the Ocean Sea* (London, 1942), chap. IX.

[2] Until the fifteenth century, it was the custom to take down these "castles" when the danger was past. After that date, they were sometimes, and eventually always, left on, probably because the owners needed their protection in the days when piracy was in national favour.

[3] See Corbett, *Drake and the Tudor Navy*, 24; Lewis, *England's Sea Officers*, 23-4; von Maltzahn, *Naval Warfare*, 16-17; A. P. Usher, "Spanish Ships and

There is still a good deal of confusion in definition—even in Tudor times the new galleons were sometimes called great-ships, galleases,[4] and galleots—for these are matters on which not even the experts are agreed. It is sufficient here to say that this offspring of the "cog," longer, speedier, and more easily manœuvrable than its parent, became from the time of Henry VIII onwards the first English man-of-war.

In the sixteenth century, however, this new fighting galleon or man-of-war had no place in any system of fleet tactics, because no such system for sailing ships had been developed. There was no plan of co-operative action, as in the case of the Mediterranean rowing galleys, with each ship taking its assigned position subject to central command. Partly responsible for the lack of method, was the difficulty inherent in the nature of the new instrument. Obviously there were limits to the manœuvrability of the sailing-ship which severely handicapped it as a unit in any tactical formation. The rowing-galley, or later on the steamship, presented no such problem because it was self-propelling and could go in any direction irrespective of wind and tide. In Elizabeth's time, even the fastest and best designed square-rigged ship could not beat close to windward, and many times action was interrupted or prevented by a fall of wind which becalmed the engaging fleets.

Yet, once the architecture of the fighting ship had been mastered, some kind of battle order was bound to evolve. "All systems of tactics are ultimately based on the dominant weapon to be used,"[5] and the weapon which did most to establish a system of naval tactics was Henry VIII's new gun. In the early days ships were mainly armed as man-killers with small breech-loading guns for repelling boarders. With the introduction of the heavy gun in the reign of Henry VIII, we have a "ship-killing" weapon placed, because of its weight, not in the castles at either end, but on the deck of the ship.[6]

Shipping," 190-1; Corbett, *Papers Relating to the Navy during the Spanish War*, App. B, 337-41; and W. L. Rodgers, *Naval Warfare under Oars, 4th to 16th Centuries* (Annapolis, Md., 1939), 288-91.

[4]The galleas was an attempt to unite galley and sailing ship to produce a vessel larger and faster than either, but it never succeeded for it possessed the virtues of neither. It carried three lateen-rigged masts and, like the galleon, high castellated structures at each end. The oars were long and heavy, from twenty-five to thirty-two on a side, and each was manned by from six to seven men. But the sail area was smaller than a galleon's, and the supplementary oars proved useless except in the smoothest weather. Moreover, it proved too expensive to maintain. See Haring, *Trade and Navigation between Spain and the Indies in the Time of the Hapsburgs*, 265.   [5]Corbett, *Fighting Instructions*, ix.

[6]Lewis, *England's Sea Officers*, 29.

Fighting on sea, which had been hitherto a matter of hand-to-hand "hammer and tongs" on high-walled floating citadels, became less intimate when there was danger of losing masts and possibly the whole ship as a result of gun-fire.

With the "big gun," naval fighting in the modern sense of the word was born.   Broadside firing from ports cut through the sides of the ship took the place of grappling and boarding, and although the Elizabethan admirals had no understanding of co-ordinated fleet tactics there gradually developed in the following century the practice of *line ahead*, based on the thesis that a succession of broadsides from a column of ships in line was the most effective means of damaging an enemy fleet.   In short, instead of many ships advancing in a swarm against an enemy mass, the leading ships were ordered to steer against the enemy's van, the centre at his centre, and the rear against his rear, a system which was to become incorporated in the seventeenth century into the sacrosanct *Fighting Instructions*.[7]

When the main theatre of naval operations had passed from the Mediterranean to the Atlantic, and when the galleon with sails and heavy guns took the place of the rowing-ship with its beak and small arms, Spain simply failed to adapt herself to the new medium.[8] The transition was not, indeed, an easy one for any state.   The building of land armies demanded far less technical preparation (as Napoleon discovered) than that required for equipping a fighting fleet.   Armies could be and were quickly improvised for defence, but not so the new navies.   Apart from national support in terms of industrial and scientific resources, navies had certain special needs, such as bases.[9] Moreover without the foundation of a merchant marine or fisheries, it was a slow business developing a seafaring class competent to work a ship as well as man her guns.

Hence, while the sixteenth century gradually learned the use of the sailing-ship as an instrument of war, no nation as yet contem-

[7]See Corbett, *Fighting Instructions*, 28; also Admiral Lisle's "Fighting Orders of 1545," (item 3), quoted in D. Hannay, *A Short History of the Royal Navy, 1217-1688* (London, 1898), 66.

[8]Spain hardly ranked as a true sea power in the modern sense, until the conquest of Portugal in 1580 provided her with a nucleus of first-rate crews and galleons. See Duro, *Armada Española*, III, 175-6.

[9]The "invincible Armada" was perhaps the first naval expedition of importance whose action was seriously hindered by the lack of bases. In the Channel, far from their ports at Corunna and Lisbon, the Spanish vessels were as good as lost. The open roadsteads of Calais and of Gravelines provided them with neither shelter from bad weather nor a refuge from their enemies. See R. Castex, *Théories stratégiques* (Paris, 1931), III, 185.

plated controlling the sea by organized fleets. No nation had created a navy in the sense of established fleets of fighting vessels built and maintained for purely military purposes. The word "navy" was used, but in a general sense, meaning the shipping and seamen of the state; there was no clear-cut distinction between ships of war and merchantmen. With a few alterations, such as the cutting of gunports, or the addition of an extra deck to accommodate the soldiers, a merchantman could still become a man-of-war. The famous *Henry Grâce à Dieu* of Henry VIII was simply a King's Ship of exceptional size and structure, a notch or two above the ordinary merchantman. Elizabethan ships like the *Revenge* represented a further advance in the direction of the specialized war-ship, but for many years after 1588, when an English fleet was needed for war, it was composed largely of merchantmen, either pressed or hired from English owners or, on occasion, rented from other countries.[10] Parsimonious monarchs like Elizabeth were loth to spend too much of their incomes on construction of special war-ships, and preferred to raise their fleets like regiments. By hiring or commandeering merchant vessels, in most cases already armed against pirates, the monarch was relieved of the expense of maintaining a large standing force in a state of efficiency in time of peace.[11]

[10]Oppenheim, *A History of the Administration of the Royal Navy*, 32; Oppenheim, *The Naval Tracts of Sir William Monson* (Navy Records Society, 5 vols., London, 1902-14), XXII, vol. I (1902), 3-5; Williamson, *Hawkins*, 306-7; Corbett, *Drake and the Tudor Navy*, I, 16.

[11]Armed merchantmen were still serving in the line of battle in considerable numbers as late as Charles II's war of 1665-67. The proportion was about one merchantman to four regular men-of-war, as compared with the period of Cromwell's Dutch War, when the proportion was one in three.

APPENDIX B

TYPES OF BRITISH SHIPS AND GUNS IN THE EIGHTEENTH CENTURY

IT IS no credit to the English shipwright that during the period of the second Hundred Years' War Britain achieved command of the sea. Not until the change from oak to iron, and the transfer of the ancient yards of the Thames and south coast to the mineral regions of the north, did the marine engineers of Mersey, Tyneside, and Clyde give ship-building its present pre-eminence.[12] And not until the days of Fisher's dreadnought (1905) could it be said that Britain took the initiative in designing a single new type of fighting ship. There was no serious school of naval architects until Napoleonic days, and building was chiefly by rule of thumb.[13] There were no set standards of design, and ships of the same rate were often of unequal dimensions which meant that stores and rigging were not always interchangeable. Moreover, changes in size and rating were taking place almost constantly. For the purposes of this book, however, a rough classification may be useful.

A first-rate line-of-battle ship mounted 100 guns; the "110" was a rarity, although one or two were in use at the end of the century. A second-rate carried 90 to 98, and the third-rate from 64 to 80 guns. The third-rates were the most numerous class, chiefly because they were the most effective in combining fire-power and manœuvrability.

The fourth-rate of 50 guns represents the transitional stage between the line-of-battle ship and the frigate. In Anne's reign, the "50" was the cruiser *par excellence*, although counted as a ship of the line until the end of the Seven Years' War; after 1763 she was finally classed "under the Line."

The true frigates in the eighteenth (and nineteenth) century sense were the fifth- and sixth-rates. Before 1756 or thereabouts, they carried 40-44 and 20-24 guns respectively. They were followed

[12]See G. Blake, *British Ships and Shipbuilders* (London, 1946), 30-2.
[13]Albion, *Forests and Sea Power*, 78-9.

319

by two main types, the "32's" and the "28's," until about 1780, when there appeared the single-decked "38" and "36" which had approximately the same weight of metal as the old "44." The merit of these new ships lay in their ability to fight in all weathers, whereas the "44's" were forced to keep their lower deck ports closed in heavy seas. The smaller sixth-rates were still being built during the American Revolution, and some of them (22-24 guns) were serving at the time of Trafalgar.

Sloops and brigs from 10 to 20 guns operated as small frigates. In addition, there were various types of light, fast, and easily handled craft, such as luggers, cutters, and schooners. Bomb-ketches mounting mortars in the bows were maintained for attack on coastal fortifications and harbour defences.

The range and size in eighteenth-century ships may best be appreciated by citing parallel examples, as follows:

BEGINNING OF CENTURY				END OF CENTURY			
Date	Name	Guns	Tons	Tons	Guns	Name	Date
1701	*Royal Sovereign*	100 (occasionally 110)	1880	2500	110	*Hibernia*	1804
1710	*Neptune*	96	1580	2120	98	*Neptune*	1797
1700	*Essex*	70	1090	1720	74	*Elizabeth*	1807
1695	*Severn*	54	680	1060	38	*Shannon*	1806
1702	*Nightingale*	24	250	385	18	*Frolick*	1806*

*See Admiralty Library, *List Books* and *Abstracts of Progress*.

The average life of the wooden ship was ten to twenty years, but the numerous exceptions should not go unnoticed. At the Battle of the Saints (1782) 14 ships were under ten years of age, 11 between ten and twenty, and 7 over twenty. In 1805 at Trafalgar, 10 ships were under ten years, 7 were between ten and twenty, and 10 were over twenty. Nelson's *Victory* was forty years old.

In both France and Britain, great attention was paid to the refitting of old ships. Sometimes life was prolonged by reducing the number of guns, rather than supplying lighter ones. For example, the *Royal William*, built in 1719, was cut from 100 to 84 guns in 1757; in 1749 the *Neptune* (90 guns) built in 1730, was reduced to a "74."[14] France had greater natural resources of wood than Britain, but ordinarily such advantages did not prevent her from building up emergency reserves of Baltic timber and naval stores. In Britain the best forests of oak were nearing exhaustion, and during the

[14]For this information and other data, I am indebted to Commander J. H. Owen, R.N.

eighteenth century reserves of foreign timber were always insufficient. As a consequence, in the Seven Years' War, pressure of events frequently forced the use of green timber that had a constant tendency to warp and rot. The use of copper sheathing in British ships during the War of the American Revolution put an end to external decay, but inside the ship the ravages continued undiminished.[15]

In estimating the power of a ship or squadron, it is a mistake merely to count the total number of guns by which the ships are rated. Fire power lay not only in number but in size of guns, and the larger ships carried heavier guns. Although there were many protests regarding "under-gunning" early in the eighteenth century, only too frequently the reverse was true; British ships were apt to suffer from the overcrowding of the quarter-deck and forecastle with small guns. During the century, there was a steady increase in the weight of the batteries, corresponding to the increase in size. Roughly, the increase may be summarized thus:

Class of Ship	1700-1715 Heaviest Gun	1780-1800 Heaviest Gun
90 guns and above	32 pdrs.	32 pdrs.
70's and 80's	24 "	32 "
60's and 64's	18 "	24 "
50	12 "	24 "

In neither France nor Britain were there any revolutionary improvements in the design of guns during the eighteenth century. Efficiency certainly increased, but most weapons were handled in the same rudimentary fashion as a century earlier. The gun, mounted on four wheels, was run out again after each shot, at first by sheer manpower, subsequently with the aid of tackles. Most seamen looked askance at the backsight as too delicate an instrument for the sea, and gunners usually aimed along the metal. About 1780, the British introduced the carronade (first manufactured at the River Carron Ironworks near Stirling), a short, light iron cannon of heavy calibre, without trunnions, with fixed breeching and no recoil. Its range was short, but it could fire three times as fast as the average gun, and the effect of heavy shot at short distances was devastating. By the middle of the eighties, it was in general use as auxiliary to

[15]See Albion, *Forests and Sea Power*, 84.

the main armament; and at the end of the century, almost all line-of-battle ships and frigates mounted 32-pounder carronades on the forecastle, quarter-deck, and, in the case of ships of the line, on the poop. Sloops and other of the smaller vessels mounted them as their main armament, as well as old ships of higher rates, which were regarded as too weak to carry their normal proportion of heavy guns.

APPENDIX C

The La Pérouse Expedition to Hudson Bay

THE French attack on Hudson Bay in 1782 was an anticlimax but, like the attack on Newfoundland in 1762, it was carried out with a privateering boldness that deserves recording even though its success had no effect on the making of the peace.

On May 31, M. La Pérouse, with a 74-gun ship and two 36-gun frigates, set out from the West Indies, and entered the Bay on July 17. Forcing his way slowly through the fog and floating ice, he was able, by August 8, to reach Prince of Wales Fort on the estuary of the Churchill River. The Hudson's Bay Company had taken some pains to fortify their posts, all of which possessed artillery and some reserves of stores; but the small garrisons were without military training. They were civilians, and not the most adaptable civilians, for five years of desperate war combined with the increasing competition of the North-west Company on the Saskatchewan had drained the labour market of its best pioneer quality.

Moreover, the forts, however imposing in appearance, were not stoutly built. York was a timber structure capable of resisting little more than small-arms fire; the masonry of Prince of Wales was composed of boulder rubble held together with a minimum of mortar.[16] Even had the walls been proof against bombardment, the inhabitants of Prince of Wales could not have withstood a long siege. The fort had no well, and there was no means of getting drinking water within the limits of the defences. Furthermore, although the governor, Samuel Hearne, had forty guns at his disposal, his total complement of thirty-nine men would hardly have sufficed to man five guns.[17] Finally, the fort had no protective moat or ditch, and a vigorous

[16]See J. Robson, *An Account of Six Years Residence in Hudson's Bay from 1733 to 1736 and 1744 to 1747* (London, 1752), 9-11, 15, 19, 36.

[17]I am indebted for this and other information on the defences of the forts to Professor R. G. Glover of the University of Manitoba, who generously placed at my disposal notes based on his own careful investigations.

night raid by La Pérouse's four hundred must have been a comparatively simple and almost certainly a successful operation.

As it happened, Hearne was taken completely by surprise, and surrendered without even a parley. From available evidence, it seems that when the French arrived the garrison were away in the marshes shooting ducks for winter rations,[18] an impression which is vaguely confirmed by Umfreville's reference to officers "shooting birds in the Factory avenues."[19]

On August 20, La Pérouse weighed anchor off the Nelson River, landed the troops on the following day, and then marched his men some twenty miles over rough ground through thickets and bogs to confront the English garrison—sixty white men and twelve Indians —in Fort York. Cut off from his ships by wilderness and facing siege operations under conditions of cold, hunger, and fatigue, La Pérouse realized he had to win immediately or not at all. But his anxieties proved to be short-lived. The occupation of York took scarcely more than ten minutes. Hardly had his force appeared, when the ailing and panic-stricken governor, Humphrey Marten, without waiting for a summons, raised the white flag and handed over the entire fort to the besiegers, who could hardly believe their good fortune.[20]

La Pérouse might have continued his successful adventures and added to his rich stock of furs by capturing Fort Severn. Normally the middle of September was a safe time of departure from the Bay; but the French commander apparently preferred not to gamble with his two weeks' margin. After firing York on August 31, he set sail for France.

His little force had come out of the inhospitable waters of Hudson Bay almost intact; his losses occurred when he had reached the comparative security of the Atlantic. During the return voyage of six weeks, 70 men died of scurvy, and 400 sick were disembarked at Cadiz. It was a grim, but for the eighteenth century a not unusual, home-coming; scurvy had always killed men more quickly than guns. La Pérouse was given a hero's reception. The king read his account of the campaign "avec beaucoup d'attention" and expressed satisfaction with the resourcefulness and energy that the commander of his little company had shown.[21]

[18]L. J. Burpee, *The Search for the Western Sea: The Story of the Exploration of North-Western America* (London, 1908), 164.
[19]E. Umfreville, *The Present State of Hudson's Bay* (London, 1790), 137.
[20]*Ibid.*, 127-8; see also Beatson, *Naval and Military Memoirs*, V, 540-3.
[21]See G. Lacour-Gayet, *La Marine militaire de la France, sous le règne de Louis XVI*, 414-15.

APPENDIX D

"Of the Convoys required to ports abroad whether to our own settlements or to foreign ports, specifying the force of the ships which can be spared for this service from those in commission; and the probable time of their absence from Britain."

From whence trade is to be carried	To what ports trade is to be carried	Ships of the Line No. Ships	No. Guns	Frigates No. Ships	No. Guns	Probable time of absence from Britain	Whether the ships can return with the trade or not
London	East Indies	1	74	1	18	one year	To return with the trade
St. Helena	London	—	—	1	50	6 months	To sail again with India ships
London, etc.	Jamaica	—	—	1	44	8	To bring back the trade
"	"	—	—	1	14	8	" "
"	"	—	—	1	44	8	" "
"	"	—	—	1	14	8	" "
"	Leeward Is.	—	—	1	44	8	" "
"	"	—	—	1	14	8	" "
"	"	—	—	1	44	8	" "
"	"	—	—	1	14	8	" "
"	Canada	—	—	1	44	8	" "
"	Spain, Portugal, Gibraltar	—	—	1	14	6	" "
London, etc.	"	1	64	1	32	2	" return with "
"	Newfoundland	1	64	1	14	2	" "
"	"	—	—	1	14	2	" the same ships as first mentioned
"	"	—	—	1	32	8	To Portugal and Spain and return in time to go out next year
"	Coast of Guinea	—	—	1	50	8	To West Indies and return with trade
"	North America	—	—	1	50	7	To return with the collected trade from the coast of N. America
Turkey, Italy, etc.	Gibraltar	—	—	2	12	To continue in Mediterranean with the ships in the North Sea	To carry the trade from Gibraltar to Turkey, Italy, etc.
London, Hull, Newcastle, Leith	Baltic	—	—	1	50		To go and return with convoys to Flambro Head, where they part North and South witht he sloops
"	"	—	—	2	44		
"	"				18		

Contained in Statement IV, Patton to Middleton, June 27, 1794, *Letters and Papers of Charles, Lord Barham, 1758-1813,* edited by Sir John Laughton (Navy Records Society, 3 vols., London, 1907-11) XXXVIII, vol. II (1910), 400. See also, Statements on Convoys provided after Trafalgar; P.R.O., *Convoy Books,* vols. 1097-1114.

Index